This book comes with access to more content online.

Quiz yourself, track your progress,
and score high on test day!

Register your book or ebo[ok]
www.dummies.com/go/ge[t]

D1402048

Select your product, and then follow the prompts
to validate your purchase.

You'll receive an email with your PIN and instructions.

LSAT®

3rd Edition
with Online Practice

by Lisa Zimmer Hatch, MA, and Scott A. Hatch, JD

for
dümmies®
A Wiley Brand

LSAT® For Dummies®, 3rd Edition with Online Practice

Published by: **John Wiley & Sons, Inc.,** 111 River Street, Hoboken, NJ 07030-5774, www.wiley.com

Copyright © 2021 by John Wiley & Sons, Inc., Hoboken, New Jersey

Published simultaneously in Canada

For general information on our other products and services, please contact our Customer Care Department within the U.S. at 877-762-2974, outside the U.S. at 317-572-3993, or fax 317-572-4002. For technical support, please visit https://hub.wiley.com/community/support/dummies.

Wiley publishes in a variety of print and electronic formats and by print-on-demand. Some material included with standard print versions of this book may not be included in e-books or in print-on-demand. If this book refers to media such as a CD or DVD that is not included in the version you purchased, you may download this material at http://booksupport.wiley.com. For more information about Wiley products, visit www.wiley.com.

Library of Congress Control Number: 2020950312

ISBN 978-1-119-71627-3 (pbk); ISBN 978-1-119-71629-7 (ebk); ISBN 978-1-119-71628-0 (ebk)

Manufactured in the United States of America

10 9 8 7 6 5 4 3 2 1

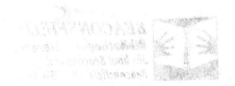

Contents at a Glance

Table of Contents

Introduction

Welcome to *LSAT For Dummies,* 3rd Edition! This book contains updates to familiarize you with the LSAT's Digital format so that you're comfortable with taking the test on a tablet. Even though the delivery is modern, the content of the Law School Admission Test (LSAT) hasn't changed. You may have heard horror stories about the LSAT, especially about the infamous "logic games." Yes, the LSAT is no walk in the park, but it's not the hardest test in the universe. It doesn't require you to brush off your math and science texts from high school, and it doesn't expect you to remember anything from your history classes. It really just expects you to be able to read and analyze. If you can read carefully and quickly and then apply what you've read, you already have the skills you need to succeed on the LSAT.

This book helps you refine those skills and apply them to the particular tasks on the LSAT. If you go through this book and work through a healthy number of practice questions, you should have a good idea of what awaits you on test day.

About This Book

First, allow us to tell you what this book *can* do: This book introduces you to the LSAT and helps you get a handle on how to take it. It describes the three types of multiple-choice sections — analytical reasoning, logical reasoning, and reading comprehension — and provides guidance on how to handle them, with plenty of practice questions and explanations. It also touches on the writing sample, which is unscored but still merits a bit of attention. The first three chapters discuss some basics of law school admissions, test-taking strategy, and other logistical entertainment.

On to what the book *can't* do: This book doesn't give you a bunch of tricks to help you "crack" the LSAT. The LSAT isn't a nut; it's a test, and to do well on it you have to apply your natural intelligence and experience. We give you plenty of advice on how to approach each question type to maximize your talents and train your mind to think in the most effective way.

Included in this book are three full-length practice tests, which you can use to try out the tips and techniques we provide throughout the chapters. The difficulty levels and thought patterns on the practice tests are similar to those on real LSATs. Actual LSAT test-prep instructors and LSAT-takers assisted us by massaging and tweaking the questions to make sure that they're equivalent to the real LSAT questions. You can get real and valuable practice by using the questions in this book. But the fact is, no one makes real LSAT questions but the real Law School Admission Council (LSAC). If you want real LSAT questions, get yourself some LSAT PrepTests, which are real LSATs administered in previous years. That's the most authentic practice you can find, and we highly recommend it. (You can order these official tests in text or digital form from the LSAC website: www.lsac.org. They come with answers but [in most cases] not explanations, so they're great practice, but to figure out why your answers are right or wrong, you should work through this book first to get a sense of how the questions work.)

To help, we italicize any new LSAT-related terms that you're likely to be unfamiliar with the first time we use it.

Because this book is a test-prep, you probably want to read most everything here. Besides, we worked really hard on this book! However, if you're pressed for time or just have a short attention span, you can skip the sidebars and any text marked with a Technical Stuff icon without missing out on too much.

Foolish Assumptions

We make a few assumptions about you, the reader (we hope you don't mind):

>> Call us crazy, but we're guessing you've signed up to take the LSAT or you're at least seriously considering taking the LSAT.

>> We know, of course, that you're not a dummy. You've likely received or are in the process of receiving an undergraduate degree and are no stranger to thinking analytically. You simply need guidance regarding how to apply your already sharp skills to the unfamiliar question types on the LSAT.

>> Our third and final assumption is that you've chosen this book for one of several reasons — the fabulous *For Dummies* reputation for providing information in an easily accessible format, the price, or the attention-grabbing yellow-and-black cover — but mainly because you think you want to go to law school, and the LSAT is the primary way to that destination.

Icons Used in This Book

This book, like all *For Dummies* books, uses icons to help you spot important tidbits of information and break up the monotony of otherwise plain and ordinary pages. Here are the icons you'll encounter in this book:

TIP

This icon marks useful bits of information that may come in handy when you study for or take the LSAT.

REMEMBER

This icon reminds you of valuable strategies to keep in mind as you work through the test content.

WARNING

This icon marks stuff to avoid, potential mistakes, and traps for the unwary.

EXAMPLE

This icon identifies practice questions that demonstrate how to apply specific techniques.

TECHNICAL STUFF

This icon highlights extra tidbits of info that enhance your reading but aren't essential to preparing for the LSAT.

Beyond the Book

By now we're hoping that you're impressed with the wealth of content contained in this book. But to quote your favorite infomercials: Wait! There's more!

In addition to what you're reading right now, this book comes with a free access-anywhere Cheat Sheet that includes tips to help you prepare for the LSAT. To get this Cheat Sheet, simply go to www.dummies.com and type "LSAT For Dummies Cheat Sheet" in the Search box.

You also get access to four full-length online practice tests and approximately 500 flashcards. To gain access to the online practice, all you have to do is register. Just follow these simple steps:

1. Register your book or ebook at Dummies.com to get your PIN. Go to www.dummies.com/go/getaccess.

2. Select your product from the dropdown list on that page.

3. Follow the prompts to validate your product, and then check your email for a confirmation message that includes your PIN and instructions for logging in.

If you don't receive this email within two hours, please check your spam folder before contacting us through our Technical Support website at http://support.wiley.com or by phone at 877-762-2974.

Now you're ready to go! You can come back to the practice material as often as you want — simply log on with the username and password you created during your initial login. No need to enter the access code a second time.

Your registration is good for one year from the day you activate your PIN.

Where to Go from Here

If you bought this book, you must have some plan — definite or tentative — to take the LSAT. But just buying the book alone won't help you much. To get the full benefit, you have to open it up, read it, and work the problems.

There are two approaches you can take:

>> Read all the explanatory materials, work your way through all the practice problems, and then take the practice tests at the end and see how you did.

>> Take one of the full-length tests to see how well you do. Score your test. Then study the sections that give you the most trouble, concentrating on the questions you find difficult.

It's up to you. You're the one taking the test, and you're the one who has to decide what you need to study and how much time you want to allocate to the process.

1

Getting Started with the LSAT

IN THIS PART . . .

Gain insight into the minds that create the LSAT.

Discover tips for managing the LSAT and each of its question types.

Be prepared for exam day by knowing exactly what and what not to bring to the testing site.

Discover other important considerations for getting into your top-choice law school.

Chapter **1**

The L Team: The LSAT and Its Administrators

If you want to go to law school, you'll likely take the *Law School Admission Test*, also known as the LSAT. The more than 200 law schools that belong to the Law School Admission Council (LSAC) require the LSAT (see the later section "What Have You Done for Me Lately? The LSAC" for info about the LSAC). Some schools may allow you to substitute a GRE score for the LSAT. Law schools that don't require either the LSAT or GRE for admission may not be approved by the American Bar Association (ABA), which in turn may not qualify you for admission to a state bar, so be careful about choosing a school that doesn't require the LSAT.

The LSAT, annoying though it can be, provides a significant metric for law schools to evaluate their applicants on the same playing field. Colleges are different, backgrounds are different, and cultures are different, but the LSAT is the same for everyone. The LSAT is carefully designed so that the testing experience of test-takers is virtually identical. Each LSAT test is crafted so that test-takers have a 90 percent chance of scoring the same on a different version. So, law schools feel confident that the LSAT is an objective measure of student ability.

Grade point averages, unlike the LSAT, are highly subjective; they vary depending on the difficulty of a school, the difficulty of particular courses, and other random and unpredictable factors (like the grading policies of individual professors). Law school applications include other information like personal statements that can give schools an idea of a student's abilities, but the schools still can't know for sure that they're getting the real goods — plenty of students get help writing those essays. That leaves the LSAT as one of the most reliable and objective means to compare candidates.

In this chapter, you get an introduction to the LSAT and its various parts and learn all about registering and preparing for the big day. You also get a peek at the organization behind all this madness, the LSAC.

WARNING

If you're going to be a lawyer, you have to get used to disclaimers, and here's ours for this chapter. The technical information we offer about fees and procedures is subject to change, so refer to the official website (www.lsac.org) to verify the facts and figures for yourself.

Getting to Know the Enemy

If you want to get a decent score on the LSAT, you need to know the test. You can't expect to walk into a test center cold, never having encountered an LSAT in your life, and just ace the questions.

You don't necessarily have to study for a long time. If you're good at standardized tests, you may be able to flip through one or two sample tests, work a few of the problems, get the idea, and score in the 95th percentile. Some people can. If, on the other hand, you find standardized tests generally challenging, and the LSAT difficult in particular, you probably need to devote yourself to more practice time to master the proven strategies provided by this book. Whatever your situation, keep motivated and prepare with the certainty that you can and will improve with dedicated practice.

The LSAT is offered digitally and consists of four different question types:

>> Analytical reasoning questions

>> Logical reasoning questions

>> Reading comprehension questions

>> Writing sample

The analytical reasoning, logical reasoning, and reading comprehension sections consist of multiple-choice questions. You take these questions at a testing center in a format called the Digital LSAT, which delivers these questions via an electronic tablet rather than a paper booklet. The tablet format is similar to a paper test, but instead of marking answers with a No. 2 pencil, you mark and eliminate answers and highlight portions of the questions with a stylus. The testing center supplies you with scratch paper and a pen to work through problems; you can also bring in your own pencils and eraser.

The Digital LSAT consists of five separate test sections presented in no particular order:

>> Two scored sections of logical reasoning

>> One scored analytical reasoning section

>> One scored reading comprehension section

>> One unscored section that can be another section of any of the three multiple-choice question types

You don't know which section is unscored, and the unscored section looks just like any other LSAT test section. Every section lasts 35 minutes.

TECHNICAL STUFF

The unscored section that you take is a collection of questions that the LSAC is considering using on a future LSAT. The LSAC wants to see how well these new questions work when presented to actual LSAT-takers. This section can be analytical reasoning, logical reasoning, or reading comprehension; you don't know which section is unscored.

The writing sample isn't offered at the test center. You prepare an essay on your own computer at home (or some other secluded place free of interruptions) in response to a specific prompt. The scheduled writing session is timed and remotely proctored. You must complete at least one writing sample before the LSAC will report your LSAT scores to law schools, but you don't need to complete a writing sample every time you take the Digital LSAT.

TIP

The quickest way to get your hands on an actual LSAT is to take the free sample tests available at the LSAC website (www.lsac.org). Completing the samples is a good way to familiarize yourself with the test and its digital format.

Taking a Quick Look at the Types of Questions

The LSAT has three different kinds of multiple-choice questions and an unscored written essay. Each questions type has its own virtues and vices, and you'll come to know and love them all (though we won't blame you if you pick a favorite).

Analytical reasoning — playing games with your head

The analytical reasoning section consists of four logic problems — the infamous "logic games" — each of which is followed by between five and eight questions. These games involve a group of players (or game pieces) that you need to arrange or assign and the rules that govern how you go about it.

You may get something like: "Five college students — B, C, D, E, and F — must share three rooms in a house. B can't stay with D. E must stay with F." This fact pattern is followed by several questions that allow you to explore your understanding of the relationships between the students and the dorm rooms. One question may propose five possible roommate arrangements and ask you to choose which one is the only one that could work.

This kind of puzzle commonly appears on IQ tests or in books of games to amuse travelers on airplanes. What they have to do with law school is a mystery to many people. The LSAC PrepTest booklets say that these types of problems "simulate the kinds of detailed analyses of relationships that a law student must perform in solving legal problems." And it's true that the skills the analytical reasoning section tests are important in law school. To answer these questions correctly, you must read carefully and accurately. You have to apply rules to a system, which is similar to applying statutes or case law to a problem. You have to restrict your analysis to what's directly stated or to what can be logically inferred. So the analytical reasoning section is fairly useful at predicting who might succeed in law school.

The analytical reasoning section is worth about 25 percent of your LSAT score. See Chapters 4 through 6 for more on analytical reasoning.

Logical reasoning — putting your arguing skills to good use

The logical reasoning section consists of about 25 short (for example, three or four sentences) passages about various topics. Each of them is followed by one question. The questions ask you to identify the point of an argument, to make deductions about what the author is assuming, to draw conclusions, to identify principles or argument structures, to spot logical errors, and so forth.

Most of these questions involve informal or casual logic, the kind you use to make everyday decisions. All you have to do is read carefully (and quickly) and think clearly. Sometimes the wording is tricky, and you have to concentrate to avoid getting confused. Jotting down some notes or paraphrasing the passage in your own words can help you focus.

Every LSAT has two logical reasoning sections. Together, they're worth about 50 percent of your LSAT score. Chapters 7 through 10 are full of information about logical reasoning.

TIP

Because the logical reasoning section is worth a considerable percentage of your total LSAT score, work hard on your technique for these problems. You get twice the benefit if you do well on this section!

Reading comprehension — concentrating and remembering what you read

In the reading comprehension section, you read three fairly long and one pair of shorter passages on particular topics and answer several questions about them. The questions ask about the author's conclusion, the author's tone, the meaning of words, how the passage is organized, and other points designed to test your ability to understand what you read. The good news: The LSAT uses a limited pool of question types over and over again. Because you can predict the types of questions being asked, you can practice reading to answer the questions you know you'll see.

Topics range from humanities and science and social science disciplines to law-related writing. You don't need any expertise in any particular area; in fact, if you have expertise in the subject of a passage, try to forget your outside knowledge. You want to answer all the questions from the information given to you in the passage. Outside knowledge may actually distract you!

This section tests your ability to read and understand a fairly long reading passage. Reading and understanding a long passage is applicable to law school because most law classes consist of reading long, densely worded passages on obscure topics and then answering questions about them.

The reading comprehension section accounts for about 25 percent of your LSAT score. See Chapters 11 and 12 for the lowdown.

The writing sample — jumping the final hurdle

The other part of the LSAT is the digital writing sample. You get 35 minutes to write your essay on your own computer. The essay topic lets you exhibit your skills at using a set of facts to defend one course of action over another.

For example, your question may ask you to decide which dog a widow should buy: a German shepherd, which would be a good guard dog but not very affectionate, or a Pekingese, which would make a good companion but be utterly useless for home defense. (You can explore this question further in Chapter 13.)

Your selection doesn't matter. There's no right or wrong answer. All you have to do is pick a side and justify your decision. Chapters 13 and 14 go over this process in detail.

You don't get a score on the writing sample, but the Credential Assembly Service (CAS) sends a copy of your essay to every law school that receives your LSAT score.

REMEMBER

Some folks wonder why they should prepare for the writing sample section if it's unscored. Law schools often read essays in deciding borderline cases or comparing similar applicants. If your profile is substantially similar to hundreds of others, law schools often look at the essays to compare like candidates.

You Gotta Score!

The LSAT is scored on a scale from 120 to 180; every year a few people attain the Everest-like peak of 180, and they can pretty much write their own tickets to law school. Although percentile charts vary slightly among test administrations, the average LSAT score is around 152. Any score higher than 160 is quite good and puts you in the top 20 percent of test-takers (80th percentile). A score of around 164 puts you around the 90th percentile, and a score of 173 or above is where the top 1 percent of test-takers usually reside.

To get a 160, you need to answer about 75 percent of the answers correctly. To get a 150, you need to answer correctly about 55 percent. If you get 95 percent or more right, your score will be up in the stratosphere, around a 175. The LSAT scoring is straightforward. Your raw score is the number of questions you get right; no points are deducted for wrong answers. You plug that raw score into the score chart to determine what your LSAT score would be. So if, say, your test has 100 questions on it, and you get 75 of them right, your raw score is 75 and your LSAT score may be 161. If you get 44 right, you'd get more like a 144. The raw score to scaled score conversion changes very slightly from test to test to account for the minor differences in difficulty of each test.

TECHNICAL
STUFF

The LSAT-writers work hard to ensure that the test is reliable. That means that the same test-taker should get scores in a similar range on two or three different tests and that luck in getting an easy test shouldn't be a factor in scores. In practice, luck is always something of a factor, but it shouldn't be a major one.

Still, you've probably taken a metric ton of tests by now, and you know that everyone has good days and bad days, good tests and bad tests (hey, even good hair days and bad hair days!). The combination of a bad test and a bad mood (say, for instance, despite our advice to the contrary, you pull an all-nighter before exam day) can lead to a misleadingly bad score. If that happens, you can cancel your score and try again (see more about doing this in Chapter 2). On the other hand, you may be in the test-taking zone on test day, and every question seems laughably easy to you. It can happen that way. If you have a good day, thank your lucky stars because that'll probably result in a good LSAT score and law school admission.

TIP

What if you get a 160 and your friend gets a 163? Does that mean your friend is a better law school prospect than you? Probably not. Small differences among test-takers aren't usually due to actual differences of ability. Your score will be in the range of scores you're capable of, but if you take the LSAT several times within a short period of time, you probably won't get the same score every time. It may go up or down slightly, but it should be within 3 points up or down of your original score (though your mileage may vary).

Registering for the LSAT

The LSAT typically happens eight times a year: one Saturday every month except for March, May, September, and December. If you want to enter law school the next fall, you should take the LSAT by the prior December, or February at the latest, though we recommend taking it earlier. August, October, and November are the most popular test dates because some law schools start taking applications in the fall and begin accepting applicants early in the winter; the earlier you apply, the better your odds of acceptance.

The registration fee for the LSAT is currently $200. (Prices are subject to change — and likely will — so be sure to check with the LSAC to find out current charges.)

Keep the following things in mind when registering for the LSAT:

>> **Be sure to register.** Okay, duh. But really, be sure to register. The deadlines for registration fall well ahead of test dates, so you need to be on the ball. You can find the deadlines on the LSAC website (www.lsac.org). Plan accordingly. And make sure you're free the day of the test!

>> **When you register, be very careful to enter the correct code for your test center.** If you get the code wrong, you may be assigned a test center in a different state — not convenient. (The LSAC doesn't check for accuracy; the LSAC has no idea where you really want to take the test, so it doesn't know if you make a mistake.) Driving several hours the day before your test definitely won't calm your nerves. You can change your test center through the LSAC website for a fee, but you don't want to have to worry about that if you can avoid it.

>> **Upload your picture before the deadline.** When you register for the LSAT, you need to include a picture of your face. You don't need to upload the picture at the time of registration, but you should. Your picture must be in the system by the upload deadline (about a month before the test date), or you won't be able to take the test on that day.

>> **If something comes up — you catch the flu, you get sent overseas to war, you go into labor — and you're unable to take the LSAT, you can get a partial refund.** Granted, you get only a small portion of your registration fee back, but that's better than nothing. The LSAC website has deadlines for sending in the request.

>> **If you discover before the test date that you won't be able to make it that day, you can change your test date.** Of course, you have to pay a fee. The LSAC website has the deadlines for sending in a written request.

TIP

If you absolutely can't afford the cost of the LSAT, you can apply for a fee waiver on the LSAC website. The LSAC doesn't want to deny access to the legal profession solely on the basis of economic disadvantage. Be warned, though; the requirements are quite strict.

Preparing for the LSAT

Helping students prepare for the LSAT has become a multimillion-dollar (at least) industry. Test-prep companies promise huge score increases; students spend thousands on semester-long courses and tutors. Every major bookstore is full of books to help prospective lawyers on their way.

WARNING

Be wary of expensive classes or snake oil salesmen that promise to reveal secrets or give you huge score increases. Usually, all that most people need is a good LSAT prep book (such as this one!) and a few recent LSAT tests to do their best on test day. Save your money for law school! But be warned: Many folks lack the motivation and discipline for self-study. If this describes you, buckle down and sign a contract with yourself, form a study group, or consider enrolling in a reasonably priced test prep course.

What really helps

What really helps you succeed at the LSAT is exposure to the test. Exposure may mean something as simple as taking one or two sample tests the days before you take the official one. More often, though, it may mean several weeks — or even months — of practice.

WHAT STUDY METHOD WORKS BEST FOR YOU?

No one wants to spend too much of her life thinking about the LSAT. Studying as efficiently as possible makes sense. Here are some possible plans for your LSAT studying.

- **The slow and careful approach:** You should go with this approach if you take preparing for the LSAT very seriously and are willing to spend a good deal of time on it. Start at least two months before you plan to take the LSAT. Go to the LSAC website (www.lsac.org) and order official LSAT exams, either the paper books or the digital access or both. Read all the chapters in this book carefully, working all the practice questions. Then take the three practice exams at the end of the book and the others available online. When you feel comfortable with the material, take as many official LSAT tests as you can. When the time comes to take the real LSAT, fear not — you'll be ready for anything it throws at you.

- **The quick and dirty route:** Okay, so you've put off studying for the LSAT to the last minute (a habit we recommend you overcome before you enter law school!) and need to maximize the little amount of time remaining before you take the test. Here's what you should do: Begin at least the week before the LSAT. Read Chapters 4 through 12. Work some of the questions available online. If you can't answer the questions quickly and easily, check back to the appropriate chapters to find out more about your problem areas. Access the two full-length Digital LSAT practice tests from the LSAC website, take one of the tests under timed conditions, and review your answers to discover your areas of weakness. Work as many of the practice problems in this book as you can, concentrating particularly on the question types that give you the most trouble. Outline a writing sample essay in your head to make sure you're familiar with how to organize a response to an essay prompt. Take the other official practice test. Show up at the LSAT and do your best.

- **Riding the fence:** Most of you probably fall somewhere in the middle. That's fine; you're the one who knows what you need and how much time you can afford.

No matter how you choose to study, start sooner rather than later. The more time you spend working on the LSAT, the better you'll get at it, so you don't want to shortchange yourself by procrastinating.

If you need extra prep materials, you can't do better than the official LSATs sold by the LSAC; compilations of prior paper tests are available in texts called *PrepTests,* and they're the actual LSATs that have been administered to willing victims over the last decade. Be warned, though; the LSAT has increased in difficulty and changed slightly in format over the years, so you'll get your most valuable practice from the most recent tests. You can take two Digital LSATs for free from the LSAC website and also buy access 60 official tests in the digital format for one year.

Practice makes perfect

Any book you consult will recommend that you prepare for the LSAT by taking a full, official practice test or two under simulated test-day conditions. That means sitting down on a Saturday morning (or some other day when you have three hours unscheduled) with access to an official Digital LSAT practice test from the LSAC website, some scratch paper, a No. 2 pencil, and an eraser, working your way through the test, section by section, stopping work when the timer buzzes.

Taking a timed, full-length practice test is ideal, but if you're unable to carve out three hours to complete this useful exercise, don't despair. Your valuable (and presumably limited) study time may be better spent working through questions slowly and carefully, making sure that you really know how to work the analytical reasoning problems and analyze the logical reasoning questions. Then take timed practice sections to hone your time-management skills for each question type.

However you decide to practice, just be sure you give yourself enough time. Try to start at least a couple of weeks before the test date. The more exposure you have to test questions, the more comfortable you'll be on exam day.

What Have You Done for Me Lately? The LSAC

Did you ever wonder who makes up the LSAT? It comes from the minds of the *Law School Admission Council,* or LSAC, a nonprofit corporation in Newtown, Pennsylvania. The LSAC comprises the majority of law schools in the United States and Canada; the member professors and attorneys volunteer their time to the council. The LSAC offers a number of services designed to facilitate applications to law school and improve legal education, and it also sponsors research into issues such as minority representation in the legal profession.

If you're serious about applying to law school, familiarize yourself with the LSAC and its offerings because the LSAC will be part of your life for a while. You can visit the LSAC, register for the LSAT online, and do various other fun activities at the LSAC's website, www.lsac.org.

Creating and administering the LSAT

The LSAC administers the LSAT to more than 100,000 people every year. The organization creates at least eight complete tests every year and constantly works to develop new questions and refine the LSAT's accuracy — that's one reason why you get to take an extra, unscored section of multiple-choice questions when you take the LSAT. The LSAC compiles statistics on the number of people that take the tests and the scores they receive, schedules test dates, fields questions and complaints from test-takers, and generally makes it possible for many people to apply to law school every year.

Aiding in law school applications

The LSAC also plays a major role in law school applications. When you register for the LSAT, you can also sign up to participate in the *Credential Assembly Service,* or CAS, for an extra fee. Law schools require you to use the CAS to send your application documentation.

The CAS streamlines the law school application process by assembling most of the information needed to apply to law schools and sending it to the schools in one package. A CAS report includes

>> Summaries of transcripts from all your undergraduate and graduate schools

>> LSAT scores and copies of the LSAT writing sample section

>> Letters of recommendation

The LSAC gets you coming and going. In addition to paying the CAS fee, you need to purchase a report for each law school on your application list. CAS registration lasts five years. Almost all the law schools approved by the ABA require that their applicants use the CAS, which makes your life much easier. Rather than having to assemble all that information for every school to which you apply, you just give the information to the LSAC (along with your money), and it takes care of everything. When you apply to a law school, the school requests the report from the LSAC, the LSAC sends the report, and you just sit back and wait.

You can register for the CAS on the LSAC website (www.lsac.org) at the same time that you register for the LSAT. When you do this, you authorize the LSAC to release information about you to eligible law schools, which means law schools that are interested in you may contact you.

REMEMBER

If you don't register for the CAS at the same time that you register for the LSAT, you still must register before you apply to law schools. Do this at least six weeks before you start applying.

Providing other goods and services

The LSAC does a number of other good deeds for the legal education system:

>> The *Candidate Referral Service* allows law schools to search CAS data for students who match particular profiles (for example, LSAT scores of a certain level, minorities, women, students from a certain region, and so on) so that they can contact them and invite them to apply.

>> Law school forums held in different states give prospective law students an opportunity to find out more about law school and the legal profession.

>> The LSAC sells LSAT prep materials and other information; you can buy these materials on the website. Buying recently administered LSATs is one of the most useful tools. They come with answers, not explanations, but they're the real thing and make great practice tests.

>> The LSAC also works to increase minority representation in the legal profession.

Chapter **2**

Test-Taking Basics: Setting Yourself Up for Success

f you're contemplating law school, you're almost certainly a veteran of standardized tests. You know what to expect. Just like the SAT, ACT, GMAT, and GRE, the LSAT is another morning of eliminating four answers out of five and maintaining your cool under pressure. You've been there, done that. Getting up early, walking into an unfamiliar testing center, and joining a group of nervous strangers tapping ubiquitous No. 2 pencils is old hat. You know this drill.

In this chapter, you discover some strategies and considerations specific to the LSAT, as well as some general test-taking basics, in the hope of making your experience as painless as possible. You also find out what to do after the test, including considering whether you need to retake the test.

Planning Your LSAT Test-Taking Tactics

You'll have an easier time on test day if you consider some strategic matters beforehand. The following sections provide a few simple strategies to ease your test-taking venture.

REMEMBER

You can't "beat" the LSAT; no one can. These strategies aren't tricks to outsmart the test, but they can help you do better.

Maximizing your chances

Some people are naturally good at taking standardized tests. This strength doesn't mean they make better law students or better lawyers; they just find these tests easy. Other people have a harder time. They find tests stressful in general and LSAT questions especially annoying.

Whichever type you are, you can undertake some basic strategies to help you improve your score and have a more pleasant test-taking experience. (Well, maybe not as pleasant as a spa visit, but better than a root canal.)

TIP

Here are a few things you can do to maximize your chances of getting a good score:

>> **Answer every question.** The LSAT test-makers don't penalize you for guessing, so you'd be crazy not to make sure every number on the answer sheet has a bubble filled in, even if you don't have time to read the question that goes with it. See the section "To Guess or Not to Guess" later in this chapter for more on guessing.

>> **Take your time.** You may get better results by answering three-quarters of the test accurately and then guessing on the last quarter than by racing through the whole thing too fast to be accurate.

>> **Budget your time.** You get 35 minutes for each section. Decide how to spend it. Allotting each question exactly 1.3 minutes may not be the most effective approach, but be careful not to get so caught up in the first analytical reasoning problem that you have only 5 minutes to work the last three.

>> **Don't worry about answering questions in order.** Especially in the analytical reasoning and reading comprehension sections, some questions may be easier to answer after you tackle others regarding the same passage or logic game. You don't get extra points for answering the questions in the way they're presented, but you may earn points by answering them in the order that works best for you.

>> **If you get stuck on a question, forget about it.** Move on to another question. (But be sure to flag the question in case you have time to come back to it.)

>> **Ignore your companions.** What they do makes no difference to your score. If you have a major problem with your surroundings — the stench of cheap perfume from the woman next to you, the snuffling of the allergy sufferer behind you — speak to the proctor, but don't count on getting moved; test centers are often fully booked. If you're positive your performance has suffered, you can always cancel your test score and try again later.

>> **Stay on target.** You may get bored, and your mind may want to wander somewhere more pleasant, but don't let it. Use visual cues to help yourself stay focused. Point to questions with your pencil or finger, and underline key words in the questions that help direct you to the correct answer.

REMEMBER

Don't forget to answer every question!

Taking the straight or the winding road

Should you start with the first question and work every subsequent question until you get to the last one? Or should you jump around? It's entirely up to you.

The analytical reasoning and reading comprehension sections are both divided into four approximately equal parts, and if you want to pick the easiest part first and work your way to the hardest, by all means do so. Just remember that initial assessments of difficulty are rarely accurate; a more productive way of choosing your first problem is to pick the analytical reasoning problem or reading comprehension passage with the largest number of questions — that way you maximize the number of questions you actually answer.

WARNING

Although starting with a reading comprehension passage or analytical reasoning problem that isn't the first one in your test is okay, after you pick one, stick with it until you're done. Trying to jump between two or three passages or problems at the same time will likely confuse you.

Skipping around on the logical reasoning sections works too. If your practice reveals that you're great at answering questions that ask for the answer that weakens the argument, tackling all questions of that type first fosters confidence and ensures that you have time to maximize your strengths.

REMEMBER

If you don't answer questions in order, make sure you mark those you skip with the tool included in the software, so you know to go back to them when you're ready.

TIP

Some test-prep experts recommend that if you really can't finish an analytical reasoning or a reading comprehension section, you cut your losses and just do your best on three of the four problems, tackling the scariest at the end if you have time. Sounds crazy, but this approach actually makes more sense than trying to speed through all four passages or problems; you maximize your accuracy on the parts you do instead of doing the whole section too fast and getting half of it wrong. If you do three-quarters of a section and get all those questions right, you get 75 percent, which is better than finishing the section and getting only half right. Of course, you should still mark answers for the questions you don't answer because there's no penalty for wrong answers. See "To Guess or Not to Guess" later in this chapter for more info on guessing.

Taking the occasional break

When you take the LSAT, you spend about three hours staring at a tablet full of questions. The only break you get comes after Section III, and it only lasts about 10 or 15 minutes — enough time to dash to the bathroom and wolf down an energy bar. The entire day may take four hours with the registration business you have to do before and after the test.

So the LSAT is a test of stamina as much as anything else. It's a long test, and it's tiring.

That's why pacing yourself is crucial. When you finish a chunk of test — an analytical reasoning problem or seemingly endless logical reasoning questions — take a break. Close your eyes, twist your neck, loosen those tight muscles in your shoulders, breathe, and let your eyes focus on a distant object. Don't take more than ten seconds or so, but do take the break. It helps you more than fretting about how little time you have left.

Have you heard the story about two guys who were cutting wood with axes? They worked side by side from morning until evening. The first man worked straight through without a break, swinging that axe from dawn 'til dusk. The second man sat down and rested for ten minutes every hour. At the end of the day, the men compared their piles of wood. The man who rested every hour had a pile much bigger than that of the other man. The first man asked the second one how he managed that feat, especially because he spent so much of the day resting. The second man replied, "While I rested, I sharpened my axe."

REMEMBER

Your brain is like that axe. You bring it to the test sharp, but the LSAT is designed to make it dull. Take those breaks and sharpen (and rest) your brain — the breaks really help.

To Guess or Not to Guess

When in doubt about the answer to a question, guess. Always guess. The LSAT test-makers don't penalize you for wrong answers, so guessing doesn't hurt, and you always have the chance that your random pick may be the correct answer. What's certain is that you won't get credit if you don't answer it at all.

The joy of statistics

How likely is it that you'll get a question right by random guessing? Not very.

TIP

On questions where you have no idea of the correct answer, you have better luck if you pick a letter and stick to it for all your shots in the dark. Why? Each answer choice appears at more or less the same frequency. If you answer an entire test with one letter, you'll probably get about 20 percent right. You'd get the same results if the test were in a language you couldn't read or if you didn't bother to read the questions or answers. If you vary your answer choices from question to question, you just may miss everything.

Is Choice (B) really best?

Many people talk about which letter is statistically most likely to be the right answer. Many people recommend Choice (B) as the best choice. We conducted a little survey of some recent LSATs to see how many times each answer choice was correct.

In some sections, Choice (B) was more frequently correct; in others, the winner was Choice (D). All in all, the percentage that each of the five answer choices was correct didn't vary greatly. Based on this information, we can't come up with any letter that would always be better than any other, though we'd probably stick with Choice (B) or Choice (D) if we had to choose.

Increase your odds: Eliminate the duds

A better strategy than random guessing from a pool of five choices is random guessing from a pool of two or three choices. Your odds of getting a right answer improve if you can eliminate a wrong answer or two.

To increase your odds, use a process of elimination to get rid of wrong answers on every question. Take this step first, unless you get one of those rare questions where the right answer jumps out at you. Crossing out the wrong answers — crossing them off using the tablet's marking tool so they don't distract you — makes spotting the possible right answer easier.

Readying Yourself for Battle

All your preparation will be in vain if you don't get to take the test. And if you don't feel calm and collected, you may blow questions that you should get right. So keep in mind the following checklist to help you before and during test day:

>> **Prepare your 1-gallon maximum zip-lock bag the night before.** Make sure you have your valid identification and several sharpened No. 2 wooden pencils (mechanical pencils aren't allowed) and an eraser without a sleeve to work out problems on the provided scratch paper.

You may also include a pencil sharpener, a 20-ounce maximum beverage in a plastic container or juice box (no aluminum cans), a snack for the break, some tissues, your wallet, car keys, and medical products. All items must fit in the sealed bag, and no other stuff is allowed. Collect your supplies the night before so you aren't frantically trying to find a pencil sharpener the morning of the test! No need to add to your stress.

>> **Leave prohibited items behind.** You can wear a silent analog watch, but digital watches and all other electronics aren't allowed, including cell phones and calculators.

>> **Don't stress yourself out that evening.** The night before the LSAT, if you feel compelled to study (I know, you can't help yourself), *don't* do a new test. Instead, review a section you've already done and know the answers to, which can reinforce strategies and boost your confidence.

>> **Get enough sleep the night before the test and several nights before that.** Don't stay up partying. Definitely don't stay up studying; you're not going to discover anything extra at that point.

>> **Wake up on time.** If you live far away from the test center, set your alarm extra early — or even consider spending the night at a hotel nearby. Staying alert through the test is hard enough without combating a lack of sleep, too.

>> **Eat breakfast.** Your brain functions better if you feed it. Drink coffee if you like to drink coffee (though not too much — it's a *diuretic,* which makes you have to use the restroom more often). Try to eat something sustaining — protein and whole grains last longer than a sugary donut. For suggestions, see the nearby sidebar, "The test-day diet."

>> **Make sure you know how to get to the testing site.** Don't wait until the morning of your test to find directions. Take a test drive a day or two before. If you don't know exactly where the site is or where to park, call the test center earlier in the week for complete directions. If you have trouble parking, leave extra early. If you have to feed a parking meter, bring enough coins.

>> **Get to the center early.** Doing so gives you time to get settled in, handle any last-minute emergencies, and make a last preemptive bathroom stop.

After you finish these steps, you're ready to take the test!

If your test starts at 8:30 a.m., you must be at the testing center by 8 a.m. If it starts at 12:30 p.m., you must be there by noon.

REMEMBER

THE TEST-DAY DIET

A growling stomach and a full bladder can drive you crazy when you're trying to work out the details of an LSAT question. Are there ways to prevent these problems? Sure! Protein, fat, and salt are the keys. One of the reasons low-carb diets work is that protein and fat prevent your appetite from rumbling back too soon. For example, if you eat a meal heavy in protein, you don't get hungry for several hours. Try it — eat something like two eggs with cheese cooked in olive oil and see how long it takes you to get hungry again. As for the full bladder, you can do two things: Don't drink too much, and consume salt. Water, coffee, tea, cola, and orange juice all have a diuretic effect, which can send you running to the bathroom or wishing you could. Salty snacks can reverse this phenomenon, helping your body hold on to its fluids. Beef jerky, peanuts, and sports drinks with electrolytes can prevent your bladder from filling too fast. Hey, it may not be the healthiest diet, but desperate times call for desperate measures.

What to bring

Don't sabotage your LSAT score by forgetting the essentials. The following items are imperative for a smooth test experience:

>> **Your admission ticket and a valid photo ID (such as a passport, driver's license or other state-issued ID, or military ID):** You can't get into the test without them.

>> **Sharpened No. 2 pencils, functional eraser, and maybe even a small sharpener:** The eraser can be attached to the pencils or separate; just make sure it fully erases, doesn't leave smudges, and isn't enclosed in a sleeve.

>> **A sweatshirt or jacket:** Wear something with short sleeves underneath. An overenthusiastic climate control system can cool exam rooms to about 50 degrees in fall and spring, and warm them up to 85 degrees in the winter. Like an explorer in the wild, you need to be prepared for any eventuality.

>> **A snack:** Don't eat it during the test, but if you're hungry, definitely shove it into your mouth at break time. Try to make it something sustaining — an energy bar, nuts, or a candy bar packed with peanuts. Protein helps alertness; carbohydrates make some people sleepy.

What to leave behind

When taking the LSAT, you and your fellow test-takers should be focused on the test. You want to avoid anything that could bother you or others. The following list includes items you can't (or shouldn't) bring into your test site:

>> **A calculator, a dictionary, an LSAT strategy book, or any other reading material:** These items are all taboo in LSAT Land.

>> **A cellphone:** No electronics are allowed at the testing site, and their use is banned even during the break.

>> **Heavy perfume:** Other test-takers may be sensitive to it, and you really don't want to sabotage their efforts.

>> **Worries, anxieties, and angst:** Worrying doesn't help now. Breathe deeply and remember everything you read in this book.

Life after the LSAT: What to Do Now?

So you've done it; you've completed an LSAT. What now? Are you happy with your performance? Great! Sit back and wait for your score. Unhappy? You don't have to accept your score; you can cancel it if you really want to. Got a score that you don't like? Try, try again, if your heart is still in it.

Yeah, that worked for me

If you liked what you did or you're just relieved that you're finished and can't be bothered to worry about it now that it's done, you don't have to do anything except wait for your results. If you registered online, your score arrives by email in about three weeks. Printed score reports arrive about four weeks after the test for those without online accounts. The LSAC website (www.lsac.org) has more information.

Wait, I can do better than that!

What if you weren't happy with your performance? You may have choked on an analytical reasoning problem and not managed to finish the section. You may have been too sick to think straight. You may have kept a running tally of questions you thought you got wrong and decided that this test wasn't going to give you a score that you wanted.

Canceling a score

If you decide that your life would be better if your score on this test never saw the light of day, you can cancel it. You can cancel your score in your LSAC account status page from the day after you take the test to up to six days after.

If you cancel your score, that's the end of it. Neither you nor anyone else will ever see the score, though your score report will indicate your decision to cancel.

Previewing a score

If you're a first-time test taker, you can opt to preview your score. For an additional fee, you sign up for score preview. This gives you the option to view your score and then decide within six days whether you wish to cancel it. If you cancel your score, the cancellation will appear in your LSAT report but not the actual score.

If you encountered a problem at the test center — for example, if you had no desk and had to hold your tablet on your knees — report it to the test supervisor. To make sure the problem is considered, you must also report it in writing to the LSAC; you have six days to do this.

Repeating the LSAT

If you're disappointed with your score and you're sure you can do better, you can take the LSAT again. The LSAC's data shows that scores often improve (slightly) for repeat test-takers. Scores also sometimes drop.

WARNING

Before you commit to retaking the LSAT, look at the policy of the law schools you want to apply to. Some law schools average your LSAT scores, so even a big improvement may not make that much difference. However, most schools consider just your highest LSAT score.

The LSAC limits the number of times you can take the LSAT:

REMEMBER

>> **Three times in one year.** The LSAT testing year begins on June 1 and ends on May 31.

>> **Five times during the current and past five testing years.**

>> **Seven times during your lifetime.**

That means you can't just take the LSAT every time it's offered, hoping to get the perfect test that gives you the perfect score.

Even if your score improves dramatically the second or third time you take the test, law schools still see your lower scores. The LSAC sends all LSAT scores in its reports to law schools. In the score report, your scores appear individually and averaged.

TIP

You don't have to let your scores speak for themselves. If something happened that made you score badly, tell the law schools when you send in your application. Think of this as an opportunity to practice your persuasive writing skills. If you do a good job, the law school may be so impressed with your potential as an advocate that it will accept you despite a low LSAT score.

The LSAC's score report automatically includes the scores of all the LSATs you've taken (or registered for and missed) during a five-year period; cancellations also appear.

REMEMBER

Looking to the future, some (but not all) state bar associations demand the law school admission records of applicants. To be safe, keep records from your law school admission process until you've been sworn in and added that lovely "Esq." to your name.

Chapter **3**

The Lowdown on Law School Admissions

If you're reading a book about the LSAT, you're probably considering applying to law school. Well, get ready for a great adventure. Applying to law school can be a rough ride, not to be attempted by the lazy or ambivalent. If you're truly committed to acquiring a legal education, though, the application process can be challenging and even sort of exciting. And if you get into law school, you may get to live someplace new, meet new friends, and broaden your horizons in ways you never considered.

In this chapter, we discuss the ins and outs of choosing schools and applying for admission, as well as the importance of the LSAT in this process.

Choosing a Law School

Not all law schools are created equal. You may still be able to get a fine legal education at most of them, but understand that different law schools have different characteristics. Some are extremely competitive, while others are easier to get into. Some have excellent practical legal programs, while others take a more theoretical approach to the law. Some offer better financial aid packages than others. You need to decide what you want in a school before you let schools decide whether they want you.

Where to go for information

Sifting through the vast amount of often conflicting information about law school can be a daunting task. Finding that information in the first place, though, doesn't have to be hard. Tons of sources are available, some more subjective than others. Here are a few places to look for info:

>> **Career placement or guidance offices at colleges and universities:** Not only do these offices have lots of information on various schools and career options, but they also may even have real people who can give you sensible advice.

- **Friends and acquaintances who've gone to law school:** Don't neglect your personal network! If you know someone who's gone through this process, pump her brain.

- **The Internet:** If you're interested in a particular law school, check out its website. You can also find numerous websites devoted to legal issues, including law school.

- **LSAC law school information:** The Law School Admission Council (LSAC; www.lsac.org) provides detailed information about law school in a searchable format.

- **Bookstores and libraries:** Plenty of books are available about law school, legal practice, and similar topics. (Check out *Law School For Dummies* by Rebecca Fae Greene [John Wiley & Sons, Inc.].)

- **Law school forums:** The LSAC also holds several law school forums in major cities each fall. At a forum, you can speak with real people about selecting a law school, the admissions process, whether law school is right for you, and other concerns.

A wealth of information is out there, so you don't have to apply to law school in the dark. Read the next section to help you decide which law school is right for you.

Important considerations

Keep these important considerations in mind when choosing law schools to which you want to apply:

- **Cost:** This is a biggie. Some law schools are expensive; others are extremely expensive. You need to decide how much money you want to spend (or are able to spend) on your education, bearing in mind that law school debts can stick with you for much of your working life. (**Note:** Cost often goes hand in hand with exclusivity and prestige, which may mean that spending more on a prestigious school results in a better payoff after graduation.)

- **Location:** Where do you want to live? Do you want to be near your family? Do you want to be able to drive to the beach or the mountains (when you're supposed to be in class)? Do you hate harsh winters? Do you consider yourself an East Coast, West Coast, or Midwestern person? You're going to live near your law school for nearly three years, so liking the location is important. Location also plays a role in cost considerations; living in New York City is more expensive than living in Baton Rouge.

- **Public or private:** Some law schools are affiliated with state university systems, while others are part of private universities. Some public schools are cheaper than private ones, especially for in-state residents. On the other hand, public schools tend to suffer more at the whim of state legislators, who can cut their budgets at the drop of a hat. As for prestige, some public institutions regularly appear in the top of the law school rankings, so you can't assume that a private school is more prestigious than a public one.

- **Selectivity:** Does getting into a school with a minute acceptance rate matter to you? Some schools accept a large proportion of applicants, while others skim the thin layer of cream off a giant vat of applications. This point goes with school rank (see the next section); if selectivity matters to you, then keep it in mind. If you have ambitions of working in the nation's top firms or climbing the judicial ladder all the way to the bench of the U.S. Supreme Court, you will likely be better situated if you attend an exclusive, highly ranked school. If you want a JD so you can make a better living in your hometown, an exclusive school may not be worth the money it will cost you.

- **Reputation:** Reputation is such a nebulous concept; the American Bar Association (ABA) especially hates this aspect of the *U. S. News & World Report* ranking scheme. Still, reputation can matter. Consider where you plan to practice law; you want to attend a school that people in that area respect.

>> **Attrition rate:** At some law schools, if you can get in, you're virtually certain to graduate (barring extreme circumstances). Other schools let in a wider variety of applicants but get rid of many of them before graduation by failing a number of students in their first year. No one wants to get weeded out. On the other hand, schools with high attrition rates can be easier to get into in the first place. If your scores are a bit low but you plan to work like crazy in law school, a law school with a high attrition rate may work well for you.

>> **Quality of life:** Some law schools are known for being happy places to get a legal education. Students are friendly to one another, social events are at least as important as classes, and the surrounding area is bucolic. Other places aren't as pleasant, with more competition among students and crowded, ill-equipped facilities. You can get a decent education at either type, but you'll have more fun at some schools than at others.

>> **Campus life:** You want to spend your law school years among friends, if at all possible, which often means finding a school attended by people similar to you. Some schools attract younger students, those who have recently graduated from college and attend full time. Other programs may have a higher percentage of older students, many of whom may have day jobs and families and may prefer to attend law school part time. If any aspect of campus life is particularly important to you, take some time to research whether the schools that interest you are congenial places to spend three years of your life.

>> **Grading practices:** Grades are extremely important to law students; some law firms base most of their hiring decisions on law school grades. Not all schools grade alike, though. Many schools grade on a *mean,* in which the majority of students get a particular grade (such as B) with only a few getting grades above or below. Other schools grade most classes pass-fail. Still others don't control grading at all, and grades depend on the professors' whims.

>> **Curriculum:** What do you want to study in law school? Do you like large lectures or small seminars? Some schools offer joint degrees, such as JD-MBA combinations. Some schools are known for specialties, such as international or environmental law. Some law schools are very liberal; others are extremely conservative. Bear these points in mind when choosing your school — and your future friends — for the next three years.

>> **Opportunities for practical experience:** Clinical programs offer students the opportunity to put their legal skills in practice early on, which can be invaluable for finding jobs and working after graduation. Some schools emphasize this more than others, providing ample opportunity for students to get hands-on practice during the school year through clinics and internships.

>> **Bar pass rate:** You can't practice law if you can't pass the bar exam. Some schools have a higher bar-pass rate than others. Don't think, though, that no one passes the bar from schools with low pass rates. All a lower bar-pass rate means is that the school's students overall aren't as well prepared for the bar exam. (Not that law school prepares you to pass the bar; that's what postgraduation bar review is for.)

>> **Where you want to live after law school:** This point is more significant than you may realize. If you want to live on the East Coast, you'll have better luck finding a job there if you attend a nearby law school than if you go off to Washington State. If you want to practice in South Carolina, a degree from the University of South Carolina may be more useful than a degree from the University of Michigan, even though Michigan is ranked higher.

>> **Alumni network:** You'll spend much more of your life as a law school graduate than as a law school student. Knowing that the friends you make in law school can help you down the road is great. A strong alumni network can be a valuable resource for the rest of your life.

Choosing a law school is a lot like choosing a college. A wide variety of choices is out there; try to find a selection of schools that really suits you.

REMEMBER

Keeping ranking in mind

Nearly 200 law schools in the country are approved by the ABA. (Incidentally, you should go to an ABA-approved school; lots of state bars don't admit graduates of schools that aren't approved.) Naturally, people have tried to rank the nation's law schools. (See the nearby sidebar, "Law school rankings and accreditation," for more about these organizations that rank law schools.)

In a field as competitive as law, are you really surprised to know that people are constantly trying to come up with ways to look superior to one another? Law firms like to know the relative rankings of the schools from which they recruit. Law students like to compare their school to others, usually in the hopes of bragging that their school is better than another one. Law school recruiters like to emphasize how attractive their graduates are to prospective employers.

TIP

What do you think is one of the main things that *U. S. News & World Report* looks at when ranking schools? You guessed it — LSAT scores! The higher the average LSAT score of admitted students, the higher the school's ranking. Other things count, but LSAT scores are very important. These schools are best because their students' LSATs are best, which means the schools are best (wait, that's circular reasoning!).

The ABA and the LSAC (the folks who create and run the LSAT; see Chapter 1) disapprove of commercial rankings, which try to reduce every law school to a single numeric value, and they have a point. There's a lot more to an individual school than a number published in *U. S. News & World Report*. Rankings are random and don't reflect the true value of the education available at any given institution.

WARNING

Unfortunately in the real world, rank sometimes matters. Certain law firms and other employers take their new hires from a specific group of schools, and they very rarely consider applications from anyone who didn't attend that select group, no matter how good the person's grades or outside experiences are. The rationale behind this practice is that top law schools have already selected the "best" law students — the ones with the highest grades and LSAT scores — and these people will naturally make the best lawyers. Although in practice that doesn't always turn out to be the case, you'll have a hard time convincing those employers otherwise.

REMEMBER

However, the law school rankings are far from perfect. Law school rankings change from year to year, sometimes dramatically. A school may be ranked 7th one year, fall to 14th the next year, and jump back to 6th the next. That fluidity alone should be a warning to you not to take rankings too seriously; there's no way a school's total quality can change that much that fast.

Are you wondering about how schools are ranked? The following list breaks down the law school rankings (which *doesn't* list specific schools):

> » **Top ten:** These are the top of the pile.
>
> » **First tier:** These are the top 50 schools.
>
> » **Second tier:** Schools ranked 51 through 100.
>
> » **Third tier:** Schools ranked 101 through 150.
>
> » **Fourth tier:** Schools ranked 151 through 186 (or so).

Firms that care about these rankings restrict their recruiting to particular tiers. Other firms are more interested in the whole applicant — his grades, interests, commitment to living in a particular place, work ethic, and so on — and interview dedicated students from any school if they seem like good prospects.

LAW SCHOOL RANKINGS AND ACCREDITATION

Every year, *U. S. News & World Report* publishes rankings of colleges and universities; you may remember looking at these rankings when you applied to undergrad. Law schools don't escape this ranking system. When *U. S. News* sets out to rank law schools, it concocts a numerical score based on several criteria, including the school's assessment by lawyers and peer institutions (that is, the opinion that other law schools and legal professionals hold about the school), average LSAT scores and undergraduate GPAs of the current entering class, percentage of applicants who are accepted, student-faculty ratios, employment rate of graduates at graduation and nine months after graduation, and the school's bar passage rate in its state.

ABA accreditation is a whole different ballgame. The ABA keeps tabs on law schools in an effort to make sure that all law school graduates receive a meaningful legal education; it has kept a list of accredited schools since 1921. It doesn't accredit schools where the average undergraduate GPA or LSAT score of the students is below a certain level (143 is the cutoff score for the average LSAT). After a law school applies for accreditation, the ABA evaluates it based on the school's admissions standards, its faculty, its facilities and library, and its program of instruction. ABA committee members actually visit the school for several days and attend classes. If a school passes the test, the ABA gives it provisional approval for three to five years, followed by full approval if it maintains its standards. (Read more about this on the ABA's website, www.americanbar.org.) ABA accreditation is currently a touchy topic for several law schools that want accreditation but haven't yet received it, especially with the advent of online law schools in recent years.

Why do some firms rely on these rankings? Reading résumés takes a lot less time if they throw out all the ones from lower-ranking schools. They figure the law schools have already selected a good batch of future lawyers and find it easier to limit their recruiting to those elite schools.

Rank also affects future salaries and career possibilities. Graduates of the highest-ranked law schools tend to have the highest salaries. People who eventually become law professors and major judges also come more often from higher-ranked schools.

Okay, that's depressing. So let us give you some better news. People who barely scrape through the lowest-ranked school still get employed as lawyers, and plenty of them make good money, too. And plenty of folks who graduate from top-ten law schools don't end up practicing law at all.

REMEMBER

What's the moral of all this? Rankings do matter, but not for everyone and not in every case. So take them seriously, but not too seriously. More important, look at what you want out of law school and what you want to do afterward.

Filling Out All the Forms — Applying to Law School

Applying to law school is an art all its own. You have to choose several schools, go through the expensive and complicated application rigmarole, scrounge around for financial aid, and then decide which one of the schools that accepts you is the one you want to attend. The whole process is daunting and really not much fun, but it's the only way to get where you want to go (assuming law school *is*, in fact, where you want to go).

Pick more than one

Back when you applied for undergrad, you probably picked out several schools that interested you and applied to them all (unless you got in somewhere early). You probably knew that you couldn't count on getting into them all, but if you applied to several places, you'd most likely get into at least one and wouldn't be stuck after high school with no college to attend. (If you were fortunate, several schools accepted you, and then you got to choose the one that best suited your needs.) The same principle holds true in law school.

Unless you're sure you'll get into a particular school or there's only one place you could feasibly attend, pick several schools that you think satisfy your craving for legal education. The prevailing wisdom is to apply to at least one or two safety schools, where you're pretty sure you'll be accepted; four or five schools where you have a reasonable chance of getting in; and one or two "reaches," schools where you probably won't be accepted but still have a chance of getting in.

WARNING

Applying to law schools isn't cheap. At about $60 to $100 a pop, the cost can really add up if you apply to several schools. Spend your money wisely; only send applications to schools you'd seriously consider attending. If you already know that you can attend only your local law school, don't waste money applying anywhere else.

How admissions work

Law school admission offices run on a yearly cycle. In the fall, the admissions folks begin accepting applications. In the winter and spring, they read these applications and send out letters of acceptance. They spend the late spring and summer assembling the entering class — fielding letters of commitment, accepting students off the waiting list when spots open up, and getting ready for the next admission cycle. Most law schools promise to send out letters of admission by April 15, though many of them begin sending them out much sooner.

The early bird . . .

Most law schools stop accepting applications in January and give students until March to get in all their supporting materials. That doesn't necessarily mean you can wait until January with impunity. Many schools start reviewing applications in the fall and may begin sending out acceptance letters in November. As a result, students whose applications aren't complete until March are competing for fewer spaces in the entering class, which decreases their chances of acceptance.

TIP

Some law schools offer an early notification option. Students who get their applications in really early — during September, October, or November of the year before they want to matriculate — receive a decision by December. This option doesn't necessarily commit a student to that particular law school; make sure to check the rules at individual schools.

REMEMBER

If you know you're going to apply to law school, take the LSAT the spring, summer, or early fall of the year you want to apply. You can take it in late fall and still get in, but you risk losing a space to someone who gets her documents in earlier. Some law schools accept February LSAT results, but don't wait that late; most of the spaces in a class are gone by the time the results come in.

A complete application

Are you wondering what comprises a complete law school application? Don't worry. Check out this list for a complete inventory of what most law schools consider a complete application:

>> Completed, signed application form

>> LSAT score

>> Transcripts of prior academic record, submitted through the Credential Assembly Service (CAS)

>> Dean's certification forms from your prior institutions of higher education (to prove that you went there)

>> Letters of recommendation, submitted through the CAS or independently

>> Personal statement — an essay you write, usually explaining why you want to go to law school

>> Application fee — $60 to $100, though this number tends to creep upward year by year

You may also have to send in forms about your state residency, financial needs, or other relevant bits of information. Every school's admission form tells you exactly what to send.

WARNING

If one single piece of your application isn't in place by the deadline (or whenever the admissions committee stops considering applications), no one will read any of it. So if the form for your dean's certification goes missing or one of your recommenders forgets to send in his letter, your application is no good and you've wasted your money.

Review of applications

Many law schools receive far more applicants than they have spaces in an entering class. Obviously, the first thing admissions committees look at is academic credentials and LSAT scores, but numbers definitely aren't everything. Every year, competitive law schools admit some students with fairly low scores and grades and reject some with stellar numbers.

Law schools are interested in more than mere academic ability. They hope to create law school classes that represent a diversity of backgrounds and interests and that have the potential to do great things. Nothing makes a law school look as good as an illustrious group of alumni. Here are a few of the factors that admissions committees consider:

>> Geography (where students come from); schools like to get people from all over the place

>> Ideological background

>> Race and ethnicity

>> Unique experiences and responses to hardships

Your personal statement is a good place to mention anything you want the admissions committee to know about you — anything that makes you unique.

Law schools take great pains to assure everyone that their admissions committees and faculty members really do read every single application, regardless of how low the applicant's numbers are. Usually at least two people review each file. Each reader makes a recommendation — whether to admit, deny, wait-list, or put on hold to reconsider later. If the two readers disagree about an application, it goes to a third reader. At the end of the admission cycle, the committee ranks everyone who is left; some get in, some don't, and some get wait-listed.

REMEMBER

If you're wait-listed, don't despair. Every year, many students receive phone calls from law schools during the summer, often as late as the week before classes begin, informing them that they've been admitted. This doesn't give you much time to prepare or find housing, but it's not a bad deal if you're flexible.

Don't forget the money

Law school is expensive and seems to get pricier every year. The good news is that most people who need it can get financial aid from their law school or from other sources. The bad news is that the vast majority of this aid is in the form of loans, not scholarships or grants, which means you have to pay it back after you're done with law school. (The large loans are one of the factors that keep many recent and not-so-recent law school grads working outrageous hours for law firms.)

If you need financial aid, you have to fill out the correct paperwork fairly early, by March of the year in which you'll matriculate. The financial aid office at your future law school can tell you what you need to do.

TIP

Some law schools offer merit scholarships to applicants with very high LSAT scores. Some schools also waive application fees for high scorers, which is less lucrative than free tuition but still pleasant.

2

Analytical Reasoning: Following the Rules of the Logic Game

Overcome the often-overwhelming analytical reasoning (also known as *logic games*) questions and maybe even learn to love them.

Distinguish between ordering and grouping logic games.

Discover how to create a useful game board for each logic game so that you can answer the questions more efficiently.

Find out why the first question in the set is almost always the easiest to answer.

Analyze each logic game's rules more thoroughly by knowing about contrapositives.

IN THIS CHAPTER

» Knowing analytical reasoning
section basics

» Establishing a strategy to tackle
analytical reasoning problems

» Using certain tactics to maximize
your analytical reasoning score

Chapter **4**

Gaming the Analytical Reasoning Questions

The LSAT's analytical reasoning section intimidates most LSAT-takers. It's the bugaboo, the bête noir, the boogeyman, the nemesis of otherwise calm, cool, and collected would-be law students. No one does problems like these logic brain-drainers in school, so they're a completely new experience for many people.

But here's the good news: These problems are totally teachable, and in fact they can be fun! So fun we also refer to them as logic *games.* This chapter provides you with tips that can improve your score significantly. After you crack the code of a particular fact pattern, answering every single question in the set correctly is entirely possible. You may even find that the analytical reasoning section becomes one of your favorites.

In this chapter, we introduce the analytical reasoning section and describe techniques to tackle the two main problem types: ordering and grouping. In keeping with the spirit of seeing analytical reasoning problems as games, we show you how to set up a game board and then manipulate the game pieces according to the rules of each question set. We also introduce the three general question types and give you insight on how to approach each one. Master the game plan, and before long you'll know exactly how to play this section successfully.

Analyzing the Analytical Reasoning Section

The analytical reasoning section lasts 35 minutes. During that period, you experience four fact patterns with conditions followed by 5 to 8 questions, for a total of about 23 questions. So you have about 8 minutes and 45 seconds to work through each set of questions. The fact patterns present scenarios with a set or two of variables we call *game pieces* — people, dorm rooms, places around an office table, stuff like that — and introduce rules that govern how to use them. The questions test your ability to apply the given rules and make deductions, which (believe it or not) is a skill you use a lot in law school and the practice of law.

The thought processes involved in applying statutory and case law to a scenario aren't very different from the thinking and method involved in applying the rules to the facts in analytical reasoning problems. Furthermore, lawyers concentrate on arcane laws for long periods of time, and the LSAT indicates whether you can maintain that kind of attention to detail for an extended period. So, although working analytical reasoning problems won't be part of your grueling first year of law school, you need the analytical skills and attention to detail these problems test to endure the Socratic teaching methods that your law professors may implement.

Setting Yourself Up for Success Step by Step

Analytical reasoning problem sets vary in topic. You may be asked to undertake a somewhat silly task, such as choosing toppings for ice cream flavors, or you may find yourself taking on the role of city planner, positioning buildings on a new construction site. Regardless of their subject matter, you tackle every analytical reasoning problem in much the same way.

1. **Read the facts.**

   Each logic game introduces the scenario with a paragraph or two that indicates whether the problem involves ordering or grouping, lists the variables *(game pieces)*, and otherwise provides the information you need to set up a diagram we call the *game board*.

2. **Analyze the rules.**

   Also referred to as *conditions*, the rules dictate the limitations for arranging or grouping the game pieces on the game board.

3. **Answer the questions.**

   After you've analyzed the effects of the rules and recorded them and their corollaries on your game board, you've established the foundation for tackling the questions that follow.

The rest of this chapter provides you with the details on how to follow these three steps for every logic game you encounter. We're very thorough, but if you want even more detailed information about how to master this section of the LSAT, we suggest you read *LSAT Logic Games For Dummies*, by Mark Zegarelli (John Wiley & Sons, Inc.). This helpful text devotes itself to only the analytical reasoning section; it covers how to deal with some of the more unusual logic games and provides you with many more practice questions.

Get the facts, decide between ordering and grouping, and set up your game board

The first paragraph of a logic game sets up the facts. As you read the information, complete these tasks:

>> **Establish whether the logic game is an ordering or grouping problem.** We define these two types of logic games in much more depth in Chapters 5 and 6, but the general difference between them is that ordering problems require you to place game pieces in relationship to one another and grouping problems ask you to group game pieces together in two or more sets.

>> **List the initials of the elements you need to order or group.** These are your game pieces. Each element always begins with a different letter, so referring to pieces by their first initial is quick and easy. You have scratch paper provided by the test center and your own pencil and eraser to create your game board.

>> **Create the foundation of your game board.** The most common game board for logic games is a very simple box chart with the positions or group names as column headers, below which you place the game pieces according to the rules.

So if the LSAT presents you with this sample first paragraph for an ordering logic game, you know what to do:

EXAMPLE

A college radio station schedules six disc jockeys — Gary, Harriet, Jamal, Lucy, Marco, and Penelope — during a 24-hour period. Each one of the six disc jockeys hosts exactly one 4-hour program, and the programs are scheduled one after the other during that period.

As you read the example paragraph, note the key word *schedules*. This is a big clue that you're dealing with a logic game that requires you to place the pieces in order according to some type of schedule. You have six game pieces — the six disc jockeys. Although the paragraph doesn't clearly specify that you're dealing with six positions, you can gather this fact from the wording. Knowing there are six 4-hour programs in a 24-hour period, one scheduled right after the other, tells you that you need to list the six disc jockeys in six scheduled spots from first to last. Every possible ordering in this game includes all six game pieces and all six spots.

Create your game board as you read. List the initials of the disc jockeys — G, H, J, L, M, and P — on your scratch paper. Draw a simple box chart with six columns headed 1, 2, 3, 4, 5, and 6 to designate the six daily program spots from first to last. Your board looks something like this:

G H J L M P

1	2	3	4	5	6

Consider the rules and modify your game board

The second half of the logic game is a list of conditions that specify how the game pieces may be arranged or grouped. Some rules allow you to place a game piece in a permanent spot on the game board. We call these *target* rules. An example of a target rule is, "Gary is scheduled last." Unfortunately, very few rules in LSAT logic games are targets. Some indicate where game pieces don't belong, such as, "Gary is not scheduled last." Others give you information about where pieces belong relative to one another, such as, "Lucy is scheduled before Marco." And others tell you something is true about a game piece contingent on when the condition is true of another game piece, such as, "If Marco is scheduled before Penelope, Harriet is scheduled before Gary."

As you read the rules, record them in shorthand under your game board. Shortcuts save time and space and allow you to refer the rules just by looking at your game board. Different kinds of rules call for different recording methods, and rules for ordering games may be worded a bit differently from those for grouping games. We cover analyzing the rules and writing them in shorthand in more detail in Chapters 5 and 6, where we provide specific information about how to handle the two general types of logic games.

TIP

Your rule shortcuts don't have to be fancy as long as you use them consistently. Some common shorthand symbols include:

>> Arrows (→) to mark the spatial relationship between pieces

>> = or ≠ to mark positive or negative relationships between pieces

>> A strikethrough through a letter to indicate that a piece can't be someplace or do something

>> Underscores (_) to mark spaces that must be filled by unknown pieces

Check out the conditions that apply to the sample logic game.

EXAMPLE

A college radio station schedules six disc jockeys — Gary, Harriet, Jamal, Lucy, Marco, and Penelope — during a 24-hour period. Each one of the six disc jockeys hosts exactly one 4-hour program, and the programs are scheduled one after the other during that period. To accommodate each disc jockey's schedule, the station must abide by the following conditions in setting up its daily programming:

Both Lucy and Marco are scheduled before Harriet.

Both Lucy and Penelope are scheduled before Jamal.

If Marco is scheduled before Penelope, then Harriet is scheduled before Gary.

Gary's program is not the last program of the day.

Analyze each condition.

>> The first tells you that both Lucy and Marco come before Harriet. You can write this rule in shorthand next to your game board: L → H; M → H. Note that this rule means that L and M can occupy any position before Harriet, not necessarily the one immediately before Harriet.

>> The second condition is similar. Write its shortcut next to the game board: L → J; P→ J.

>> The third rule provides a contingency, an "If/then statement." You can write this rule next to the game board like this: If M → P, H → G. The contrapositive, if G → H, P → M, is also true. We discuss contrapositives in more detail in Chapters 5 and 6.

>> Condition four tells you where Gary doesn't go. You can record this rule directly on the game board by writing a G in the sixth spot and crossing it out.

None of the four rules is a target, so you don't know exactly where any one of the game pieces fits on the board.

As you examine each rule, pay attention to the consequential truths that arise and look at your shorthand list for rules that concern the same piece. Record your findings on the board.

>> If L is scheduled before H, L can't be 6, and H can't be 1. Furthermore, if M is before H, M can't be 6, and H can't be 1 or 2. Record these truths by adding the pieces to the game board with slashes through them.

>> If L is before J (and also before H according to the preceding rule), L can't be 5 or 6, and J can't be 1. If P is before J, P can't be 6, and J can't be 1 or 2.

>> Because the third rule is conditional, you can't represent it permanently on your game board, but you can show the conditions of the two alternatives for when P is before M and when M is before P, like this:

G H J L M P

If P→M (or G→H)	1	2	3	4	5	6
If P→M (or G→H)	~~H~~ ~~J~~ ~~M~~ G, L, or P	~~H~~ ~~J~~			~~J~~	~~G~~ ~~J~~ ~~M~~ ~~P~~ H or J
If M→P (or H→G)	~~H~~ ~~J~~ ~~P~~ G, L, or M	~~H~~ ~~J~~	~~H~~ ~~J~~		~~J~~ ~~M~~	J

L → H
M → H
L → J
P → J
If M → P, H → G
If G → H, P → M

Your game board reveals that when M is before P (and thus H is before G), J has to be 6, and only L or M can be 1. Focus on what's true for the first and last positions, but fill in the available pieces for the middle spots, too, as we've done in the game board.

When P is before M, only G, L, or P can be 1, and only H or J can be 6.

You can take your deductions even further by writing out some of the possible orders whenever M is scheduled before P:

G H J L M P

	1	2	3	4	5	6
If P→M (or G→H)	~~H~~ ~~J~~ ~~M~~ G, L, or P	~~H~~ ~~J~~			~~J~~	~~G~~ ~~J~~ ~~M~~ ~~P~~ H or J
If M→P (or H→G)	~~H~~ ~~J~~ ~~P~~ ~~G~~ L or M	~~H~~ ~~J~~ ~~G~~	~~H~~ ~~J~~ ~~G~~	~~J~~	~~J~~ ~~M~~	J
"	L/M	M/L	P/H	H/P	G	J
"	L/M	M/L	H	G/P	P/G	J

L → H
M → H
L → J
P → J
If M → P, H → G
If G → H, P → M

So whenever M is before P, the following are true:

>> L or M must be 1.

>> M must be 1 or 2.

>> H must be 3 or 4.

>> G must be 4 or 5.

>> P can be 2, 3, 4, or 5.

>> J must be 6.

Congratulations! You've just completed your working game board. Now you can tackle the questions.

WARNING

Not every logic game allows you to come up with just a few possible orders or groups. If you don't come up with a few possibilities right away, begin answering the questions. Don't spend so much time considering all options that you don't have time to finish the section.

Answer the questions

Creating the game board for logic games is key, but you don't get points unless you answer the questions. Most of the questions you experience in this section fall into four types:

» **Possible listing/assignment questions:** Almost all logic games begin with a question that asks you for the answer that provides a possible listing (for order problems) or assignment (for grouping problems) of the game pieces.

» **Quantity questions:** For these questions, you usually determine how many game pieces could occupy a particular position, so they're most common in ordering-problem sets.

» **Add-a-rule questions:** Some questions provide an additional condition to use to answer only that question.

» **Open questions:** This question type simply asks what's true, false, or possible based on the original conditions.

We show you how to answer each type of question in the rest of this section.

Possible listing/assignment questions

The easiest logic game question type to answer is the possible listing/assignment question. It's usually the first question of the set. You don't need to refer to the game board to answer it; you simply apply each condition to the answer choices and eliminate the four answers that violate a condition.

These questions ask you for the answer that provides an accurate ordering or grouping of the game pieces. The five answers supply five potential orders or groups for the logic games. Four of the orders or groups violate at least one condition and are therefore not possible. Only one provides a possibility that doesn't violate a rule.

TIP

The key to answering every possible listing/assignment question correctly is to read a rule and then eliminate the answer (or answers) that violates it rather than reading an answer choice and finding the rule(s) it violates. Here's a sample possible listing/assignment question for the disc jockey scenario to demonstrate what we mean.

EXAMPLE

Which of the following could be the programming order of the disc jockeys from first to last?

(A) Penelope, Marco, Lucy, Jamal, Gary, Harriet

(B) Lucy, Penelope, Marco, Harriet, Jamal, Gary

(C) Harriet, Lucy, Penelope, Jamal, Gary, Marco

(D) Gary, Marco, Penelope, Lucy, Harriet, Jamal

(E) Gary, Lucy, Jamal, Penelope, Marco, Harriet

This is an ordering problem, so the question asks for a possible order. When you see this question type for a grouping problem, it will likely ask for a possible assignment or matching of elements to groups. Here are the steps to answering this question:

1. **Read the first condition.**

It states that both L and M are before H. Look through the five answer choices to find the one that doesn't place L and M before H. Choice (C) puts H first, so neither L nor M is before H. Cross out Choice (C).

2. **Read the second condition.**

   Both L and P are before J. Choice (E) positions J between L and P, so it can't be a possible order. Eliminate Choice (E).

3. **The third condition pertains to when M is before P.**

   Of the remaining answers, only Choice (D) positions M before P. H is definitely after G in Choice (D), so that answer violates the third rule and is incorrect.

4. **Check the last condition.**

   It's an easy one to evaluate. Gary can't be last, but Choice (B) puts Gary at the end. So Choice (B) must be wrong.

5. **Do a quick rule check for the remaining answer Choice (A).**

   L and M are before H, L and P are before J, the third condition doesn't apply, and Gary isn't last. Its order is entirely possible.

Choice (A) is the answer.

See how easy this question type is when you approach it methodically? The good news is that virtually every logic game begins with one of these easy question types, so you're bound to answer the first question of every problem set correctly.

TIP

Note that you don't need to use the game board to answer this question. So even if you're having trouble setting up a board for a problem set, at least attempt to answer the first question.

Quantity questions

When the answers to a logic game question are all numbers, you're likely dealing with a question that asks how many of the elements could occupy one of the positions in an ordering problem or be a group member in a grouping problem. Usually a question set contains no more than one of this type. You'll be glad you spent a little time creating your game board when you encounter a question that asks for *how many*.

1. **First, check the position on your game board to see whether you've eliminated any of the pieces from the position in question.**

2. **Eliminate answers that are greater than the number of remaining possibilities.**

   So if your game board shows that three of six game pieces can't occupy the position in question, you can eliminate any answer that's greater than 3.

3. **Test each of the remaining possibilities to see whether an arrangement exists that places it in the position in question without violating a rule.**

4. **Choose the answer that reflects the number of game pieces that could occupy the position.**

For the sample logic game, you may see a quantity question like this one:

EXAMPLE

Exactly how many of the disc jockeys could be the one scheduled sixth?

(A) 1

(B) 2

(C) 3

(D) 4

(E) 5

When you look at the sixth position on your game board, you see that four disc jockeys — G, L, M, and P — can't possibly occupy that spot. Eliminate Choices (C), (D), and (E). You know that when M → P, only J can be sixth. But it appears that when P → M, H could also occupy the sixth position. You could trust that both H and J are possible in the sixth position and pick Choice (B). If you wanted to be absolutely sure, though, you could try H in the sixth spot to see whether it works. You could order the schedule like this: L, G, P, J, M, H. That arrangement puts H last and violates no conditions. So you know for sure that both H and J could be scheduled sixth, and Choice (B) is the answer.

TIP

If you're unable to limit your game board to the extent demonstrated by the example, you may find it helpful to skip the quantity question until you've answered a few of the other questions in the set. Sometimes your answers to other questions provide further enlightenment on which game pieces can occupy which positions. Eliminate as many answers as you can, mark the question to show that you still need to answer it, and go back to it after you've answered the other questions in the set.

Add-a-rule and open questions

The remaining questions in a problem set are usually ones that either add a temporary condition or ask an open question about the original conditions. Both types ask for answers that are true, false, or possible. Read the question carefully to make sure you know which answer type you're looking for and which answers to eliminate.

» **True:** For questions that seek a true answer, eliminate answer choices that either must be false or could be false. These questions may be worded like these:

- Which one of the following must be true?

- Each one of the following could be false EXCEPT:

- Which one of the following CANNOT be false?

- Which one of the following must be selected?

» **False:** For questions that seek a false answer, eliminate answer choices that either must be true or could be true. These questions often look like these:

- Which one of the following CANNOT be true?

- All the following could be true EXCEPT:

- Which one of the following must be false?

» **Could be true:** For questions whose answers are possible or true, eliminate answers that must be false. The questions may look like these:

- Which one of the following could be true?

- Each one of the following must be false EXCEPT:

>> **Could be false:** For questions whose answers are possible or false, eliminate answers that must be true. Questions could be worded like these:

- Which one of the following could be false?
- Each one of the following must be true EXCEPT:

Generally, add-a-rule questions are faster to answer than the open type because they allow you to limit your game board a little more. To answer the questions that add a rule, apply the temporary condition to your game board and play with the new possible arrangements. Then, depending on whether the question asks for what's true, false, or possible, eliminate answers as we specify in the preceding list.

Here's a sample add-a-rule question for the disc jockey logic game.

EXAMPLE

If Lucy is scheduled directly before Gary, then which one of the following must be true?

(A) Penelope is scheduled first.

(B) Marco is scheduled before Gary.

(C) Lucy is scheduled in one of the first three programming spots.

(D) Harriet is scheduled last.

(E) Gary is scheduled in one of the last three programming spots.

This question adds the temporary condition that L comes immediately before G and asks for the answer that *must be true.* So add the rule to your game board and eliminate answers that either could be false or must be false.

Look at your original game board. None of the possible orders allows for L to come right before G whenever M → P because M → P forces H between L and G, which violates the first rule. So you're dealing with arrangements where P → M. If G comes right after L, then L can't occupy the fourth position because now there has to be room for G, J, and H after L. So when L is right before G, L can't be 4, 5, or 6, which is the same as saying that L has to occupy 1, 2, or 3. That's Choice (C).

Eliminate Choice (A) because it could be false. P doesn't have to be first. This order places L before G and doesn't violate any rules: L, G, P, M, H, J.

This arrangement also reveals that Choices (B), (D), and (E) could be false and are therefore wrong. M doesn't come before G, H isn't last, and G is in the 2 spot.

Choice (C) is correct.

REMEMBER

Questions don't build on one another, so the temporary condition supplied by an add-a-rule question applies only to that question. Don't take it along with you to the next question in the set.

You handle open questions much the same way you do those that add a rule, except that you don't enter additional information on your game board. Focus on what type of answer — true, false, or possible — you seek, and eliminate choices accordingly.

Here's an open question that could appear in the disc jockey example:

EXAMPLE

Which one of the following CANNOT be true?

(A) Penelope is scheduled in the second programming spot.

(B) Penelope is scheduled before Marco.

(C) Lucy is scheduled in the fifth programming spot.

(D) Harriet is scheduled in the last programming spot.

(E) Harriet is scheduled before Gary.

An answer that can't be true must be false, so eliminate any answer choice that could or must be true. Your game board reveals that L is never 5, so the likely answer is Choice (C). See whether you can eliminate the other choices to be sure.

The game board shows P as a possibility in the second position, so Choice (A) could be true and is therefore wrong. All the options for when M is before P have H before G, so Choice (E) could be true. You were able to put H last when you worked out the answer to the quantity question, so you know Choice (D) could be true. And the order you created to answer the add-a-rule question shows P before M, so Choice (B) is wrong.

The correct answer absolutely must be Choice (C).

Open questions can be the most time consuming. If your game board is thin, sometimes the only way to answer them is to apply each answer choice to the game board. So you may find it easier to answer some of the other question types in a set before you tackle this type.

In Chapters 5 and 6, we provide more strategies for answering logic games questions and talk a little about how to handle some of the rare questions that don't fit into one of the four main categories.

Attending to Some Analytical Reasoning Do's

As you tackle the logic games in the analytical reasoning section, follow these "to do's" to optimize your experience.

Take time to develop your game board

You may feel you're wasting precious time analyzing the rules and creating a game board. But if you spend several minutes setting up the board and extending the conditions, you'll spend very little time actually answering the questions.

Pick your battles

You don't have to answer the questions for a logic game set in order. In fact, sometimes working out answers to later questions in a set gives you the information you need to answer an earlier question.

When you get stuck on a question, mark it, skip it, and move on. If answering other questions in the set doesn't help you solve it, eliminate answers that must be wrong, guess from the remaining ones, and get on with the rest of the test. (See Chapter 2 for some guidance on guessing.)

Don't skip the first question in the set, though. You can almost always answer this question by simply applying the rules one by one and eliminating answers that violate them.

Remember that four wrongs make a right

Identifying wrong answers is often a lot easier than searching for the right one. For many questions, violations of rules are easy to spot; answers that don't violate any rules can be harder to see. When you eliminate four of the answers, the right answer remains.

Stay calm

Panic destroys some potentially brilliant LSAT scores. A student starts to work on a problem, doesn't immediately see the relationships among the characters, looks at the clock, realizes she only has five minutes left and seven questions left to answer, looks back at the problem, gets increasingly flustered, looks at the clock again, sees her future sinking into the mire, and suddenly she's blown the whole thing. It happens all the time.

Guess what? That approach doesn't help! Sure, it's nerve-racking, facing down this scary test amidst a roomful of strangers and knowing that your professional life could be on the line. Take a deep breath and remind yourself you're just playing a few games. Get back on course by applying the game method we outline in this chapter and Chapters 5 and 6.

Decide which problem to confront first

Each analytical reasoning section contains four logic games. You don't have to work them in order. You can work the second one first, and then the fourth, the first, and the third if you want to. No one cares — as long as you answer them all.

How do you decide which problem to work first? One method is to skim all four logic games, rank them in order of difficulty, and then work them in order from easiest to hardest. The problem with this method is that distinguishing between the easy sets and the difficult sets may not be obvious at first and takes away from time you could be using to work the problems.

TIP

A less time-consuming method is to work the problems with the most questions first. If you see a logic game with eight questions and another one with five, work the one with eight questions first. Each fact pattern takes about the same amount of time to figure out, so if you choose the problem with the greatest number of questions, you maximize the payoff from your time investment.

Maintain your perspective

Don't let this section psych you out. The test provides you with every piece of information you need to answer each question. The LSAT doesn't expect you to have experience in cupcake decorating or city planning when it presents you with a logic game. It does try to make this section difficult by making problem sets seem more complex than they are. Simply remind yourself that you have the tools you need to ace this section.

TIP

If a particular logic game or question spikes your adrenaline and sparks your natural flight reaction to the point where you'd like to flee the room, give yourself a break. Sit back in your chair, close your eyes, and take a deep, cleansing breath to get the oxygen flowing to your brain.

REMEMBER

You can solve every analytical reasoning problem on the LSAT. The test-makers have checked to make sure. When doubt arises, combat it with this important truth.

Keep practicing

The best way to get better at answering logic games is to apply the strategies to a bunch of them. This book gives you access to three complete analytical reasoning sections in Chapters 15, 17, and 19. Additionally, we suggest that you work on the questions from prior LSAT exams that are available from the LSAC. Access copies of more than 60 LSAT exams from www.lsac.org and work as many of them as you have time for before you sit for the exam.

Chapter 5

Proper Placement: Analytical Reasoning Ordering Games

At least one of the four logic games in any 35-minute LSAT analytical reasoning section requires you to order its elements. To make sure you're ready for this common question type, this chapter gives you tips on recognizing ordering games, dealing with their rules, and answering their questions correctly.

Spotting Ordering Games

Chapter 4 outlines the three steps to approaching logic games as read the facts, analyze the rules, and answer the questions. As you read the facts, your first job is to decide whether the game involves ordering or grouping.

The way you approach ordering games differs a bit from the way you handle grouping games, so distinguishing between the two is one of the first steps in your overall approach to the analytical reasoning section. (For the 411 on grouping games, see Chapter 6.) The LSAT is inconsistent in the number of ordering logic games it presents and the order in which they appear, so you have to rely on clues to know for certain whether you're dealing with an ordering problem.

Fact patterns and rules that deal with scheduling, ranking, or positioning are usually ordering games. You can spot them by looking for these word clues:

>> **Temporal references:** Words such as *day, year,* and *month* indicate scheduling.

>> **Ranking terms:** Comparison language — such as *best/worst, greatest/least,* and *highest/lowest* — show ranking.

>> **Positioning terms:** References to positions — such as *first/last* and *before/after* — designate order.

Although the LSAT may throw in an unusual arrangement every once in a while, the most common ordering problems position elements (or game pieces) in a straight line from left to right.

TIP

If you're still not sure about the type of logic game after you read its setup, check the first question. The first question of each logic game usually asks you to choose a possible listing or assignment of the elements. First questions that ask for a possible listing, ordering, positioning, or ranking of the game pieces belong to ordering games.

Here's a fact pattern for a sample ordering game:

> For its annual holiday concert, a high school orchestra performs exactly eight musical pieces — an aria, a concerto, a march, a polka, a rhapsody, a sonata, a tango, and a waltz — one immediately after the other. The conductor observes the following conditions in determining the order in which the orchestra plays the eight pieces for the concert:

This looks like an ordering game that involves positioning; it contains references to *after* and *order* in the facts.

To confirm your decision, see what you can glean from the first question:

> Which of the following could be the order, from first to last, in which the orchestra plays the pieces at the holiday concert?
>
> (A) polka, march, sonata, aria, waltz, concerto, tango, rhapsody

The references to *order, first,* and *last* in the question tell you that this is most definitely an ordering game. The ordered list of eight musical pieces in the answer choice further confirms the classification.

After you know that you're working with an ordering game, immediately begin building your game board.

Becoming Chairman of the (Game) Board

Begin creating your game board as you read through the fact pattern. Putting a board together requires four steps: listing the game pieces, drawing the box chart, recording the rules, and analyzing them. You should spend only about four or five minutes completing this process. This section describes how to make the game board and analyze the rules for ordering games.

Putting together the game pieces

The first sentence usually tells you how many game pieces you're dealing with. Although ordering games commonly have six or seven game pieces, some may have fewer and some may have more.

The sample game we introduced in the preceding section has eight: "For its annual holiday concert, a high school orchestra performs exactly *eight* musical pieces . . .." On your scratch paper, write out the game pieces using their first initials. For the sample game, you record A, C, M, P, R, S, T, and W to represent aria, concerto, march, polka, rhapsody, sonata, tango, and waltz.

Drawing the box chart

The box chart for most ordering problems is a simple table with as many columns as there are positions. The column headings for position and rank games are usually a number sequence, and the headings for scheduling games are time designations (such as hours in a day, days in a week, or months or quarters in a year).

The sample problem has eight positions designating the order in which the orchestra plays the eight musical works from first to last. Its column headings are simply 1, 2, 3, 4, 5, 6, 7, and 8, like this:

A C M P R S T W

1	2	3	4	5	6	7	8

TIP

Draw only as many lines as you need to separate the elements in each column. On the LSAT, neatness doesn't count, but speed does.

Recording the rules

Most logic games have three, four, or five conditions or rules that restrict how you play with the pieces. For ordering games, the restrictions provide clues to how the pieces may be positioned in relation to one another. Common types of ordering rules are targets, spacers, and arrangers.

Target rules

Targets give you concrete evidence about where a game piece belongs or doesn't belong on the board. You can record a target directly on the box chart.

Clues that tell you exactly where a piece belongs are rare on the LSAT. Here's an example:

The orchestra plays the march third.

You can record this target directly on the box chart like this:

A C M P R S T W

1	2	3	4	5	6	7	8
		M					

More common on the LSAT are clues that narrow a piece's options on the board or that tell you where a piece doesn't fit. An example of the first type is this:

The third piece must be either the march or the polka.

You can indicate this restriction on the box chart by recording both options in the third column, separated by a slash to mean *or:*

A C M P R S T W

1	2	3	4	5	6	7	8
		M/P					

Restrictions that tell you where a piece doesn't belong may be simply stated, like this:

The march is not played last.

You can record that clue by writing M in the last column and striking through it, like this:

A C M P R S T W

1	2	3	4	5	6	7	8
							~~M~~

Another way a rule may indicate that a piece doesn't belong is by giving you a few options where it may belong, like this:

The orchestra plays the sonata first, fourth, or sixth.

Record this clue on the box chart by showing the columns where S doesn't belong. You can keep track of where S can be by writing its options under the chart:

A C M P R S T W

1	2	3	4	5	6	7	8
	~~S~~	~~S~~		~~S~~		~~S~~	~~S~~

S = 1, 4, or 6

Spacing rules

Some ordering rules indicate the number of spaces that separate certain pieces. Without additional information or analysis, you can't record these *spacing rules* directly on the chart, so remember them by recording them next to the chart.

When there are no spaces between pieces, they're ordered consecutively. A rule like this one tells you that one piece comes right after another:

The tango is played immediately after the rhapsody.

Record that the pieces are ordered consecutively by writing RT next to the box chart on your game board.

WARNING

Read rules carefully. The rule mentions T first, but that doesn't mean that T comes before R and the order is TR. Because the rule states that T comes *after* R, the order is R before T, or RT.

Spacing rules may be precise or ambiguous. The preceding rule about the relative order of R and T is precise. You know that R is always immediately before T. A spacing rule may be worded more ambiguously, like this:

> The tango is played either immediately before or immediately after the rhapsody.

You can record the two options next to the box chart on your game board like this:

> RT *or* TR

We show you more tips for recording this rule on the game board in "Expanding rules" later in this chapter.

Sometimes, a rule may tell you that pieces *can't* be next to each other:

> The sonata is not played either immediately before or after the rhapsody.

We use strikethrough to indicate that S and R can't be consecutive, like this:

> S̶R̶ and R̶S̶

Spacing rules may tell you the exact number of spaces that separate certain pieces. A rule like this one indicates the precise number of spaces between two particular pieces but is ambiguous about the order:

> The orchestra plays exactly two musical pieces between its performance of the march and its performance of the polka.

Use underscores to stand for the number of spaces between the playing of the two musical pieces:

>
> M_ _P *or* P_ _M

REMEMBER

The rule doesn't tell you whether M is before or after P, so either order is possible.

Arranging rules

Rules that indicate the general arrangement of pieces without precisely stating how many spaces separate them are common on the LSAT. These rules tell you to order game pieces somewhere before or after other pieces. Here's an example:

> The orchestra plays both the polka and the waltz after the concerto.

You know that C precedes P and W, but you don't know how many other pieces separate C from P and W. And you don't know the relative order of P and W. P could be played either before or after W, as long as both are played after C. We use a right arrow to designate arranging rules on the game board:

> C → P
>
> C → W

TIP

We use only right arrows for the arranger rule shortcut so that all the relationships go in the same left-to-right direction. So C → W is short for "C is before W" or "W is after C." We'll show you how you can record this rule on the game board in "Expanding rules" later in this chapter.

Analyzing the rules

As you record each condition, consider how you may extend it to further develop your game board. You can better complete your board by expanding on the implications of individual rules and by combining rules that involve the same game pieces. Rules that offer contingencies may allow you to split the box chart and open up your ordering options. When you spend quality time extending your game board, you spend less time answering the questions.

Expanding rules

One way to extend an ordering game board is by getting as much mileage from each rule or condition as you can. Spacing and arranging rules provide you with more information than just which piece comes before or after another. When you know the relative order of particular pieces, you can eliminate them from specific positions on the chart.

The sample rule that the tango is played immediately after the rhapsody not only indicates that R and T are consecutive but also that R can't be last and T can't be first. (If T is first, R can't precede T, and if R is last, there's no space for T to follow.) You can record this information directly on your chart:

A C M P R S T W

1	2	3	4	5	6	7	8
~~T~~							~~R~~

RT

The sample rule that C precedes both P and W reveals several additional conditions:

>> C can't be last, because it precedes another game piece.

>> C also can't be seventh, because it must have at least two spaces after it to accommodate both P and W.

>> P can't be first.

>> W can't be first.

You record these truths like this:

A C M P R S T W

1	2	3	4	5	6	7	8
~~P~~						~~C~~	~~C~~
~~W~~							

C → P
C → W

WARNING

Because the rule doesn't give you the relative order of P and W, you can't know whether P precedes W or W precedes P. So you can't say that P or W can't be second. You only know that neither can be first because you have to leave a space for C.

TIP

Whenever an ordering game tells you the relative positions of its game pieces, you can eliminate each of these game pieces from either end of the order. Strike the piece that comes before another from the last position and the piece that comes after another from the first position.

Combining rules

Examining the rules in combination often provides you with valuable insight. As you record the rules on your game board, evaluate and combine the rules with common game pieces. For example, your game board could list the following conditions:

$$C \rightarrow P$$

$$C \rightarrow W$$

$$W \rightarrow R$$

$$R \rightarrow T$$

$$T \rightarrow M$$

You know that C comes before both P and W, W comes before R, R is before T, and T precedes M. You can rewrite your rules in shorthand, like this: $C \rightarrow W \rightarrow R \rightarrow T \rightarrow M$.

P can be anywhere in the order as long as it's after C. So the order could be CPWRTM, CWPRTM, CWRPTM, CWRTPM, or CWRTMP. And because the sample game contains eight positions, the other two musical pieces could fit anywhere in between as long as one of these relative orderings is maintained.

TIP

You can use an expanded sequence to eliminate additional pieces from positions on the chart. For example, because C must be followed by W, R, T, M, and P, C can't occupy the last five positions on the chart. When you draw similar conclusions for W, R, T, and M, you can expand the chart. Here is a partially complete game board that combines the sample rules we've covered so far for the concert game example with their expansions and combinations:

A C M P R S T W

1	2	3	4	5	6	7	8
~~P~~	~~R~~	~~T~~	~~C~~	~~C~~	~~C~~	~~C~~	~~C~~
~~W~~	~~T~~	~~M~~	~~M~~		~~W~~	~~W~~	~~W~~
~~R~~	~~M~~					~~R~~	~~R~~
~~T~~							~~T~~
~~M~~							
A/C/S							

$C \rightarrow P$

$C \rightarrow W \rightarrow R \rightarrow T \rightarrow M$

Because you've eliminated four pieces from the first spot, you know that only A, C, or S can be played first.

When you start focusing your reasoning powers, you find that you can draw conclusions based on other spacing rules. Add this condition to the existing game:

Exactly three musical pieces separate the performance of the concerto from the performance of the sonata.

You can write this rule on the board like this: C _ _ _S *or* S _ _ _ C.

Additional consideration of the board reveals that S _ _ _ C isn't possible, because C can occupy only the first three positions. Therefore, S can be only fifth, sixth, or seventh. Your game board looks something like this:

ACMPRSTW

1	2	3	4	5	6	7	8
P	R	T	C	C	C	C	C
W	T	M	M		W	W	W
R	M	S	S			R	R
T	S						T
M							S
S							
A/C							

C→P
C→W→R→T→M
C _ _ _ S

That's a lot to work with, but there's still more. Notice that only two possible game pieces can occupy the first position: A or C. Knowing that either A or C can be first sets up a contingency, which may allow you to narrow the possible orders even further.

Working with contingencies

When you're left with two possible pieces for a particular position or when a given condition provides you with an either/or contingency, you may be able to split your board into more manageable possible orderings.

For example, you can continue building the board you just created in the preceding section by splitting the chart into possible orderings when A is first and when C is first:

ACMPRSTW

1	2	3	4	5	6	7	8
P	R	T	C	C	C	C	C
W	T	M	M		W	W	W
R	M	S	S			R	R
T	S	C				S	T
M							S
S							P/A/M
A/C							
C	P/W/A			S			P/A/M
A	C				S		P/M

C→P
C→W→R→T→M
C _ _ _ S

Placing C first puts S fifth and limits the second spot to P, W, or A and the last spot to P, A, or M. When A is first and C is second, S must be sixth, and only P or M can occupy the last spot. That's likely enough to get you going on the questions. You can consider the other possibilities when you start answering them.

Sometimes, a given condition sets up a contingency. You may see rules worded like this:

> If the polka is played before the waltz, then the aria is played before the concerto.

Based on this rule, either of two possible rule pairings exists because either P comes before W or it comes after W. The first is a direct statement of the rule: P → W and A → C.

The other possibility, then, is W → P.

When you see such a contingency in the list of conditions for an ordering logic game, you likely can split your chart. In this case, you have one for when P → W (which also means that A → C) and one for when W → P.

Notice that applying this contingency to the game board you've developed for the orchestra game provides you with additional information to narrow the two existing options. When P is before W, you get two possible results:

>> The first two rules can be combined as C → P → W → R → T → M.

>> A must be before C, which places A in the first spot, C in the second, and S in the fifth.

When W is before P, you can come up with fewer deductions, but you can still create some possibilities that place P somewhere after W. In this case, W has to be second or third because W can never be first, and P, R, T, M, and S have to occupy the remaining spaces after W. You can record the possibilities on your chart like this:

A C M P R S T W

	1	2	3	4	5	6	7	8
	P̶ W̶ R̶ T̶ M̶ S̶ A/C	R̶ T̶ M̶ S̶	T̶ M̶ S̶ C̶	C̶ M̶ S̶	C̶	C̶ W̶	C̶ W̶ R̶ S̶	C̶ W̶ R̶ T̶ S̶
When W→P	C	W	P/R/A	P/T/R/A	S	P/T/A/R	P/T/A	P/A/M
	A/C	A/C	W	P/R	P/R/S	P/R/T/S	P/T/M	P/M
When P→W and A→C	A	C	P	W	R	S	T	M

C→P
C→W→R→T→M
C _ _ _ S
P→W = A→C

These orderings show you that when P precedes W, you know the exact program schedule for the holiday concert.

WARNING

Don't spend too much time coming up with all possible orderings. Get a handle on what's available given the two main options and draw additional conclusions as you answer the questions.

Answering Ordering Questions

When you've assembled your game board to the best of your abilities and within a reasonable time frame (about four to five minutes), you're ready to tackle the set of five to eight questions that follow the ordering game's facts and rules.

In Chapter 4, we discuss the four general logic game question types: possible listing/assignment, quantity, add-a-rule, and open. Less frequently you may see a couple of additional question types in one of the ordering games on your LSAT.

Substitute condition questions

One question type asks you to choose a condition in the answer choices that could replace one of the original conditions without changing anything about the orders. This twist on analyzing conditions appears in some grouping games, but it's more common in ordering games. It's unlikely to appear more than once on your LSAT, and it's often the last question in the set, which is great because by the last question, you've established several possible orderings to draw from. Here's an example:

EXAMPLE

A circus performer includes exactly six activities in an act — bungee jumping, flame throwing, juggling, lion taming, sword swallowing, and trapeze swinging. The performer carries out each activity one at a time and no more than once during the act. The order in which the performer carries out the activities is subject to the following conditions:

Lion taming occurs before bungee jumping.

Flame throwing occurs immediately before bungee jumping.

Trapeze swinging occurs before sword swallowing.

Trapeze swinging occurs either immediately before or immediately after juggling.

Which one of the following, if substituted for the condition that trapeze swinging occurs before sword swallowing, would have the same effect on determining the order of the performer's act?

(A) Sword swallowing occurs before juggling.

(B) Sword swallowing occurs before flame throwing.

(C) Juggling occurs before sword swallowing.

(D) Sword swallowing occurs either immediately before or immediately after juggling.

(E) Sword swallowing may not occur first, second, or third.

To answer this question, create a game board:

1. List the game pieces: B, F, J, L, S, and T.

2. Create a box chart with six columns numbered 1 through 6.

3. Record the first rule: L → B.

4. Record the second rule: FB.

5. **Record the third rule: T → S.**

6. **Record the fourth rule: TJ or JT.**

7. **Extend the board by entering on the chart where pieces don't fit and by combining rules, such as L → FB and TJ/JT → S.**

8. **Consider possible orderings.**

The board looks something like this:

B F J L S T

1	2	3	4	5	6
B̶ S̶ F̶	B̶ S̶			T̶	T̶ F̶ J̶ T̶ B/S
L	F	B	T/J	J/T	S
L	T/J	J/T	S	F	B
T/J	J/T	L	F	B	S
T/J	J/T	S	L	F	B

L → FB
JT → S or TJ → S

Here are the steps to answering questions that ask for a substitute condition:

1. **Determine what effect the original condition has on the board.**

   It places T before S.

2. **Check the answers to see which one would place T before S in all orderings.**

3. **Eliminate answers that don't jibe with your game board.**

   Choice (E) has to be wrong because S *can* be third in some orderings. Choice (A) puts S before T in all orderings, so it's out.

4. **Rule out answers that don't have the same effect on the orderings as the original.**

   Choice (B) affects the order of S and F, but it doesn't put T before S in all orderings. You could have LSFBTJ, which doesn't maintain the third condition that T occurs before S. Choice (D) swaps S for T, which doesn't ensure that T occurs before S in all orderings.

5. **Check the remaining answers to determine whether they affect the orders in the same way.**

   Choice (C) looks promising. Notice that whatever holds true for T is also true for J. The two acts, which are always consecutive, may hold the same positions, regardless of the orderings. Therefore, Choice (C) provides the same condition as the one that requires T to occur before S. T is interchangeable with J, so pick the answer that exchanges T for J in the original third condition. Choice (C) is correct.

Completely determined order questions

Another, even less common question is one that asks you to choose the condition that would allow you to create an exact ordering of the pieces. This question type may appear in an ordering set, such as the one we discuss in the earlier section "Working with contingencies." The ordering game's conditions narrowed the possible orderings to these:

1	2	3	4	5	6	7	8
C	W	P/R/A	P/T/R/A	S	P/T/R/A	P/T/A	P/A/M
A/C	C/A	W	P/R	P/R/S	P/T/R/S	P/T/M	P/M
A	C	P	W	R	S	T	M

$C \rightarrow P$
$C \rightarrow W \rightarrow R \rightarrow T \rightarrow M$
$C \_ \_ \_ S$
$P \rightarrow W = A \rightarrow C$

And you may be asked this question:

The order in which the orchestra plays the musical pieces at the holiday concert is completely determined if which one of the following is true?

EXAMPLE

(A) The polka is played second.

(B) The concerto is played first.

(C) The march is played last.

(D) The waltz is played fourth.

(E) The sonata is played last.

Attack this question methodically:

1. Eliminate obviously incorrect answers.

Choice (E) can't be right. The orchestra never plays the sonata last. Also notice that P can never be second, so Choice (A) is wrong. If P were second, C would have to be first, but that would put C before A and P before W, which violates the condition that A is before C when P is before W.

2. Dismiss conditions that could apply to more than one possible order.

Many of the possible orders have C in the first spot and M last, so Choices (B) and (C) are incorrect.

3. Check the remaining answer.

The last order on the chart is the only one with W in the fourth spot. When the waltz is fourth, all the other pieces fall into place. The four spots after W have to be filled by S, R, T, and M, so P and A have to join C in the first three spots. P comes before W, and when P is before W, A is before C. So A has to be first and C second. With C second, S has to be sixth, and R, T, and M fit into the fifth, seventh, and eighth spots, respectively, to retain their relative order. Choice (D) is the answer.

Ordering the Approach to an Advanced Game

LSAT ordering games are often closed, which means they involve an equal number of game pieces and positions to put them in. You use each game piece once and only once and fill each spot once and only once. However, not all ordering games are so, well, orderly. Some may use game pieces more than once; others may have fewer positions to fill than game pieces, meaning that you don't use all the pieces. Still others may require you to fill a position with more than one game piece. We refer to these more complex ordering games as *open* rather than *closed*. When you encounter an open ordering game, don't panic. You handle them in much the same manner as you do the more traditional variety. We show you how in this section with a sample practice problem.

EXAMPLE

A pastry chef must choose which four of five cake layers — chocolate, lemon, red velvet, strawberry, and vanilla — will make up the individual layers of a four-layer wedding cake. Each of the chosen layers will make up exactly one of the cake's four layers in order from bottom to top. The pastry chef is restricted by the following conditions in selecting the layers:

> If chocolate is included, then strawberry is the layer immediately above chocolate.
>
> Red velvet is neither the second layer nor the top layer.
>
> If vanilla is not one of the layers, then lemon is the second layer.
>
> If lemon is the second layer, then vanilla is not one of the layers.

You know this is an ordering game because the facts reference order and the conditions include ordering language, such as *above*, *top*, and *second*.

The five game pieces are C, L, R, S, and V, but your box chart has only four columns, one for each of the four layers represented from left to right in order from bottom to top. So you won't use one of the pieces when you put together your orders. Record the rules in shorthand:

>> If C, CS.

>> If R, R = 1 or 3.

>> If no V, L = 2.

>> If L = 2, no V.

Your board may start out looking like this:

C L R S V

1 - bottom	2	3	4 - top

If C, CS
If R, R = 1 or 3
If no V, L = 2
If L = 2, no V

TIP

If the open nature of this game unsettles you, gain your composure by working with the first question before you try to expand the conditions on your game board. Just run through the conditions and eliminate the answer choice(s) that violates each one.

Which one of the following could be the order of the layers from bottom to top?

(A) chocolate, strawberry, red velvet, lemon

(B) vanilla, lemon, chocolate, strawberry

(C) strawberry, red velvet, lemon, vanilla

(D) red velvet, lemon, strawberry, chocolate

(E) lemon, vanilla, red velvet, strawberry

To answer this first question, consider each condition. The first says "if C, CS." Choice (D) places S before C, so it's out. The next states "if R, R = 1 or 3." R is second in Choice (C), so it has to be wrong. For the third condition, eliminate answers that don't have V but put L somewhere other than second. Choice (A) has no V but puts L last, so it's out. Consider the fourth condition and look for answers that include V but put L in the 2 spot. Choice (B) does that, so it's incorrect. The only answer that doesn't violate a condition is Choice (E).

The first question of the set is almost always a possible listing/assignment question that doesn't require you to refer to a game board. So you can answer it before you create a board.

After you master the first question, return to your game board with renewed confidence. Examine the conditions again. Each one presents a contingency, and none allows you to add a permanent piece to the box chart. So try to come up with possible orders.

Notice that the third condition gives you a target clue in certain circumstances: If no V, L = 2. So create a possible layering for when there's no V.

When V isn't a layer, the four layers must be R, L, C, and S. L has to go in the 2 spot. C and S have to be 3 and 4 because they need to be next to each other in that order. The remaining first spot is for R. Only one order exists when V isn't a layer: RLCS.

Consider what happens when R isn't a layer and C, L, S, and V make up the cake. L can't be second, because V is a layer, and you need space for CS. Record these possible orders for when R isn't a layer on your game board: CSVL or CSLV, LVCS, or V/L C S V/L.

What happens when C isn't a layer? L, R, S, and V must be layers. So L can't be in the 2 spot, and R must be 1 or 3. Write out the possibilities for when R is 1: RS/VLS/V or RS/VS/VL. When R is 3, you can have these orders: S/VS/VRL or LS/VRS/V.

Exclude L and work with C, R, S, and V. R has to be 1 or 3, and C and S have to be together. When R is 1, you can have these orders: RCSV or RVCS. When R is third, you have this possibility: CSRV.

Consider your options when S isn't a layer and C, L, R, and V are. Wait! That's not possible. You can't have C without S, so S has to be a layer in every cake.

Your expanded game board may look like this:

C L R S V

	1 - bottom	2	3	4 - top
NO V	R	L	C	S
NO R	C	S	V/L	V/L
	L	V	C	S
	V/L	C	S	V/L
NO C	R	S/V	L	S/V
	R	S/V	S/V	L
	S/V	S/V	R	L
	L	S/V	R	S/V
NO L	R	C	S	V
	R	V	C	S
	C	S	R	V

If C, then CS
If R, then R = 1 or 3
If no V, then 1 = 2
If L = 2, then no V

TIP

If you don't have time to come up with every one of these possible options, don't despair. At least get started on narrowing the possibilities so you get accustomed to the way you need to think to master the game.

Because you've spent quality time developing your game board, answering the questions shouldn't take much time at all. Consider this quantity question:

EXAMPLE

If the cake includes both a chocolate layer and a red velvet layer, then how many layers are there, any one of which could be the bottom layer?

Refer to your game board to see that when both C and R are cake layers, the only possible bottom layers are C and R. The answer must be two.

An add-a-rule question like this one is easy, too:

EXAMPLE

If the cake's bottom layer is vanilla, then which one of the following must be true?

(A) The cake doesn't have a chocolate layer.

(B) The cake doesn't have a red velvet layer.

(C) The cake's second layer is chocolate.

(D) The cake's strawberry layer is second.

(E) The cake's top layer is lemon.

According to your game board, the possible orderings when V is in the 1 spot are VSRL (if C is left out) and VCSL (if R isn't a layer). The only answer that's common to both options and therefore must be true is Choice (E). The top layer has to be lemon whenever the bottom layer is vanilla.

Try another question:

EXAMPLE

Which of the following CANNOT be true?

(A) The lemon layer is immediately below the red velvet layer.

(B) The red velvet layer is immediately below the chocolate layer.

(C) The red velvet layer is immediately below the strawberry layer.

(D) The strawberry layer is immediately below the lemon layer.

(E) The vanilla layer is immediately below the strawberry layer.

Compare the answer choices to your game board and eliminate all that could be or must be true. R is right before C when there's no L, so Choice (B) is out. R is right before S when there's no C, so Choice (C) is wrong. You see S right before L in one of the options when C isn't a layer, so Choice (D) isn't right. V comes right before S in the no C options, so Choice (E) is out. In no order does L come right before R, so the correct answer is Choice (A).

TIP

Other variations of the open ordering game exist, and you can handle them all when you apply what you know about working with the traditional types. To get more experience with the ordering logic game type, go to the practice exams in Chapters 15, 17, and 19 and online, purchase a copy of *LSAT Logic Games For Dummies* (John Wiley & Sons, Inc.), and order official LSAT exams from the official LSAT website: www.lsac.org.

Chapter **6**

Type Casting: Grouping Games

In addition to ordering games, which we cover in Chapter 5, the LSAT analytical reasoning section presents another logic game type we call *grouping games*. These games ask you to categorize the elements, or game pieces, into two or more groups in accordance with several rules or conditions. Grouping games may appear at first to be more complicated than they are. This chapter provides you with an approach that breaks down and simplifies them and puts you in control of the game board.

Several kinds of grouping games exist, but the general way you handle them doesn't vary. Consider the facts and rules, create a game board, and leap into the questions with confidence.

Classifying Grouping Games

One way to identify grouping games is by recognizing the language the facts and rules *don't* use. Although some grouping games may also include an element of ordering, most are noticeably bereft of ordering references, such as first/last, higher/lower, and before/after. Instead, the facts and rules contain wording that suggests matching one set of elements to another set or two of elements. Look for words that indicate group membership, such as *included, on the team, with,* and *together.*

TIP

Another way to confirm whether a game is of the grouping variety is by reading its first question. Usually, the first question of a grouping game asks you for a possible assignment of game pieces to categories. The answer choices often list each group name followed by a colon and a list of the game pieces included in that group. When the first question in the set exhibits this format, you're likely dealing with a grouping game.

After you know you have a grouping game, engage in another categorization. Grouping games come in two general types:

» **In/out:** The facts for this game type reference *one* group, to which game pieces either belong or don't belong. If a game piece belongs, it's in. If not, it's out. You can designate these two options on your game board as in/out, yes/no, +/−, or whatever works for you.

» **Classification:** This type's fact pattern names *two or more* groups to which you assign the game pieces. Designate the groups on your game board by name.

To help you distinguish between the two grouping game types, take a look at a couple of simple sample fact patterns. An in/out type mentions just one group, like this:

A stylist has access to exactly seven accessories — belt, earrings, hat, glasses, necklace, ring, and scarf. The stylist accessorizes one outfit with exactly five of these accessories. The stylist selects the five accessories for the outfit in accordance with these specifications:

From these facts, you create one group of accessories, the group of five that beautifies the outfit. Five accessories belong on the outfit, and two don't. To record this information on a game board, list the game pieces (first initials of the seven accessories) and create a box chart that indicates that five pieces belong and two don't:

B E H G N R S

					+	−

A classification fact pattern, like this one, specifically names two or more groups:

Exactly five zoo animals — gnu, peacock, snake, yak, and zebra — are moved into three habitats — A, B, and C. Exactly two animals are moved into A, exactly two animals are moved into B, and exactly one animal is moved into C. The assignment of animals to habitats must adhere to the following conditions:

These facts define three groups — A, B, and C — and five game pieces — g, p, s, y, and z. List the game pieces and form a box chart with the group designations as column headings. This simple scenario states exactly how many members exist in each group, so you can record the appropriate number of spaces under each group name, like this:

g p s y z

A		B		C

Most LSAT grouping games are more complex than these sample scenarios. The facts may provide additional qualifiers. (For example, the stylist scenario could also state that each accessory is colored either silver or gold.) Group assignments may be left open. (For example, the zoo animal scenario may not clarify exactly how many animals are moved into each habitat.) Regardless of the grouping game's complexity, the game board you construct usually follows the same general format as the ones you've constructed for the sample scenarios.

Following the Rules of Division

In grouping games, the fact pattern is followed by the set of rules or conditions that restrict the group arrangements. Grouping game rules generally fall into three types: targets, joiners, and if/then statements.

Target rules

Targets give you concrete evidence about which group a game piece belongs or doesn't belong to. You can record a target directly on the box chart.

Clues that tell you exactly which group a piece belongs to are rare on the LSAT. Here's an example of a target rule for the in/out game in the preceding section:

> The stylist does not select the belt.

You can record this target directly on the box chart, like this:

BEHGNRS

					+	-	
						B	

A sample target rule for the classification game in the preceding section could be this:

> The gnu is moved into habitat C.

And the box chart would look like this:

g p s y z

A		B		C	
				g	

Some rules don't tell you exactly which group a piece belongs to, but they narrow the options so significantly that we classify them as targets as well. Here's an example for the in/out game:

> The stylist selects either the hat or the glasses, but not both.

These two conditions allow you to record information on the box chart. Knowing that either the hat or the glasses (but not both) are selected gives you two options for the box chart:

BEHGNRS

					+	-	
H						G	
G						H	

The LSAT may also convey this same condition with a set of two if/then rules, like this:

> If the hat is selected, the glasses are not selected.

> If the glasses are not selected, the hat is selected.

WARNING

Knowing that if the hat is selected, the glasses aren't selected doesn't give you enough information to determine that H and G are always separate. Without the presence of the second rule, you only know what happens when each item is selected. You can't make assumptions about what happens when one is not selected. So without the presence of the second rule, it may be possible that both H and G are *not* selected. We further discuss the implications of if/then rules in the upcoming section "If/then rules."

For the classification game, you may see a target rule like this one:

> The yak is moved to either habitat A or habitat C.

If the yak is in either A or C, you know the yak can't be moved to habitat B. Record this rule by showing where the yak *can't* belong:

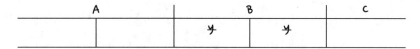

Joining rules

Joining rules specify game pieces that are always assigned to the same group. Depending on the game, you may or may not be able to record joining rules in the box chart. In/out games have only two possible groups, so for these games, joining rules provide two possible assignments. The game pieces are either both in or both out. Here are some examples of joining rules for the in/out game regarding the stylist:

> Either both the ring and the scarf are selected or neither is selected.

> The ring is selected if and only if the scarf is selected.

These two rules give you the same information: If S = in, R = in, and if S = out, R = out. Record the options on your box chart:

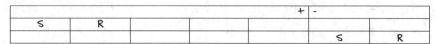

A possible joining condition for the classification game could be this:

> The peacock is moved into the same habitat as the zebra.

This rule gives you two valuable clues:

>> The peacock and zebra are together.

>> The peacock and zebra can't occupy habitat C because it has space for only one animal.

You can record these clues on your game board by writing *pz* under the box chart and entering *p* and *z* with slashes through them in the C column of the box chart.

g p s y z

A		B		C
				p̸ z̸

pz

If/then rules

Grouping games commonly provide or suggest *if/then statements* in the rules. These statements are logically equivalent to their *contrapositive* statements, which are created by inverting and flipping the two parts of the statement.

Every if/then statement has two parts: the *if* and the *then*. In a *conditional* statement, these two parts are both positive, like this:

> If the earrings are selected, the necklace is selected.

The contrapositive of a conditional statement reverses the order of the two parts and makes them negative:

> If the necklace is not selected, the earrings are not selected.

The contrapositive of an *inverse* statement (where both parts are negative) is also true. So knowing that "if the earrings are not selected, the necklace is not selected" also tells you that "if the necklace is selected, the earrings are selected."

You may also find the contrapositive of statements with negative and positive parts. So "if the necklace is not selected, the earrings are selected" also means that "if the earrings are not selected, the necklace is selected."

REMEMBER

To find the contrapositive of any if/then statement, follow these two steps:

1. **Put the second part of the statement first and the first part second.**

2. **Make the positive statements negative and the negative statements positive.**

Apply the two steps to this if/then condition:

> If the necklace is not selected, the ring is not selected.

Start the contrapositive statement with the second part, the ring, and change the original negative statement to a positive: "If the ring is selected." End the statement with the first part and change its negative to a positive: "the necklace is selected." The contraposition statement is this:

> If the ring is selected, the necklace is selected.

Record the if/then and its contrapositive on the game board like this:

B E H G N R S

					+	–

If R = –, then N = –
If N = +, then R = +

TIP

Whenever you see an if/then statement in a logic game, you know that its contrapositive is also true.

WARNING

Follow the steps to forming contrapositives exactly. You can't form the contrapositive of an if/then statement by just reversing the parts. You must also switch the positives and negatives. So knowing that "if the necklace is not selected, the ring is not selected" does *not* tell you that "if the ring is not selected, the necklace is not selected."

As you record each condition, consider how you may extend it to further develop your game board. You can better complete your board by expanding on the implications of individual rules and by combining rules that involve the same game pieces. Rules that offer contingencies may allow you to split the box chart and open up your ordering options. When you spend quality time extending your game board, you spend less time answering the questions.

Expanding the Grouping Game Board

Before you leap into the questions for a grouping game, you want to extend the rules and play with a few possible group assignments to become familiar with how the rules limit the game. Take a look again at the zoo animal game with a couple of rules included:

Exactly five zoo animals — gnu, peacock, snake, yak, and zebra — are moved into three habitats — A, B, and C. Exactly two animals are moved into A, exactly two animals are moved into B, and exactly one animal is moved into C. The assignment of animals to habitats must adhere to the following conditions:

> The peacock is moved into the same habitat as the zebra.
>
> The yak is moved to either habitat A or habitat C.

When you create a game board for this game and record the rules, you get something like this:

g p s y z

A		B		C
		~~y~~	~~y~~	~~p z~~

pz

This board may not seem like much to go on at first, but consider some of the possible assignments. The yak (*y*) can occupy only A or C. Moving *y* to A is very limiting. The animals *p* & *z* have to be moved to B because B would be the only habitat with two spots for them to share. Only two possible combinations exist when *y* = A. They are A: *y* & *g*; B: *p* & *z*; C: *s* or A: *y* & *s*; B: *p* & *z*; C: *g*.

Moving *y* to habitat C is also limiting; *p* & *z* occupy either A or B, and *g* & *s* occupy whichever habitat *p* & *z* don't. After careful consideration of the two rules, you can record the four possible combinations on your game board:

g p s y z

A		B		C
		~~y~~	~~y~~	~~p z~~
y	g/s	p	z	g/s
p	z	g	s	y
g	s	p	z	y

When you take a few moments to consider the implications of the rules, you often find that you're left with a limited number of possible assignments.

The grouping games you encounter on the LSAT aren't usually as simple as the zoo animal scenario. Most make the problem more complex by introducing an additional grouping factor or by leaving open the number of pieces assigned to each group. For example, the zoo animals may be additionally classified as mammal or non-mammal, or the game may not specify the number of animals moved to each of the three habitats. Regardless of the game's complexity, however, you create each grouping game board in the same general way:

1. **Record the game pieces on your game board.**

2. **Isolate the main groupings and use them to head the columns of your box chart.**

3. **Record the rules.**

4. **Consider several possible group assignments.**

When you finish these four steps, you're ready to tackle the questions. Refer to Chapter 4 to review the approach to answering logic game questions. We cover the process in detail in the next section, where you work through examples of a simple and more complex grouping logic game.

Mastering Practice Grouping Games

The best way to get a handle on the grouping logic games is to walk through a few games step by step. The first few logic games you face can be a bit daunting (okay, very daunting), but remember, you can solve them by following the steps. And with practice, the steps will become as familiar as your walk home. If you start to feel panicky, take a deep breath and just take the next step. Don't get caught up in what you don't know; apply what you do know. Here are a couple of practice problems to help you out.

An in/out grouping game

Try your skills on an in/out grouping game.

A building contractor creates a team of exactly six professionals to work on a construction site. He chooses from three plumbers: Harry, Ingrid, and James; three carpenters: Mary, Nick, and Oliver; and three tile installers: Andrew, Bert, and Ernestine. The contractor observes the following conditions in forming the team:

> If Oliver is selected for the team, Andrew is not selected.
>
> If James is selected for the team, Harry is not selected.
>
> If James is selected for the team, Mary is also selected.
>
> If Mary is selected for the team, Oliver is also selected.

The construction workers are either among the six who are in the group (+) or among the three who are out of the group (−). You know exactly six of the nine workers will be in and three will be out.

Start building your game board immediately. Forget the names; list the workers by letter underneath the headings of P, C, and T to keep track of each worker's profession. Create a box chart with nine columns, six for the team members and three for those who are left out. You start with a game board like this:

Analyze the rules. All provide if/then statements. The first tells you that if O is in, A is out. So it's also true that if A is in, O is out, and O and A are never both in. Record these facts on your game board. The second rule is the same: If J is in, H is out, and if H is in, J is out. Keep track on your game board.

The third rule is a little different. It tells you that if J is in, M is in. You also know the contrapositive — that if M is out, J is out. That's the same as saying that you can't have J without M (but you can have M without J). The fourth rule is similar to the third. It states that if M is in, O is in. So you also know that if O is out, M is out. Record these rules on your game board.

Expand the game board by considering possible group assignments. Start with J because he's a part of many rules. When J is in, M is in, and when M is in, O is in. Add J, M, and O to the + side of the box chart. When J is in, H is out, so put H on the − side. O is in, so add A to the − side, too. The remaining three spots could be filled with I, N, B, or E.

When A is in, O is out, and when O is out, M is out. Add an option to your game board with A on the + side and O and M on the − side. One space remains on the − side. That space has to be either J or H because they can't both be in, and it has to be J because if you put J on the + side, you have to have M there too. So J is on the − side, and H, I, N, B, and E have to be on the + side of the chart.

The second option provides one possible assignment with H on the + side and J on the − side. Is there another possibility? With H on the + side, the − side could be J, A, and any one of I, N, B, E, or M. The four remaining pieces belong on the + side with O. Your game board looks like this, which should give you enough information to tackle the questions:

	P	C	T
	H, I, J	M, N, O	A, B, E

						+	−	
J	M	O	I/N/B/E	I/N/B/E	I/N/B/E	H	A	I/N/B/E
A	I	N	B	E	H	O	M	J
H	I/N/B/E/M	I/N/B/E/M	I/N/B/E/M	I/N/B/E/M	O	J	A	I/N/B/E/M

If O = +, then A = −; If A = +, then O = −

If J = +, then H = −; If H = +, then J = −

If J = +, then M = +; If M = −, then J = −

If M = +, then O = +; If O = −, then M = −

Which one of the following is an acceptable team of construction workers?

(A) Ingrid, James, Mary, Oliver, Bert, Ernestine

(B) Ingrid, James, Nick, Oliver, Bert, Ernestine

(C) Harry, James, Mary, Nick, Bert, Ernestine

(D) Harry, James, Mary, Oliver, Andrew, Bert

(E) Harry, Ingrid, Mary, Nick, Bert, Ernestine

The first question almost always asks for an acceptable assignment. Despite the work you've devoted to developing the game board, ignore it for now and answer this question by examining each of the four rules. The first rule says that if O is in, A is out. Choice (D) puts both O and A on the + side, so it's wrong. The second rule states that if J is in, H is out. Eliminate Choice (C) because it has both J and H on the + side. The third rule specifies that when J is in, M is in. Choice (B) has J with no M, so it's incorrect. The fourth rule requires O to be in when M is in. Choice (E) has M with no O, so it's out. The correct answer that doesn't violate a rule is Choice (A).

If Harry and Oliver are included on the team, then which one of the following must be true?

(A) Exactly two tile installers are on the team.

(B) All three carpenters are on the team.

(C) Mary is not a member of the team.

(D) James is a member of the team.

(E) Andrew is not a member of the team.

This add-a-rule question requires an answer that must be true. (For more information on question types, see Chapter 4.) The temporary rule is that H and O are on the + side. The third line of the box chart gives you possible arrangements when H and O are on the team. Refer to that line to eliminate answers that either could be true (but don't *have* to be) or must be false. Choice (A) could be true if the team included H, B, E, I, N, and O, but it isn't true when the team assignment is H, B, M, I, N, and O. Choice (A) doesn't have to be true, so it's wrong. Likewise, M, N, and O could be on the team together but don't have to be, so Choice (B) is out. Mary either could or couldn't be a member of the team, so Choice (C) is wrong. In no case can J be on the + side, so Choice (D) has to be false. The only answer that must be true is Choice (E). In all cases where H and O are on the + side, A is on the − side.

EXAMPLE

Each of the following pairs of workers could be included together on the team EXCEPT:

(A) Ingrid and James

(B) Mary and Oliver

(C) James and Andrew

(D) Bert and Ernestine

(E) Mary and Ernestine

Eliminate answers that could be pairs of team members. The first option in the box chart shows I and J on the team together, so cross out Choice (A). It also puts M and O on the team together, so Choice (B) is wrong. No option shows J and A on the team together, so it's likely the correct answer. Check the last two answers to be sure. B and E work together in most assignments, so Choice (D) is out. You can put M and E together when J is on the team and when H is on the team, so Choice (E) is wrong. The correct answer is Choice (C).

A more complex grouping game

Some of the more complex logic grouping games introduce an element of ordering. We classify them as grouping games, though, because they require more grouping than ordering. Here's an example of one of these more complicated grouping games.

EXAMPLE

Five graduate assistants — Quinlan, Roberts, Solomon, Trujillo, and Verma — are assigned to supervise recitation sessions in three classrooms — Fox Hall, Hepburn Hall, and McIntyre Hall. Each classroom is supervised by at least one of the graduate assistants, and each graduate assistant supervises exactly one classroom. Each of the three recitation sessions takes place on a different day. The supervisory schedule must adhere to the following specifications:

(A) The Fox Hall recitation must be held before the Hepburn Hall recitation.

(B) The Fox Hall recitation is supervised by only one of the graduate assistants.

(C) The recitation that is supervised by Quinlan must be held before the recitation that is supervised by either Roberts or Trujillo.

(D) The recitation that is supervised by Solomon cannot be held after any recitation that is supervised by Verma.

At first the ordering language may lead you to believe that this is just an ordering game, but when you check the answers to the first question, you see that the five graduate assistants are also grouped together by recitation location. That indicates that you're working with a grouping game with ordering thrown in to make things interesting.

First list the game pieces, the first initials of the graduate assistants — Q, R, S, T, and V. The three groups in this classification grouping game are the three recitation classrooms: F, H, and M. These are the column headings for your box chart. But note that the order of the columns matters, so you may want to wait until you've evaluated the rules before you create the box chart.

Before you check out the rules, however, consider the grouping possibilities. You're putting five game pieces into three groups. You use all five pieces and classrooms, so the possible groupings could be two in one group, two in another, and one in the other or three in one group, one in another, and one in the other.

The first rule says that F is before H, or F → H. Record that rule on your game board, along with the three possible orders of the recitations: (1) FHM, (2) MFH, or (3) FMH. The next rule says that F has only one member. For now, remember the rule by writing F = 1 on the board.

The third rule says that Q → R and Q → T. The last rule states that S can never supervise a session after V, so S → V or S supervises with V. Record these rules and expand the board by considering their implications. If Q → R and Q → T, Q can't be last, and R and T can't be first. For more about evaluating ordering rules, see Chapter 5.

WARNING

Be careful with the last rule. It states that S can't be included in a recitation after one that V is part of. So S → V or S can = V. S and V can be in the same recitation without violating the condition that S can't be after V. You know that V can't be first without S and S can't be last without V.

You don't know the order of the recitations, so start out by creating a box chart with three columns. The first column heading can be either F or M; the last column heading can be either M or H. If F is first, the first group can include only Q or S because F has only one supervisor, R and T can't supervise first, and V can't supervise in the first position alone. If M is first, then the first group could have one (Q or S), two (QS or SV), or three (Q, S, V) supervisors. Initially, your game board may look something like this:

Q R S T V

F	H/M	M/H
~~R T V~~ Q/S		~~Q~~ R/T/V/S

M	F	H
~~R T~~ Q/S/V		~~Q~~ R/T/V/S

F → H
F = 1
Q → R; Q → T
S → V or SV

If the first group is F, it includes either only Q or only S. If only Q supervises first, the possible groupings are numerous. Your main job is to make sure V doesn't come before S, so S could be in the second column with or without V or in the third column with V. R and T can be in either column as long as no column is empty. If the first group is supervised by only S, R and T have to be in the third column so they can follow Q, which therefore must be in the second column. V can be in either column.

If the first group is M, F must head the second column, and H must head the third column. F can have only one supervisor. If that supervisor is Q, then R and T have to be in the third column, and S must occupy the first column. V could go with S in the first column or with R and T in the third column. If R is alone in the second column, Q has to be before R in the first column, and T has to be in the third column. S and V can occupy the first or third column as long as V isn't before S. If S is alone in the second column, V has to be in the third column, R and T have to join V, and Q has to be in the first column. If T is in the second column, Q has to be in the first column, and R has to be in the third column; S and V can be in the first or third column as long as V isn't before S. If V is alone in the second column, S has to be in the first column with Q, and R and T have to be in the third column.

You can record some of the possible groupings on your game board, like this:

F	H /M	M/H
Q	R T S	V
	SV	RT
	RT or RS or ST	SV or TV or RV
S	Q or QV	RTV or RT

M	F	H
S or SV	Q	R T V or RT
Q or QS or QSV	R	TSV or TV or T
Q	S	VRT
Q or QS or QSV	T	RSV or RV or R
SQ	V	RT

Use the rules to eliminate answers to the first possible assignment question.

EXAMPLE

Which one of the following could be the graduate assistants assigned to each of the recitation classrooms, with the recitation classrooms listed in the order in which they are supervised?

(A) Fox Hall: Quinlan
   Hepburn Hall: Roberts, Solomon
   McIntyre Hall: Trujillo, Verma

(B) Fox Hall: Quinlan
   Hepburn Hall: Roberts, Verma
   McIntyre Hall: Solomon, Trujillo

(C) Fox Hall: Roberts
   McIntyre Hall: Quinlan, Trujillo
   Hepburn Hall: Solomon, Verma

(D) Hepburn Hall: Solomon
   Fox Hall: Quinlan
   McIntyre Hall: Roberts, Trujillo, Verma

(E) McIntyre Hall: Quinlan
   Fox Hall: Roberts, Solomon
   Hepburn Hall: Trujillo, Verma

Eliminate answers that violate rules. The first rule is F → H. Choice (D) puts H before F, so it's out. Choice (E) violates the second rule that F has only one member, so cross it off. The third rule is that Q → R and T. Choice (C) puts Q after R, so it's wrong. The last rule says that S is not after V. Eliminate Choice (B) because it violates this final rule. The remaining answer, Choice (A), is correct.

EXAMPLE

If one of the recitations is supervised by both Quinlan and Solomon, which one of the following could be true?

(A) The recitation in Fox Hall is the first of the three recitations.

(B) The recitation in Hepburn Hall is the second of the three recitations.

(C) One of the recitations is supervised by only Verma.

(D) The second of the three recitations includes Solomon as a supervisor.

(E) The second of the three recitations includes exactly two of the graduate assistants as supervisors.

This question adds the rule that Q and S are included in the same group. According to your game board, that group has to be M and must be first. So Choice (A) has to be false. When M is first, F is second, so Choice (B) is incorrect. It's possible that the second visit could include only V. R and T would then be in the third group. Choice (C) is possible, but check the last two answers to be sure. S must be in the first group, so Choice (D) is wrong. Only one graduate assistant can supervise the second group, so Choice (E) is out. Choice (C) is correct.

EXAMPLE

Which of the following must be true?

(A) The recitation in Fox Hall is held before the recitation in McIntyre Hall.

(B) The recitation that includes Verma is held earlier than the recitation that includes Roberts.

(C) One of the first two recitations includes Solomon as a supervisor.

(D) The second of the three recitations includes at least two graduate assistants as supervisors.

(E) At least one of the first two recitations includes only one of the graduate assistants as a supervisor.

Eliminate answers that could be true but don't have to be and answers that are always false. M can be held before F, so Choice (A) is out. Several groupings put R before V, so Choice (B) is wrong. One grouping where S is in the third group could be 1: Q, 2: RT, 3: SV, so eliminate Choice (C). When F is second, the second group has just one member, so Choice (D) doesn't have to be true. In all groupings, either the first or second group has just one member, so Choice (E) is correct.

REMEMBER

When you spend more time upfront considering the possible options for grouping games, you spend much less time answering the questions.

This last sample grouping game is just one of many ways the LSAT may test your ability to logically assign game pieces to groups in the analytical reasoning section. To expose yourself to the different kinds of possible grouping games, take the practice tests in this book, study a copy of *LSAT Logic Games For Dummies*, by Mark Zegarelli (John Wiley & Sons, Inc.), and purchase official LSAT exams from the LSAC at www.lsac.org.

3

Logical Reasoning: Picking Apart an Argument

Get the scoop on the components of logical arguments to better analyze LSAT logical reasoning questions.

Determine what sort of answer best weakens or strengthens a conclusion.

Find the flaw in a logical argument with one hand tied behind your back.

Discover the approach to a variety of logical reasoning question types.

Spot elements in logical reasoning answer choices that immediately signal an incorrect response.

Chapter 7

Analyzing Arguments: The Basics of Logical Reasoning

The LSAT logical reasoning questions test your ability to deconstruct statements. This section, like the rest of the LSAT, measures your ability to read carefully and quickly. Unlike the other sections (analytical reasoning and reading comprehension), the logical reasoning section doesn't immerse you in one text or one problem for several minutes. Logical reasoning rewards speed and flexibility. It primarily tests your informal logic ability, which is a lot like the kind of reasoning you use to determine whether you should purchase a $200 facial cream because an advertisement claims that applying it will make you look ten years younger.

REMEMBER

To add to the fun, every LSAT has two logical reasoning sections. The LSAT-makers think logical reasoning questions prove to be valuable in predicting law-school success, so on test day you spend at least 70 minutes answering these lovely little questions. Preparing for this section should be a priority; it makes up half your score, which is a big deal.

The good news is that you analyze arguments all the time, even though you may not know that's what you're doing. When you see a commercial advertising a new product that claims it'll make your life better, you probably question that claim. If a weight-loss drug helped someone lose 50 pounds, you may ask, "Is that a typical result?" If four out of five dentists recommend a chewing gum, you may say, "Did they ask only five dentists?" When a mutual fund boasts of its performance, you may ask, "Is that better than the market average?" This is the same kind of thinking that you use to ace the logical reasoning section on the LSAT.

In this chapter, you learn the basics of logical reasoning — how the sections are set up, the type of logic you apply to the argument, and the general approach to the section. Check out Chapters 8 through 10 for details about specific logical reasoning question types.

What You Can Expect in the Logical Reasoning Sections

A section of logical reasoning contains about 25 or 26 questions that you must answer in 35 minutes. Every question consists of a short statement called an *argument* — usually three to five sentences — followed by a question about that argument. You encounter short passages from a variety of sources, such as speeches, advertisements, newspapers, and scholarly articles.

For example, you may see an argument like this: "The local sales tax must be raised to fund city services. Admittedly, this increased sales tax will impose a greater hardship on the poorest citizens. But if the sales tax is not increased, all city services for the poor will have to be cut."

The paragraph reflects the type of arguments that you encounter in the news every day. The questions may ask you to strengthen or weaken an argument, identify the argument's conclusion, or duplicate the argument's pattern of reasoning.

REMEMBER

The question contains all the information you need to answer the question. Don't rely on any outside information! Even if you happen to be an expert in the area a question covers, don't rely on your expertise to answer the question.

Each question has five possible answer choices, which are often long — sometimes even longer than the argument or question. For this reason, you spend most of your time for each question examining the answer choices.

TIP

As with most LSAT questions, often you can quickly eliminate one or two of the answers because they're obviously wrong. The remaining answers are more difficult to eliminate, so spend your time analyzing these better answer choices.

Taking a Systematic Approach

What do lawyers do? They argue. They make statements and support them with evidence to convince a judge or jury that they're right or that their opponents are wrong. They read statutes, cases, and briefs, looking for tidbits of information that they can use to prove that their side is right or the other side is wrong — all under an intense time crunch.

What don't lawyers do? They don't argue from personal conviction or emotion. They don't base their arguments on their own feelings but on the facts and the laws. They don't always get to choose the side they represent, which occasionally results in a lawyer's having to support a side that she personally believes should lose. In every logical reasoning argument, the author states some conclusion and attempts to support it with evidence. Your job is to identify this conclusion, figure out how the author is supporting it, and then determine why it's successful or not.

To break down a logical reasoning question, follow these steps:

1. **Read the question.**

2. **Read the argument paragraph, focusing on the specific information you need to know to answer the question and looking for inconsistencies and/or assumptions in the logic.**

3. **Come up with your own idea of a possible correct answer.**

4. **Evaluate the answers.**

Reading the question first

Tackle a logical reasoning question by reading the question first to determine its type. Following are some of the main types of logical reasoning questions you may encounter:

> **Assumptions:** Which one of the following is an assumption required by the argument above?

> **Flaws:** A reasoning flaw in the argument is that the argument . . .

> **Logical conclusions:** Which one of the following most accurately expresses the main conclusion of the argument?

> **Strengthen:** Which one of the following, if true, most strengthens the argument?

> **Weaken:** Which one of the following, if true, most seriously weakens the argument above?

> **Inference:** If the statements above are true, then which of the following must also be true?

> **Role played by a claim:** The claim that attorneys sometimes serve as their own secretaries plays which one of the following roles in the argument?

> **Resolving discrepancies or paradoxes:** Which one of the following, if true, most helps to resolve the apparent paradox described above?

> **Disagree:** The statements above provide the most support for holding that X would disagree with Y about which one of the following statements?

> **Patterns of reasoning:** Which one of the following exhibits a pattern of reasoning most similar to that exhibited by the argument above?

> **Principles:** Which one of the following conforms most closely to the principle illustrated by the statements above?

> **Structure of argument:** In responding to Larry, Stephen . . . (criticizes, accuses, explains, challenges, assumes)

Chapters 8, 9, and 10 show you how to distinguish logical reasoning question types. When you first read the question, don't read all the answer choices; doing so takes way too much time and clutters your thinking. Instead, concentrate just on the information you need to answer the question. Then you can read the argument with the specific question in mind. For example, if a question asks you to reconcile an apparent discrepancy, read the argument looking for a discrepancy. If a question asks you for an assumption, read the argument looking for an assumption. Reading the argument before the question doesn't hurt, but most arguments lend themselves to several different question types, and if you read the argument first and only then read the question, you may have to backtrack through the argument.

TIP

Underlining the key words in the question may help. For example, if you get a question that asks you to resolve a discrepancy, underline the word *discrepancy*. If the question asks you for the author's conclusion, underline the word *conclusion*.

Reading the argument

After you figure out what kind of question you're dealing with, read the paragraph very carefully. Be sure to locate the argument's conclusion, which may come at the beginning, middle, or end of the argument. When you've identified the conclusion, you can better understand the rest of the argument. As you read the argument, look for inconsistencies or gaps that may help you answer the question. Look for whatever the question asks for. If it asks for an assumption, look for an assumption — you know one is in there. If it asks for a flaw, find a flaw. Isolating the argument's premises, assumptions, and conclusion helps you determine the method of reasoning. We cover how to go about these tasks in the later section "Making a Case: Essentials of Informal Logic."

The argument usually isn't too complicated, and therefore, you may be tempted to read it too quickly. Force yourself to read slowly and carefully so you don't skim over the word or words that provide the keys to the argument. If you read thoroughly enough, you'll be able to eliminate some — or even most — of the answer choices. When you're down to two possible answers, you can then easily refer back to the text to make sure you choose the correct answer.

Here's an example: "My house is full of bees. I need to call an exterminator." What's the argument's conclusion? I need to call an exterminator. What evidence is used to justify this conclusion? My house is full of bees.

This basic statement, simple though it is, could become the basis for a variety of logical reasoning–style questions. For example, what assumptions does this statement make? It assumes that an exterminator can eradicate bees in a house. What information could strengthen the conclusion? Maybe something like, "Exterminators are specialists in ridding houses of insect pests." What information could weaken the conclusion? How about a statement such as, "Ordinary exterminators don't handle bee swarms and recommend that customers call animal control specialists to take care of them."

TIP

Logical reasoning questions, like all LSAT questions, include all the information you need to answer them correctly. That means you don't have to be an expert in any esoteric topic — say, bees or exterminators — to answer them. That doesn't mean, however, that you don't have to understand what they're talking about. Logical reasoning questions presume a fairly high level of reading proficiency and vocabulary; you have to be a skilled reader to understand the arguments well enough to work with them. So you should still leave your preconceived notions about a subject at home, but you should definitely keep thinking actively and put your vocabulary and reading skills to work.

REMEMBER

Most logical reasoning questions are a bit longer than this example, and they're usually not as straightforward. At heart, though, they're not that different. Each one offers a proposition and supports it with evidence. The proposition may be right or wrong, and the evidence may or may not support it, but the basic structure doesn't change.

Again, if it helps you to highlight key words, use the highlighter tool. Be careful, though, because you don't want to highlight too much, which won't help you. If you're a chronic highlighter or if you find the exercise of highlighting to be distracting, forget about it and just read carefully.

REMEMBER

LSAT arguments seem like fairly scholarly or specialized statements, but they're really just made-up paragraphs. So if their facts seem wrong or if an argument makes a point that you disagree with, don't let it bother you. You need to find the argument structure, that's all. Forget about the actual accuracy of the facts — it doesn't matter.

Formulating an answer

Now try to answer the question in your head before you read the answer choices. If you do, the correct answer may just jump right out at you. The wrong answers will be glaringly wrong, and crossing them off should take no time.

Of course, you can't always concoct the exact right answer. For example, if a question asks what information would strengthen the author's conclusion, you can't always hope to imagine the exact factoid that'll be in the right answer, but you probably can come up with something in the ballpark. Actively approach the answers already armed with an idea of what you want to find.

REMEMBER

Many students overlook this step, not realizing what a valuable tool anticipating the answer can be. Don't make this mistake yourself. Always try to concoct an answer before you check out the choices. Paraphrasing the right answer in your head saves time in the long run. The answer choices are meant to confuse you, but if you have a solid idea of what you're looking for, the right answer will appear more obvious, and you won't be led astray by wrong choices.

TIP

You can't answer one kind of question beforehand: A question that asks you which of the five answer choices is most similar to the pattern of reasoning in the argument. You can, however, break down the pattern of reasoning before you confront the choices, so really you're still coming up with an answer first. See Chapter 9 for more information.

Reading the answers and eliminating the wrong ones

Now read the answers. Having one obviously correct choice and four obviously wrong ones would be nice, but of course, the LSAT doesn't work that way. All five choices seem plausible. The LSAT-makers want you to spend your time agonizing over the answer choices, fretting because two of them look right and you just can't figure out which is which. Remember, though, there are never two right answers. Four answers are always wrong, one answer is always right, and the test-makers have to be very clear about which is which. Choices that seem ambiguous really aren't.

Even when you know which answer you want to find, reading through all the choices may take a little time. Logical reasoning answer choices can sometimes be nearly as long and complicated as the actual arguments. You know what to do, though: Read each answer quickly but carefully. Cross it off if you know for sure that it's wrong; leave it alone if you think it may be right.

REMEMBER

Don't get too caught up in the quest for speed. If you feel like you need to read an argument twice to find the answer, go ahead and do it, and don't fret because you had to backtrack. You've already put the time into reading the argument, so you may as well give it a fair shake.

After reading all the answer choices, pick an answer. If you cross off four obviously wrong answers and find one obviously correct one, great. If you can't decide between two answers, think about them for a little while, no more than 30 seconds or so. If you still can't decide which one is right, pick one, move on, and perhaps mark the question for review later if you have time. You have other fish to fry.

THE WINDING OR THE STRAIGHT ROAD?

Do you work logical reasoning sections straight through, from first to last question? Or does it make more sense to jump around, answering the questions you like first and saving the ugly ones for later?

We don't think it matters. There's no reason not to begin on the first question and work your way to the last, selecting the answers as you go. Then again, if you find jumping around easier, go for it. And if you get stuck on a question, it makes sense to skip it and move on, flagging it to return later if you have time.

If you do jump around, realize that rating questions for difficulty uses up some of your valuable test time. There's not all that much variation in difficulty from problem to problem, so you may get better results just tackling each question without categorizing it first.

TIP

Take a break after answering five or six questions. Your brain gets tired after several straight minutes of logical reasoning. These questions are tiring because there are so many of them and because you're constantly stuffing new information into your already overstuffed mind. So every time you finish a few questions, take a break. Not a long break — just a few seconds is enough. Close your eyes, roll your head around, stare out the window, and let your brain recharge. Then forge ahead.

WARNING

While you look around the room or out the window, be sure you *don't* look at anyone else's tablet or even seem like you may be. LSAT proctors don't tolerate even a suspicion of cheating. If you cherish hopes of a legal career, you won't ever cheat or look like you're cheating on the LSAT.

Making a Case: Essentials of Informal Logic

You can score well on the LSAT logical reasoning questions without knowing the elements of informal logic, but if you understand a few terms and concepts, you'll score even higher. You really just need to know the two basic components of a logical argument and a few methods of coming up with a conclusion.

Fighting fair: The elements of an argument

A logical argument consists of premises and a conclusion, and when you're analyzing arguments, identifying what parts are premises and what makes up the conclusion can help. The *premises* give the supporting evidence that you can draw a conclusion from. You can usually find the *conclusion* in the argument because it's the statement that you can preface with "therefore." The conclusion is often, but not always, the argument's last sentence. For example, take a look at this simple argument:

All runners are fast. John is a runner. Therefore, John is fast.

The premises in the argument are "All runners are fast" and "John is a runner." You know this because they provide the supporting evidence for the conclusion that John is fast, which is the sentence that begins with "Therefore." Not all conclusions in LSAT arguments begin with "therefore" or other words like it (such as "thus" and "so"), but you can try adding "therefore" to any statement you believe is the conclusion to see whether the argument makes sense.

Getting from point A to point B: Types of reasoning

Each logical argument has premises and a conclusion, but not every argument comes to a conclusion in the same way. For the purposes of the LSAT, you should be familiar with two basic types of logical reasoning: deductive and inductive. LSAT logical reasoning questions primarily test your inductive reasoning ability.

SURE SEEMS GREEK TO ME: ORIGINS OF LOGICAL THOUGHT

Legend has it that a Greek philosopher named Parmenides in the fifth century BC had plenty of time on his hands while living in a Greek colony off the west coast of Italy. So he whiled away the hours contemplating logical thought and became one of the first Westerners to record his findings. He penned a philosophical poem in which an unnamed goddess instructs him in the ways of determining truth about the universe. His poem explored the contrast between truth and appearance and portrayed truth to be firm and steadfast, whereas appearance (the way mortal men usually think) was unstable and wavering. Parmenides's work influenced other great Greek thinkers, like Plato, Aristotle, and Plotinus.

Unfortunately, you won't have a goddess to guide you through the LSAT's logical reasoning questions, but you can rely on Aristotle's method of developing syllogisms to examine LSAT arguments. He's the one who came up with this famous syllogism: All humans are mortal; Socrates is human; therefore, Socrates is mortal.

Elementary, my dear Watson: Deductive reasoning

In simple terms, in *deductive reasoning*, you come up with a specific conclusion from more-general premises. The great thing about deductive reasoning is that if the premises are true, the conclusion must be true! The following is an example of a deductive reasoning argument:

> All horses have hooves. (General premise)
>
> Bella is a horse. (More specific premise)
>
> Therefore, Bella has hooves. (Very specific conclusion)

If the premise that all horses have hooves is true, and if Bella is, in fact, a horse, then it must be true that Bella has hooves. The same holds true for all examples of deductive reasoning. Here's another example:

> All who wish to report an LSAT score must complete a writing sample. (General premise)
>
> You wish to report an LSAT score. (More specific premise)
>
> Therefore, you have to complete a writing sample. (Very specific conclusion)

This example shows the relationship between the truth of the premises and that of the conclusion. The first premise is categorically true: reporting an LSAT score requires you to write an essay. The second premise, however, may not be true. Certainly, you're thinking of taking the LSAT or you wouldn't be reading this book, but you may still decide not to report a test score. This possibility doesn't affect the argument's logic. Remember, in deductive reasoning, the conclusion must be true *if* the premises are true. If you wish to have your LSAT score reported, you have to write an essay, so this argument is valid.

Perhaps I'm just generalizing: Inductive reasoning

In deductive reasoning, you draw a specific conclusion from general premises. With *inductive reasoning*, you do just the opposite; you develop a general conclusion from specific premises. Inductive reasoning differs from deductive reasoning in that the conclusion in an inductive reasoning argument could be false, even if all the premises are true. With inductive reasoning, the conclusion is essentially your best guess. That's because an inductive reasoning argument relies on less complete information than deductive reasoning does. Consider this example of an inductive argument:

Bella is a horse and has hooves. (Specific premise)

Smoky is a horse and has hooves. (Specific premise)

Nutmeg is a horse and has hooves. (Specific premise)

Shadow is a horse and has hooves. (Specific premise)

Therefore, it is likely that all horses have hooves. (General conclusion)

Because an inductive argument derives general conclusions from specific examples, you can't come up with a statement that "must be true." The best you can say, even if all the premises are true, is that the conclusion can be or is likely to be true.

TIP

Inductive reasoning arguments come in all sorts of flavors, but the folks who create the LSAT tend to favor three types: cause and effect, analogy, and statistical. To excel on the LSAT, you want to get familiar with these three methods of inductive reasoning:

>> **Cause-and-effect arguments:** This argument concludes that one event is the result of another. These types of arguments are strongest when the premises prove that an event's alleged cause is the most likely one and that there are no other probable causes. For example, after years of football watching, you may conclude the following: "Every time I wear my lucky shirt, my favorite team wins; therefore, wearing my lucky shirt causes the team to win." This example is weak because it doesn't take into consideration other, more probable reasons (like the team's talent) for the wins.

>> **Analogy arguments:** This argument tries to show that two or more concepts are similar so that what holds true for one is true for the other. The argument's strength depends on the degree of similarity between the persons, objects, or ideas being compared. For example, in drawing a conclusion about Beth's likes, you may compare her to Alex: "Alex is a student, and he likes rap music. Beth is also a student, so she probably likes rap music, too." Your argument would be stronger if you could show that Alex and Beth have other similar interests that apply to rap music, like hip-hop dancing or wearing bling. If, on the other hand, you show that Alex likes to go to dance clubs while Beth prefers practicing her violin at home, your original conclusion may be less likely.

>> **Statistical arguments:** This argument relies on numbers to reach a conclusion. These types of arguments claim that what's true for the statistical majority is also true for the individual (or, alternately, that what's true of a member or members of a group also holds true for the larger group). But because these are inductive reasoning arguments, you can't prove that the conclusions are absolutely true. When you analyze statistical arguments on the LSAT, focus on how well the given statistics apply to the conclusion's circumstances. For instance, if you wanted people to buy clothing through your website, you may make this argument: "In a recent study of consumers' preferences, 80 percent of shoppers surveyed said they prefer to shop online; therefore, you'll probably prefer to buy clothes online." You'd support your conclusion if you could show that what's true for the majority is also true for an individual.

TIP

To do well on logical reasoning questions, you need to recognize stated premises, assumed premises, and conclusions in arguments; determine the method of reasoning; and establish whether premises adequately support the conclusion. As you can induce, knowing a little about logical reasoning is essential to scoring well on the LSAT!

Chapter **8**

Conclusions, Inferences, Assumptions, and Flaws in Logical Reasoning Questions

Logical reasoning questions come in various types, which require you to focus on different aspects of each argument. The most basic task involved in logical reasoning questions is identifying the argument's conclusion. To answer most questions, you first have to spot the conclusion and then figure out how and why the author reached that conclusion. For some questions, though, all you have to do is identify the conclusion. Look at those questions as a gift. Other logical reasoning questions are a bit more complicated; you must not only spot the conclusion but also figure out how the author uses evidence to support the conclusion, either effectively or not so effectively.

In this chapter, you discover how to approach questions that ask you to spot a conclusion and figure out how the author reached that conclusion, or questions that ask you to draw a conclusion from a set of premises. The most basic conclusion-type questions simply require you to spot the conclusion or draw your own. The more complicated *assumption* and *logical flaw* questions ask a bit more of you; you first have to spot the conclusion, and then you figure out what facts the author assumed to reach that conclusion or point out a mistake the author made in applying the evidence.

Jumping to Logical Conclusions

The LSAT tests your ability to identify conclusions in two ways. One type presents a full argument with premises and a conclusion and then asks you to identify the statement that constitutes the conclusion. These questions are relatively easy. Classify each statement in the argument as either one that leads to a conclusion or one that contains the ultimate opinion that results from the other statements. This type of question may be worded like these:

>> Which one of the following most accurately expresses the main conclusion of the argument?

>> Which one of the following most accurately expresses the conclusion drawn in the paragraph?

More frequently, the LSAT tests your ability to draw logical conclusions (or hypotheses) from a series of premises (the evidence). You choose an answer that best concludes the information. Questions that ask you to draw conclusions from premises may be worded like this:

>> Which one of the following is most strongly supported by the information above?

>> If the statements above are true, which one of the following is most strongly supported on the basis of them?

>> Which one of the following most logically completes the argument?

As you read through the premises, think of a logical conclusion of your own. Then look through the answer choices to see whether one comes close to matching what you've thought up.

TIP

The key to correctly answering these more common conclusion questions is to look for the answer choice that addresses most of the information contained in the premises. Eliminate any choices that are off-topic or incomplete. A conclusion that addresses only part of the information may be plausible, but it probably isn't the best answer. For example, consider the following premises:

Five hundred healthy adults were allowed to sleep no more than five hours a night for one month. Half of the group members were allowed 90-minute naps in the afternoon each day; the remaining subjects were allowed no naps. Throughout the month, the subjects of the experiment were tested to determine the impact of sleep deprivation on their performance of standard tasks. By the end of the month, the group that was not allowed to nap suffered significant declines in performance, while the napping group suffered more moderate declines.

The best conclusion for these premises would have to address the following:

>> The nightly sleep deprivation of healthy adults

>> The allowance for naps for half of the study group

>> The smaller decline in performance of standard tasks for the group that took naps

Any conclusion that fails to address all three points isn't the best conclusion. For example, the statement "Sleep deprivation causes accumulating declines in performance among healthy adults" wouldn't be the best conclusion because it fails to address the effect of naps. A better conclusion would be, "Napping helps reduce the declines in performance caused by nightly sleep deprivation among healthy adults."

WARNING

You'll often see more than one plausible conclusion among the answer choices. Your task is to identify the best choice. Don't fall for the trap of choosing an answer that just restates one of the premises. Answer choices that restate a premise may entice you because they echo part of the information in the argument, but the best choice must contain an element of each of the pieces of information presented in the question.

The process is pretty simple, really. Try this sample question to see for yourself:

EXAMPLE

Over the last eight years, the Federal Reserve Bank has raised the prime interest rate by a quarter-point more than ten times. The Bank raises rates when its Board of Governors fears inflation and lowers rates when the economy is slowing down.

Which one of the following is the most logical conclusion for this paragraph?

(A) The Federal Reserve should be replaced with regional banks that can respond more quickly to changing economic conditions.

(B) The Federal Reserve has raised the prime rate in recent years to try to control inflation.

(C) The economy has entered a prolonged recession caused by Federal Reserve policies.

(D) The monetary policy of the United States is no longer controlled by the Federal Reserve.

(E) The Federal Reserve has consistently raised the prime rate over the last several years.

You know from the language that this is a conclusion question, so you don't have to look for a conclusion in the argument. Just read through the premises and formulate a quick conclusion, something like, "Because the Federal Reserve has raised interest rates many times over the last eight years, it must fear inflation."

Eliminate answer choices that aren't relevant or that contain information not presented by the premises. The paragraph says nothing about regional banks or the termination of the Federal Reserve's control over U.S. monetary policy, so you can disregard Choices (A) and (D). Then get rid of any choices that don't take all premises into consideration. Choice (E) just reiterates the first premise, so it's wrong. You're left with Choices (B) and (C), but Choice (C) contradicts the information in the premises. The problem says the Federal Reserve responds to the economy, not the other way around, so it would be wrong to say the Federal Reserve causes a recession. Choice (B) is clearly the best answer. It takes into consideration the information that the Federal Reserve has raised rates and that raising rates is its response to inflation.

WARNING

Be careful to avoid relying on outside knowledge or opinions when answering conclusion questions. You may have studied the Federal Reserve Bank and have opinions about monetary policy. Choices (A), (C), and (D) reflect some possible opinions about the Federal Reserve. Don't get trapped into choosing an answer just because it supports your opinion.

Using Your Noggin to Make Inferences

Logical reasoning inference questions ask you to make an *inference* from a series of statements. These questions may contain the word *infer*, but more often they ask you to choose the answer that is most strongly supported by the statements. So you may make inferences for questions worded like these:

>> Which of the following can be properly inferred from the statements above?

>> If the statement above are true, then which one of the following must also be true?

>> Which one of the following is most strongly supported by the consumer's statements?

>> The information above provides the most support for which one of the following statements?

The key to answering these questions correctly is to remember that they usually ask you to make an inference based on information in the paragraph's statements rather than draw an overall conclusion based on all of them. So you should choose an answer that makes a plausible inference about or connection between one or more of the statements. Like the correct answer choices for the conclusion questions, the best answers to this type of question don't go beyond the scope of the information provided in the passage. So eliminate answer choices that concern information not specifically addressed by at least one of the statements.

EXAMPLE

Television ratings are based on the number of overall viewers, but the highest-rated television shows do not always command the most advertising dollars. Many advertisers are willing to pay more for spots that run during shows that attract a high proportion of males between the ages of 19 and 34 than for ads that run during other, more highly rated shows that do not attract as large a proportion of males aged 19 to 34. Ads that run during televised sporting events are often more expensive than ads that run during other types of programs.

Which one of the following is most strongly supported by these statements?

(A) Advertisers have done little research into the typical consumer and are not using their advertising dollars wisely.

(B) Sports programs are viewed by a greater proportion of males aged 19 to 34 than are other prime-time network programs.

(C) The ability to reach a particular demographic is more important to many advertisers than reaching the greatest number of overall viewers.

(D) Many advertising executives prefer sports programs and assume that other Americans do as well.

(E) Ads that run during the most popular sporting events are the most expensive of all ads.

You know you're dealing with an inference question because the question asks for the most strongly supported answer based on the statements. Focus on the paragraph's statements as you read. Then look through the answer choices and eliminate any that don't address or connect the statements.

The statements say nothing about advertising research and don't make value judgments about particular advertising practices, so you can eliminate Choice (A) immediately. Likewise, Choice (D) mentions the program preferences of advertisers, but none of the statements concerns what advertisers like to watch, so you can get rid of Choice (D). Choice (E) is wrong because the statements don't support an inference about what would constitute the most expensive ads. Just because sporting events ads are "often more expensive" than other ads doesn't necessarily mean that they're always the most expensive. This leaves you with Choices (B) and (C).

The author implies that some televised sporting events have lower overall ratings, even though they have higher advertising rates. Plus, the statements don't indicate who watches televised sporting events. So you can't justify Choice (B). You're left with Choice (C), which provides an explanation for the information in the second sentence that states that advertisers are more willing to pay more for lower-rated shows that are nevertheless viewed by a larger proportion of males between 19 and 34. This practice makes sense if the advertisers are trying to attract young male consumers. Choice (C) is best.

WARNING

Remember to check your outside knowledge about the subjects at the door! You may know that Super Bowl ads are the most expensive ads, which may tempt you to pick Choice (E). Using your own knowledge rather than what's expressly stated in the test questions will cause you to miss questions that someone with less knowledge may answer correctly.

Making Assumptions

Making an argument without assuming at least one or two points is nearly impossible. If you back up everything you say, it can take forever, and sometimes you have to assume something just for the sake of argument. Assumptions aren't necessarily bad, but you do need to recognize them when they occur.

Seeking-assumptions questions ask you to identify a premise that isn't present in the argument. For these types of questions, the author directly states a series of premises and provides a clear conclusion, but in getting to that conclusion, the author assumes information. Your job is to figure out what the author assumes to be true but doesn't state directly in drawing the conclusion.

For example, if the argument says, "My house is full of bees, so I need to call an exterminator," you know the author must assume that the exterminator can do something about the bees, even though the argument doesn't explicitly state this fact.

Seeking-assumptions questions may look like these:

>> Which one of the following is an assumption required by the argument above?

>> The professor's conclusion follows logically if which one of the following is assumed?

>> Which one of the following is an assumption on which the scholar's reasoning depends?

>> The politician's argument depends on assuming which one of the following?

>> On which one of the following assumptions does the argument rely?

>> Which one of the following, if assumed, would allow the conclusion to be properly drawn?

>> Which one of the following, if assumed, enables the argument's conclusion to be properly inferred?

>> The argument requires the assumption that . . .

TIP

Words like *assume, rely, presume, depend on,* and their derivatives usually indicate seeking-assumptions questions. Remember, these questions ask you to look for the ideas the author relies on but doesn't state.

As you read seeking-assumptions questions, look for information that's necessary to the argument but isn't stated by the author. In these questions, the author always takes for granted something on which the entire argument depends. You just need to identify what that is. To do so effectively, choose an answer that links the existing premises to the conclusion. The assumption you're seeking always bears directly on the conclusion and ties in with one or more premises, often with the last premise. Therefore, the best answer often contains information from both the last premise and the conclusion. Try on this one for size:

EXAMPLE

Women receive fewer speeding tickets than men do. Women also have lower car insurance rates. It is clear that women are better drivers than men.

On which of the following is an assumption on which the conclusion relies?

(A) Men drive cars more frequently than women do.

(B) The percentage of female drivers in the population is greater than the percentage of male drivers.

(C) Women do not receive more parking tickets than men do.

(D) Most men prefer sports cars to sedans.

(E) Having lower car insurance rates indicates that one is a better driver than those who have higher rates.

As always, read the question first. Because it references assumptions, we bet you figured out pretty quickly that it's a seeking-assumptions question.

Next, read through the argument and try to figure out the assumption or assumptions the author makes in reaching the conclusion that women are better drivers. The author moves from the premises to the conclusion pretty quickly and assumes that fewer speeding tickets and lower car insurance rates indicate better driving skills. The author also assumes that men and women have equal driving experiences because the evidence is about the number of ticketed men and women, not the percent of ticketed men and women (if women just drove less than men, then they could easily have fewer tickets without actually being better drivers). Use this information to examine each of your options.

The author uses the premise that women have lower insurance rates to support the conclusion that women are better drivers, so the author must assume that better drivers enjoy lower insurance rates, so the answer must be Choice (E). Choice (A) may provide an explanation for why more men receive speeding tickets, but it doesn't lead to the conclusion that women are better drivers. Choice (B) is wrong. The conclusion may presume that the number of men and women drivers is equal, but the conclusion that women are better drivers than men doesn't rely on the assumption that there are more women drivers. Choice (C) is irrelevant to an argument that uses number of speeding tickets to reach its conclusion, and Choice (D)'s reference to sports cars is completely off base.

TIP

Often, the correct answer to an assumption question is the one that links one of the premises directly to the conclusion.

Finding Flaws in an Argument

Not every argument is convincing. In fact, many (if not most) arguments have something wrong with them. As a lawyer, you have to spot your opponents' bad arguments so you can attack them and spot bad arguments in your own work so you can fix them. Many logical reasoning questions have flaws. The LSAT-makers place the flaws there to test your ability to spot them.

These problems are a bit more complicated than questions that simply ask you to draw a conclusion. First you find the conclusion, then you figure out how the author reached it, and finally you determine what's wrong with that reasoning process.

Take a look at some examples of spot-the-flaw questions:

> » Which one of the following most accurately describes a flaw in the argument?

> » The reasoning above is flawed because it fails to recognize that . . .

> » The argument is vulnerable to criticism on which one of the following grounds?

> » The reasoning in the argument is flawed because the argument fails to take into account that . . .

> » The argument is questionable because it fails to consider . . .

Occasionally, the LSAT asks you to find the flaw in a formal argument. Usually the author draws a faulty conclusion by confusing a sufficient condition with a necessary one. For example, an argument may fallaciously conclude that because only girls wear pink and Jane is a girl, Jane must be wearing pink. Notice that if the first premise stated that *all* girls wear pink, the conclusion that Jane is wearing pink would be justified. The majority of finding-the-flaw questions, however, concern informal arguments and are easier to answer when you're familiar with informal fallacies. Some of the informal fallacies most commonly tested on the LSAT are these:

> » **Fallacies of relevance occur when the conclusion isn't relevant to the premises offered to support it.**
>
> - An *appeal to force* specifies that you better believe a conclusion is true or you'll suffer harm.
>
> - The *bandwagon approach* requires you to accept a conclusion because everybody else does.
>
> - The *red herring* introduces a premise that has nothing to do with the argument and then bases the conclusion on that irrelevant point.
>
> - An *ad hominem* attack opposes another's argument by attacking the person rather than the conclusion's reasonability.

> » **Fallacies of weak induction occur when the premises don't adequately support the conclusion.**
>
> - An *appeal to authority* is fallacious when the authority used to support a claim isn't an expert in the argument's subject.
>
> - A *hasty generalization* occurs when the sample size provided to support a claim is inadequate.

> » **Fallacies of ambiguity use unclear or undefined meanings.**

> » **Fallacies of presumption occur when someone's claim presumes an unsubstantiated truth.**
>
> - *Circular reasoning* occurs when the premise used to support a conclusion is the conclusion itself.
>
> - A *complex question* is a question presented in such a way that you can't answer it without implicating yourself.
>
> - A *false dichotomy* occurs when an argument provides only two options, provides evidence to reject one of those options, and then concludes that the other option is the only viable truth without recognizing that other options exist.

> » **Fallacies of analogy result from comparing entities that aren't sufficiently similar to warrant a comparison.** They may also occur when one claims that because the parts of a whole are a certain way, the whole is also that way, or because a whole is a certain way, the parts individually are also that way.

Watch for these informal fallacies when you approach a question that asks you to find the flaw, such as the following example.

EXAMPLE

Some southern towns have quaint downtown areas, and some southern towns have small colleges. Therefore, some southern towns with small colleges also have quaint downtown areas.

The reasoning in the argument is flawed because the argument

(A) implies a definite causal relationship from a coincidence that could be explained in other ways.

(B) contains a premise that cannot be true unless the conclusion is known to be true.

(C) employs the word "quaint" to mean two different things.

(D) fails to acknowledge that one group could have members in common with each of two other groups without those other two groups sharing any members in common.

(E) mistakes towns that have quaint downtown areas for towns that have small colleges.

As always, your first step is to read the question. It asks you to figure out what's wrong with the argument's reasoning. Now read the argument. It concludes that because some southern towns have quaint downtowns and some have small colleges, some have both. This sounds like a fallacy of analogy. The problem with the argument's conclusion is that it assumes overlap between two sets ("southern towns with quaint downtown areas" and "southern towns with small colleges") that don't necessarily have to overlap. It's entirely possible that the two sets of towns aren't similar at all and that no town has both a quaint downtown and a small college.

Now read through the answers, looking for a choice that suggests a problem with the analogy. Choice (A) is wrong because no causal relationship is implied. Choice (B) is wrong because no premise of the argument depends on the conclusion; in other words, the first statement can stand on its own without the conclusion. Choice (C) is wrong because the word "quaint" is used the same way both times to describe downtown areas. Choice (D) looks correct; the argument does illogically suppose that because one group (southern towns) has members in common with two other groups (towns with quaint downtown areas and towns with small colleges), those two latter groups must also share members. Choice (E) is wrong because the argument doesn't confuse the two types of towns with each other; it keeps them distinct while reaching the erroneous conclusion. Choice (D) is the best answer.

TIP

If the argument had used the word *most* instead of *some*, you could assume overlap. The statement "Most southern towns have quaint downtowns, and most southern towns have small colleges; therefore, some southern towns have both" would be perfectly acceptable.

Chapter 9

Strengthening and Weakening Arguments

When a lawyer argues a point, she must support it with evidence. Her opponent argues the opposite point, and she must find evidence that can weaken his argument. Law students take an entire class on evidence in which they explore how to use evidence to support their cases or to destroy the other side's evidence. Using evidence to support arguments is a constant requirement in all their other classes. To succeed as a law student and a lawyer, you absolutely must have a good understanding of how evidence can strengthen or weaken a conclusion.

The LSAT-writers design logical reasoning questions to test your ability to strengthen or weaken arguments. These questions present an argument and then ask you to strengthen it, weaken it, criticize it, or some other similar exercise.

In this chapter, we show you how to identify strengthen/weaken questions and provide strategies for working them.

Understanding How These Questions Work

Logical reasoning questions that ask you how to best support or damage an argument are some of the easiest to answer. You probably analyze ideas every day and think of evidence to attack or defend those ideas. Because you already have the skill to evaluate arguments, it doesn't take much work for you to modify that skill to fit this specific LSAT question format. This question category has two subtypes: One asks you to strengthen an argument, and the other asks you to weaken it. You'll recognize these questions because they include words that mean to strengthen or weaken (like *support, bolster,* or *impair*), and they almost always contain an "if true" qualifier.

WARNING

Nearly all these questions contain the words "if true," but not all questions that have "if true" in them are strengthening-or-weakening-the-argument types. To make sure an "if true" question is really a strengthening-or-weakening question, look for the identifying language that asks you to either strengthen or weaken the argument.

Here are three simple steps to follow when approaching strengthening-or-weakening-the-argument questions:

1. **Read the question very carefully so you know exactly what it is you're strengthening or weakening.**

   In most cases, it's the main argument's reasoning. But in less frequent cases, you may be asked to support or impair a different line of reasoning, like the view of the author's opponent.

2. **Examine the argument to find the premises and conclusion and to determine what method of reasoning the author uses to reach the conclusion.**

   Usually the author uses inductive reasoning, so you need to figure out whether the argument relies on analogy, statistics, or cause and effect to arrive at the conclusion. In the upcoming sections, we tell you what to look for in each type of reasoning.

3. **Evaluate the answer choices to determine which choice best fits with the author's conclusion and method of reasoning.**

   Assume all the answer choices are true and then determine which one best either supports or undermines the specific line of reasoning addressed in the question.

WARNING

Always assume that all the answers to strengthening-or-weakening-the-argument questions are true. Almost all these questions include the words "if true" in them to remind you that you're supposed to assume that each answer choice presents a true statement. Don't fall into the trap of trying to evaluate whether answer choices are true or false! Your only job is to determine whether the choices help or hurt the argument. This means that a statement like "humans do not breathe air" could be a correct answer choice even though you know it's not true. Perhaps you're supposed to weaken an argument that concludes that a company must pump air into an underwater habitat for humans. If humans don't breathe air, pumping in air may not be necessary. Make sure you don't dismiss any answer choices simply because you know or suspect they aren't true in the real world.

Affecting cause-and-effect arguments

Questions that ask you to evaluate arguments often feature cause-and-effect reasoning. If the argument uses cause and effect to make its point, focus on the causes. Almost always, the right answer to a question that asks you to strengthen the argument shows that the cause mentioned is the most likely source of the effect. The best answer for a question for which you have to weaken the argument points to another probable cause of the effect. Here's how you apply this reasoning to a sample question:

EXAMPLE

Average hours of television viewing per American have sharply increased for more than three decades. Over the same period of time, there has been an increase in obesity rates in America. To fight the rise in obesity, Americans must limit their hours of television viewing.

Which one of the following, if true, would most weaken the author's argument?

(A) A person burns more calories while watching television than while sleeping.

(B) Over the last 30 years, there has been an increase in the number of fast food restaurants in the United States.

(C) Americans spend most of their television time watching sports events rather than cooking shows.

(D) Television viewing in Japan has also increased over the past three decades.

(E) Studies show that the number of television commercials that promote junk food has risen over the past ten years.

To tackle this question, first identify the conclusion and the premises the author states or implies to reach that conclusion. The conclusion is pretty easy to spot. The last thought of the argument is that Americans must limit their hours of TV viewing to curb the rise in obesity. The author makes this judgment using the following evidence:

>> The author directly states that the number of TV viewing hours has increased over the last 30 years.

>> According to the author, the number of obese Americans has also increased.

>> The author implies that TV viewing causes obesity.

To weaken the argument that Americans have to reduce their TV watching, you have to find the answer choice that shows that there could be another cause for the rise in obesity.

You may have been tempted to select Choice (A) because it shows that TV watching may be less fat-producing than another activity, sleeping. But it doesn't give you another reason for the rise in obesity. Choice (A) could be right only if it showed that Americans are sleeping more than they were 30 years ago. It doesn't, so move on.

On the other hand, stating that during the same time period the number of fast food restaurants also increased introduces another possible cause of obesity and weakens the conclusion that Americans have to stop watching so much TV to get slimmer. Maybe it's the popularity of fast food that's the culprit! Choice (B) is a better answer than Choice (A), but read through all the possibilities before you commit. Choice (C) is wrong because the argument contains nothing that suggests that the type of TV Americans watch affects their obesity, nor does Choice (C) show that viewing patterns have changed over the last three decades. You can eliminate Choice (C) from contention. And Choice (D) is also out because it doesn't correlate what's happening in Japan with what's happening in the United States. You don't know whether Japanese citizens weigh more now than they did 30 years ago, so the information in Choice (D) is useless.

If the question had asked you to strengthen the conclusion, Choice (E) would be a good option. It shows a reason that increased TV watching could cause obesity. But the question asks you to weaken the conclusion, so Choice (B) is the best answer. It's the only one that shows that there could be another cause for the rise in obesity.

Analyzing analogy arguments

Remember that analogy arguments rely on the similarity of the two persons, things, or ideas being compared. Therefore, if the author uses an analogy to reach a conclusion, answer choices that show similarities between the compared elements support the conclusion, and choices that emphasize the differences between the elements weaken the conclusion. Take a look at this example of an analogy argument:

EXAMPLE

Hundo is a Japanese car company, and Hundos run for many miles on a gallon of gas. Toyo is also a Japanese car company; therefore, Toyos should get good gas mileage, too.

The author's argument would be best supported by which one of the following, if that statement were true?

(A) All Japanese car manufacturers use the same types of engines in their cars.

(B) British cars run for as many miles on a tank of gas as Hundos do.

(C) The Toyo manufacturer focuses on producing large utility vehicles.

(D) Toyo has been manufacturing cars for more than 20 years.

(E) All Japanese cars have excellent service records.

Recognizing the premises and conclusion in this argument is simple. The author states directly that Hundo cars are Japanese and get good gas mileage and that Toyo cars are Japanese; therefore, Toyos also get good gas mileage. Your job is to find the answer that bolsters the similarity between Hundos and Toyos.

TIP

You can generally eliminate answer choices that introduce irrelevant information, such as Choices (B), (D), and (E). The author compares Japanese cars, so British cars have nothing to do with the argument. The length of time that Toyo has been in business tells you nothing about how similar its cars are to Hundo's. And the question is talking about gas mileage, not service records, so don't spend too much time considering Choice (E).

Choice (C) tells you the focus of Toyo producers, but it doesn't give you any information about how that compares to Hundo, so the best answer is Choice (A). If all Japanese manufacturers supply their cars with the same engines, and Hundo and Toyo are both Japanese manufacturers, it's more likely that Toyos will achieve a gas mileage similar to that experienced by Hundos.

Stabbing at statistical arguments

If you see statistics used to promote an argument, look for an answer that shows whether the statistics actually relate to the conclusion's topic. If they do, you'll strengthen the conclusion. On the other hand, an answer that shows the statistic is unrelated to the conclusion significantly weakens that conclusion. The following is an example of a statistical logical reasoning question you could find on the LSAT:

EXAMPLE

In a survey of 100 pet owners, 80 percent said that they would buy a more expensive pet food if it contained vitamin supplements. Consequently, CatCo's new premium cat food should be a top seller.

Which one of the following, if true, would most weaken the author's argument?

(A) Some brands of cat food contain more vitamin supplements than CatCo's does.

(B) CatCo sells more cat food than any of its competitors.

(C) Some of the cat owners surveyed stated that they never buy expensive brands of cat food.

(D) Ninety-five of those pet owners surveyed did not own cats.

(E) Many veterinarians have stated that vitamin supplements in cat food do not greatly increase health benefits.

Because the argument hinges on statistics, eliminate answers that don't directly address the statistical evidence. Those surveyed stated they would pay more for pet food with vitamin supplements, but they didn't provide information on whether the amount of vitamin supplements was important. So even though Choice (A) may entice you, it isn't the best answer because it doesn't address the statistics used in the argument. Choice (B) doesn't regard the survey results either, and it seems to support the conclusion rather than weaken it. The argument has nothing at all to do with veterinarians, so Choice (E) can't be right. Only Choice (C) and Choice (D) deal with the survey the author uses to reach the conclusion that CatCo's premium cat food will be a big seller.

TIP

You can eliminate answer choices that show there's an exception to the statistical evidence. Exceptions don't significantly weaken a statistical argument.

Therefore, Choice (C) is wrong and Choice (D) is the best answer because it demonstrates a weakness in the statistics the author uses to support the conclusion. The preferences of dog or bird owners wouldn't be a good indicator of the habits of cat owners.

TIP

Strengthen/weaken questions lend themselves quite well to the technique of trying to answer the question before reading the answers. If you can identify the conclusion, take a moment to think about how you'd answer the question if you didn't have an array of answers to choose from. Consider what the author is claiming, and then consider how you'd strengthen it, weaken it, or whatever the question wants you to do.

Build It Up: Strengthen/Support Questions

Sometimes lawyers want to bolster their arguments. They look for evidence, court decisions, and laws that support the claims they're making. Spotting evidence that can support an argument is a real skill; law schools teach it, but they want their students to arrive already understanding the basic concept. That's why the LSAT includes logical reasoning on the test.

The logical reasoning section includes some questions that ask you to pick answers that can strengthen the argument. The questions may use the word *strengthen*, but they may also ask you to support a position or justify reasoning. No matter how they're phrased, they're all asking you to do the same thing — to spot the answer that can make the argument's conclusion more likely.

Check out some examples of strengthen/support questions:

>> Which one of the following, if true, most strengthens the argument?

>> Which one of the following, if true, most strongly supports the statement above?

>> Which one of the following, if true, would provide the most support for the teacher's assertion?

>> Which one of the following, if true, most helps to support the position of the second group of economists?

>> Which one of the following discoveries, if it were made, would most support the hypothesis stated above?

>> Which one of the following, if true, most supports Martin's counter to Jessica?

>> Which one of the following principles, if valid, most helps to justify the reasoning above?

>> Which one of the following principles, if established, most helps to justify Susan's position?

>> Which one of the following principles, if valid, most helps to justify the bookstore owner's argumentation?

>> Which one of the following principles, if valid, most justifies the physicist's conclusion?

REMEMBER

The approach to answering all these strengthen/support questions is the same: Figure out what the conclusion is and what the premises are, and then figure out what would make the connection between them stronger and more believable. Try to come up with your own answer before you consider the choices.

Tear It Down: Weakening Questions

Almost as important as strengthening your own arguments is tearing down your opponent's. Lawyers spend at least as much time attacking their opponent's arguments as they do bolstering their own. No matter how strong your case is, your opponent will have a tough case in response. Even if the opposing case is flimsy as gauze, you still have to go through the necessary steps of taking it apart. That's why the LSAT tests for this skill.

The logical reasoning section contains several questions asking you to weaken an argument. These questions may use the word *weaken.* They also may ask you to criticize, undermine, or attack the argument.

Here are some weaken questions:

>> Which one of the following, if true, most weakens the argument?

>> Which one of the following, if true, most seriously weakens the argument?

>> Which one of the following statements, if true, most seriously weakens the argument above?

>> Which one of the following, if true, most undermines the doctor's argument?

>> Which one of the following, if true, most undermines George's objection to Marisol's analysis?

The approach to these questions is exactly like the approach to strengthen/support questions, except that you want to hurt the argument, not help it. Find the conclusion, figure out what evidence and reasoning the author used to get there, and come up with something that makes the relevance of that evidence to that conclusion seem less likely.

A Twist: EXCEPT Questions

Many strengthen/weaken questions don't ask for the choice that best strengthens (or weakens, or supports, or undermines) the argument but instead for the one choice that *doesn't* do one of those things. These questions end in the extremely important word *EXCEPT*. It's always capitalized, so you can't miss it.

These questions look like this:

>> Each of the following, if true, supports the argument above EXCEPT:

>> Each of the following, if true, would weaken the commentator's argument EXCEPT:

>> Each of the following, if true, supports the physicist's hypothesis EXCEPT:

>> Each of the following, if true, weakens the argument EXCEPT:

>> Each of the following, if true, strengthens the argument EXCEPT:

They can also look like this:

>> Which one of the following, if all of them are true, is LEAST helpful in establishing that the conclusion above is properly drawn?

>> Which one of the following, if all of them are true, is LEAST effective at undermining the politician's argument?

They're still strengthen/weaken questions, but instead of finding one answer to strengthen/weaken/support/undermine, you want to find four.

REMEMBER

As always, first read the question *carefully*. These questions aren't your standard strengthen/weaken questions. Instead, they offer four choices that do strengthen or weaken the conclusion, and one that doesn't. You don't necessarily have to find an answer that strengthens or weakens the conclusion; you just want an answer that doesn't do what the other four do. For example, if the question reads, "Each of the following, if true, weakens the argument EXCEPT:" the correct answer doesn't necessarily strengthen the argument, but it definitely doesn't weaken it.

Here's an example of a question that has four answers that weaken the argument and one that doesn't:

EXAMPLE

Some workers in microwave popcorn factories have contracted a rare lung disease. Experts have linked this disease to a chemical used in the process of mixing popcorn and flavorings. Consumers should, therefore, stop buying and eating all types of microwave popcorn to avoid the risk of contracting this lung disease.

Each of the following, if true, weakens the argument EXCEPT:

(A) The lung disease is caused by being exposed to the chemical for many hours at a time over a period of years.

(B) The chemical only becomes toxic when it is held at a temperature much higher than that reached by popcorn in a microwave.

(C) The lung disease has only been found in workers who handled the Cajun Spice flavor of popcorn.

(D) In 20 years of widespread microwave popcorn consumption, no consumer has ever contracted this rare lung disease.

(E) The EPA has not yet done any research to determine whether the chemical that causes the lung disease is present in the steam and air that come out of a bag of popcorn when it is opened.

From reading the question first, you know you want an answer that doesn't weaken the argument. The conclusion is that consumers should stop eating all types of microwave popcorn to avoid catching a disease. The evidence for this conclusion is that a chemical in microwave popcorn caused this disease in popcorn factory employees.

What weakens the argument? Any evidence that makes consumers seem safe. If you can prove that the disease is somehow restricted to the factory workers, you can reassure consumers that they can eat microwave popcorn with impunity. What doesn't weaken the conclusion? Any evidence indicating that consumers can catch the disease from eating microwave popcorn, or any evidence that's of unclear relevance or simply off-topic.

>> Choice (A) weakens the argument because most consumers aren't exposed to the chemical in question for long periods of time.

>> Choice (B) weakens the argument because consumers aren't keeping their popcorn hot enough.

>> Choice (C) weakens the suggestion that consumers should avoid all kinds of microwave popcorn, though possibly not the suggestion that they should avoid Cajun Spice flavor.

>> Choice (D) weakens the suggestion because it makes the risk to consumers appear almost negligible.

>> Choice (E) doesn't weaken the argument; if the EPA hasn't yet done any research into the chemical's presence in popcorn steam, then the chemical could well be lurking in there, ready to sicken hapless consumers.

Choice (E) doesn't especially strengthen the argument, but it doesn't weaken it, either. Choice (E) is the correct answer.

» Determining points of agreement and disagreement

» Analyzing patterns of reasoning

» Spotting principles

» Deciphering argument structure

» Figuring out the role of a claim

Chapter **10**

Examining Other Logical Reasoning Question Types

Lawyers are artists of a sort — or maybe *craftspeople* is a better word. They build arguments. Lawyers use as much craft in drafting a brief or presenting a closing argument as craftspeople do in building a fine cabinet. The LSAT tests to see whether you have the natural aptitude for this craft, whether you understand how arguments hold together, and why an author uses particular words.

The questions we discuss in this chapter tend to appear less frequently on the LSAT; these questions generally concern the ways arguments and their elements are constructed, and examine the thought processes that underlie statements. To succeed on these questions, you can't just ask "what." You must also ask "why" and "how." Think like a craftsperson, an artisan of arguments, and you'll be fine.

Reconciling Discrepancies and Paradoxes

Sometimes a set of facts just doesn't seem to hold together. One of the pieces seems to, if not quite contradict another, at least create a questionable relationship. That is, the passage contains a discrepancy or paradox that requires explanation.

Looking for paradox questions

The logical reasoning sections include a number of questions designed to test your ability to resolve paradoxes or discrepancies. They almost always contain the word *explain* or *resolve*, followed by a word like *paradox, discrepancy, surprise,* or *conflict.* To answer these questions, you have to figure out what piece of information would help you explain why the apparent conflict is not in fact a conflict at all.

The following list includes some examples of paradox and discrepancy questions:

» Which one of the following, if true, most helps to resolve the apparent paradox?

» Which one of the following, if true, would most effectively resolve the apparent paradox above?

» Which one of the following, if true, most helps to resolve the apparent discrepancy in the passage above?

» Which one of the following, if true, most helps to resolve the apparent discrepancy described by the representative?

» Which one of the following, if true, contributes most to an explanation of the behavior of chimpanzees describe above?

» Which one of the following, if true, most helps to resolve the apparent conflict described above?

» Which one of the following, if true, most helps to reconcile the specialists' two claims?

» Which one of the following, if true, most helps to reconcile the experts' belief with the apparently contrary evidence described above?

You answer these questions by reading the passage to figure out which two facts seem to be at odds with each other. Then try to come up with an idea that would reconcile the inconsistency and make the paradox disappear. You probably won't be able to envision the exact answer before reading the choices, but you can come up with something in the ballpark.

Perusing a paradox example

Here's an example of a paradox question:

EXAMPLE

Skydiving experts have noted that improvements in gear and training techniques have led to fewer fatalities than occurred in the sport's earlier years. However, fatalities among very experienced skydivers, who use the most modern gear equipped with a device that automatically opens the reserve parachute if the skydiver has not opened the main parachute by a certain altitude, have held steady for the last 12 years.

Which one of the following, if true, most helps to resolve the apparent paradox in this passage?

(A) Most skydivers prefer not to buy improved gear as it appears because it costs too much.

(B) Experienced skydivers favor tiny parachutes that fly at high velocities and that must be landed precisely, which makes them more likely to hit the ground at an uncontrolled high speed, even under an open parachute.

(C) Not all jumpers choose to use the device that automatically opens their reserve parachute for them.

(D) The U.S. Parachute Association's recommended minimum opening altitude for reserve parachutes has increased over the last 12 years.

(E) Most inexperienced skydivers rent gear from drop zones instead of owning their own gear.

Read the question. The passage contains an apparent paradox. Despite advancements in safety, skydiving fatalities have not decreased among experienced skydivers. This fact is surprising because experienced skydivers use modern gear that guarantees that their parachutes will open. An open parachute must not be the only guarantee of a safe landing. If experienced skydivers are dying despite open parachutes, their fatalities must result from another cause. Snipers aren't picking them off from the ground, so they must be dying on landing. Perhaps experienced skydivers land differently from novices. See what the answer choices have to offer.

>> Choice (A) doesn't explain the specific paradox related to the fates of experienced skydivers. The buying habits of other, less experienced skydivers are irrelevant.

>> Choice (B) does explain the results; experienced skydivers land differently and more dangerously than novices do, which could explain why the safer parachutes aren't leading to fewer deaths.

>> Choice (C) is also irrelevant because it doesn't pertain specifically to the experienced skydivers who are at the heart of the paradox.

>> Choice (D) makes the paradox even more surprising. If the reserve parachutes activate at higher altitudes, fewer fatalities should result.

>> Choice (E) doesn't explain anything about fatalities. It may explain why inexperienced and experienced skydivers use different gear, but it doesn't explain why experienced skydivers die despite having good, high-tech, perfectly functioning equipment.

Choice (B) is the correct answer.

Finding Points of Agreement and Disagreement

Some LSAT questions present you with two separate arguments followed by a challenge to determine on what point the two opinions either agree or disagree. Answering these questions can be pretty straightforward as long as you know where to place your focus. The following sections give you some pointers.

Assessing points that intersect and divide

Questions that ask you to find an element of agreement or disagreement between two related but different opinions are usually easy to recognize. The LSAT presents you with two separate arguments, each preceded by a person's name. You are then asked to find a specific statement that both speakers would agree or disagree on. Answer choices supply you with five statements related to the two arguments.

The following list includes some examples of the wording of agreement and disagreement questions:

>> Joe and Sue are committed to disagreeing over the truth of which one of the following statements?

>> Valerie's and Armando's statements provide the most support for concluding that they disagree over which one of the following?

» Shea's and Charmaine's statements provide the most support for the claim that they agree about which of the following?

» The dialogue provides the most support for the claim that Grant and Howell agree that. . .

When you encounter these dialogues, examine each of the two arguments separately. Isolate the premises and conclusion of the first speaker and do the same for the second. Then look for areas where the components of the two arguments are the same for questions that ask for agreement, or different for those that ask for disagreement. As you read through the answer options, eliminate those answers that relate to only one of the opinions, and also answers that are unstated by either argument. The correct answer pertains to a point that is common to both arguments. For disagreement questions, this common point will be one that the two arguments differ on; for agreement questions, the point will be one that both arguments would say is true.

REMEMBER

The point of agreement or disagreement can be any element of the arguments. Although you may tend to focus on the conclusions of the arguments, the correct answer more often results from a careful examination of each commentator's premises.

Analyzing an agreement/disagreement example

Here's an example of a question that asks for a statement upon which two people disagree:

EXAMPLE

Sergio: The Internet has made public libraries obsolete. A person can find free information just by searching for online articles from magazines. Free resources for downloading ebooks and audio titles are prevalent. There is no reason for someone to enter the doors of a building of books in the modern age.

Belinda: It is true that many online resources provide the public with free information and digital books. However, obtaining information is not the only way the public benefits from libraries. Libraries provide a relaxing place for people to browse for tangible books and enjoy the tactile nature of turning pages.

This interchange provides the most support for the claim that Sergio and Belinda disagree over whether

(A) the information people receive online is more current than information conveyed in tangible books.

(B) libraries provide value to the public.

(C) it is better to read ebooks and print books or listen to audiobooks.

(D) county governments should continue to fund public libraries.

(E) libraries provide a relaxing environment for the public.

Read Sergio's argument. He makes the claim that there is no reason for people to visit libraries based on the premise that the Internet has replaced them as a source for books and information. Read Belinda's response. She acknowledges that the Internet supplies free information, but she concludes that libraries provide additional benefits. Based on your analysis of the two positions, review the answer options.

> » Choice (A) provides a consideration that neither Sergio nor Belinda address: how current the information on the Internet is relative to the information available in books. If neither party addresses the point, then they likely aren't disagreeing about it.

>> Choice (B) is promising. Both parties mention the value of the library. Sergio discredits the value of libraries when he states that there is no reason to visit a library. Belinda believes that libraries provide value when she espouses the benefits of browsing print books in a relaxing atmosphere.

>> Choice (C) addresses elements Sergio touches on (ebooks and audiobooks), but he never contrasts the two. Belinda never mentions ebooks or audiobooks. So the preference of ebooks and print books over audiobooks doesn't provide a point of disagreement.

>> Choice (D) requires you to read more into the two arguments than they provide. Neither Sergio nor Belinda discusses the funding of libraries. Their arguments may eventually support or challenge library funding, but you can't deduce that without more information.

>> Choice (E) presents a point that Belinda would agree with, but you don't know Sergio's position on the library's environment. You know that Sergio sees no reason to visit a library, and you may think you can conclude that he would therefore disagree that libraries provide relaxation. But you could also infer that Sergio would agree that libraries are relaxing but not consider that a good reason to visit them.

Choice (B) is the best of the five options.

Reasoning by Pattern

A well-structured argument is a beautiful thing. A reader can follow the steps of the reasoning from start to finish with no effort at all, and the conclusion should seem self-evident if the author has done her job right. Structuring an argument well isn't that easy, though. Lawyers spend years perfecting the art of putting arguments together and taking apart their opponents' arguments. The first step toward doing both is understanding how existing arguments work. The LSAT exists partly to test your ability to do this.

Finding pattern-of-reasoning questions

These logical reasoning questions ask you to choose an answer that uses the same method of reasoning as the argument or, less often, directly ask you what type of reasoning the author uses to make an argument. Look over these examples of pattern-of-reasoning questions:

>> Which one of the following exhibits a pattern of reasoning most similar to that exhibited by the argument above?

>> Which one of the following arguments is most similar in its pattern of reasoning to the argument above?

>> The reasoning in which one of the following arguments is most similar to that in the argument above?

>> Which one of the following most closely parallels the newscaster's argument in its reasoning?

>> Which one of the following is most closely parallel in its flawed reasoning to the flawed reasoning in the argument above?

>> Which one of the following employs a flawed argumentative strategy that is most closely parallel to the flawed argumentative strategy in the letter above?

>> Which one of the following uses flawed reasoning most similar to that used in the argument above?

>> The flawed reasoning in the argument above is most similar to that in which one of the following?

For the purposes of the LSAT, the chief methods of reasoning are as follows:

>> *Deductive,* which is reaching a specific conclusion from general premises.

>> *Inductive,* which is drawing a general conclusion from specific premises and which includes the following methods:

- *Cause and effect,* which shows that one event resulted from another.

- *Analogy,* which shows that one thing is sufficiently similar to another thing such that what holds true for one is true for the other.

- *Statistics,* which uses population samples (surveys) to reach conclusions about the population as a whole.

When you know you're dealing with a pattern-of-reasoning question, you just need to focus on the way the author makes the argument to make sure you choose an answer that follows the logic most exactly.

Don't choose an answer just because it deals with the same subject matter as the given argument. These choices are often traps to lure you away from the answer that more exactly duplicates the author's logic but addresses another topic.

It doesn't matter whether the argument makes sense. If the given argument isn't logical, pick an answer choice that isn't logical in the same way.

You may focus on the method of reasoning better if you substitute letters for ideas in the argument. For instance, say you're presented with this argument: "Balloons that contain helium float. Jerry's balloon doesn't float, so it doesn't contain helium." You can state this logic with letters, like this: "All A (helium balloons) are B (floaters). C (Jerry's balloon) isn't B (a floater), so C isn't A." Then you can apply that formula to your answer choices to see which one matches best.

You may have noticed that many of the questions mention the *flawed reasoning* or the *flawed argumentative strategy* in the arguments. You know what that means — something's wrong with the argument. And it likely contains one of the informal fallacies we list in Chapter 8.

Patterning a reasonable example

Here's an example of a pattern-of-reasoning question:

Formaldehyde is a known carcinogen. Many nail polishes contain formaldehyde. Therefore, anyone who wears nail polish will get cancer.

Which one of the following is most closely parallel in its flawed reasoning to the flawed reasoning in this argument?

(A) Hot dogs can contain insect parts. Insects are dirty and carry disease. Therefore, people should not eat hot dogs.

(B) Ultraviolet rays can cause skin cancer. Sunscreen can prevent damage from ultraviolet rays. Therefore, people who wear sunscreen will not get cancer.

(C) Sodium can cause high blood pressure. Potato chips contain sodium. Therefore, anyone who eats potato chips will get high blood pressure.

(D) Beans contain a large amount of dietary fiber. Dietary fiber may be able to prevent some kinds of cancer. Therefore, people who do not eat beans will get cancer.

(E) Alcohol consumed during pregnancy can cause fetal brain damage. Wine contains alcohol. Therefore, pregnant women should not drink wine.

Read the question. You need to find the answer that uses the same process of reasoning as the argument. You know that this process of reasoning is flawed because the question tells you so. So, how is it flawed? The flaw is in the conclusion, which makes an unjustified assumption that the presence of a known carcinogen in nail polish means that everyone who wears nail polish will get cancer.

The problem with the conclusion is that it assumes that a carcinogen automatically causes cancer in everyone who encounters it, which isn't justified by the evidence presented in the argument. The argument doesn't say that formaldehyde always causes cancer or that nail polish causes cancer; all it says is that formaldehyde can cause cancer and that nail polishes contain formaldehyde. You can't assume based on that information that nail polishes inevitably cause cancer.

Truthfully, though, the flaw isn't the important thing here. The reasoning process is all you really care about. You want to find the answer choice that uses the same process of reasoning as the argument. For the purposes of finding the answer with parallel reasoning, break down the argument's structure. You can rewrite it in a formula, like this: F can cause C; NP contains F; therefore, NP always causes C.

TIP

In questions like this, it can be helpful to abbreviate players, just as you do in analytical reasoning questions. When writing equations, single letters are faster and easier to use than full words and can make the pattern of reasoning clearer.

Which answer choice makes this same kind of logical leap?

» Choice (A) says that H can contain I; I causes disease; therefore, don't eat H. That's not the same as the argument.

» Choice (B) says that U can cause C; S prevents damage by U; therefore, S prevents C. That's not the same as the argument.

» Choice (C) says that S can cause H; P contains S; therefore, P always causes H. That looks identical to the argument's reasoning.

» Choice (D) says that B contains F; F can prevent C; therefore, B prevents C. That's not the same as the argument.

» Choice (E) says that A during P causes BD; W contains A; therefore, P shouldn't drink W. That's not the same as the argument.

Choice (C) is the correct answer because it exactly parallels the argument's reasoning.

Exploring Arguments Based on Principles

Lawyers often base their arguments on particular principles or propositions. These propositions sound like statements of truths, especially universal truths — "we hold these truths to be self-evident" sort of statements. How well these principles apply or closely adhere to a particular situation is the matter up for debate.

Pinpointing principles questions

These logical reasoning questions test your ability to identify principles stated in arguments and then pick the answer that describes an action that conforms most closely to or violates most clearly that principle. Alternatively, a principle question may ask you to pick an answer that most accurately expresses a particular action's underlying or supporting principle. These questions can look like this:

>> Which one of the following most closely conforms to the principle above?

>> Which one of the following judgments best illustrates the principle illustrated by the argument above?

>> Which one of the following judgments conforms most closely to the principle stated by Laila?

>> To which one of the following principles does the critic's commentary most closely conform?

>> Which one of the following conforms most closely to the principle illustrated by the statements above?

>> Which one of the following most accurately expresses the principle underlying the argumentation above?

>> Which one of the following best illustrates the proposition above?

TIP

When you see the word *principle,* or occasionally *proposition,* read the argument looking for some fairly general statement about what's necessary or proper given the circumstances. These arguments often start with the words "it is," as in "it is crucial" or "it is essential."

REMEMBER

A *principle* is a kind of abstract rule or concept that applies to most situations. On the LSAT, laws themselves can be principles because they make statements about correct or incorrect action. When you see a principles question, try to come up with an abstract rule or unstated law that guides the passage's author.

Read the argument looking for a principle. The argument may state it explicitly or just imply it. Definitely try to formulate an answer to principles questions before you look at the answer choices. Stating the principle in your own words usually isn't that difficult, and it can save you tons of time spotting the right answer.

Parsing a principles example

Here's an example of a principles question:

EXAMPLE

When deciding which colleges to include on her application list, Alicia researched university mission statements and found that College X, a small private college with a cost of attendance of $50,000 per year, was dedicated to producing compassionate and curious leaders. College Y, a large public university with a cost of attendance of $35,000 per year, promoted itself as a leading scientific research facility. Alicia's future goals include working as an executive of a nonprofit organization designed to provide assistance to underrepresented populations. Therefore, she decided to apply to College X rather than College Y.

Alicia's decision most closely conforms to which one of the following principles?

(A) A direct relationship exists between a college's cost and the quality of the education it provides.

(B) Students should apply to smaller colleges that offer more personalized attention from professors.

(C) A large research university cannot prepare students for a career as a nonprofit executive.

(D) Students should apply to colleges with mission statements that align with their goals.

(E) The best way for students to know which college is the best fit for them is by researching each college's mission statement.

Break down Alicia's decision process. Her main activity was researching mission statements. Although the paragraph provides each college's cost and size, it doesn't mention that Alicia used these factors in her comparison of the two colleges. The statement leading to Alicia's conclusion regards her plans to lead a nonprofit organization, so she most likely based her decision on a determinate of which college provides a better preparation for her goals and used the college's mission statement to make that determination. Therefore, the underlying principle guiding her decision is that she should put colleges on her application list based on how well their mission statements fit her goals.

>> Choice (A) regards college cost, but no evidence exists to indicate that Alicia considered price in her decision, so it can't be the right answer.

>> Choice (B) can't be the underlying principle. It concerns college size, and Alicia researched college mission statements rather than college sizes.

>> Choice (C) may seem applicable at first, but it actually regards what universities can and cannot do rather than what a student like Alicia should rely on during the college application process. So the principle in Choice (C) doesn't specifically relate to Alicia's decision-making process.

>> Choice (D) is the best answer. It specifically relates to Alicia's decision regarding whether to apply to a particular college and supports her use of mission statements in the process.

>> Choice (E) seems very similar to Choice (D). It acknowledges the importance of college mission statements. However, the principle supports Alicia's research activity rather than her decision to apply to a college based on her research. So Choice (D) is a better answer than Choice (E).

Choice (D) best expresses the principle upon which Alicia based her decision to add College X to her application list. It verifies that applying college mission statements to one's goals is a good way to create a college list.

Figuring Out an Argument's Structure

Arguments are like wars; individuals who argue use a variety of tactics to make their points and disarm their opponents. They may deny something the other person says, challenge their opponent's evidence, explain what they mean, or use analogies to illustrate their points. Lawyers, being in the business of argument, use these tactics all the time. Law schools want to pick students who already understand the rudiments of this art.

Spotting structure questions

A number of logical reasoning questions focus on the structure of arguments. These questions usually involve two speakers who disagree with each other in some way. The question usually asks you to explain how the second speaker responds to the first. These questions can look like this:

>> Yolanda responds to Javier by . . . (arguing, denying, using analogy, challenging, showing evidence)

>> In responding to Penelope, Odysseus . . . (accuses, criticizes, challenges, explains, assumes)

>> Carter counters Yvette's argument by . . . (questioning, suggesting, denying, pointing out, calling into question)

>> This advertisement proceeds by . . . (using analogy, proving, understating the role, demonstrating, asserting)

>> Seth challenges Arne's reasoning by . . .

>> Kelsey's criticism suggests that he interpreted Mac to be . . .

>> Landrieu and Blanco disagree about whether . . .

>> Marquis responds to Theodora's argument in which one of the following ways?

>> Rinn responds to Julio's criticism by . . .

Your goal is to figure out how the second speaker's argument relates to the first. The second speaker addresses the first speaker in some way; you have to figure out how. If there's only one speaker, you simply have to describe how the speaker constructs the argument.

Tackling a structure-of-argument example

Here's an example of a structure-of-argument question:

EXAMPLE

Gabrielle: The man who invented the shopping mall in the United States envisioned it as the heart of a pedestrian community, much like the centers of European towns, with their sidewalk cafes, boutiques, and pleasant boulevards. Malls now provide a safe environment in which people can walk from shop to shop and meet with their friends.

Antonia: Although people walk within a mall, the very existence of the shopping mall has killed pedestrian culture. American town centers are now wastelands where no one goes, and malls themselves exist in the center of massive parking lots. People isolated in their cars drive to suburban malls and then wander around the mall ignoring and avoiding their fellow shoppers.

Antonia responds to Gabrielle by

(A) arguing that the invention of the mall has led to consequences that are exactly opposite what the mall's inventor intended.

(B) proposing that sensible urban planning could result in the shopping mall becoming a positive force in communities.

(C) using an analogy to illustrate the detrimental effects of malls.

(D) pointing out that European cities now have shopping malls in their suburbs.

(E) explaining why American cities have developed in such a way that private automobiles are the only practical form of transportation.

Read the question first. It asks how the second speaker responds to the first. The answers to this sort of question always start with verbs, such as *criticize*, *argue*, *point out*, and things like that. You want to decide for yourself how Antonia responds before you start reading the answer choices.

Gabrielle suggests that the shopping mall has evolved as its creator envisioned — as a safe, enclosed, walkable community. Antonia disagrees with her, contending that malls have ended pedestrian culture and community spirit. So you want to find an answer that disagrees with Gabrielle's argument and claims that the mall isn't the institution its creator imagined.

>> Choice (A) looks like exactly the answer you want; Antonia does argue that the mall's consequences are opposite those intended by its creator.

>> Choice (B) is wrong because Antonia doesn't mention sensible urban planning.

>> Choice (C) is wrong because Antonia doesn't use an analogy.

>> Choice (D) is wrong because Antonia doesn't mention Europe.

>> Choice (E) is wrong because Antonia doesn't mention automobiles.

Choices (B) through (E) all bring up points that Antonia might use if she were to continue her argument, but they're not relevant here. Choice (A) is the correct answer.

Knowing the Role Played by a Claim

If you make a statement in an argument, you have a reason for doing so. You may want to provide an example to illustrate your point, you may want to respond to your opponent's conclusion, or you may want to provide evidence to back up your conclusion. Law students have to be able to not only form arguments but also analyze their opponents' arguments. A large part of that analysis lies in understanding why their opponents say particular things. These sections provide more tips to help you with these types of questions.

Determining a claim's purpose

Almost all the logical reasoning questions that test your ability to determine the purpose of a certain sentence or claim in an argument use the word *role*, as in, "What role does this statement play in the argument?" Glance at some of the following examples:

>> The claim that people have positive or negative responses to many nonsense words plays which one of the following roles in the argument?

>> Which one of the following most accurately describes the role played in the teacher's argument by the assertion that participating in organized competitive athletics may increase a child's strength and coordination?

>> Which one of the following most accurately describes the role played in the psychologist's argument by the claim that the obligation to express gratitude cannot be fulfilled anonymously?

>> The claim that humans are still biologically adapted to a diet of wild foods plays which one of the following roles in the nutritionist's argument?

>> Which one of the following most accurately describes the role played in the scientist's argument by the claim that recent scientific research can often be described only in language that seems esoteric to most contemporary readers?

>> The statement that inventors sometimes serve as their own engineers plays which one of the following roles in the argument?

When you encounter one of these questions, remember an argument's elements. The claim may supply evidence to support a conclusion or it may be a premise used to attack someone else's conclusion. It may be the conclusion of the argument or something else particular to that argument's structure. Before you look at the answers, formulate your own idea regarding the purpose of the claim in question. The correct answer is more likely to jump out at you if you know what you're looking for.

Trying out the role of a claim example

Look at this example of a role-played-by-a-claim question:

EXAMPLE

When selecting a horseback-riding vacation, it is important to be honest about your actual riding ability. Some vacations require riders to handle spirited horses in open terrain or to spend six hours a day in the saddle, which for a beginner would be uncomfortable at best and dangerous at worst. Even for novice-level vacations, you should be able to post a trot, control a slow canter, and care for your horse's tack. Most people can learn to ride a horse well, provided they are willing to put in the effort, but it is never wise to overestimate your ability.

The claim that some vacations require riders to handle spirited horses in open terrain plays which one of the following roles in the argument?

(A) It is the main conclusion of the argument.

(B) It undermines the argument's main conclusion.

(C) It is evidence that supports the argument's conclusion.

(D) It summarizes the evidence in support of the conclusion.

(E) It is an assumption on which the argument's conclusion depends.

Read the question first. Note the words "plays which one of the following roles." That means you have to figure out why the author included the point about handling spirited horses in open terrain.

Now read the argument, looking for where the author mentions the spirited horses. If you find highlighting helpful, highlight those words when you see them. You can find this tidbit in the second sentence. Now, what is this argument trying to do? The author's conclusion, stated at the beginning and the end of the paragraph, is that anyone going on a horseback-riding vacation should evaluate his or her riding ability honestly. Why? Because taking a riding vacation may require more skill than a rider has and could be dangerous or unpleasant.

So why does the author mention the need to handle spirited horses in open terrain? In this case, she's using this information as an example of something a rider on a horseback-riding vacation may have to do and telling you that it's something a beginner shouldn't attempt. In effect, the "handle spirited horses" statement is evidence that the author uses to support the conclusion.

Now go through the answer choices and look for a response that matches this conclusion. Choice (A) is wrong because the argument's conclusion is that people shouldn't overestimate their riding ability. Choice (B) is wrong because that factoid doesn't undermine the conclusion; instead, it supports it. Choice (C) looks good; the author is using the fact that riders must be able to handle spirited horses in open terrain as an example of something that beginners shouldn't attempt, which supports her conclusion. Choice (D) is wrong because that fact doesn't summarize the evidence at all. Choice (E) is wrong because it's not an assumption but a stated fact. Choice (C) is the only answer that works.

4

Reading Comprehension: Read 'Em but Don't Weep

Chapter 11

Rites of Passage(s): Types of Reading Passages and Questions

One of the four scored sections on the LSAT is reading comprehension. Like the other multiple-choice sections, it lasts 35 minutes. Expect about 27 questions distributed across four passages. One passage actually consists of two short comparative passages, each of which presents its take on a common theme. You may think this section sounds fairly straightforward — after all, you've been reading and understanding what you read for years. But LSAT reading comprehension questions aren't designed to test your ability to just pick information out of a text. They're meant to also encourage you to use logical reasoning to figure out *why* the author wrote the text, make connections between the author's ideas, and determine what the text implies. In fact, you may see some questions in the reading section that look a lot like the questions in the logical reasoning sections.

Reading comprehension questions are designed to test how well you understand unfamiliar reading material. But you're probably less concerned with the reason these passages are included on the LSAT than you are with getting through all that reading and question-answering within the 35-minute time limit. You certainly don't want to limit your chances of going to a great law school just because you experience brain droop while reading about the history of the Italian textile industry!

What you need is a proven strategy. This chapter introduces you to the types of passages and questions you'll encounter, and in Chapter 12, we show you the strategies for dealing with those questions.

Presenting Reading Passages

The approximately 27 questions in the LSAT reading comprehension section break down into four sets to accompany three single passages and a pair of comparative passages. You can count on passage length to be about 450 to 500 words each. Even the set of comparative reading passages maintains overall word count; each contains roughly 225 words. The number of questions per passage varies. Some may have as few as five and others as many as eight. Each reading comprehension section covers four general categories of information: natural sciences, social sciences, humanities, and law. The LSAT wants to see how well you analyze a variety of topics, unfamiliar and familiar, so it presents you with articles about everything from the steel-making process to the quality of artifacts from the Bronze Age.

Experimenting with natural science passages

Physical and biological sciences play a big role in a host of legal issues. Some attorneys specialize in negotiating water and mineral rights. Patent attorneys often begin as engineers. Even product liability and personal injury cases require a general understanding of the way the physical world works.

Although you may concede the importance of the natural sciences, you may not be eager to find that 25 percent of your reading score is based on a chemistry passage. The good news is that the reading comprehension questions don't assume that you have any previous knowledge of the subject. If you do come across a reading passage on chemistry and it's been 20 years since you've studied the periodic table, relax. The answer to every question is located somewhere in the passage.

You really don't need to know a lot about a passage topic to answer the questions correctly. Although it's true that chemistry majors may read a passage about polymers more quickly than someone who never took a college chemistry course, that doesn't necessarily mean chemistry experts will answer more questions correctly. In fact, they may actually be at a disadvantage because they may try to answer questions based on outside knowledge instead of using the information stated in the passage.

WARNING

Reading comprehension questions test reading skills, not the plethora of details you keep tucked away in your long-term memory. When you come across a passage on a subject that you're pretty familiar with, don't rely exclusively on your outside knowledge to answer the question! Make sure the answers you choose can be justified by information contained in the passage.

REMEMBER

Natural science passages tend to be more objective and neutral than persuasive in tone. So often, the main theme of a natural science topic is to explain, describe, or inform about a scientific event. Here's a shortened version of a nice, neutral natural science passage that may appear on the LSAT:

EXAMPLE

A logarithmic unit known as the *decibel* (dB) is used to represent the intensity of sound. The decibel scale is similar to the Richter scale used to measure earthquakes. On the Richter scale, a 7.0 earthquake is ten times stronger than a 6.0 earthquake. On the decibel scale, an increase of 10 dB is equivalent to a tenfold increase in intensity or power. Thus, a sound registering 80 dB is ten times louder than a 70 dB sound. In the range of sounds audible to humans, a whisper has an intensity of 20 dB; 140 dB (a jet aircraft taking off nearby) is the threshold of immediate pain.

The perceived intensity of sound is not simply a function of volume; certain frequencies of sound appear louder to the human ear than do other frequencies, even at the same volume. Decibel measurements of noise are therefore often "A-weighted" to take into account the fact that some sound wavelengths are perceived as being particularly loud. A soft whisper is 20 dB, but on the

A-weighted scale, the whisper is 30 dBA. This is because human ears are particularly attuned to human speech. Quiet conversation has a sound level of about 60 dBA.

Continuous exposure to sounds over 80 dBA can eventually result in mild hearing loss, while exposure to louder sounds can cause much greater damage in a short period of time. Emergency sirens, motorcycles, chainsaws, construction activities, and other mechanical or amplified noises are often in the 80 to 120 dBA range. Sound levels above 120 dBA begin to be felt inside the human ear as discomfort and eventually as pain.

Don't let the unfamiliar scientific concepts worry you. You're probably familiar with the term *decibel*, but you may have never encountered the *A-weighted decibel* or *dBA*, as it's abbreviated. Focus on the main point, which in this passage is to describe dBAs and how human ears perceive them.

Observing social science passages

The reading comprehension section includes a passage about a different kind of science: social science. This passage type includes topics like philosophy, history, political science, archaeology, sociology, and psychology. The good news about social science passages is that their topics tend to crop up more in the news and in daily conversation than does, for example, physics! So you may be more comfortable with social science topics. Although passages about the social sciences are still mostly descriptive and informative, they're more likely to be persuasive than natural science passages, so you may see more variety in the kinds of tones these passages display. For instance, the personality and opinion of the author of this excerpt of a sample philosophy passage are more apparent than those of the author who wrote the natural science passage in the preceding section:

EXAMPLE

For most Americans and Europeans, this should be the best time in all of human history to live. Survival — the very purpose of all life — is nearly guaranteed for large parts of the world, especially in the West. This should allow people a sense of security and contentment. If life is no longer, as Thomas Hobbes famously wrote, "nasty, brutish, and short," then should it not be pleasant, dignified, and long? To know that tomorrow is nearly guaranteed, along with thousands of additional tomorrows, should be enough to render hundreds of millions of people awe-struck with happiness. And modern humans, especially in the West, have every opportunity to be free, even as they enjoy ever-longer lives. Why is it, then, that so many people feel unhappy and trapped? The answer lies in the constant pressure of trying to meet needs that don't actually exist.

The word *need* has been used with less and less precision in modern life. Today, many things are described as needs, including fashion items, SUVs, vacations, and other luxuries. People say, "I need a new car," when their current vehicle continues to function. People with many pairs of shoes may still say they "need" a new pair. Clearly, this careless usage is inaccurate; neither the new car nor the additional shoes are truly "needed."

This author conveys a clear opinion regarding Western interpretations of needs. The dubious tone and clear opinion of this social science passage comes through in the placement of copious quotation marks and the introduction of rhetorical questions.

Entertaining a humanities passage

Humanities passages explore topics related to the arts and literature. So you may read about the message of a Mexican muralist, the techniques applied by a modern composer, or the themes advanced by a particular playwright. This passage excerpt interprets the impact of a popular Latin American poet:

EXAMPLE

The Chilean poet Pablo Neruda joined the Communist Party in 1939 and, according to Jean Franco, began to write social poetry shortly thereafter. But Neruda's social philosophy is apparent in the poems he wrote before his formal Communist affiliation. In 1924, Neruda published *Twenty Love Poems and a Song of Despair*, a compilation of 21 poems through which Neruda reveals the compassion for common humanity that formed the foundation of his political choices. Neruda's use of familiar images and common experience in his poetry makes his art accessible to the average person, and because art attempts to make sense of the often ambiguous objective world by presenting it in a more easily grasped form, Neruda's poems carry out the Communist ideal of collective equality by offering everyone the opportunity to better comprehend the world. Therefore, *Twenty Love Poems* achieves a more powerful purpose than merely exploring the relationship between a man and a woman; Neruda's poems provide a means by which to explore the complexities of the world and perhaps catch a glimpse of something more eternal.

The excerpt reveals the author's positive view of Neruda's compilation through a relatively objective account of the work's influence. Like many humanities passages, this paragraph incorporates historical and political references in its discussion of the artist.

Laying down the law-related passages

Every reading comprehension section includes a passage that deals with an aspect of law. You may read an interpretation of a public policy, an opinion on the significance of a court decision, an explanation of the effect a new law may have on the lawyer–client relationship, and so on. Law passages may be persuasive or more descriptive, such as this sample excerpt:

EXAMPLE

In personam actions are said to be either *local* or *transitory*. The plaintiff's attorney may file a local action only where the subject matter of the litigation is located. For example, a party suing to foreclose a mortgage on real property must file the action in the county where the property is situated. Transitory actions, on the other hand, are much broader. The plaintiff may bring a transitory action in any county in any state where the defendant may be found and served with process. An action for personal injuries resulting from a defective bottle of beer is an example of a transitory action.

In the present court system, the law determines *in personam* jurisdiction through mutual consent of the parties much more heavily than it used to. Corporations who do business in a state and motorists who drive across a state are said to have consented to the jurisdiction of that state's trial court under the long-arm statute, which makes it easier for a state to prosecute lawbreakers who don't reside in the state where they violated the law.

Approaching Reading Questions

The LSAT gives you 35 minutes to answer around 27 reading questions. That boils down to just a little over a minute to answer each question, including reading time! So having a system for tackling reading questions is imperative. Your approach to each question should include these steps:

1. **Recognize the type of question.**

2. **Quickly eliminate incorrect answer choices.**

3. **Know how to manage questions that ask for the answer that *isn't* supported by the passage.**

Identifying the question type

The first step in answering a reading question correctly is identifying what type of question it is. We've found that most reading comprehension questions fall into one of these three broad categories:

>> Summarizing the passage as a whole

>> Finding directly stated information

>> Making inferences and logical deductions

Each of these question types requires a slightly different approach. Answering whole passage questions requires you to consider the big picture. When you know that a question is about specific details in the passage, you can focus your attention on the portion of the passage that's relevant to the information in the question. Inference questions require you to make logical deductions based on information in the passage.

Big picture questions

Main idea questions and those that ask you to identify a passage's primary purpose regard the whole passage. Almost every passage has at least one question that asks you to see the big picture, and often it's the first question you answer for a particular reading passage.

TIP

You can identify main idea questions by the language they contain. Here are some examples of the ways main idea questions may be worded:

>> Which one of the following most accurately expresses the main point of the passage?

>> The author's primary goal (or purpose) in the passage is to do which one of the following?

>> An appropriate title that best summarizes this passage is

As you examine the passage, look for its main idea and primary objective because you know you'll probably be asked about them. For instance, as you read through the dBA passage presented in "Experimenting with natural science passages" earlier in this chapter, you recognize that the author is clearly concerned about hearing loss and the effects of loud noises, specifically exposure to very loud human-generated noises. You may state the passage's primary purpose like this: "The author seeks to educate people about the way noise is measured and warn them of the danger of hearing loss from exposure to loud noises." If you're asked a question about the passage's main idea, look for an answer that conveys an idea similar to your statement of the author's purpose.

TIP

The best answer to a main idea question is general rather than specific. If an answer choice concerns information that's discussed in only one part of the passage, it probably isn't the correct answer. Here are some other ways to eliminate answer choices for main idea questions:

>> Eliminate answer choices that contain information that comes only from one part of the passage. The main idea is one that can be supported throughout the entire passage.

>> Eliminate any answer choices that contain information that you can't find in the passage. These choices are irrelevant.

>> Sometimes you can eliminate answer choices by concentrating on the first words. For example, if you're trying to find the best answer to the author's purpose in an objectively written natural science passage, you can likely eliminate answers that begin with less objective terms, like *to argue that, to criticize,* and *to refute the opposition's position that.*

Just the facts: Direct information questions

Some LSAT reading questions ask you about specific statements from the passage. These questions are potentially the easiest type of reading question because the information you need to answer them is stated in the passage, and the correct answer is usually a pretty good paraphrase. You just need to locate exactly where the passage supplies the relevant facts. This information may be quantitative, such as years, figures, or numbers, or it may be qualitative, like ideas, emotions, or thoughts.

Spot specific information questions by noticing how they're phrased. Those that contain verbs that indicate direct statements, such as *states*, *indicates*, or *claims*, are likely ones whose correct answer is a paraphrase of information in the passage. Usually, questions that ask for answers that are "according to the passage" are also specific information questions. So look for a direct answer to a question that's phrased like these examples:

>> The passage states that Neruda's Communist beliefs were evident in his poetry as early as which one of the following years?

>> According to the passage, which one of the following is true about the primary intensity of sound?

>> In the passage, the author indicates that transitory actions can be filed in which one of the following?

TIP

Because specific information questions seek an answer that derives directly from information in the passage, look for answers that come straight from the passage and eliminate answer choices that require you to make any inferences. If you have to make a logical deduction to justify an answer choice for this question type, it's probably wrong.

Reading between the lines: Inference questions

Inference questions ask you about information that's *implied* by the passage rather than directly stated. These questions test your ability to draw conclusions using evidence that appears in the passage. For inference questions, you're required to do one of a number of logical exercises:

>> Identify a logical consequence of a statement or of two statements taken together.

>> Infer the intended meaning of a word that's used figuratively in the passage.

>> Determine the author's attitude toward or level of agreement with the passage's topic or subtopics.

>> Analyze a method of reasoning provided in the passage.

>> Determine what would strengthen or weaken an argument.

>> Infer from attitudes portrayed in the passage how the author or others feel about different theories or events.

For instance, suppose you read a passage that compares the rapidity of wing beats between houseflies and horseflies. Information in paragraph two may state that the wings of horseflies beat at 96 bps (beats per second). Information in paragraph four may say that a Purple Winger is a type of horsefly. From this information, you can infer that the wings of the Purple Winger beat at a rate of 96 bps. This is an example of the first bullet in the preceding list: recognizing a logical consequence of the author's statements.

TIP

The horsefly conclusion doesn't require that you make great leaps of logic. When you're answering an inference question, look for the choice that slightly extends the passage's meaning. Choices that go beyond the passage's scope are usually incorrect. Don't choose an answer that requires you to assume information that isn't somehow addressed by the passage.

As you read the passage, look for clues to the author's tone as well as his or her purpose. You're bound to see questions that ask you to gauge how the author feels about the topic. Tone and style questions commonly ask you to figure out the author's attitude or complete the logical flow of the author's ideas. The author may be neutral, negative, or positive and may have different attitudes about different types of information within the same passage. It's up to you to determine the nature and degree of the author's feeling from the language used in the passage. With practice, you'll figure out how to distinguish between an enthusiastic author and one who's faking enthusiasm to mock the passage's subject.

WARNING

When making determinations about the author's style and tone, consider the passage as a whole. You may find one or two examples of praise in an article that's otherwise overwhelmingly critical of a subject. Don't make the mistake of quickly categorizing the passage from a few words that happen to catch your attention. Instead, determine the passage's main idea and the author's purpose (you need to do this to answer other questions, anyway), and use that information to help you discern the author's style and tone. For example, if an author's purpose is to argue against a particular point of view, critical words regarding the proponents of that viewpoint reveal an overall critical attitude. However, you wouldn't say the same about an author of a passage that supports a viewpoint overall but includes one or two criticisms of some supporters of the viewpoint.

REMEMBER

Style and tone questions may point you to a specific portion of a passage, or they may be about the whole passage. Even if a question does reference a specific part of the text, it does so in relation to the passage as a whole. For example, you can usually answer a question that asks you why an author chose to use certain words in a particular sentence only within the context of the entire passage. So if you know the main idea, author's purpose, and tone of the entire passage, you should be able to effectively deal with questions about the use of a particular word or phrase in one part of the passage.

The reading comprehension questions resemble those in the logical reasoning sections. Expect to be asked how to strengthen or weaken arguments, find flaws in arguments, duplicate methods of reasoning, and find points of agreement and disagreement as you would for logical reasoning questions.

The LSAT primarily tests your logical reasoning ability, so expect to see a lot of these types of questions in the reading comprehension section. They're easily recognizable because they often contain *infer*, *suggest*, or *imply* in the question or contain wording similar to those found in the logical reasoning sections. Here are some:

>> It can be inferred from the passage that the Western concept of "need" differs from other definitions of need in which one of the following ways?

>> Which of the following, if true, would most strengthen the conclusions of the author regarding the effect of loud sounds on hearing loss?

>> Information in the passage implies that which one of the following is often the subject of Neruda's poetry?

>> The method of reasoning used to analyze the finding of the commission is most like which one of the following?

>> The author's stance toward the Western concept of "need" can best be described as

>> The author brings up southern migration patterns most likely to suggest which one of the following?

REMEMBER

Sometimes knowing a great deal about a passage's topic can be a detriment because you may be tempted to answer questions based on your own knowledge rather than the passage itself. Simply answer the questions as they're asked, and make inferences that can be justified by information in the passage.

Eliminating answer choices

One of the most effective ways of moving through reading comprehension questions is to eliminate incorrect answer choices. That's because you're looking for the best answer choice, not necessarily the perfect answer choice. Sometimes you have to choose the best out of five pretty close choices, and other times you choose from five less-than-ideal options. Because the definitive answer usually doesn't pop right out at you, it's almost always easier to find the wrong answers. Get rid of choices that contain any element that can't be justified by the passage contents. Chapter 2 gives you general tips for eliminating answer choices. In this section, we show you how to apply those techniques specifically to reading questions.

TIP

Sometimes you can eliminate wrong choices without referring back to the passage. Usually two of the five options contain an element that makes them clearly incorrect. Some common wrong answers include the following.

>> **Choices that concern information that isn't found in the passage:** Some answer choices contain information that's beyond the passage's scope. Even if you know from experience that the information in these choices is true, you can't choose them. You have to choose answers based on what's stated or implied in the passage. Eliminate these choices, no matter how tempting they may be.

>> **Choices that contradict the main theme, author's tone, or specific information in the passage:** After you've read through the passage, you should be able to quickly eliminate most of the choices that contradict what you know about the passage.

>> **Choices that go counter to the question's wording:** You can also eliminate some answer choices by paying careful attention to the question's wording. For example, a question may ask about a *disadvantage* of something discussed in the passage. If one of the answer choices lists an advantage instead of a disadvantage, you can eliminate that choice without thinking too much about it. Or a question may ask you to choose which answer the author is most optimistic about. If one of the things listed is something the author is negative about, you can eliminate that choice.

WARNING

The LSAT may try to entice you with answer choices that contain information directly stated in the passage but that don't relate to the actual question at hand. Don't choose an answer just because it looks familiar. Make sure it actually answers the question.

>> **Choices that contain extremes:** Question any answer choice that uses absolutes. Examples are *all, always, complete, never, every,* and *none.* An answer choice that contains a word that leaves no room for exception is probably wrong. ***Beware:*** Usually the rest of an answer choice that includes an extreme word sounds pretty good, so you may be tempted to choose it.

WARNING

Don't automatically eliminate an answer choice that contains an extreme. If information in the passage justifies the presence of *all* or *none* in an answer choice, it may be right. For instance, if a passage tells you that all horseflies beat their wings at a rate of 96 bps, the choice with *all* in it may be accurate.

Dealing with exception questions

Most questions ask you to choose the one correct answer, but some questions are cleverly disguised to ask for the one false answer. We call these gems *exception questions.* You'll recognize these questions by the presence of a negative word in all capital letters, usually *EXCEPT* or *NOT.* When you see these words capitalized in a question, you know you're looking for the one answer choice that *doesn't* satisfy the question's requirements.

You won't see many exception questions on the LSAT reading section, but when you do see that word in all caps, take a moment to make sure that you know exactly what the question is asking. Don't get confused or rush and automatically choose the first choice that looks good. Remember, the question is asking for the one answer out of five that's false or not part of the information stated or implied in the passage.

Exception questions aren't that difficult if you approach them systematically. Determining that an answer definitely *isn't* discussed in the passage takes time. You have to carefully look through the passage for the choice and *not* find it — then check again just to be sure. But there's a better way. Instead of determining if an answer isn't discussed, eliminate the four true answers, which leaves you with the one false (and therefore correct) answer.

Identifying those choices that *do* appear in the passage is much easier than determining the one choice that isn't there. After you've identified the four correct answers, you can choose the one false answer as the correct one for that question.

REMEMBER

Exception questions can take some time, but they're among the easier reading comprehension questions because often the answers are right there in the text! So don't get in a hurry and make a mistake. Relax and use the proper approach, and you'll do exceptionally well on exception questions.

Chapter **12**

Safe Landing: Mastering the Approach to Reading Comprehension

The LSAT's reading comprehension section is less about reading than picking up information on the fly. If you approach this section the way you do, say, a bestselling novel or a trade magazine article, you'll likely run out of time. If you're having difficulty answering reading comprehension questions correctly, it's probably not because you lack reading skills. It's more likely that you're not familiar with the specific way you have to read for the LSAT. The best approach to LSAT reading passages is to get in and get out quickly, focusing mostly on just what you need to answer the questions.

Reading Comprehension Strategy

You should use much more of your precious time analyzing reading comprehension questions than reading the passages. For tips on breaking down questions, see Chapter 11. The plan is to read just as much of the passage as you need to answer the questions.

The Digital LSAT presents reading questions one at a time. The full passage text appears on the left side of the page, and the question is presented on the right side. You can move back and forth between questions, view a record of the questions you have and haven't answered at the bottom of the screen, and mark questions for future review. Given this format and the limited time provided, you may want to adjust your approach to this section.

Skimming the questions

Back in the day when print tests were king and you were handed a flimsy paper booklet rather than an electronic tablet, you may have approached reading questions by skimming through them before you read the passage, intending to pick up bits and pieces to mark as you perused the material. The Digital format doesn't lend itself well to this approach. Moving from question to question with the sole intention of finding key words to home in on during your initial read-through isn't efficient when the questions appear one at a time. But you probably won't miss that page of questions when you discover the beauty of encountering one question per page.

To read or not to read

As you prepare for the reading section of the LSAT, determine whether you prefer to read the entire passage first, or skip it and jump straight to the questions. Some people feel more comfortable when they read the passage first, but you may find the alternative strategy of reading the passage as you answer questions to be more successful and time-efficient. If you prefer to begin with the passage, you can find tips on how to use the provided tools to maximize the benefits of this approach in "Pacing Yourself through the Passages," later in this chapter. However, we suggest that you try the approach of skipping the initial full read-through at least a few times to determine whether this may be a better option. We cover this strategy in "Starting with the Questions."

In or out of order?

You can answer the questions from first to last, or you can jump around from question to question. It doesn't really matter, as long as you select an answer for each question before time runs out. If you spot a question that you like, go ahead and do it first. Each question can stand alone, and they're not intentionally organized by difficulty. The first question very often is a main-point question that requires you to understand why the author wrote the passage.

Eliminating the duds

Four answer choices are wrong. It's always that way. Knocking off wrong answers is just as valuable, and possibly more so, than spotting right answers. It's often easier to spot what makes an answer wrong than it is figure out whether it's right. When you find an answer that's obviously wrong, select the elimination bubble (with a diagonal slash) to the right of the choice to eliminate it. You can always toggle back if you change your mind. If you can't decide whether an answer is wrong, leave it; chances are you'll be able to resolve that conflict by the time you've read all the choices or if you decide to revisit the question after tackling a few others for the same passage. After you've eliminated four wrong answers, the remaining choice has to be the best answer.

TIP

Typically, any question has at least two and usually three obviously wrong answers. Normally, you will narrow your choices to two answers that look plausible. The LSAT-makers deliberately create some answers that are very close to the correct answers, but there's always something wrong with them that makes them less than best. For more about how to eliminate wrong answers in the reading comprehension section, see Chapter 11.

Picking an answer and moving on

If you find an answer that you know is right, good for you! Mark it and move on. If, after careful scrutiny and contemplation, you're still stuck between Choices (A) and (C), fret not; pick one of them and move on to the next question. You can mark the question to remind yourself to review it later if you have time. Spending too much time on any one question doesn't help the answer magically materialize before your eyes, but it does use up time you could employ answering more promising questions.

Pacing Yourself through the Passages

You have a little over a minute to answer each reading question, and that includes the time you spend reading the passage. Generally, you shouldn't spend more than about a minute or two on a passage before you answer its questions, so you have to read as efficiently as you can. If you choose to read through the passage before you begin reading the questions, you need a plan for getting through the passage in a way that allows you to answer questions correctly and quickly.

What to read for

When you read a passage, focus on the following elements:

>> The passage's general theme

>> The author's tone

>> The way the author organizes the passage

TIP

Unless you have a photographic memory, you won't be able to remember all of a passage's details long enough to answer the questions. Don't spend time trying to figure out the passage's minutiae while you're reading it. If you encounter a question about a little detail, you can go back and reread the relevant section. Instead of sweating the small stuff, make sure you understand the author's main point, the tone the author uses to make it, and the overall way the author presents the information.

Getting the main point

Generally, people write passages to inform or persuade. Passages on the LSAT are often argumentative; they advance a particular opinion. For those, the main purpose may be to attack, criticize, or advocate a position. But some passages present a neutral, objective tone. Their purpose may be nothing more than to explain, describe, or explore a theory, law, or phenomenon.

Because most authors present the main theme in the first paragraph or two, you'll probably figure it out in the first few seconds of your reading. If the main idea isn't clear in the first paragraphs, it probably appears in the last paragraph, when the author sums up the ideas. After you figure out the author's overall theme, quickly jot down on your scratch paper a word or two to help you remember it. For a passage that describes the differences between the flight patterns of houseflies and horseflies, you could write down *compare flight — house/horse.* Your notation gives you something to refer to when you're asked the inevitable big-picture questions (which we discuss in greater detail in Chapter 11).

Absorbing the author's tone

In addition to understanding the author's point, you need to know how the author feels about the issue to help you answer inference questions. You get clues to the author's tone or mood by noticing the words he or she uses. LSAT passages either inform the reader about something or try to persuade the reader to adopt the author's viewpoint. Informative passages are often more objective than persuasive ones, so the author's tone is usually neutral. Authors of persuasive passages may exhibit more emotion. You may sense that an author is critical, cynical, pessimistic, optimistic, or supportive. Knowing the tone of a passage helps you choose answers that exhibit the same tone or subjectivity.

WARNING

Regardless of the author's mood, don't let your personal opinions about a passage's subject matter influence your answer choices. Getting emotionally involved with the passage's content can cloud your judgment and may cause you to subconsciously rely on your opinions as you answer questions. To avoid doing so, you may find it helpful to remind yourself that correct answers are true *according to the passage* or *according to the author*.

Forming the framework: The passage's outline

Knowing the passage's structure is much more important than understanding its details. You should spend no more than two minutes to absorb the passage's information, so instead of trying to comprehend everything the author says, focus on how the author lays out the information. That way, when you're asked a question about a particular topic, you'll know where to go to answer it.

Standard essay format includes an introduction with a thesis, two or three supporting paragraphs, and a conclusion. Many LSAT passages are excerpts from larger works, so they may not exhibit precise five-paragraph essay form, but they will contain evidence of all three elements. As you read, in addition to the passage's overall point, determine main points of each of its paragraphs.

TIP

You may find it helpful to construct a mini-outline of the passage on your scratch paper. Jot down a word or two that describes the type of information each paragraph contains. For example, you could use hints such as *diff wingspan, size diff — horse 3x bigger,* and *flight helps house* for a passage that compares houseflies and horseflies. This outline tells you that in the first supporting paragraph, you find information about how the two flies differ in wingspan. The second supporting paragraph is where you find information that explains how the greater size of horseflies affects their flight. And from the third supporting paragraph, you find out how the housefly's flight helps it in everyday life. Although you may not understand all the fascinating details of the author's account, you know where to go in the passage if you have to answer a detail question.

Building an outline as you skim helps you know where in the passage you can find answers to questions about particular details. Doing so also helps you answer any questions that ask you *how* an author develops his or her point.

Using the digital tools

The LSAT has a Passage Only button that you can select to view the passage without the accompanying questions. With the entire passage in front of you, start marking stuff. You have access to three highlighter colors, an underline tool, and an eraser. Use one color to highlight important words. Underline key statements, especially those that look like the passage's main point. Mark any obvious statements of opinion and clear transitions. If you notice any kind of obvious structure, mark it so you can see it clearly. Doing so helps you spot key ideas when you need them. Jot little notes on your scratch paper as you absorb the substance of the passage. You want to transform this undifferentiated block of text into something with noticeable breaks and pauses.

Here are some things you're trying to find:

>> The author's main idea

>> The author's purpose

>> The author's attitudes and opinions

» The passage's structure

» Transition words, such as *for example, nevertheless,* or *in sum*

» Pieces of evidence that the author uses

» Arguments made by the author or others mentioned in the passage

TIP

Spotting transition words can really help you identify the passage's structure. These words serve as kind of a road map for the passage; if you underline them and ignore the rest of the content, you should still have a good idea of the passage's direction. Look for transitions such as *moreover, for example, in contrast, however, but, furthermore,* and *therefore.* If you spot any of these, you know where the author has been and where he or she plans to go.

WARNING

Whatever you do, don't underline or highlight too much! Many students highlight or underline nearly every word in their textbooks or notes, which has the virtue of canceling out anything they've underlined and making plain text stand out. If you don't know how much is too much, aim to not use emphasis more than 20 times, including highlighted words and phrases and underlined sentences.

Deciding whether to work in or out of order

No one says you have to work the reading comprehension section in order. If you want to spend half a minute or so at the beginning of the section moving back and forth and ranking the passages from your favorite to your most detested, go right ahead. If you prefer to save that half a minute and work the section from start to finish, that's great, too.

TIP

As with analytical reasoning, if you choose to work the passages out of order, your best criterion for ranking them may be the number of answers attached to them. If you anticipate running out of time, concentrate on the passages with a large number of questions first. So if one passage has eight questions and another has only six, choose the one with eight questions first. You may also select passages based on their content; some people have an easier time with scientific data, while others better understand topics from the humanities.

Although hopping around within the reading comprehension section is fine, working two or more passages at once isn't a good idea. Loading a passage's information into your brain takes time, and you don't want to interfere with your concentration by hopping around. When you pick a passage, stick with it until you've answered all the questions, and then move on.

Starting with the Questions

Many test takers find reading the entire passage first to be time consuming and inefficient. If you're like most people, your mind will begin to wander by the second or third paragraph. You'll realize that you haven't paid attention to a single point and may feel the need to reread the paragraph, which is a colossal waste of precious time. Additionally, when you read the passage in full before you tackle the questions, you may be tempted to answer questions based on your memory of what you've read rather than taking the time to refer back to the material. Answering LSAT reading questions correctly depends on an excruciatingly detailed reading of the text, which you're more likely to commit to if you haven't spent much time initially reading the passage.

Jumping into the questions without having read the passage may feel uncomfortable at first, so practice on several passages before you decide whether it works for you. To apply the approach successfully, follow these steps:

1. Choose the question you think will be easiest to answer first.

You won't answer the questions in order, so you need a method for picking the best candidate. Start with questions with highlights. They steer you directly to the point in the passage that likely contains clues to the answer. Remember, though, that you almost always have to read more sentences than just the one or two indicated by the line reference.

2. When you've exhausted questions with line references, check questions that contain key words that are easy to scan for, such as capitalized or italicized words or specific nouns.

3. After you've answered four or five questions, you should have a pretty good sense of what the passage is about.

You're then ready to tackle the big-picture questions.

When you forgo reading the passage before you answer the questions, you have more time to spend on the questions, so use it wisely. Remember these tips:

» Questions with verbs such as *states*, *indicates*, and *claims*, as well as those that ask for answers "according to the passage," seek an answer that is a direct statement or nice paraphrase of information straight out of the passage.

» If you have trouble finding key words or topics, be sure to read the first sentence or two of each paragraph to determine what type of information that paragraph covers.

» If a question doesn't provide you with easily scanned-for key words, check the answer choices for easily spotted ideas. Scan the passage for words in the answer choices and eliminate answers that don't work.

» Read the questions and answer choices very carefully. Make sure every part of the answer is true.

» Rely on the process of elimination to whittle your way down to the correct answer. Cross out choices you know can't be true so you can concentrate on narrowing the better-sounding answers.

» Don't spend a lot of time on any one question. If a question appears easy to answer at first but you find it to be more time-consuming than you thought, eliminate wrong choices, mark that question, and move on to another question in the passage set. Return to the skipped question after you've answered the other questions. You'll approach it again with additional information about the passage.

TIP

Because you haven't read the passage before answering the questions, take the time to read the text carefully as you answer the questions. When a question gives you a line reference, read the entire paragraph that contains that information. To recognize the passage's main point, read the beginning and ending paragraphs.

Giving Sample Passage 1 a Shot: Influenza Vaccination

In this section, you find a typical reading comprehension passage followed by questions about the passage. We use this sample passage to show you how to work through the reading passages and answer the questions.

Reading and highlighting or underlining

Whether you read the passage initially or while you're answering the questions, underline or highlight anything that may help you answer a question. (Don't underline the entire passage!)

TIP

You can also make little notations on your scratch paper, highlight words in different colors, underline key sentences — anything that makes finding what you need easier. Don't sweat this process too much; you don't have to mark everything, and you'll have access to the passage while you answer the questions.

Okay, here's Passage 1. For your convenience, we've marked various words and phrases that may be important to answering the questions:

> Every winter, public health officials warn people that a major influenza outbreak could occur and encourage all vulnerable people to get vaccinated. They have good reason to do this; the flu is a major inconvenience at best and deadly at worst. The Spanish flu epidemic of 1918 killed more than 20 million people worldwide. More Americans died from this flu than were killed during all the wars of the 20th century; a disproportionate number of the dead were young adults in the prime of life.

> The name *influenza* is an Italian word meaning "influence"; Italians in the mid-18th century called the illness *influenza di freddo,* which means "influence of the cold." The disease is usually not fatal — it kills about one tenth of 1 percent of the people who catch it — but it can be extremely dangerous in vulnerable groups, such as the elderly, young children, pregnant women, and anyone with a compromised immune system, diabetes, or heart or lung disease. The precise strain of the disease changes every year as new viruses arise. The flu virus originates in birds, usually in south-east China. The birds give the virus to pigs, who then pass it on to humans, although scientists are now concerned that some strains of the virus can jump straight from birds to humans, bypassing the pig vector.

> Because influenza is caused by a virus, there is no way to treat it. The best approach to flu is to prevent it by vaccination. Public health officials in the United States developed a vaccine for the flu in 1944, which they produced by cutting a hole in the shell of a fertilized hen's egg, injecting the virus into the amniotic fluid, and allowing the chick embryo to breathe in the virus. The virus would multiply inside the chick and then be exhaled back into the amniotic fluid, which gradually became cloudy with viruses. Scientists still use this technique today, which is why it takes so long for pharmaceutical manufacturers to make flu vaccines each year.

> Vaccines have been extremely effective at reducing the severity of flu outbreaks. Unfortunately, the swine flu vaccination fiasco of 1976 gave many people a mistaken view of the vaccine's dangers. That year, the Centers for Disease Control and Prevention feared a devastating flu epidemic and urged the government to implement a nationwide vaccination campaign, which President Ford agreed to do. People were vaccinated in droves, but then two bad things happened: The swine flu epidemic never materialized, and some people claimed the vaccine gave them a nerve disease, Guillain-Barré syndrome, and nearly 4,000 of them filed lawsuits against the government. There has been no scientifically proven link between the flu vaccine and Guillain-Barré syndrome. Some

people still fear vaccinations, and the federal government has become more hesitant to recommend mass vaccination schemes, but there is no need for this. The flu vaccine is a tremendously successful product with few detrimental side effects, and people should get their flu shots every year with confidence.

Thinking about the passage

Before you start on the questions, think a bit about the passage you just read. What's the main point? Well, the author obviously thinks the flu vaccine is a good thing; he includes a bit of information about influenza and its virus, a bit of history of the flu vaccine, and a lamentation about the unfortunate lawsuits surrounding the 1976 vaccination program. The piece is mostly informative but also expresses a definite opinion. All that information is relevant to the questions.

Knocking down the questions

Now tackle the questions. Try to answer them yourself first. Use a blank sheet of paper to cover the answers and explanation, and then see whether you answered each question correctly. Don't peek.

TIP

Regardless of whether you can answer the question on your own, make sure you read the explanation of how to arrive at the correct answer. You may find this information helpful later, when working on other reading comprehension passages.

1. The passage is primarily concerned with discussing which one of the following?

(A) The symptoms of the flu and the effects of the 1918 influenza pandemic

(B) The 1976 swine flu vaccination fiasco and its detrimental effects on subsequent vaccination drives

(C) The constant mutation of the flu virus in birds and pigs

(D) The efforts of the scientists who first identified the cause of influenza

(E) The effects of the flu and the history and benefits of the influenza vaccine

This is a big-picture question; all you have to do is understand what the passage — the *whole passage* — is about. In this case, the passage is primarily concerned with providing some information about the flu, the virus that causes it, and the history of the vaccine, arguing that the vaccine is beneficial and not at all dangerous.

Now consider the answer choices: Choice (A) is wrong because the author doesn't actually describe flu symptoms anywhere. Choice (B) is too specific. It would be correct if the question asked about just the third paragraph. The author mentions Choice (C) but as part of his discussion of the flu virus, so it's also too specific to be the answer to a big-picture question. Choice (D) isn't right; the author doesn't really say anything about the scientists' efforts beyond describing the egg-injection process. Choice (E) looks correct; it's an overall theme, not restricted to a particular paragraph, that pretty well sums up the passage. Choice (E) is the correct answer.

2. Which one of the following best describes the author's attitude toward influenza vaccination?

(A) conviction that the vaccine is the best way to prevent a flu epidemic and that people should not fear it

(B) skepticism as to whether the vaccine's benefits outweigh its risks

(C) annoyance that the government has tried to interfere with people's lives by encouraging them to get vaccinated

(D) admiration for the heroic efforts of the scientists who developed the flu vaccine in the 1940s

(E) disgust at the attorneys who took advantage of the government's vulnerability in the Guillain-Barré lawsuits

The author quite clearly thinks the flu vaccine is a good thing. He calls it a "tremendously successful product with few detrimental side effects"; claims that "the best approach to flu is to prevent it by vaccination"; and says that "people should get their flu shots every year with confidence."

Skim the first words of the answers and knock out anything that's obviously wrong. Choice (A) looks promising; it sums up the author's attitude toward the vaccine. Choice (B) should go because the author displays no skepticism. Choice (C) is likewise wrong because the author isn't at all annoyed at the government's efforts. Choice (D) is also probably true of the author's attitudes, but he doesn't really get into scientists' efforts in the passage. Choice (E) describes an attitude that the author probably has, but it doesn't answer this question. Choice (A) is the correct answer.

3. The passage suggests which one of the following about current techniques of producing the flu vaccine?

(A) Scientists have taken advantage of technological developments in the second half of the 20th century to make the process more efficient and precisely tailored to specific strains of the influenza virus.

(B) Because scientists use chicken embryos in eggs to incubate the virus, they can only create vaccines that are effective against flu transmitted by chickens.

(C) Because the technique has not changed appreciably since it was developed in the 1940s, it is a fairly inefficient process with some major limitations.

(D) It is unfortunate that scientists use fertilized hens' eggs to create the flu vaccine because this means that the developing chicken embryos will die before they hatch.

(E) There are many better ways of creating vaccines, but scientists are unable to put them into practice because of economic restrictions.

What does the author say about current techniques? "Scientists still use this technique today, which is why it takes so long for pharmaceutical manufacturers to make flu vaccines each year." That sounds like he thinks the process is slow and possibly inefficient. Be careful about assuming that he thinks the process is outdated because he doesn't suggest that scientists should use a different, more efficient method.

Now, consider the options. Choice (A) is wrong because scientists haven't in fact updated the flu vaccine creation process. Choice (B) is wrong; the author says nothing about this. Choice (C) restates the author's words but with a little more judgment; this works as an answer because the author does note that it takes pharmaceutical companies a long time to generate vaccines, which is limiting. Choice (D) doesn't work; the author says nothing about the sad implications to the chick embryos. Choice (E) is wrong; the author doesn't mention newer and better techniques of producing vaccines. Perhaps there aren't any, and the egg method is still the best way. Choice (C) is the best answer.

4. Which one of the following best describes the author's opinion of the lawsuits brought by people claiming to have contracted Guillain-Barré syndrome from flu vaccine?

- **(A)** They were justified because the flu vaccine had caused people to contract Guillain-Barré syndrome.

- **(B)** They were frivolous lawsuits that did not prove a connection between the vaccine and Guillain-Barré syndrome and did major damage to the public health drive to vaccinate people against influenza.

- **(C)** They were an important cautionary lesson for the government about the dangers of getting involved in public health matters.

- **(D)** They are an example of unscrupulous lawyers and runaway juries taking advantage of a defendant with deep pockets and a cause of action that is too complicated for a typical juror to understand.

- **(E)** They illustrate the necessity of government indemnification of pharmaceutical companies that manufacture necessary but potentially dangerous substances such as vaccines.

A couple of things should give you a clue about the author's attitude: the use of the word "unfortunately" to describe the events following the 1976 vaccination program, and the statement that there has been no link proven between the vaccine and Guillain-Barré syndrome. You know that this author believes strongly in the value of the flu vaccine and thinks everyone should get it, and he thinks that the damage done by the 1976 lawsuits is unfortunate.

Look for an answer that says something like that. Choice (A) is definitely wrong because the author doesn't think the lawsuits were justified, and he notes the lack of a proven connection between vaccine and disease. Choice (B) looks very good. The author mentions the lack of a connection and goes on to describe the aftereffects, including government reluctance to try another vaccination program and unfounded public fears of the vaccine. Choice (C) may well be true, but the author doesn't seem to think the government should use the 1976 story as a cautionary tale. In fact, he says there's "no need" for the government to hesitate to vaccinate people. The author may secretly believe Choice (D), but he never mentions either unscrupulous lawyers or runaway juries in this passage, so you can't assume anything about his opinions of them. Choice (E) doesn't work because the author never mentions the fact that the government indemnified the pharmaceutical companies in these cases. Choice (B) is the correct answer.

5. Which one of the following states the primary purpose of the passage?

- **(A)** To encourage all American citizens to receive the flu vaccine every year

- **(B)** To criticize the government's drive to vaccinate all Americans against the 1976 swine flu, which was a premature action that led to unfortunate product liability lawsuits and large damage awards

- **(C)** To discredit any claims of a link between the influenza vaccine and nerve diseases such as Guillain-Barré syndrome

- **(D)** To suggest that vaccinating people against influenza is the best way to respond to the threat of a major global epidemic, several of which have already occurred with devastating consequences

- **(E)** To argue against allowing product liability lawsuits against the manufacturers of vaccines

The author has a definite axe to grind. He wants to convince people that the flu vaccine is safe and effective, along with providing a little information about the process of creating the vaccine and the devastating consequences of the disease.

See which answer choice best fits this agenda. Choice (A) isn't exactly right; the author isn't addressing this piece specifically to the government, and he's not really suggesting that the government take this exact action, though he probably does think a yearly vaccination program would be a good idea. See whether there's a better answer. Choice (B) is totally wrong, the complete opposite of what the author thinks. Choice (C) isn't the primary purpose of the passage. The author mentions this lack of a link once, in the last paragraph, but it would have to appear more often than that to be the primary purpose. Choice (D) looks pretty good. The author does emphasize the benefits of vaccination and mentions the devastating consequences of a previous flu epidemic, the 1918 pandemic. Choice (E) is just plain wrong; the author doesn't say anything about product liability at any point in the passage. Though he certainly thinks the lawsuits were wrong, you can't assume anything he doesn't state explicitly or implicitly. Choice (D) is the best answer.

6. Which one of the following presents the primary purpose of the second paragraph?

(A) To provide some background information about influenza, such as the origin of the name and the way the virus mutates

(B) To suggest that pregnant women in particular should receive the flu vaccine

(C) To describe the method scientists use to replicate the flu virus inside fertilized hens' eggs

(D) To speculate on possibly unverified ways in which the flu virus can jump from animals to humans

(E) To criticize the way influenza received its name because the Italian version of the name gives the mistaken impression that influenza is caused by cold temperatures

Paragraph 2 describes the origin of the name *influenza*, lists the people most at risk from the disease, and briefly describes the way the virus develops.

Look for an answer that hits those points. Choice (A) actually looks good; keep that in mind as a possible answer. Though the author mentions that pregnant women should get vaccinated, that isn't the only thing he says in this paragraph, so Choice (B) doesn't work. Choice (C) is simply wrong; that information is in the third paragraph. Choice (D) is wrong, too, because the author doesn't speculate about virus transfers. Likewise, Choice (E) is wrong. The author simply states that the word *influenza* comes from an Italian phrase, but he doesn't suggest that this is in any way misleading to English speakers. Choice (A) is by far the best answer.

7. According to the passage, who should make the greatest effort to receive vaccination against influenza?

(A) medical workers such as nurses and doctors, who are most likely to be exposed to the flu on a daily basis and then transmit the virus to their own patients

(B) young children and people who work around children, such as day-care workers and elementary school teachers

(C) people who are most vulnerable to dying from the flu, such as the elderly, young children, pregnant women, and people with compromised immune systems, diabetes, or heart or lung disease

(D) scientists who work with flu viruses

(E) people who are planning to travel to Asia, particularly southeastern China, at the time of year when the flu virus tends to jump from birds to pigs to humans

In the first paragraph, the author mentions that vulnerable groups in particular should get vaccinated against the flu. In the second paragraph, he writes that the flu "can be extremely dangerous in vulnerable groups, such as the elderly, young children, pregnant women, and anyone with a compromised immune system, diabetes, or heart or lung disease."

Skimming the first words of the answers results in the following: Choice (C) jumps out as a near-perfect answer. Double-check the others to be sure, though. The author doesn't mention medical workers or teachers, so Choices (A) and (B) are wrong. He doesn't mention scientists or travelers, so Choices (D) and (E) are wrong. Choice (C) is the only answer that works here.

8. Which one of the following best describes the author's opinion of the role the government should take in public health matters?

   (A) The government should take an active role in informing people of the dangers of diseases such as influenza and encouraging people to receive vaccines to prevent national or international epidemics.

   (B) The government should avoid taking any extreme stands on public health matters because of the danger of lawsuits, frivolous or otherwise.

   (C) The government should subsidize research into better vaccines for dangerous illnesses such as influenza.

   (D) The government should quarantine people who contract dangerously communicable diseases such as influenza to prevent the diseases from spreading rapidly throughout the population.

   (E) The government should increase the budget of the Centers for Disease Control and Prevention because the CDC is the organization most capable of preventing a major outbreak of influenza.

You're pretty familiar with the author's attitudes by now; he certainly thinks the government can have a role in preventing influenza epidemics.

So which answer choice works best here? Choice (A) looks like a good answer. Choice (B) isn't right because the author actually says that there's no reason for the government to hesitate to recommend vaccination. Choice (C) is wrong because nowhere does the author address funding for research. Choice (D) is also wrong because quarantine isn't a topic in this passage. The author may agree with Choice (E), but he doesn't mention funding for any group, including the CDC, so that can't be right. Choice (A) still looks best.

Conquering Sample Passage 2: Manifest Destiny

You can tackle the following reading passage just as you did the one in the preceding section.

Answering questions and highlighting or underlining

Now you're ready to tackle this second passage. If you didn't try reading the passage as you answered the questions in the previous example passage, you may want to try it now. Skip the passage and jump right into the questions. Choose the ones that are easiest to tackle first, and accumulate information about the passage as you continue through the questions in the order that makes the most sense to you. As you answer questions, you can record what you find out about the passage on your scratch paper, such as noting that the second paragraph is about Texas or highlighting words and phrases that help you keep information in mind. Here's how you could mark up this passage as you answer the questions:

During the middle of the 19th century, the United States increased its geographical area by 1.2 million square miles. Many Americans justified this tremendous expansion, which inevitably came at the cost of the lives and way of life of Native Americans and other colonists, with the self-righteous claim that the United States was divinely ordained to spread democracy over the world. They summed up this belief in the phrase *manifest destiny*, a term invented in 1845 by writer John O'Sullivan in an editorial defending the United States' claim to Texas. In this editorial, O'Sullivan argued that the United States was destined to be the great nation of the future because of its superiority in individual freedom, equality, and progress, and therefore had a divinely granted right to expand its government everywhere. Americans of that time, at the height of the American Romantic movement, sincerely believed that it was their country's duty to spread the American way of life as far as possible, and therefore willingly supported the federal government's expansionist policies. At the same time, many citizens disliked the German and Irish immigrants crowding into northeastern cities and wanted to force these newcomers to move elsewhere.

James K. Polk campaigned for the 1844 presidential election on a wildly popular expansionist platform and won handily. He immediately set about adding to U.S. territory and, in the process, precipitated a major war with Mexico. The territory of Texas was hotly contested at that time; Mexico considered it Mexican territory, but American settlers in the area had declared Texas an independent republic in 1836. The previous U.S. administrations had hesitated to annex Texas as a state, fearing to anger America's southern neighbor, but Polk had no such qualms. He admitted Texas to statehood in 1845, and, as expected, Mexico ended diplomatic relations with the United States. Soon afterward, Polk sent his envoy to Mexico to discuss the purchase of California, but the Mexican minister refused to receive the man, and Polk used this as an excuse to send American troops to the Rio Grande, which the American residents of Texas considered their southern boundary.

Mexico disagreed, and Mexican troops crossed the river to attack American troops. Polk bullied a reluctant Congress into declaring war on Mexico, assuring them that the conflict would resolve itself after a few minor skirmishes. Instead, the Mexican-American War lasted from 1846 until 1848 and cost a multitude of lives, to say nothing of the vast monetary expense. Ultimately, the investment paid off as Polk had hoped it would. Mexico surrendered and relinquished the land from Texas to California, effectively ceding half its territory to the United States. The war also functioned as a training ground for several army officers, including Robert E. Lee and Ulysses S. Grant, who became key figures in the next major conflict fought by Americans, the Civil War.

Answering the questions — full speed ahead

Try to answer the questions on your own first before peeking at the answer. Read the answer explanations regardless — doing so is good practice. The explanations help you think more about the passage and about the way LSAT questions are constructed, and may give you some insights when you take the test for real.

1. Which one of the following most accurately states the main point of the passage?

   (A) Without the Mexican-American War as a training ground for military officers, the outcome of the American Civil War may have been quite different.

   (B) A belief in manifest destiny, a desire for more land, and the election of an aggressive president led the United States into a war with Mexico and generated tremendous territorial expansion in the mid-19th century.

   (C) Manifest destiny — a belief that the United States was destined to be the great nation of the future because of its superiority in individual freedom, equality, and progress — was the predominant philosophy of Americans in the 1840s.

   (D) Polk was a strong president who managed to force his ideas about war through Congress despite the fact that most of America was ambivalent about the republic of Texas and aggression against Mexico.

   (E) The Mexican-American War was a worthwhile investment of time, money, and lives because it added a huge chunk of territory to the United States, including land on the Pacific Coast.

You've already thought about the main point, so see whether one of the answers matches your thinking. Choice (A) doesn't look right. The passage mentions the Civil War only in the very last sentence, so the Mexican-American War's effects on the Civil War can't be the main point. Choice (B) looks pretty good; it hits all the passage's highlights. Choice (C) looks like it could be the answer, except that it stops with manifest destiny and ignores the two-thirds of the passage concerned with the Mexican-American War, so it's not right. Choice (D) also seems plausible, but Polk's aggression toward Congress really isn't the main point, only part of the passage's point. Choice (E) makes a claim about the value of the Mexican-American War that the author really doesn't make; she expresses no opinion as to whether that endeavor was worthwhile (in fact, her negative comments about manifest destiny in the first paragraph suggest that she may think the war wasn't valuable). Choice (B) is the best answer.

2. Given the information in the passage, which one of the following best summarizes the concept of manifest destiny?

   (A) It was a concept created by a newspaper writer who used the phrase in an editorial supporting the United States' claim to Texas.

   (B) It was a religious belief cherished by many American Protestants, particularly those who settled in the western and southwestern territories, that God had given them the entire North American continent for their own purposes.

   (C) It was the political platform on which James K. Polk based his 1844 presidential election campaign.

   (D) It was a racist sentiment that American citizens used to justify their hatred of new immigrants.

   (E) It was an idea born of 19th-century romanticism that claimed that the United States had a divinely ordained duty to spread its ideas about government and social equality as far as possible, even if that meant conquering other lands and people.

First, make sure you know what the question is asking; highlight the word "summarize" so you remember your mission. Here's what the author says: "Many Americans justified this tremendous expansion . . . with the self-righteous claim that the United States was divinely ordained to spread democracy over the world. They summed up this belief in the phrase *manifest destiny*, a term invented in 1845 by writer John O'Sullivan . . . O'Sullivan argued that the United States was destined to be the great nation of the future because of its superiority in individual freedom, equality, and progress, and therefore had a divinely granted right to expand its government everywhere."

Consider which answer choice works best. Choice (A) isn't right because it doesn't address the concept of manifest destiny, just the phrase's origin. Choice (B) isn't right; manifest destiny wasn't explicitly a religious or Protestant belief, though it did have a religious component to it. (And the author never mentions Christianity or Protestants anywhere in the passage.) Choice (C) doesn't summarize the concept, though Polk did campaign on an expansionist platform; note, too, that Polk ran for president in 1844 and O'Sullivan coined the phrase in 1845. Choice (D) isn't right; the passage doesn't say that manifest destiny was an explicitly racist philosophy. Choice (E) looks good because it focuses on the American sense of having a divinely ordained mission to spread democracy, which is exactly what the passage says. Choice (E) is correct.

3. Which one of the following is NOT identified by the author of the passage as a consequence of the United States' war with Mexico?

   (A) The U.S. Congress came to resent Polk's imperious attitude.

   (B) Many soldiers died in the conflict.

   (C) Officers who later became major figures in the Civil War had their first combat training.

   (D) The United States added the entire southwest, from Texas to California, to its territory.

   (E) Mexico lost approximately half its territory.

Skim the answers and cross off the ones that you can find in the passage; the last one standing is your answer. The only fact that the author doesn't mention is Congress's growing resentment of Polk's attitude, so Choice (A) looks right. Many soldiers died in the war with Mexico, so Choice (B) is out. The last sentence of the passage mentions Choice (C). Choice (D) is mentioned in the last paragraph, as is Choice (E). Choice (A) is indeed the correct answer.

4. Based on the passage, the American people of the early 19th century would be most likely to hold which one of the following views of America's movement toward the Rio Grande?

   (A) It was a mistake because it ran the chance of alienating Mexico.

   (B) It was economically sound because it would provide territory for new immigrants to settle far away from the cities of the eastern seaboard.

   (C) It was an excellent means of spreading Protestant Christianity among the predominantly Catholic Mexicans.

   (D) It was a dangerous maneuver likely to spark a war with Mexico.

   (E) It was the right thing to do because the United States had been created by God to spread democracy and equality throughout as much of the world as possible.

You know what 19th-century Americans thought of expansion — they liked it and thought it was their country's duty; that's what the whole manifest destiny business is about. Choice (A) is wrong; the passage gives you no reason to believe that ordinary Americans worried about alienating Mexico by settling Texas. The same reasoning invalidates Choice (D). Choice (B) is wrong; the passage suggests that American citizens wanted more territory for immigrants but doesn't specifically state that they thought Texas was the place for these newcomers. This is a tricky answer, though, because it could plausibly seem right. Choice (C) is wrong; the passage doesn't suggest that Americans wanted to proselytize the Catholic Mexicans. Choice (E) sums up the prevailing philosophy nicely. Choice (E) is correct.

5. The phrase "fearing to anger America's southern neighbor" in the second paragraph is most likely intended to

   (A) justify Polk's agreeing to annex Texas as a state.

   (B) argue that the annexation of Texas was precipitous and done out of anger at Mexico.

   (C) suggest that Mexico had plans to go to war with the United States to reclaim the Texas territory.

   (D) describe the effect that Polk's predecessors believed annexing Texas as a state would have on Mexico's government.

   (E) condemn the actions of the American residents of Texas who declared the territory an independent republic without Mexico's permission.

"America's southern neighbor" in this sentence is, of course, Mexico. (The LSAT assumes a bit of rudimentary geography — you do, of course, know that Mexico is south of the United States.) Presidents before Polk hadn't wanted to annex Texas as a state because they were afraid Mexico would get angry if they did.

Choice (A) doesn't work because the phrase doesn't justify Polk's actions. Choice (B) is wrong because it has nothing to do with fearing to anger Mexico but in fact suggests that the United States didn't care if it did anger Mexico. Choice (C) is the opposite of the answer. Polk's predecessors didn't want to anger Mexico, fearing that would spark a war, but didn't think Mexico would start a war unprovoked. Choice (D) is the best answer to this question. Polk's predecessors didn't take action on Texas because they were afraid Mexico would get angry and go to war. Choice (E) totally doesn't work; it's not condemning Texans, who certainly weren't concerned about angering Mexico. Choice (D) is correct.

6. The passage suggests which one of the following about Polk's attitude toward expansion?

(A) Polk believed that, as president, he was justified in bullying Congress into approving troops and funding for the Mexican–American War, even if most legislators disagreed with him.

(B) Until his envoy was turned away at Mexico City, Polk thought he would be able to purchase California from Mexico without recourse to violence.

(C) Polk was determined to expand U.S. territory and power, but he did not want to jeopardize good diplomatic relations with other countries.

(D) Polk disapproved of the residents of Texas taking matters into their own hands by declaring Texas an independent republic.

(E) Polk wanted to continue the policies of previous administrations with regard to Texas and Mexico.

According to the passage, Polk wanted to expand the United States regardless of whom he had to alienate, whether it be Congress or Mexico. Choice (A) looks like a good answer. Choice (B) doesn't look so good. If Polk used Mexico's refusal to receive his envoy as "an excuse to send American troops to the Rio Grande," he probably didn't expect his offer to buy California to go over well in the first place. Choice (C) is obviously wrong; the passage provides no evidence that Polk cared about good diplomatic relations with other countries. Choice (D) doesn't work, either; Polk had no problem with independent Texans and was quite willing to annex them as a state, even when he knew Mexico wouldn't like it. Choice (E) is also explicitly wrong; Polk most definitely didn't continue the previous administration's policies. So Choice (A) is correct.

7. Which one of the following most accurately describes the organization of the passage?

(A) A description of American philosophy and prevailing opinions in the early to mid-19th century, followed by an account of the start of the Mexican–American War and its effects on the United States

(B) A description of the philosophy called *manifest destiny*, introduced as justification for the war against Mexico

(C) A description of a newspaper editorial that introduced a phrase that became very popular in 19th-century American literary circles, followed by a condemnation of the expansionist policies of Polk and an account of the injustices forced on Mexico

(D) A detailed account of U.S. territorial expansion in the 19th century, beginning with the war against Mexico and ending with the Civil War

(E) An analysis of the philosophy of manifest destiny, followed by a description of Congressional action to expand U.S. territory, followed by an account of the Mexican–American War, and concluding with the years preceding the Civil War

Make a quick mental outline of the passage (or look at your notes if you've jotted down main points of each paragraph). It starts with a description of manifest destiny, followed by a paragraph on Polk's expansionist tendencies and the start of the Mexican–American War, and concludes with a paragraph on the results of that war.

Look for an answer choice that echoes this organization. Choice (A) looks like a good answer. Choice (B) is wrong because the passage doesn't just address manifest destiny. Choice (C) is wrong because the passage doesn't condemn Polk or describe injustices inflicted on Mexico. Choice (D) is wrong, too, because it skips the paragraph on manifest destiny and includes material that's not in the passage; the only territorial expansion that appears is what resulted from the war with Mexico, and you can't assume that's all the expansion that occurred in the 19th century. Choice (E) starts well, with the analysis of manifest destiny, but the passage doesn't actually discuss Congressional action, nor does it address the years preceding the Civil War. Choice (A) is correct.

5

The Writing Sample: Penning a Persuasive Argument

Chapter 13

Pick a Side, Any Side: Responding to the Writing Sample Prompt

You have to prepare at least one LSAT writing sample for your LSAT score to count, and here's the good part: You write the essay in the comfort of your own home (or any place of your choosing) on your own computer using a special secure software program that remotely proctors your progress. If you don't have access to a computer, you can use computer labs at local colleges and universities, public libraries, or other locations. When you download the software on your computer, you have immediate access to the Get Acquainted With LSAT Writing tool to get used to the essay software's features. You can cut, copy, and paste text and check your work with a spellcheck tool. The essay opens up eight days before each test administration, but you don't have to write an essay every time you take the LSAT; one is enough for the LSAC to report your LSAT score to law schools.

This essay doesn't factor into your LSAT score. The people at the Law School Admission Council (LSAC) don't read it, so many students don't take this part of the LSAT very seriously. They should, though. Do you want to know what happens to your writing sample? The good folks at the LSAC send a copy of it with your score report to every law school that receives your LSAT score.

The people who decide whether to admit you to law school are the only ones who get an opportunity to read your LSAT-inspired prose. Chances are they're not going to read it very carefully. After all, they have plenty of other stuff to read, and a short essay written in 35 minutes isn't very informative. But your essay may make a difference.

Because you have no idea who will read your writing sample, you want to be sure you produce your best effort. So spend a little time thinking about the exercise and polishing your writing skills. At the very least, preparing for the LSAT writing sample prompt allows you the opportunity to practice crafting the traditional five-paragraph essay. (Flip to Chapter 14 to read some sample essays.)

Picking a Side — No Ridin' the Fence

The writing sample is a 35-minute exercise in written advocacy. The test gives you a situation in which someone has to choose between two alternatives, each of which has advantages and disadvantages.

Some recent topics have included the following:

>> Picking a travel package for a tour of South America on behalf of a travel club

>> Deciding which archaeological dig would most benefit the career of a young scholar

>> Choosing which school a local school board should close

>> Picking a city in which to hold a scholarly convention

>> Deciding whether to publish a famous manuscript or donate it to a university library

REMEMBER

You can argue every topic equally well in either direction. The object is to convincingly construct an argument for one side or the other.

REMEMBER

When you plan your LSAT essay, keep in mind your likely audience. The people who read these essays are usually law professors on the admissions committees of their respective law schools. They're academics, so write as if you were writing something for school. Be intelligent, thoughtful, organized, and lucid. Don't be too conversational, don't use slang, never use sarcasm, and be very careful with humor. You don't want to annoy your reader with a flippant tone.

Walking through a Practice Essay

Here's a writing sample topic of the type that appears on the LSAT:

EXAMPLE

Marilyn, a widow, wants to buy a pet and is trying to decide between two available dogs. Write an argument for Marilyn's choosing one dog over the other, keeping in mind the following goals:

Marilyn wants a dog to guard her house.

Marilyn wants a dog that's affectionate and inexpensive to feed.

The first dog is a German shepherd. This dog is large, strong, and well trained and is particularly recommended for use as a guard dog. It weighs 85 pounds and eats several pounds of dog food a day. It is neither vicious nor particularly affectionate toward humans.

The second dog is a Pekingese. This dog is small, has a long, silky coat, and makes an excellent lap dog. It formed a strong attachment to its former owner and is a devoted companion. At 20 pounds, this dog does not require much food. Its small stature makes it somewhat ineffective as a guard dog, though it will growl aggressively when angered.

Organizing your argument

Take up to five minutes to think about how to answer this question and make an outline. Pick a side — either side, though you probably feel a stronger gravitation toward one dog or the other. If you have a real preference, go with it. If you don't, quickly pick a side to argue. Both sides have good and bad points, so either one lends itself to a good, strong essay. You don't want to waste precious time agonizing over which pet to pick. You need every precious second to type the essay.

When you organize your thoughts, think about how you'll make your point. Create a five-paragraph outline:

1. **Introduce your thesis.**
2. **Make your strongest point and support it.**
3. **Continue with your second point and support it.**
4. **Give a nod to the opposing viewpoint.**
5. **Summarize your points.**

Consider how you'll transition from one thought to another. The best essays flow smoothly from sentence to sentence and from paragraph to paragraph.

Setting priorities

Choosing a side is simply a matter of setting priorities. For example, in the dog case, if you decide that companionship is what Marilyn needs, choose the Pekingese. If, on the other hand, you think she needs a guard dog more than a lap dog, select the German shepherd. When you write the essay, you still make a case for why your choice satisfies the lesser priority as well.

Making an outline

After you pick your side and before you type your essay, create a quick outline. You have lots of ways to write this kind of essay, but during the LSAT really isn't the best time for you to get creative. If you follow the same basic five-paragraph structure, you'll get a serviceable essay every time. It won't be great literature, but it'll do the job.

Here's one way you can organize the essay about the dog, singing the praises of the Pekingese:

Introduction: The widow should pick the Pekingese because companionship is more important to her well-being than guarding.

Paragraph 2: Pekes are excellent companions, and widows living alone need companions.

Paragraph 3: Pekes are inexpensive to feed, and a widow on a fixed income should make this a priority.

Paragraph 4: Pekes aren't the best guard dogs, but they can bark and growl ferociously, and anyway, the widow's need for a guard dog is overstated.

Conclusion: The widow really ought to pick the Peke over the German shepherd.

Structuring the essay

Based on your outline, the essay will include these five paragraphs:

>> **Make the introduction about three or four sentences long.** Provide a brief summary of the prompt and a statement of your position. Include one or two sentences that discuss the goals your party wants to achieve; focus on the ones that your choice would meet.

The last sentence of the first paragraph should include the word "because." This is your *thesis sentence,* the one that explains why you've chosen the side you have. For example, it could read, "Because the Pekingese would make the best companion and also be somewhat effective as a guard dog, the widow should pick the Pekingese for her pet."

>> **Write your first two body paragraphs to explain the reasons why the side you've chosen is best, and compare its advantages to the disadvantages of the other side.** Make each of these paragraphs four or five sentences long; you don't have space for more than that.

>> **Use the fourth paragraph to discuss disadvantages of the side you've chosen.** No argument is perfect, and pointing out the failings of your side yourself is better than waiting for an opponent to spot them. If you do this, you can then argue that they're not really disadvantages at all. Minimize your side's weaknesses at the same time as you acknowledge them. In the same paragraph, you may want to point out the apparent advantages of the other side, but solely so you can explain why the other side's strengths aren't in fact strengths at all.

TIP

One effective way of writing is to start each paragraph with a sentence that first states a disadvantage of your choice but then follows it with an advantage. Use the remaining sentences in the paragraph to back up the advantage. That way, the last thing the reader encounters is an advantage.

>> **Draft your last paragraph to be your conclusion, where you sum up your argument and state for the last time why the side you've chosen is the best.** Don't repeat your thesis statement verbatim, and don't mention a point you haven't already examined in the previous paragraphs, but do say something that leaves your reader with a positive sense of your argument. One or two sentences are enough. Don't skip a conclusion; you want to let your reader off smoothly with a definite sense of finality. Remember, this is the last thing the reader sees; you want it to leave a good impression.

This structure is very basic. You can probably think of other more exciting ways to approach the writing sample, and if you're experienced at doing that sort of thing, go right ahead. Otherwise, follow this outline and you'll always be able to toss off a decent short essay. It doesn't need to be brilliant; it just needs to be coherent and mistake-free.

TIP

Another way to organize the essay is to write it in four paragraphs. Paragraph 1 is the introduction and Paragraph 4 is the conclusion. In Paragraph 2, discuss all the advantages of your choice. In Paragraph 3, discuss all the disadvantages of the other choice.

REMEMBER

The key to good writing is simplicity. Say what you have to say in the simplest way possible to make sure your readers understand you. Use precise words instead of long ones. Contrary to what many people believe, using longer words doesn't make your prose seem more intelligent.

You absolutely must observe proper grammar and usage rules in your essay. You also must write out all words — no abbreviations.

WARNING

One topic, two different essays

As you learn when you study law, there's always another side to the story. You can write equally cogent arguments for either position presented by the writing sample prompt. The rest of this chapter presents you with two ways of responding to the same essay task.

The pro-Pekingese approach

Say you decide to argue for the Pekingese, using the outline from the earlier "Organizing your argument" section. Here's how the essay could go:

> *Marilyn should choose the Pekingese to be her canine companion. She's a widow living alone on a fixed income, and what she needs most is a friendly dog that won't eat her out of house and home. She has found a loving Pekingese and a protective German shepherd. Because it will be more affectionate than*

the German shepherd and more friendly to her pocketbook and because its barking would in fact make it an effective guard dog, the Pekingese would be the best choice to offer the widow both friendship and protection.

Every week, the television news runs stories about the dangers of the elderly living alone; they suffer depression, don't eat enough, and decline much faster than their biology would dictate. The news has also run stories on the benefits of pets to old people; people with pets take much more interest in life and remain healthier themselves. To protect her health and ensure her general well-being, the widow requires an affectionate companion, and the Pekingese would be the best choice for companionship.

Widows are also prone to financial hardship. They must often make their husband's pensions and Social Security stretch for years without much additional income. The last thing Marilyn needs is a dog that would be a major expense to her. The Pekingese eats very little in comparison to the more voracious German shepherd and therefore would be cheaper to maintain.

A Pekingese is a small dog and therefore would likely be less effective than the German shepherd at offering defense in the unlikely event of a home invasion. Realistically, though, Marilyn has little need of a guard dog. People tend to exaggerate the likelihood of their homes being invaded, which is really a very uncommon event. In addition, the Pekingese could actually pass muster as a guard dog. A Pekingese can bark and growl ferociously, alerting Marilyn to potential intruders and frightening off criminals who hear it. The Pekingese has a growl much bigger than its stature and teeth. An angry Pekingese may be all the defense the widow needs if a stranger calls with mischief on his mind.

Marilyn most needs a loving pet that won't eat all her savings. A Pekingese would meet her needs perfectly, providing companionship for a reasonable price and actually guarding her home quite well. For this reason, she should choose the Pekingese.

Going with the German shepherd

What if you decide that the German shepherd is the better choice? Bigger teeth, fiercer growl, and all that? That's fine. Here's an example of how you could argue that point:

Life is very unsafe for older women living alone. A widow like Marilyn is virtually defenseless against burglars and ne'er-do-wells. She needs a dog that will make her feel safe. She also needs a dog for company. Because the German shepherd is by far the better dog for striking fear in the hearts of criminals and would also make a fine companion, Marilyn should choose the larger dog for her pet.

German shepherds make excellent guard dogs. They're large, imposing, intelligent, and have lots of big teeth that they're not afraid to use. The police often use German shepherds for work with criminals because they are so well suited to this task. These qualities would make the German shepherd an excellent choice as a guard for Marilyn.

This German shepherd will also make an excellent companion. It won't curl up in her lap while she watches television, but it will spend every possible minute in her presence. She will get exercise by taking it for long walks, which will improve her health and her bone density, possibly forestalling osteoporosis and hip fractures. And because the German shepherd is more intelligent than the Pekingese, Marilyn will find it easier to keep out of trouble in and out of her house.

The only drawback to the German shepherd is its size and appetite. This is a minor consideration; even the most expensive dog food is hardly ruinous, and Marilyn can always buy food in bulk at a discount warehouse, achieving substantial savings.

Marilyn's needs are clear: safety and companionship. The German shepherd is the better choice on both counts.

Chapter **14**

Practice Writing Samples

ow you have your chance to try writing LSAT–style writing sample essays. Open up your word processing program and enable the spellcheck (or use the Get Acquainted With LSAT Writing software to prepare your practice essays). Remember, there's no right or wrong answer. Just pick a side and defend it well. After the two sample topics, we include two possible responses for each. The essay positions aren't right or wrong. Read them to get an idea of how you could organize your essays.

Topic 1: Choosing a Law School

This first topic deals with picking one law school over another. Don't forget to set up your argument before you start writing. Begin by reading the prompt:

> Gael is a senior in college who plans to attend law school the following year. She has been accepted by several law schools and has narrowed her choice down to two of them. Write an argument for selecting one law school over the other, keeping two guidelines in mind:
>
> > Gael wants to go to a friendly school where she can pursue her main interest, environmental law and the preservation of resources.
> >
> > Gael wants to borrow as little money as possible and to find a lucrative job as soon as she graduates.
>
> Law School A is a small school attached to a state university in a fairly undeveloped state known for its liberal tendencies. Because of the school's small size and relaxed atmosphere, students and faculty get to know one another very well. It has one of the best environmental law programs in the country; graduates of this program usually find jobs with agencies dedicated to protecting the environment. Securing employment sometimes takes several months, and the jobs usually do not pay as well as those with private law firms. Because Gael comes from another state, she will not receive an in-state tuition discount and will have to take out a substantial loan to pay for her law school education.

Law School B is a larger law school that is part of a well-known and prestigious private university. The tuition is about the same as the tuition at Law School A, but Law School B has offered Gael a partial scholarship that would cover about one-third of her costs. This law school is known for its cutthroat environment; students compete with one another viciously, and professors devote little time to socializing with students because they are busy working on their own research. Law School B has an excellent job placement record, and nearly all its graduates accept high-paying jobs at private law firms. Law School B offers courses in environmental law but is not especially known for its environmental program.

Sample answer: Choosing Law School A

Here's a possible argument for choosing Law School A:

Law School A would be a better choice for this student. Gael wants to specialize in environmental law and to attend school in a collegial atmosphere. These priorities should come before her desire to economize and should not interfere with her wish to find a lucrative job. Because Law School A has one of the best environmental law programs in the country and is well-known for its friendly atmosphere, Gael would be much happier in the present and more satisfied with her career in the future if she chooses to attend this smaller law school.

Law School A has one of the best environmental law programs in the country. Gael is very interested in a career that would let her help protect the environment and preserve natural resources, and attending Law School A would make it very easy for her to spend the rest of her life doing this. Although she could study some environmental law at Law School B, the program there is not nearly as concentrated on the preservation side of environmental law, and she may feel somewhat isolated if she tries to pursue her interest in an atmosphere that does not value environmentalism.

Law School A also has a friendly feel that would make Gael's law school experience more pleasant and ultimately more satisfying than Law School B. At Law School A, she could form deep relationships with both students and faculty that would make it easier for her to learn more about her chosen field and find compatible colleagues for her future work life. Bonds that she forms during law school will benefit her for the rest of her career.

It is true that Law School A is slightly more expensive than Law School B because Law School A has not offered Gael a scholarship. That small difference in money is not enough to justify choosing a law school that will not offer her the opportunity to pursue her goals. It is also true that Law School A does not place nearly as many of its graduates in law firms that pay high salaries, so Gael may take slightly longer to pay off her student loans. Nevertheless, it is more important that Gael be able to study and find a job in a field that interests her than make a lot of money quickly.

Both schools have advantages, and Gael probably would be successful at either one. Nevertheless, because it would provide her a pleasant law school experience, allow her to study the field that most interests her, and secure a satisfying career in that field, Law School A would be a much better choice for Gael than Law School B.

Sample answer: Fighting for Law School B

If you prefer Law School B, here's an example of how you can state that argument:

Gael should choose Law School B. Law School B is much more prestigious than Law School A, which will provide Gael with more opportunities after she graduates. It has offered her a partial scholarship, which will decrease her financial burden upon graduation and is more likely to provide her with a lucrative job after she completes school. Because Law School B offers this prestige and financial advantage without preventing Gael from pursuing environmental law, Gael should choose to attend the larger law school.

A degree from a well-known law school is a valuable commodity. Future employers are extremely impressed with credentials such as a degree from Law School B. A degree from this school will allow Gael to pursue employment anywhere and in any field and will not restrict her to specialized environmental employers. Gael wants to find a job that will pay her well, and a degree from Law School B would be the best way to ensure that she does.

Law school is very expensive. If Gael accepts the partial scholarship from Law School B, she will be able to pay off her loans in a much shorter period of time than she would if she had to take out loans for the full amount of tuition she would have to pay for Law School A. Attending Law School B would mean that Gael would be financially free much sooner and would be able to leave her lucrative law firm job to take a lower-paying job in an environmental agency later if she wanted to. Attending Law School B allows Gael to combine financial success and career satisfaction.

Although Law School B is known for its competitive atmosphere, spending three years in a less enjoyable law school is a small sacrifice to make for a scholarship and a degree that will allow Gael to pursue employment anywhere and in any field. Even though Law School B's environmental law program is not as complete and well-known as that of Law School A, Gael will still be able to specialize in environmental law if she chooses. She may find that her interests lie elsewhere, and she will be in a better position to pursue them if she attends a school that does not specialize entirely in one area of the law.

Although Law School A does offer some benefits, Law School B would be a much better choice for Gael. It would provide her with prestige, financial independence, and an excellent job, without taking anything away from her environmental aspirations. She should therefore choose Law School B.

Topic 2: The Sporting Goods Store

This topic deals with whether the state should fund a large sporting retailer to come to the area. Read the prompt and pick your side.

A small southern town is trying to decide whether to provide financial incentives to a large national retailer that wants to open an outlet there. Town business leaders are considering offering funds raised by state taxes to pay for the store's construction. Write an argument either supporting or protesting offering the financial incentives, keeping two guidelines in mind:

The town wants to create jobs by bringing tourist dollars to the area.

The town wants to avoid putting local merchants out of business.

Town business leaders want to use state taxes to pay for the construction of the national retailer's multimillion-dollar facility right next to an exit from an interstate highway. The facility would include a giant sporting goods store, several restaurants, and a hotel. It would create at least 300 new jobs, and the town hopes that it would also attract tourists who otherwise would not bother leaving the highway. If the town does not provide the tax funds, the retailer will probably take its business elsewhere.

Local merchants in the town do not want to use state funds to finance the facility's construction. They claim that local retailers already provide all the goods that would be available at the new store, and they fear that the new store would deliberately cut its prices to drive them out of business. They believe it would be wrong for the state to fund the construction of a store for an out-of-town retailer when it does not provide the same service to local businesses. They insist that the town should treat the out-of-town retailer the same way it treats local merchants, and if the national retailer takes its business elsewhere, so much the better for local businesses.

Sample answer: Use state funds

Here's a sample answer that argues for using the state funds:

The benefits of bringing this large national retailer to the town are tremendous, and the town should do whatever is necessary to persuade the company to come. If that means the town's leaders must offer to pay for the facility's construction with state tax funds, then they should do it because the benefits of having the retailer move in far outweigh the cost of using state money to build the store.

The retailer would build a huge, multimillion-dollar facility just off an interstate exit. That exit would become a major destination; people who would otherwise never consider stopping in the town would now have a reason to get off the highway and spend their money there. After these people have stopped, it will be easier to convince them to stay a while and spend even more money, perhaps on amenities that already exist in town, away from the interstate.

Introducing the retailer would create hundreds of new jobs. First, construction workers would have ample employment. Second, all the facilities that would be part of the retailer's complex — the sporting goods store, the several restaurants, the hotel — would require a large number of employees. These would be good, stable jobs, and the local economy needs that.

The town already has several sporting goods stores and of course hotels and restaurants, but all are not located in one convenient place; people must drive around to get to them, and they will never attract anyone from out of town. The local merchants already have a loyal local clientele, and it's not likely that that will change; regardless, it is unfair to force local customers to pay high prices for goods that the major retailer can sell for less.

Bringing the retailer to town would be a win-win situation for nearly everyone. The town should bend over backward to persuade it to come; spending tax money to build the facility would be an investment with huge payoffs in the near future.

Sample answer: Don't use state funds

Here's a sample answer for the other side:

Offering to pay for the construction of this retailer's facility is a terrible idea. Because the potential consequences to the town's local merchants are horrific and the likely economic benefit to the town of the retailer's locating there is unproven at best and negligible at worst, the town should definitely not subsidize the store's construction with state funds.

The town should not pay to construct the national retailer's monstrous facility because to do so would be extremely unfair to local merchants. Local merchants have to pay their own way; no one has ever offered to build facilities for them. To add insult to injury, if the town does decide to use state taxes to build the complex, then local merchants will in effect be forced to finance the construction of a major competitor.

Countless towns have proven that introducing large national retailers with big-box stores is devastating for local merchants. The national retailers carry a larger variety of merchandise with prices set specifically to drive local merchants out of business. There is no reason to assume this retailer would be different. If this retailer comes to town, customers will flock there to do their business, abandoning the merchants who already operate in the heart of town. As for tourists, perhaps a few interstate travelers will get off the highway to do a little shopping or have a quick meal, but they are unlikely to stay very long or venture into town. Nothing about a big-box sporting goods store will impress them with "local color."

Although this retailer would provide a certain number of jobs, they would be low-paying jobs in an isolated area around a remote interstate exit. They would come at the cost of the jobs that already exist with the town's local sporting-goods merchants. All profits would leave the state to go to corporate headquarters, leaving the town with a hefty construction bill and 300 minimum-wage jobs with no security.

If the national retailer is serious about coming to this town, it can pay its own way like any other honorable vendor. There's no sense in the town's subsidizing its own economic destruction.

6

The Real Deal: Full-Length Practice LSATs

IN THIS PART . . .

See how your stamina measures up by taking a full-length LSAT practice test (or two, or three).

Score your test quickly with an answer key.

Discover how to improve your performance by reading through an explanation of the answer for each practice test question.

Simulate LSAT exam day by duplicating the testing environment as closely as possible.

Chapter 15

Some Rainy-Day "Fun": LSAT Practice Exam 1

Y ou're ready to take a crack at a full-blown practice LSAT exam. You're feeling good and ready to go (well, maybe not, but you're at least smart enough to know that this practice is good for you).

For best results, try to take this practice exam under simulated LSAT conditions.

1. **Find a quiet place to work, where you won't be distracted or interrupted.**

2. **Use the answer grid provided.**

   You'll mark answers directly next to the answer choices when you take the Digital LSAT on a tablet. You may use blank scratch paper throughout the test for making notes.

3. **Set your watch or alarm clock for 35-minute intervals.**

4. **Do *not* go to the next section until the time allotted for the current section is up.**

5. **If you finish early, check your work for that section only.**

6. **Don't take a break during any one section.**

7. **Give yourself exactly one 10-minute break between sections III and IV.**

The answers and explanations to this test's questions are in Chapter 16, along with a sample scoring chart. Go through the explanations to all the questions, even the ones you answered correctly. The answers are a good review of the techniques we discuss throughout the book.

REMEMBER

If you like to work the analytical reasoning and reading comprehension problems by picking your favorite set first, one of the best criteria for choosing a favorite is the number of questions — the problem set with the most questions has the most points attached to it. Assessing a problem's difficulty is nearly impossible before you start, and often the problems that look hard initially turn out to be easy. Maximize your investment of time — pick a problem with seven questions before you work one with only five.

Answer Sheet for Practice Exam 1

Section I

1. Ⓐ Ⓑ Ⓒ Ⓓ Ⓔ
2. Ⓐ Ⓑ Ⓒ Ⓓ Ⓔ
3. Ⓐ Ⓑ Ⓒ Ⓓ Ⓔ
4. Ⓐ Ⓑ Ⓒ Ⓓ Ⓔ
5. Ⓐ Ⓑ Ⓒ Ⓓ Ⓔ
6. Ⓐ Ⓑ Ⓒ Ⓓ Ⓔ
7. Ⓐ Ⓑ Ⓒ Ⓓ Ⓔ
8. Ⓐ Ⓑ Ⓒ Ⓓ Ⓔ
9. Ⓐ Ⓑ Ⓒ Ⓓ Ⓔ
10. Ⓐ Ⓑ Ⓒ Ⓓ Ⓔ
11. Ⓐ Ⓑ Ⓒ Ⓓ Ⓔ
12. Ⓐ Ⓑ Ⓒ Ⓓ Ⓔ
13. Ⓐ Ⓑ Ⓒ Ⓓ Ⓔ
14. Ⓐ Ⓑ Ⓒ Ⓓ Ⓔ
15. Ⓐ Ⓑ Ⓒ Ⓓ Ⓔ
16. Ⓐ Ⓑ Ⓒ Ⓓ Ⓔ
17. Ⓐ Ⓑ Ⓒ Ⓓ Ⓔ
18. Ⓐ Ⓑ Ⓒ Ⓓ Ⓔ
19. Ⓐ Ⓑ Ⓒ Ⓓ Ⓔ
20. Ⓐ Ⓑ Ⓒ Ⓓ Ⓔ
21. Ⓐ Ⓑ Ⓒ Ⓓ Ⓔ
22. Ⓐ Ⓑ Ⓒ Ⓓ Ⓔ
23. Ⓐ Ⓑ Ⓒ Ⓓ Ⓔ
24. Ⓐ Ⓑ Ⓒ Ⓓ Ⓔ
25. Ⓐ Ⓑ Ⓒ Ⓓ Ⓔ
26. Ⓐ Ⓑ Ⓒ Ⓓ Ⓔ
27. Ⓐ Ⓑ Ⓒ Ⓓ Ⓔ
28. Ⓐ Ⓑ Ⓒ Ⓓ Ⓔ
29. Ⓐ Ⓑ Ⓒ Ⓓ Ⓔ
30. Ⓐ Ⓑ Ⓒ Ⓓ Ⓔ

Section II

1. Ⓐ Ⓑ Ⓒ Ⓓ Ⓔ
2. Ⓐ Ⓑ Ⓒ Ⓓ Ⓔ
3. Ⓐ Ⓑ Ⓒ Ⓓ Ⓔ
4. Ⓐ Ⓑ Ⓒ Ⓓ Ⓔ
5. Ⓐ Ⓑ Ⓒ Ⓓ Ⓔ
6. Ⓐ Ⓑ Ⓒ Ⓓ Ⓔ
7. Ⓐ Ⓑ Ⓒ Ⓓ Ⓔ
8. Ⓐ Ⓑ Ⓒ Ⓓ Ⓔ
9. Ⓐ Ⓑ Ⓒ Ⓓ Ⓔ
10. Ⓐ Ⓑ Ⓒ Ⓓ Ⓔ
11. Ⓐ Ⓑ Ⓒ Ⓓ Ⓔ
12. Ⓐ Ⓑ Ⓒ Ⓓ Ⓔ
13. Ⓐ Ⓑ Ⓒ Ⓓ Ⓔ
14. Ⓐ Ⓑ Ⓒ Ⓓ Ⓔ
15. Ⓐ Ⓑ Ⓒ Ⓓ Ⓔ
16. Ⓐ Ⓑ Ⓒ Ⓓ Ⓔ
17. Ⓐ Ⓑ Ⓒ Ⓓ Ⓔ
18. Ⓐ Ⓑ Ⓒ Ⓓ Ⓔ
19. Ⓐ Ⓑ Ⓒ Ⓓ Ⓔ
20. Ⓐ Ⓑ Ⓒ Ⓓ Ⓔ
21. Ⓐ Ⓑ Ⓒ Ⓓ Ⓔ
22. Ⓐ Ⓑ Ⓒ Ⓓ Ⓔ
23. Ⓐ Ⓑ Ⓒ Ⓓ Ⓔ
24. Ⓐ Ⓑ Ⓒ Ⓓ Ⓔ
25. Ⓐ Ⓑ Ⓒ Ⓓ Ⓔ
26. Ⓐ Ⓑ Ⓒ Ⓓ Ⓔ
27. Ⓐ Ⓑ Ⓒ Ⓓ Ⓔ
28. Ⓐ Ⓑ Ⓒ Ⓓ Ⓔ
29. Ⓐ Ⓑ Ⓒ Ⓓ Ⓔ
30. Ⓐ Ⓑ Ⓒ Ⓓ Ⓔ

Answer Sheet for Practice Exam 1

Section III

1. Ⓐ Ⓑ Ⓒ Ⓓ Ⓔ
2. Ⓐ Ⓑ Ⓒ Ⓓ Ⓔ
3. Ⓐ Ⓑ Ⓒ Ⓓ Ⓔ
4. Ⓐ Ⓑ Ⓒ Ⓓ Ⓔ
5. Ⓐ Ⓑ Ⓒ Ⓓ Ⓔ
6. Ⓐ Ⓑ Ⓒ Ⓓ Ⓔ
7. Ⓐ Ⓑ Ⓒ Ⓓ Ⓔ
8. Ⓐ Ⓑ Ⓒ Ⓓ Ⓔ
9. Ⓐ Ⓑ Ⓒ Ⓓ Ⓔ
10. Ⓐ Ⓑ Ⓒ Ⓓ Ⓔ
11. Ⓐ Ⓑ Ⓒ Ⓓ Ⓔ
12. Ⓐ Ⓑ Ⓒ Ⓓ Ⓔ
13. Ⓐ Ⓑ Ⓒ Ⓓ Ⓔ
14. Ⓐ Ⓑ Ⓒ Ⓓ Ⓔ
15. Ⓐ Ⓑ Ⓒ Ⓓ Ⓔ
16. Ⓐ Ⓑ Ⓒ Ⓓ Ⓔ
17. Ⓐ Ⓑ Ⓒ Ⓓ Ⓔ
18. Ⓐ Ⓑ Ⓒ Ⓓ Ⓔ
19. Ⓐ Ⓑ Ⓒ Ⓓ Ⓔ
20. Ⓐ Ⓑ Ⓒ Ⓓ Ⓔ
21. Ⓐ Ⓑ Ⓒ Ⓓ Ⓔ
22. Ⓐ Ⓑ Ⓒ Ⓓ Ⓔ
23. Ⓐ Ⓑ Ⓒ Ⓓ Ⓔ
24. Ⓐ Ⓑ Ⓒ Ⓓ Ⓔ
25. Ⓐ Ⓑ Ⓒ Ⓓ Ⓔ
26. Ⓐ Ⓑ Ⓒ Ⓓ Ⓔ
27. Ⓐ Ⓑ Ⓒ Ⓓ Ⓔ
28. Ⓐ Ⓑ Ⓒ Ⓓ Ⓔ
29. Ⓐ Ⓑ Ⓒ Ⓓ Ⓔ
30. Ⓐ Ⓑ Ⓒ Ⓓ Ⓔ

Section IV

1. Ⓐ Ⓑ Ⓒ Ⓓ Ⓔ
2. Ⓐ Ⓑ Ⓒ Ⓓ Ⓔ
3. Ⓐ Ⓑ Ⓒ Ⓓ Ⓔ
4. Ⓐ Ⓑ Ⓒ Ⓓ Ⓔ
5. Ⓐ Ⓑ Ⓒ Ⓓ Ⓔ
6. Ⓐ Ⓑ Ⓒ Ⓓ Ⓔ
7. Ⓐ Ⓑ Ⓒ Ⓓ Ⓔ
8. Ⓐ Ⓑ Ⓒ Ⓓ Ⓔ
9. Ⓐ Ⓑ Ⓒ Ⓓ Ⓔ
10. Ⓐ Ⓑ Ⓒ Ⓓ Ⓔ
11. Ⓐ Ⓑ Ⓒ Ⓓ Ⓔ
12. Ⓐ Ⓑ Ⓒ Ⓓ Ⓔ
13. Ⓐ Ⓑ Ⓒ Ⓓ Ⓔ
14. Ⓐ Ⓑ Ⓒ Ⓓ Ⓔ
15. Ⓐ Ⓑ Ⓒ Ⓓ Ⓔ
16. Ⓐ Ⓑ Ⓒ Ⓓ Ⓔ
17. Ⓐ Ⓑ Ⓒ Ⓓ Ⓔ
18. Ⓐ Ⓑ Ⓒ Ⓓ Ⓔ
19. Ⓐ Ⓑ Ⓒ Ⓓ Ⓔ
20. Ⓐ Ⓑ Ⓒ Ⓓ Ⓔ
21. Ⓐ Ⓑ Ⓒ Ⓓ Ⓔ
22. Ⓐ Ⓑ Ⓒ Ⓓ Ⓔ
23. Ⓐ Ⓑ Ⓒ Ⓓ Ⓔ
24. Ⓐ Ⓑ Ⓒ Ⓓ Ⓔ
25. Ⓐ Ⓑ Ⓒ Ⓓ Ⓔ
26. Ⓐ Ⓑ Ⓒ Ⓓ Ⓔ
27. Ⓐ Ⓑ Ⓒ Ⓓ Ⓔ
28. Ⓐ Ⓑ Ⓒ Ⓓ Ⓔ
29. Ⓐ Ⓑ Ⓒ Ⓓ Ⓔ
30. Ⓐ Ⓑ Ⓒ Ⓓ Ⓔ

Section I

Analytical Reasoning

TIME: 35 minutes for 26 questions

DIRECTIONS: Each group of questions in this section is based on a set of conditions. In answering some of the questions, it may be useful to draw a rough diagram. Choose the response that most accurately and completely answers each question and blacken the corresponding space on your answer sheet.

Questions 1–7 refer to the following scenario.

Five members of the Sigma Delta fraternity — Biff, Chas, Deke, Marc, and Trip — participate in a college beach volleyball tournament. Each game in the tournament pits a team of two players from one fraternity against a team of two players from a rival fraternity. For every game, the fraternity supplies a pair of players. Each of the tournament participants from the Sigma Delta fraternity plays in at least one game. No two players play more than one game together. The following conditions apply to the Sigma Delta players during the tournament:

If Biff plays with Marc in any game, then Biff cannot play with Chas in any game.

Any player who plays on a team with Deke in any game must also play on a team with Marc in a game.

Trip plays in exactly one game in the tournament.

Deke never plays on a team with Marc.

1. Which one of the following could be a complete and accurate list of the pairs of players that play in the tournament?

   (A) Biff and Chas; Biff and Deke; Biff and Marc; Chas and Marc; Marc and Trip

   (B) Biff and Chas; Biff and Deke; Biff and Trip; Deke and Marc

   (C) Biff and Chas; Chas and Deke; Chas and Marc; Marc and Trip

   (D) Biff and Marc; Biff and Trip; Chas and Deke; Chas and Marc; Marc and Trip

   (E) Biff and Deke; Biff and Marc; Chas and Marc; Deke and Trip

2. At most, how many pairs of Sigma Delta players could play together in the tournament?

   (A) three

   (B) four

   (C) five

   (D) six

   (E) seven

3. Which one of the following could be true?

   (A) Biff and Chas play a game together, and neither Biff nor Chas plays with anyone else.

   (B) Biff and Marc play a game together, and neither Biff nor Marc plays with anyone else.

   (C) Biff and Trip play a game together, and neither Biff nor Trip plays with anyone else.

   (D) Chas and Marc play a game together, and neither Chas nor Marc plays with anyone else.

   (E) Marc and Trip play a game together, and neither Marc nor Trip plays with anyone else.

4. If exactly three players play games with Biff, then which one of the following could be an acceptable pairing of players?

   (A) Biff and Chas

   (B) Chas and Deke

   (C) Chas and Trip

   (D) Deke and Trip

   (E) Marc and Trip

GO ON TO NEXT PAGE

5. If each of four Sigma Delta players plays with the same player, then which of the following players must pair up for a game?

(A) Biff and Deke

(B) Biff and Trip

(C) Chas and Deke

(D) Deke and Trip

(E) Marc and Trip

6. Which one of the following pairs of players CANNOT play together?

(A) Biff and Deke

(B) Biff and Marc

(C) Biff and Trip

(D) Chas and Trip

(E) Deke and Trip

7. If Marc is the only player to play with Biff, then which one of the following could be true?

(A) Chas plays exactly one game.

(B) Marc plays exactly one game.

(C) Deke plays exactly two games.

(D) Marc plays exactly two games.

(E) Chas plays exactly four games.

Questions 8–12 refer to the following scenario.

A wrangler at a dude ranch in Colorado is taking a family of six on a trail ride through the mountains. She has selected six horses and assigned exactly one to each of the participants based on age, size, and disposition. The six horses include two feisty mares, two placid geldings, and two small Shetland ponies. The trails are narrow, so the horses must walk single file. In determining the order of horses, the wrangler must observe the following rules:

Either the first or second horse must be a gelding.

The last horse cannot be a mare.

The third horse cannot be a pony.
The wrangler can never put two horses of the same type immediately next to each other.

8. Which one of the following statements CANNOT be true?

(A) The first horse is a pony.

(B) The first horse is a mare.

(C) The second horse is a gelding.

(D) The third horse is a mare.

(E) The fifth horse is a pony.

9. If the third and fifth horses are the same type, then which one of the following statements must be true?

(A) The first horse is a pony.

(B) The second horse is a gelding.

(C) The fourth horse is a pony.

(D) The fifth horse is a mare.

(E) The last horse is a gelding.

10. If the third horse is a gelding, which one of the following must be true?

(A) The first horse is a gelding.

(B) The second horse is a pony.

(C) The fourth horse is a mare.

(D) The fifth horse is a pony.

(E) The last horse is a mare.

11. Which of the following pairs of horses must be of different types?

(A) the first and third horses

(B) the first and fourth horses

(C) the second and fourth horses

(D) the second and last horses

(E) the third and last horses

12. If the wrangler replaces one of the mares with a third pony, and all the other conditions remain the same, then which one of the following is a complete and accurate list of the positions that must be occupied by ponies?

(A) second

(B) fourth

(C) second, fourth

(D) fourth, sixth

(E) second, fourth, sixth

Questions 13–19 refer to the following scenario.

A fantasy gaming team has seven members: Brunhild, Cayenne, Maev, Roxanne, Solomon, Yorick, and Zilla. They each participate in exactly one of three fantasy gaming tournaments. The three tournaments are held in Fargo, Little Rock, and Omaha. In deciding who attends which tournament, they must observe the following rules:

Yorick cannot attend the tournament in Fargo.

Cayenne must attend the tournament in Fargo.

Brunhild and Roxanne must attend the same tournament.

Solomon and Yorick cannot participate in the same tournament.

Maev and Zilla cannot participate in the same tournament.

Exactly half as many team members attend the tournament in Omaha as attend the tournament in Fargo.

13. If Brunhild and Yorick attend the same tournament, then which one of the following could be true?

(A) Brunhild attends the tournament in Fargo.

(B) Maev attends the tournament in Fargo.

(C) Roxanne attends the tournament in Omaha.

(D) Solomon attends the tournament in Little Rock.

(E) Yorick attends the tournament in Omaha.

14. Which one of the following could be true?

(A) Roxanne is the only team member who attends the tournament in Little Rock.

(B) Solomon is the only team member who attends the tournament in Omaha.

(C) Solomon is the only team member who attends the tournament in Fargo.

(D) Exactly two team members attend the tournament in Little Rock.

(E) Exactly three team members attend the tournament in Fargo.

15. If exactly one team member attends the tournament in Little Rock, then which one of the following must be true?

(A) Brunhild attends the tournament in Fargo.

(B) Maev attends the tournament in Omaha.

(C) Solomon attends the tournament in Fargo.

(D) Yorick attends the tournament in Omaha.

(E) Zilla attends the tournament in Omaha.

16. Each of the following could be a complete and accurate list of the team members who attend the tournament in Omaha EXCEPT:

(A) Brunhild and Roxanne

(B) Maev and Solomon

(C) Maev and Yorick

(D) Solomon and Zilla

(E) Yorick and Zilla

17. Which one of the following is a possible allocation of some team members to tournaments?

(A) Brunhild: the tournament in Omaha; Maev: the tournament in Fargo; Solomon: the tournament in Little Rock

(B) Brunhild and Maev: the tournament in Omaha; Yorick: the tournament in Little Rock

(C) Brunhild, Solomon, and Zilla: the tournament in Little Rock

(D) Maev: the tournament in Little Rock; Yorick and Zilla: the tournament in Fargo

(E) Roxanne, Solomon, and Zilla: the tournament in Fargo

18. Which one of the following must be true?

    (A) Brunhild, Cayenne, and Maev do not attend the same tournament.

    (B) Cayenne, Yorick, and Zilla do not attend the same tournament.

    (C) Brunhild and Maev attend different tournaments.

    (D) Cayenne and Maev attend different tournaments.

    (E) Maev and Yorick attend different tournaments.

19. Which one of the following could be a complete and accurate list of the team members who do NOT attend the tournament in Fargo?

    (A) Solomon, Yorick

    (B) Yorick, Zilla

    (C) Brunhild, Roxanne, Yorick

    (D) Maev, Solomon, Yorick

    (E) Roxanne, Yorick, Zilla

Questions 20–26 refer to the following scenario.

A gourmet ice cream parlor offers a super-deluxe banana split intended to be shared by a group of people. The banana split comes in a long dish that contains five individual cups positioned side by side in a straight line. Each cup can hold up to two scoops of ice cream. A group of teenagers orders one of these banana splits. They request seven scoops of ice cream — three chocolate and four vanilla. Each scoop has one topping: Two scoops are topped with sprinkles, and five scoops are topped with nuts. The teenagers specify the following conditions:

A cup containing a scoop of vanilla with nuts cannot be immediately next to a cup containing a scoop of chocolate with sprinkles.

No cup can contain both vanilla and chocolate ice cream.

20. Which one of the following could be a complete and accurate arrangement of ice cream flavors and toppings in the five cups?

    (A) 1: two scoops of vanilla with sprinkles; 2: nothing; 3: one scoop of chocolate with nuts; 4: one scoop of chocolate with nuts; 5: one scoop of chocolate with nuts, two scoops of vanilla with nuts

    (B) 1: one scoop of vanilla with sprinkles, one scoop of vanilla with nuts; 2: two scoops of vanilla with nuts; 3: one scoop of chocolate with sprinkles; 4: one scoop of chocolate with nuts; one scoop of chocolate with nuts

    (C) 1: one scoop of vanilla with nuts, one scoop of vanilla with sprinkles; 2: one scoop of vanilla with nuts, one scoop of vanilla with sprinkles; 3: one scoop of chocolate with sprinkles; 4: one scoop of chocolate with nuts; 5: one scoop of chocolate with nuts

    (D) 1: nothing; 2: two scoops of vanilla with nuts; 3: two scoops of chocolate with nuts; 4: two scoops of vanilla with sprinkles; 5: one scoop of chocolate with nuts

    (E) 1: two scoops of vanilla with nuts; 2: one scoop of vanilla with sprinkles; 3: one scoop of chocolate with nuts; 4: one scoop of chocolate with nuts, one scoop of chocolate with sprinkles; 5: one scoop of chocolate with nuts

21. Which one of the following CANNOT be false?

    (A) At least one cup contains exactly one scoop of chocolate ice cream.

    (B) At least one cup contains exactly one scoop of ice cream with sprinkles.

    (C) At least one cup contains exactly one scoop of ice cream with nuts.

    (D) At least one scoop of vanilla ice cream has sprinkles.

    (E) At least one scoop of chocolate ice cream has sprinkles.

22. What is the maximum number of cups that could contain exactly one scoop of ice cream?

    (A) one
    (B) two
    (C) three
    (D) four
    (E) five

23. If the third cup has no ice cream in it, and no cup containing a scoop of vanilla is adjacent to another cup containing a scoop of vanilla, then which one of the following could be false?

    (A) Exactly one cup contains exactly one scoop of ice cream.
    (B) No scoop of chocolate is in a cup immediately next to a cup containing a scoop of chocolate.
    (C) None of the scoops of chocolate have sprinkles on them.
    (D) None of the cups contain exactly one scoop of vanilla.
    (E) All the scoops of vanilla are in the second and fourth cups.

24. If two scoops of chocolate with sprinkles are in the fourth cup, and at least one scoop of vanilla with nuts is in the second cup, then all the following must be false EXCEPT

    (A) A scoop of chocolate with nuts is in the first cup.
    (B) A scoop of chocolate with nuts is in the second cup.
    (C) A scoop of chocolate with nuts is in the fourth cup.
    (D) A scoop of chocolate with nuts is in the fifth cup.
    (E) Two scoops of ice cream are in the fifth cup.

25. If each of the scoops of chocolate ice cream is in its own cup, and all the scoops of vanilla have nuts on them, then which one of the cups CANNOT contain vanilla ice cream?

    (A) the first cup
    (B) the second cup
    (C) the third cup
    (D) the fourth cup
    (E) the fifth cup

26. Each of the following could be a complete description of the contents of the first and second cups EXCEPT:

    (A) 1: two scoops of chocolate with nuts; 2: one scoop of vanilla with nuts
    (B) 1: one scoop of vanilla with sprinkles, one scoop of vanilla with nuts; 2: one scoop of vanilla with sprinkles
    (C) 1: empty; 2: one scoop of chocolate with nuts
    (D) 1: one scoop of chocolate with sprinkles; 2: one scoop of vanilla with sprinkles
    (E) 1: one scoop of vanilla with sprinkles; 2: empty

Section II

Logical Reasoning

1. Tempest: I bought two urns from an auction at Christie's. Christie's advertised them as dating from the Louis XV period of the late 18th century. I now believe that they actually date from the late 19th century and are worth much less than I paid for them. Several antiques experts agree with me. Therefore, Christie's advertised them falsely and should refund my purchase price.

   Which one of the following, if true, most seriously weakens Tempest's argument?

   (A) The auction catalog described the urns as "A pair of Louis XV porphyry and gilt-bronze two-handled vases."

   (B) Dating antiques is an imprecise art, and often, several experts disagree about the date of origin of the same item.

   (C) Scientists have performed tests on the bronze linings of the urns, but they have not produced conclusive results regarding the vases' ages.

   (D) Christie's states in its auction catalogs that all buyers should consult outside specialists before bidding on antiques, especially in the case of extremely valuable items.

   (E) The experts who Tempest hired to date the urns are known as some of the best in their field.

2. The state should continue to use the death penalty to punish the most extreme criminals. The death penalty is the only way to provide closure for the families of victims. People who commit coldblooded, premeditated murders are incorrigible. Anyone whom a jury convicts of committing a truly heinous crime deserves to be executed by the state.

   Which one of the following, if true, most weakens the argument?

   (A) Surveys of the families of murder victims show that the surviving relatives overwhelmingly support the death penalty.

   (B) Simply executing convicted criminals is far cheaper than maintaining them in maximum-security prison for life, with no chance of release or parole.

   (C) Recent studies have shown that a large proportion of criminals sentenced to death are later shown to be innocent of their crimes.

   (D) Modern methods of execution such as lethal injection are much less unpleasant to watch than earlier methods such as electrocution or hanging.

   (E) Many states that had supported the death penalty are now moving in the other direction, and the number of executions has decreased dramatically in recent years.

3. The top-ranking, highest-paying law firms select their new associates exclusively from top-ten law schools. Therefore, if a student does not get into a top-ten law school, he or she should not bother attending law school at all.

The reasoning in the argument is most vulnerable to criticism on the grounds that the argument

(A) promises students that if they attend a top-ten law school, they are guaranteed a position at a top-ranking law firm

(B) suggests, without offering evidence, that the legal education provided by lower-ranking law schools is inadequate

(C) fails to criticize the biased recruiting practices of top-ranking law firms

(D) assumes that the only reason anyone would attend law school is to acquire a job at a top-ranking, high-paying law firm

(E) misrepresents the relationship between law school and future employment

4. Exterminator: In the summer, we implement a large-scale mosquito abatement program to protect the human population from West Nile virus. In addition to spraying insecticide and larvicide to kill mosquitoes, we also collect dead birds and test them for the virus. We have not found the virus in any birds tested this year, so there will not be an outbreak of West Nile virus in humans this summer.

The exterminator assumes which of the following in making the argument?

(A) Mosquitoes transmit the virus to birds by biting them, which is the same way humans catch the virus, but birds are much more susceptible than humans to dying from West Nile virus.

(B) The massive spraying of insecticide and larvicide will be more effective this year than in previous years.

(C) Birds are the only indicator species of West Nile virus for humans.

(D) It is possible to have an outbreak of West Nile virus among humans, even if no birds die of the virus, though that would be an unusual scenario.

(E) The insecticide and larvicide used to kill the adult and larval mosquitoes do not have a deleterious effect on the health of birds that eat mosquitoes.

5. Editorialist: Conservative legislators and religious groups want to ban all research involving undifferentiated stem cells, fearing that such research would be akin to abortion because it would destroy an embryo's chances at life. They could not be more wrong; stem cells are not embryos and can never develop into human beings. Stem cell research could lead to all sorts of promising treatments for diseases such as Alzheimer's, diabetes, and some kinds of cancer.

Which of the following most accurately expresses the conclusion drawn by the editorialist's argument as a whole?

(A) Stem cell research should not be banned.

(B) Stem cells research would not result in the destruction of embryos.

(C) Stem cell research offers many powerful benefits.

(D) Some legislators are pushing for a ban against research on undifferentiated cells.

(E) Any research that leads to promising treatments should not be banned.

6. Scientists have concluded that a pickled human heart long believed to be the heart of King Louis XVII of France is indeed his heart, and not that of a commoner substituted for the royal boy. Louis XVII's parents, Marie Antoinette and Louis XVI, fell to the guillotine during the French Revolution, and Louis XVII was thrown into prison, where he died at the age of 10. His heart was removed and preserved. Many people believed, however, that the young king had been spirited away and the boy who died in prison was an impostor. Scientific evidence now shows that the child who died in prison was indeed Louis XVII.

Which one of the following, if true, most strongly supports the scientists' conclusion?

(A) At that time in France, removing and preserving the hearts of royal corpses was a traditional service that was never applied to the bodies of commoners.

(B) Scientists examining the heart have concluded that it must have belonged to a male between the ages of 8 and 12.

GO ON TO NEXT PAGE

(C) DNA samples taken from the heart in question and from hair cut from Marie Antoinette's head when she was a child indicate that the heart and hair sample came from people who were closely related.

(D) The doctor who removed Louis XVII's heart preserved it in a jar of alcohol, which was so effective as a preservative that the heart's valves and muscles are still in good condition and can be easily examined by scientists.

(E) Scientists examining the heart have determined that it came from a child who suffered great physical privation in the years just prior to his death; in particular, its undeveloped muscles suggest that the heart's owner did not engage in much physical activity for several years.

7. Emilio: Every child should be encouraged to play a single team sport at a high level, perhaps on a select traveling team that plays year-round. If a child does not play on an elite team at a young age, he will not have a chance to play on his high school varsity team and will thus forgo any opportunity to win college scholarships for athletics.

Julienne: Parents should encourage their children to play a wide variety of sports. Sports teach children teamwork and leadership and encourage them to develop physically. Most of all, sports should be fun. Children who specialize in one sport too early miss out on the chance to develop a wide range of skills, are more prone to injuries, and usually don't enjoy themselves as much as those who play a variety of sports. Also, so few athletic scholarships are available that there is very little point in counting on one.

Emilio and Julienne disagree about whether

(A) sports teach children teamwork and leadership

(B) children who play a single sport on an elite team enjoy themselves

(C) parents should encourage their children to participate in organized sports

(D) early specialization in a single sport is beneficial to children

(E) children below high school age should be participating in organized sports

8. To preserve the flavor of food for the longest period of time, a home freezer should maintain a temperature of no greater than 0 degrees. Even food that is kept frozen at the proper temperature lasts no more than a year. For every 5 degrees of temperature above zero, the life of food is cut in half. Most home freezers maintain a temperature of about 10 degrees.

If these statements are true, which one of the following must also be true based on them?

(A) Most home freezers can store food for no more than three months.

(B) Most homeowners do not know the temperature of their freezers.

(C) Frozen foods can still be safe to eat, even when they have lost their optimum flavor.

(D) Commercial freezers stay colder than home freezers.

(E) Most food in home freezers has been kept past the point at which its best flavor begins to deteriorate.

9. Ichthyologist: I have discovered a new kind of mollusk that lives deep in the ocean. All animals that live in the deep sea are predators that eat other animals. Therefore, this new mollusk must be a predator.

Which one of the following exhibits a pattern of reasoning most similar to that exhibited by the ichthyologist?

(A) A yoga enthusiast discovers a new yoga studio. All yoga studios employ experienced and highly trained instructors. Therefore, the yoga enthusiast will be able to find a good instructor.

(B) A coach finds a talented new basketball player in Croatia. Most Croatian basketball players are tall and hardworking. Therefore, this new basketball player is tall and hardworking.

(C) A gardener discovers a new variety of tomato in his garden. All tomatoes are members of the same family as potatoes and eggplants, the nightshade family. Therefore, this tomato must be a member of the nightshade family.

(D) A jeweler finds a perfect sapphire. All sapphires are very hard and durable. Therefore, this sapphire must be hard and durable.

(E) A botanist finds a new kind of cactus in the driest part of the desert. All plants that live in the dry desert are extremely efficient at collecting and retaining water. Therefore, this new cactus must be extremely efficient at collecting and retaining water.

10. Counselor: People should always pick their battles. By bringing up only the issues that truly matter to them and ignoring the ones that don't, they maximize chances of getting what they want and avoid antagonizing friends and relatives unnecessarily.

Which one of the following provides the best illustration of the counselor's proposition?

(A) A brother and sister have to share a car. The brother never fills the tank with gasoline, always driving it until it is nearly empty and then waiting for his sister to fill it up. She yells at him every time she has to visit a gas station.

(B) A wife wants her husband to wash the dishes, take out the garbage, and make the bed in the morning, but she knows he will not do all three. She most dislikes taking out the garbage herself, so she makes a point of asking him to do that many times and ignores the dishes and bed.

(C) A test-prep teacher teaching an LSAT course wants to improve her students' scores in both logical reasoning and analytical reasoning, but she does not have time to do a thorough job on both, so she spends half her time on logical reasoning and half on analytical reasoning.

(D) A bride's mother wants her to have a big wedding in a church followed by a large reception, but the bride wants a small, less-formal wedding with just a few guests. They cannot agree, so the bride and groom decide to elope instead.

(E) A father wants his son to win an athletic scholarship and insists that his son spend hours every afternoon working out and practicing sports. Despite the son's strenuous efforts, he fails to win an athletic scholarship. Because he is a good student, though, he does win an academic scholarship.

11. People who live in poverty often have little money to spend on food, and as a result are often afflicted with malnutrition. Ironically, these same people have very high rates of obesity.

Which one of the following best resolves this apparent paradox?

(A) Obesity is becoming a serious problem all over the world and at all levels of income.

(B) People who live in poverty do not understand the basic rules of nutrition.

(C) American citizens have gotten out of the habit of cooking family meals, and as a result, fewer and fewer people know how to prepare healthy foods such as vegetables.

(D) The cheap foods that make up the majority of the diets of poor people are full of calories but devoid of essential nutrients.

(E) Recent statistics show that processed foods and fast food make up almost half the diet of a large number of people in the United States.

GO ON TO NEXT PAGE ▶

12. Most players of video games are male. Therefore, video game manufacturers should not bother making any games aimed at girls or women.

Which one of the following employs a flawed argumentative strategy that is most closely parallel to this flawed argumentative strategy?

(A) Most avid cyclists are male. Therefore, bicycle manufacturers should make most of their bike frames to fit men.

(B) Most Americans have cellular telephones. Therefore, most Americans should not bother to maintain normal land-based telephones.

(C) Most people use Windows computers. Therefore, software producers should not bother to make any software for Macintosh computers.

(D) Most lawyers need glasses or contact lenses. Therefore, optometrists should aim some of their advertising at the legal profession.

(E) Most Labrador retrievers are easy to train. Therefore, a person who wants an obedient dog should consider getting a Labrador retriever.

13. The legislature is considering a law banning the use of cellphones by people who are driving a moving car. Drivers talking on cellphones are distracted by their phone conversations and can't give their full attention to driving their vehicles. Banning the use of cellphones by drivers will make the roads safer.

The argument depends on assuming which one of the following?

(A) A study by a sociologist has shown that the use of cellphones is occasionally a contributing factor in traffic accidents.

(B) The proper role of the legislature is to enact laws that protect the safety of drivers and passengers in automobiles.

(C) Drivers who hold their cellphones in their hands are more distracted than drivers who use a hands-free headset or speakerphone while driving.

(D) Because drivers talking on cellphones are distracted, they are more prone to get into accidents.

(E) Many drivers engage in behavior that distracts them from their driving, such as eating, adjusting the radio, reading maps, and talking on cellphones.

14. Partner: Attorney A and Attorney B each wrote a brief arguing the same side of a case. Attorney A spent 8 hours writing his brief. Attorney B spent 12 hours writing her brief. Therefore, Attorney B's brief is better than Attorney A's brief.

The reasoning in the partner's argument is flawed because the argument

(A) equates time spent on a job with quality, without examining the products to verify the quality

(B) criticizes Attorney B for taking too long to write her brief

(C) fails to explain why the partner believes Attorney B's brief is better than Attorney A's brief

(D) takes for granted that tracking time spent on work is the best way to ensure quality work

(E) fails to identify the topic of the brief

15. High school student: My teacher defines insects as animals with six legs, a three-part body, an outer skeleton, and in most cases, wings. Ants are referred to as insects, but most species of ants don't have wings. Therefore, if my teacher is correct, ants can't be insects.

A reasoning flaw in the high school student's argument is that the argument

(A) ignores the possibility that some ants have wings

(B) relies on a single unverified source for its definition of insects

(C) fails to offer alternative categories in which to place ants

(D) exaggerates the importance of wings to ants

(E) assumes incorrectly that a characteristic found in the majority of a group must also be found in the majority of each subgroup within that group

16. This store is having a sale in which all its merchandise is 25 percent off. I plan to buy many things because the more I spend, the more I will save.

This argument is vulnerable to criticism on which of the following grounds?

(A) It assumes erroneously that the same discount of 25 percent will apply to all the merchandise in the store.

(B) It confuses percentage of discount with actual dollar reductions.

(C) It fails to realize that spending money on discounted items is still spending money and will result in no savings at all.

(D) It presupposes that the store has put its merchandise on sale in an effort to attract more customers.

(E) It neglects to consider that merchandise might be put on sale because it is of poor quality, defective, or unpopular.

17. Christina: The best way for employers to reduce their healthcare costs is to implement consumer-driven health insurance plans. These plans have high deductibles — upfront charges that encourage employees to think twice before seeing a doctor for frivolous reasons. Employers pay lower premiums for these plans and can help their employees pay for necessary care by contributing to healthcare savings accounts along with their employees.

Guthrie: But there are many complex causes for the rise in healthcare costs, such as inefficient record-keeping and the price of brand-name drugs. Higher financial hurdles to see a doctor will only make patients reluctant to seek care for minor problems, and that neglect could result in minor problems turning into major health catastrophes that will be very expensive for everyone.

Based on this dialogue, Christina and Guthrie are committed to disagreeing about the truth of which one of the following statements?

(A) An effective way for employers to reduce their healthcare costs is to discourage the use of brand-name drugs.

(B) The high deductibles of consumer-driven health insurance plans will lead to higher healthcare costs.

(C) Health insurance companies make it very difficult for smaller employers to buy affordable coverage for themselves and their employees.

(D) High deductibles are effective at deterring people from seeking medical attention for all but the most serious concerns.

(E) Healthcare savings accounts offer employees a way to save pretax income for anticipated medical expenses.

18. Context is everything. For example, on an Internet perfume discussion board, one participant posted the message, "Azkaban arrives today!" referring to an extremely popular film about a boy wizard that was opening that day. Another participant responded, "Where can you buy it?" evidently assuming that "Azkaban" must refer to a new perfume. She quickly realized her mistake, but because her mind was on perfumes, she couldn't immediately place the movie.

Which one of the following most accurately expresses the main conclusion of this argument?

(A) Internet discussion boards are especially prone to context-based errors.

(B) Even well-known and widely available information, provided in an unexpected context, can be misleading.

(C) To avoid misunderstanding, people should always introduce topics precisely.

(D) Participants on perfume discussion boards do not know much about popular movies.

(E) The names of perfumes are so fanciful that confusing them is easy.

 GO ON TO NEXT PAGE

19. Divemaster: Some scuba divers fill their tanks with nitrox instead of air. Nitrox is a combination of nitrogen and oxygen that contains more than the usual percentage of oxygen contained in air. Nitrox aficionados claim that the additional oxygen makes diving safer; they can stay down longer, decompress faster, dive again after a shorter surface interval, and feel less fatigued after extended diving than if they were breathing plain air. On the other hand, divers using nitrox face dangers and limitations, particularly the risk of convulsions and death, at greater depths that are safe for divers using air.

Which one of the following, if true, most helps to resolve the apparent discrepancy in the divemaster's statements?

(A) The higher concentration of oxygen in nitrox becomes toxic when it is compressed at increasing depths.

(B) Divers who use nitrox are likely to stay underwater too long, lulled into a false sense of security by their breathing gas.

(C) Divers who use air pay more attention to training and safety procedures and experience fewer fatal accidents because of improper procedures than divers who use nitrox.

(D) All divers face the rare risk of receiving a tank with contaminated air, which occurs when bacteria grow inside a compressor, occasionally resulting in diving fatalities.

(E) Divers who use nitrox are more likely to dive regularly, take frequent training courses, and buy more technologically advanced equipment than divers who use air.

20. Many Americans do not take all the vacation time to which they are entitled to by their jobs. There are several reasons for this: They feel that they are indispensable at work, they fear the resentment of co-workers, or they dread discovering that their workplaces can actually function perfectly well without them. This is a mistake; vacation time gives workers a chance to rest, recover, and gain perspective that in turn can lead to more creativity and better performance at work.

The claim that many Americans do not take all the vacation time to which they are entitled plays which one of the following roles in the argument?

(A) It is a recommendation of a policy that the American workplace should implement.

(B) It is evidence of the author's claim that vacation time gives workers a chance to rest.

(C) It is the conclusion of the argument.

(D) It is a statement of a principle that the author wishes all people would observe.

(E) It is a statement of fact about which the author goes on to make an opinion.

21. A large Southern state university has changed its teaching practices. Formerly, instructors without PhDs taught most introductory courses; now professors with PhDs will teach all introductory classes. That means the average class size will increase from 44 students per class to 600 per class, but overall the students' learning experience should improve.

Which one of the following is an assumption required by this argument?

(A) Requiring professors with PhDs to teach all introductory classes will mean that the university must hire more faculty with doctorates.

(B) Students tend to participate in smaller classes more than they do in large lectures, even when the lectures are supplemented by weekly discussion sections.

(C) Major private universities already have implemented a format in which professors with PhDs teach all introductory classes as large lectures.

(D) A class taught by a PhD, even in a lecture format with hundreds of students, is a better learning environment than a smaller class taught by an instructor without a PhD.

(E) Services that rank colleges and universities usually consider the percentage of classes taught by PhDs when computing rank.

22. Griselda: The United States should remember that it is part of a global community and that its actions affect other nations. The United States must avoid alienating the citizens of foreign countries. Ultimately, that is the best way to assure national security.

Theodore: The good opinion of foreign countries is largely irrelevant to U.S. national security concerns. The United States should always act in its own best interest, regardless of what other nations think. If that means sending troops off to war without the approval of the rest of the world, then so be it.

The dialogue provides the most support for the claim that Griselda and Theodore disagree over whether

(A) other nations disapprove of the United States' involvement in foreign affairs

(B) the proper response to threats from abroad is a show of military strength

(C) the United States should act in its best interest

(D) the United States should follow the dictates of the United Nations on all matters of national security and foreign intervention

(E) the opinion of the international community is important to the United States

23. Obstetrician: Children born to mothers who drink heavily during pregnancy often have severe birth defects and intellectual disability caused by prenatal exposure to alcohol. Pregnant women should never consume alcohol because it causes their children to be born with these serious problems.

The reasoning in the argument is most vulnerable to criticism on the grounds that the obstetrician

(A) assumes that consuming any amount of alcohol during pregnancy will cause birth defects and intellectual disability

(B) suggests that pregnant women should be prevented from drinking during pregnancy

(C) presumes that the state's interest in the health of newborns is greater than the rights of pregnant women to behave as they choose

(D) fails to provide evidence from reliable medical journals proving the link between heavy drinking and birth defects

(E) treats a condition sufficient to cause birth defects and intellectual disability as if it were necessary to cause those problems

24. An ounce of prevention is worth a pound of cure; it is always cheaper to head off problems before they start than to fix them after they have occurred.

Which one of the following most closely conforms to this principle?

(A) A homeowner spent hours preparing the soil for his lawn and garden, and as a result of his preparation, his grass was green and lush and his flowers bloomed with abandon.

(B) A state school board insisted that all students in public schools show evidence of vaccination against measles before being allowed to attend classes.

(C) A pre-law student spent several weeks studying for the LSAT, and as a result, she received an excellent score that, combined with the grades she had earned from years of diligent study, earned her admission to a top law school.

(D) A university that licensed a low-cost online workshop on proper citation techniques for its incoming students found itself needing to commit significantly fewer valuable staff hours to handle incidents of unintentional plagiarism.

(E) A woman who spent several months dieting and exercising and finally achieved her ideal body weight continued to watch what she ate and to exercise regularly to avoid gaining weight again.

GO ON TO NEXT PAGE ➤

25. Psychologist: Patients who feel they have a good relationship with their doctors generally show more improvement in their health than those who feel that their doctors ignore their concerns. Patients who like their doctors show improved emotional well-being, are less anxious about their symptoms, and are more likely to follow doctors' prescribed regimens.

Which one of the following, if true, would provide the most support for the psychologist's argument?

(A) Patients are more likely to sue a doctor for malpractice if they believe that the doctor ignored them or failed to listen while they explained their symptoms.

(B) When a patient begins to describe symptoms to a doctor, the average physician interrupts him after only 18 seconds of speech.

(C) A large number of studies have confirmed that the more anxious a patient is, the more protracted his or her recovery from a medical condition is.

(D) Recently, medical schools and health insurers have taken measures to improve doctor-patient communication.

(E) Doctors who work in stressful environments are much less likely to take the time to listen to patients than doctors in more relaxed settings.

DO NOT TURN THE PAGE UNTIL TOLD TO DO SO STOP **DO NOT RETURN TO A PREVIOUS TEST**

Section III

Reading Comprehension

TIME: 35 minutes for 25 questions

DIRECTIONS: Read each passage and answer the questions that follow it. Some questions may have more than one answer that looks right. In that case, pick the one that answers the question most completely and correctly. Don't assume anything that isn't stated in the passage or the questions. All the information you need to answer the questions is contained in the passage, questions, and answer choices.

Questions 1–7 refer to the following passage.

Recumbent bicycles, invented in the mid-1800s, dropped out of sight during most of the 20th century because of a historical accident. In 1934, a second-rate French bicyclist rode a recumbent in a race and not only won but also broke several speed records. The Union Cycliste Internationale (UCI) banned recumbents from competition, ruling that bicycle racing should be about the talent of the rider, not the advantages of a particular bicycle design. This decision produced an unintended result; bicycle manufacturers stopped designing and producing recumbent bicycles and instead focused on trying to improve the inherently inefficient diamond frame, which has remained essentially unchanged since 1885.

Conventional diamond-frame bicycles were designed based on the position a person assumes when riding a horse: upright with head high and legs low. Recumbents, on the other hand, are designed to maximize aerodynamic efficiency and comfort. A recumbent rider sits back on a seat resembling a lawn chair, with his legs in front. This position is extremely comfortable; recumbent riders never suffer the saddle sores or aching hands and necks of upright bicyclists, who report three times more overuse injuries and pain than recumbent riders. Recumbents are also aerodynamically efficient. A recumbent rider's legs are within the frame of his body, so he presents less frontal area to the wind than the rider of an upright bicycle, thereby minimizing wind resistance. This permanent aerodynamic tuck affords the rider a 15 percent speed increase over an upright bicycle. Adding a fairing, a kind of windshield, can increase speed a further 15 percent. All bicycling land-speed records have been set on recumbents; a recumbent was the first bicycle to break 65 mph on a flat track, and low-racer recumbents are now setting world records over 80 mph.

The popularity of recumbents has surged recently, bringing with it a flood of new bicycle designs. One major difference in types of recumbent is the length of the wheelbase. Short wheelbase bikes place the rider's feet in front of the front wheel, an extremely aerodynamic riding position that allows for high speeds. Long wheelbase bikes place the front wheel ahead of the rider's feet; these bikes are very comfortable for long-distance touring. Recumbent cyclists must also choose between two steering types. Above-seat steering places the rider's hands at chest height, within the frame of his body, which improves aerodynamics. Below-seat steering allows the rider to hang his arms from his shoulders to steer, which is more comfortable. Manufacturers have also been experimenting with different materials. Most recumbents are still made from heavy but inexpensive steel, but a few high-end models are now made from lightweight titanium or carbon fiber.

Some riders fear they will not be able to climb hills on recumbents, but most experienced recumbent riders find that they can equal their performance on an upright bike on grades of up to 12 percent. Climbing fast requires a high power-to-weight ratio and a fast cadence of about 70 to 80 rpm. Riders can improve their climbing by lifting weights to build strength and by learning to downshift early in their attack of a hill.

GO ON TO NEXT PAGE

1. Which one of the following most accurately expresses the main idea of this passage?

   (A) The UCI banned recumbent bicycles from competitions because it feared that allowing recumbents would turn bicycle racing into a design competition rather than a test of training, endurance, and skill.

   (B) Recumbent bicycles have become more popular recently after years of neglect, and this surge in popularity has brought with it a proliferation of recumbent bicycle designs, each of which offers benefits to speed or comfort.

   (C) Recumbent bicycles have a much more aerodynamic profile than upright bicycles, especially when used with a fairing, which explains why recumbent bicycles are faster than upright diamond-frame bicycles with identical riders under identical conditions.

   (D) Recumbent bicycles, which were banned from competition in the 1930s and thus neglected for much of the 20th century, offer many advantages over upright bicycles and come in many designs.

   (E) The permanent aerodynamic tuck of a recumbent rider allows recumbent bicycles to move faster than upright bicycles under equivalent conditions, which accounts for recumbents' breaking several world speed records.

2. According to the passage, why are recumbent bicycles faster than upright bicycles?

   (A) The seating position places the cyclist in a permanent aerodynamic tuck, with arms and legs contained within the rider's torso profile, thereby creating less wind resistance than an upright rider faces.

   (B) Most recumbent bicycles are made from high-tech, super-light materials such as carbon fiber and titanium, which makes them lighter and stronger than upright diamond-frame bicycles.

   (C) Recumbents are designed to maximize aerodynamic efficiency and comfort through the use of ergonomic seating and fairings, which reduce wind resistance.

   (D) Bicycle manufacturers have been experimenting with recumbent frames since they were first invented in the mid-1800s, which has resulted in greater refinement of construction techniques than are available for upright bicycles.

   (E) Recumbents can have two different steering configurations, which makes them faster than upright bicycles, which have only one basic steering structure.

3. According to the passage, why did the Union Cycliste Internationale ban recumbents from competition?

   (A) A second-rate cyclist won a race on a recumbent, and the other competitors petitioned the cycling organization to outlaw recumbents, despite the obvious aerodynamic advantage offered by recumbent bicycles.

   (B) After several cyclists set records on upright bicycles, the organization decided that upright bikes were far superior to recumbents and should therefore be the only vehicles allowed in bicycle racing.

   (C) Bicycle manufacturers petitioned the UCI to standardize the bicycle types that were allowed in racing to achieve a monopoly on the racing bike market.

   (D) In 1934, a second-rate cyclist on a recumbent attracted too much press attention due to his unusual and eye-catching bicycle, and the organization decided to ban recumbents to focus attention back on the more talented cyclists.

   (E) After a second-rate cyclist won a race and broke several records on a recumbent, the UCI decided that recumbents offered too much mechanical advantage and that, in order for races to reflect actual ability, all riders should use the same kind of bicycle.

4. Which one of the following is NOT mentioned in the passage as an advantage of recumbent bicycles over upright bicycles?

(A) Recumbent bicycles are more comfortable than upright bicycles, which allows cyclists to ride them for longer periods than they would on upright bicycles.

(B) Recumbent bicycles are lighter than upright bicycles, which gives them an advantage at hill climbing.

(C) Recumbent bicycles minimize the frontal profile of the cyclist, improving aerodynamics.

(D) Recumbent bicycles can be 15 percent faster than upright bicycles on the same terrain.

(E) Recumbent cyclists report many fewer overuse injuries than upright cyclists.

5. What is the primary purpose of the last paragraph?

(A) to argue that, contrary to what they may expect, cyclists can climb hills well on recumbent bicycles, and to suggest ways to improve climbing performance

(B) to prove that recumbents are as fast on hills as upright bicycles because a cyclist with a high power-to-weight ratio on a recumbent can climb hills just as well as she can on an upright bicycle

(C) to describe the ideal cadence a recumbent cyclist should use on a grade of up to 12 percent

(D) to dispute the contention that recumbent bicycles lose their aerodynamic advantage when climbing hills by offering anecdotal evidence of recumbent cyclists who are strong climbers

(E) to recommend that recumbent cyclists interested in improving their hill-climbing speed lift weights to increase their strength and minimize the weight of their bikes

6. Which of the following statements is best supported by the passage?

(A) A recumbent bicycle with a short wheelbase and above-seat steering is faster than a diamond-frame bicycle in all conditions.

(B) Recumbents have surged in popularity because they are more comfortable than diamond-frame bicycles.

(C) Recumbent bicycles could be improved by being produced with carbon fiber frames.

(D) If diamond-frame bicycles were fashioned with a fairing, their potential speed would increase by at least 15 percent.

(E) By building body strength and adjusting their shifting techniques, recumbent riders can climb hills as effectively as diamond-frame riders.

7. The author would be most likely to agree with which one of the following statements?

(A) A rider on a recumbent bicycle with above-seat steering should be able to climb faster than a rider on an upright bicycle of the same weight.

(B) In the near future, more cyclists will be riding recumbents than upright bicycles as more people discover the aerodynamic and comfort advantages of recumbent bicycles.

(C) A cyclist who wants to make his recumbent bicycle faster by reducing its weight should consider installing a fairing on it.

(D) An aerodynamic tuck on an upright bicycle offers as much aerodynamic advantage and comfort as the ordinary riding position on a recumbent bicycle.

(E) A cyclist who wants to maximize speed and comfort and is not interested in racing should choose a recumbent over an upright bicycle.

GO ON TO NEXT PAGE

Passage A

Controversy has haunted the diagnosis of post-traumatic stress disorder (PTSD) ever since its appearance in the third edition of the *Diagnostic and Statistical Manual of Mental Disorders (DSM-III)*. At the outset, psychiatrists opposed to the inclusion of the diagnosis in the *DSM-III* argued that the problems of trauma-exposed people were already covered by combinations of existing diagnoses.

Ratifying PTSD would merely entail cobbling together selected symptoms in people suffering from multiple disorders (for example, phobias, depression, and personality disorders) and then attributing these familiar problems to a traumatic event. Moreover, the very fact that the movement to include the diagnosis in the *DSM-III* arose from Vietnam veterans' advocacy groups working with antiwar psychiatrists prompted concerns that PTSD was more of a political or social construct rather than a medical disease discovered in nature. Although the aforementioned two concerns have again resurfaced in contemporary debates about PTSD, additional issues have arisen as well. For example, the concept of a traumatic stressor has broadened to such an extent that, today, the vast majority of American adults have been exposed to PTSD-qualifying events. This state of affairs is drastically different from the late 1970s and early 1980s, when the concept of trauma was confined to catastrophic events falling outside the perimeter of everyday experience. Early 21st-century scholars are raising fresh questions about the syndromic validity of PTSD.

Passage B

Of the many diagnoses in the *Diagnostic and Statistical Manual of Mental Disorders (DSM-III)*, very few invoke an aetiology in their diagnostic criteria: (i) organic mental disorders (caused, for example, by a neurological abnormality); (ii) substance-use disorders (caused, for example, by psychoactive chemical agents); (iii) post-traumatic stress disorder (PTSD); (iv) acute stress disorder (ASD); and (v) adjustment disorders (ADs). The latter three are all caused by exposure to a stressful environmental event that exceeds the coping capacity of the affected individual. The presumed causal relationship between the stressor and PTSD, ASD, and AD is complicated and controversial. Controversy notwithstanding, acceptance of this causal relationship has equipped practitioners and scientists with a conceptual tool that has profoundly influenced clinical practice over the past 30 years.

PTSD is primarily a disorder of reactivity rather than of an altered baseline state, as in major depressive disorder or general anxiety disorder. Its psychopathology is characteristically expressed during interactions with the interpersonal or physical environment. People with PTSD are consumed by concerns about personal safety.

They persistently scan the environment for threatening stimuli. When in doubt, they are more likely to assume that danger is present and will react accordingly. The avoidance and hyperarousal symptoms described below can be understood within this context. The primacy of traumatic over other memories (for example, the reexperiencing symptoms) can also be understood as a pathological exaggeration of an adaptive human response to remember as much as possible about dangerous encounters in order to avoid similar threats in the future.

8. The author of Passage A and the author of Passage B are most likely to agree with which of the following statements regarding PTSD?

   (A) Sufferers of PTSD are preoccupied with concerns about personal safety.

   (B) It can be argued that the very ratification of PTSD relies more on politics than medical evidence.

   (C) The diagnosis of PTSD is highly controversial.

   (D) The concept of trauma is limited to catastrophic events that most won't experience in a lifetime.

   (E) Sufferers of PTSD want to remember as much as they possibly can about dangerous encounters and situations so that they can avoid similar threats in the future.

9. Which of the following titles would most appropriately fit both passages?

   (A) PTSD: A Brief History of a Modern Controversy

   (B) Falsehoods in the *Diagnostic and Statistical Manual of Mental Disorders*

   (C) The Alarming Growth of PTSD in America

   (D) PTSD: Fact or Fiction?

   (E) PTSD: A Case Study

10. Which of the following arguments is NOT made by the author of either passage?

   (A) By today's definition of a *traumatic* event, most Americans have been exposed to one.

   (B) PTSD sufferers are more likely than an average citizen to feel that they are in danger.

   (C) Clinical practice has been heavily influenced by the presumed causal relationship between a traumatic stressor and cases of PTSD, acute stress disorder, and adjustment disorders.

   (D) The decision to include PTSD in the *Diagnostic and Statistical Manual* was encouraged by advocacy groups working on behalf of Vietnam veterans working with antiwar psychiatrists.

   (E) Sufferers of PTSD experience a lack of interest in day-to-day activities they used to find enjoyable.

11. Which of the following best characterizes suggestions made by the author of Passage A and the author of Passage B?

   (A) The author of Passage A suggests that PTSD may be an invalid diagnosis, while the author of Passage B indicates that PTSD is a valid disorder with recognizable symptoms.

   (B) The author of Passage A suggests ways in which the symptoms of PTSD may be indicators of other disorders, while the author of Passage B suggests that no other disorders share symptoms that are similar to PTSD.

   (C) Both authors suggest that PTSD should be included in the current *Diagnostic and Statistical Manual* as a valid disorder.

   (D) The author of Passage B indicates that questions regarding the validity of PTSD as a diagnosis are valid, while the author of Passage A suggests that PTSD is more a political or social phenomenon than a diagnosis.

   (E) The author of Passage B suggests that more should be done to help those with PTSD, while the author of Passage A implies that sufferers of PTSD are being treated thoroughly.

12. Which of the following is the most accurate presentation of the primary purpose of Passage B?

   (A) to explain how the symptoms of PTSD sufferers differ from the symptoms experienced by other survivors of traumatic events

   (B) to suggest that PTSD symptoms may be exhibited by a majority of the population

   (C) to expose the complications of traumatic stress disorders, such as PTSD, ASD, and AD, and to show how they affect the way their sufferers react to their environments

   (D) to list and define the causes of PTSD

   (E) to categorize the primary symptom of PTSD as a problem with the manner in which its sufferers respond to their environment

13. The author of Passage A mentions in the middle of the second paragraph that PTSD "was more of a political or social construct" to convey that

   (A) antiwar psychiatrists made up the disorder to ensure that Vietnam veterans would get medical care for their exposure to traumatic events

   (B) PTSD should be considered a medical disease rather than a disorder characterized by a single symptom such as a phobia or depression

   (C) the controversy over whether PTSD is a medical diagnosis is complicated by the motivations of the movement behind PTSD

GO ON TO NEXT PAGE ➡

(D) cobbling together several symptoms and calling them PTSD does an injustice to those suffering from medical diseases resulting from natural events rather than political and social events, such as war

(E) discovering the causal relationship between a traumatic event and PTSD requires a complex consideration of both natural medical stressors and political and social ones

Questions 14–18 refer to the following passage.

"Power" is a generic term that must be distinguished from the more specific term "authority." When party A gets party B to do what party B would not otherwise have done, party A has exercised power. Power takes many forms and appears variously in the histories of Alexander the Great and his time. Alexander enjoyed military power and delegated a portion of it to his general, Antipater. Antipater in turn used the coercive power afforded him by his army in Greece to install friendly governments and forestall concerted action against Macedonia. The politicians and public speakers in the Greek states demonstrated powers of persuasion that, at different times, affected the course of events differently. All this is not in itself particularly interesting — after all, only those with some degree of power become actors in political histories. More interesting is the particular manifestation of power that we call authority.

Authority is a kind of power, but not all power is authoritative. Authority is a matter of speaking; it is a "discursive function." Authority describes the ability to command effectively, for even when we speak of someone "acting" authoritatively, we actually mean "causing others to act by virtue of one's authoritative speech." As such, authority implies an asymmetry in the relationship between speaker and listener. Because authority demands obedience, it is associated with coercive power, and because it operates in discourse, it is associated with persuasive power. Yet these associations are uneasy. The command "Don't move or I'll shoot" is discursive and demands obedience, but while it shows that the speaker is in a position of power, it does not suggest a position of authority. Likewise, a well-argued case may effect its desired result, but argument presupposes a certain equality between speaker and listener.

Authoritative speech relies for its effect on the identity of the speaker, her or his relationship with the audience, and the audience's perception of the speaker. Coercion and persuasion may support this relationship, as the listeners assume either that dire consequences will result from disobedience or that there must be good reasons for obedience, reasons which could be given. But for us to see authority in action, both coercion and persuasion must remain in the background, occulted. If the listener demands a reason for a command or asks about the consequences of disobedience, the speaker's authority falters. At this point authority may give way to persuasion (if the speaker argues in favor of the command) or naked force (if the speaker threatens), or it may be reasserted by invoking the privileged, authoritative position of the speaker: "Because I said so!"

Alexander himself enjoyed many kinds of authority at different times: as acclaimed leader, first among equals, of the Macedonians, as presider over the Treaty of Common Peace in Greece, as Great King in Persia, and as an earthly divinity at first to the Egyptians (who were used to such things) and later to many Greeks. Other Macedonians also held authority, at various times, either by association with Alexander or according to their own abilities and positions.

14. Which one of the following most accurately states the central idea of this passage?

(A) Power and authority are the same thing but are spoken of differently depending on whether the person exercising power is a political leader.

(B) Power is a kind of authority that comes from persuasive speech and the threat of coercive force.

(C) Authority is a kind of power that does not explicitly depend on persuasion or coercion for its effect.

(D) Alexander was unique among ancient kings in exercising power and authority, but his general, Antipater, was also powerful.

(E) Alexander exercised power among the Greeks but relied on authority to govern Macedonians, Persians, and Egyptians.

15. The primary function of the second paragraph of the passage is to

(A) discuss the use of authority by Alexander the Great

(B) explore aspects of the concept of authority and its uneasy association with coercive and discursive power

(C) imply that without coercive power, there is no authority

(D) criticize scholars who have suggested different definitions of authority

(E) suggest that a speaker's authority falters if listeners question it

16. When the author refers to authority as a "discursive function," the author most nearly means that authority

(A) is primarily conveyed through commanding speech

(B) is synonymous with coercive and persuasive power

(C) is mostly conveyed through spoken communication

(D) occurs when the listener questions the reason for a command or the consequences of not following that command

(E) is largely a matter of persuasion and requires strict obedience on the part of the listener

17. According to the passage, what is the difference between power and authority?

(A) Authority is a generic term for creating an effect through persuasion, while power involves coercive force.

(B) Power is a generic term for the ability to make someone do something; authority is a particular form of power, the ability to command without explicit persuasion or coercion.

(C) Authority is exercised by virtue of political office, while power requires military command.

(D) Power exists in the eyes of the governed, while authority resides in the one employing it.

(E) Power is a generic term for the ability to make someone do something; authority is a particular form of power, the ability to command by skillfully applying persuasion and coercion as necessary.

18. With which of the following statements would the author agree regarding what happens when a listener questions a speaker's authority?

(A) The speaker's authority becomes weaker, whereupon that speaker can resort to persuasion or force, or reassert authority by invoking a privileged position.

(B) The speaker's power falters, but that speaker retains authority as long as the conversation continues.

(C) The listener and speaker change roles, with the listener becoming the one with access to authority.

(D) The speaker necessarily has to rely on coercion to assert authority.

(E) Both power and authority vanish from the relationship, which then becomes one of mutual negotiation.

Questions 19–25 refer to the following passage.

In 1897, the explosion of the USS *Maine* in the Havana harbor ignited a war between the United States and Spain over Cuba. The U.S. Navy had just constructed the USS *Oregon,* one of the first true battleships, and believed that this new ship was an important and necessary weapon in the ensuing conflict. But there was one problem — the *Oregon* was stationed in San Francisco, far from Cuba. The voyage around South America, more than 12,000 miles in all, gave the United States 67 days to worry whether its flagship could arrive in time.

The *Oregon* eventually arrived and did play a pivotal role, but military strategists in the United States were left thinking: What would the U.S. Navy have done had it not been able to transport its ship quickly enough? What would happen in future conflicts if a more powerful enemy were to attack, and there were no ships in the area to repulse them? The impossibility of sailing north of North America, and the distance of the voyage around South America, effectively divided the U.S. Naval forces into two fleets. Such a division was costly, inefficient, and ultimately less powerful than a fleet that could unify on demand. If the *Oregon* had been able to somehow pass through the Americas in a narrow point in Central America, the distance between the coasts could be cut by two-thirds.

GO ON TO NEXT PAGE

Two decades later, the questions were answered. The U.S. ships based in California and Hawaii that set out for Europe to transport soldiers to fight in World War I found their trips greatly shortened by a passage through the Isthmus of Panama, which cut nearly a month off the trip from one ocean to the other. Since 1914, the Panama Canal has provided U.S. Naval forces with a guaranteed shortcut that has conferred a great tactical advantage in all inter-ocean conflicts.

In addition to its role in ensuring security, the Panama Canal bears enormous economic significance for the United States and the world market. More than 100 million tons of U.S. cargo passes through the canal every year, comprising 14 percent of American international seaborne trade. Japan, the second heaviest user of the canal, receives most of its grain imports and sends the majority of its automobile exports through the canal. The relative importance of this trade route is even greater for many South American economies; more than 50 percent of Ecuadorian international trade passes through the canal, as does more than 40 percent for Chile and Peru. The canal, by drastically reducing the distance cargo must travel, allows merchants to profit from shipments that would not be economically feasible if sent by another route.

19. Which one of the following most accurately expresses the main point of this passage?

(A) Before the Panama Canal was built, a Navy ship took more than two months to move from California to the Atlantic; after the canal was opened, the same trip took about one month.

(B) During World War I, the U.S. Navy quickly learned to exploit its new passage through the Isthmus of Panama, which made it easy to transport troops from the West Coast and Hawaii to the European theater of war.

(C) The Spanish-American War was the impetus that persuaded the Roosevelt administration to construct the Panama Canal, intended to be a marine shortcut between the Atlantic and Pacific oceans.

(D) The Panama Canal is important to the military, but its real significance is economic, especially for nations in South America.

(E) The Panama Canal, built as a result of military strategists worried about transporting Navy ships from one ocean to another, not only expedited military transport but also made moving cargo between the oceans easier, opening a wealth of economic opportunities.

20. According to the passage, what was the logistical problem that inspired the construction of the Panama Canal?

(A) The U.S. Navy could not realistically build enough ships to man fleets in both the Atlantic and the Pacific oceans.

(B) U.S. merchants on the East Coast couldn't profitably sell their goods to markets on the Pacific because shipping them there was too expensive and time-consuming.

(C) Spain launched an attack on U.S. forces in Cuba by destroying a U.S. ship in the Havana harbor, and the U.S. Navy did not know whether the USS *Oregon* would reach Cuba in time to fight.

(D) Without the canal, the only way to transport boats from the Atlantic to the Pacific was to sail them around the entire continent of South America, which took more than two months.

(E) After the Spanish destroyed the USS *Maine* in 1897, the U.S. Navy had no major ship in the Atlantic to offer a counterattack to the massive Spanish presence near Cuba.

21. What does the author mean by the phrase "effectively divided the U.S. Naval forces into two fleets" in the middle of the second paragraph?

(A) The commanders of the U.S. Navy wanted to keep half their ships in the Pacific and half in the Atlantic to have fleets in both oceans all the time.

(B) The U.S. Navy was unable to use all its ships in the same conflicts because it took far too long to sail ships from the Atlantic to the Pacific and vice versa.

(C) Ships based in the Pacific could not sail around South America in time to play effective roles in conflicts in the Atlantic.

(D) The U.S. Navy had intended the USS *Maine* to be the flagship of its Atlantic fleet, and when it was destroyed in Cuba in 1897, the Navy had great difficulty moving its Pacific battleship, the USS *Oregon*, into the Atlantic.

(E) The U.S. Navy built all its battleships, such as the USS *Oregon*, in California, on the assumption that the Pacific theater would have more need of battleships than the Atlantic theater.

22. What does the author imply may have happened if the USS *Oregon* had not arrived in Cuba in time?

    (A) The Panama Canal may not have been built.

    (B) American ships other than the USS *Maine* could have been destroyed.

    (C) Spain could have won the fight for Cuba.

    (D) San Francisco may have been left without a ship to defend it.

    (E) The U.S. Navy may not have had a chance to test out its new battleship.

23. The passage mentions each one of the following functions of the Panama Canal EXCEPT:

    (A) It has transformed Panama into a major player in world trade.

    (B) Fourteen percent of U.S. seaborne trade passes through the canal.

    (C) Japan imports most of its grain and exports most of its automobiles through the canal.

    (D) The U.S. Navy uses it to transport ships from the Atlantic to the Pacific and vice versa.

    (E) It facilitates a large proportion of the trade of several South American nations.

24. The primary purpose of the second paragraph is to

    (A) analyze the thinking of military strategists who worried about what would have happened had the USS *Oregon* not reached Cuba in time

    (B) explain the role of the USS *Oregon* in the war with Spain over Cuba and the effects of its performance on the thinking of military strategists

    (C) weigh the costs and benefits of travel through the Panama Canal and compare them to those of sailing around South America

    (D) discuss various possible alternatives to the construction of the Panama Canal that the U.S. military strategists considered at the time, such as sailing north of North America

    (E) describe the drawbacks of sending ships around South America and the reasoning that led to the decision to build the Panama Canal

25. Which one of the following is most likely the author's overall purpose in the passage?

    (A) to argue that the U.S. Navy was severely hampered by the geographical necessity of sailing around South America before the building of the Panama Canal, and that the United States was therefore justified in digging a canal through a foreign nation

    (B) to describe the history behind the construction of the Panama Canal and the canal's importance to world trade and the U.S. military

    (C) to present the history of the founding and creation of the Panama Canal as an illustration of American exercise of imperial power in the early 20th century

    (D) to describe the construction of the Panama Canal and the Panama Canal's subsequent role as a facility used by both military and commercial shipping concerns

    (E) to explain why the explosion of the USS *Maine* in 1897 was the precipitating event in the design and construction of the Panama Canal

Section IV

Logical Reasoning

TIME: 35 minutes for 25 questions

DIRECTIONS: Read the passage and choose the best answer. Some questions may have more than one answer that looks right. Select the one that answers the question most completely. Don't assume anything that isn't directly stated, and don't let your imagination run wild; all the information you need is in the arguments and the answer choices.

1. Curmudgeon: Why should I have to pay taxes for public schools? I do not have children who can attend those schools, so I should not have to pay for something that can never benefit me.

   Which one of the following is an assumption required by the curmudgeon's argument?

   (A) In a democracy, it is essential that all citizens have at least a basic education to enable them to choose candidates and vote intelligently.

   (B) People who do not have children attending public schools cannot benefit in any way from the existence of public schools.

   (C) People who do have children in public schools are reaping an undeserved benefit from the tax dollars of other citizens.

   (D) Encouraging people to have children is in the interest of the state because these children form the next generation of citizens.

   (E) Paying for 12 years of education for a child is much cheaper than paying for 12 years of incarceration for a convicted criminal.

2. Magazine article: Scientists have found that people fall asleep faster when they go to bed with warm feet that cool off as they lie still — for instance, warming one's feet with socks before going to bed and then removing them when one lies down to sleep to let the feet cool off again. That means that anyone with insomnia should try wearing socks to bed.

   The reasoning in the magazine article's argument is flawed because the argument

   (A) concludes without justification that the technique of warming feet and then letting them cool is a valid approach to preventing sleeplessness

   (B) implies that the same advice will work for all sufferers of insomnia, regardless of the cause

   (C) assumes that the research on how foot temperature affects sleep is accurate because it came from scientists, without further investigation into the source of the information

   (D) misinterprets the results of the research by failing to note that the sleep technique suggested by scientists requires the sleeper to remove the socks before trying to sleep

   (E) criticizes those suffering from insomnia for not taking well-known steps to solve their problem

3. Everyone knows that mothers love their babies more than anything else in the world, and mothers are the ones who should raise their children. No one can do the job of raising a child as well as that child's mother, so all mothers should stay home to care for their young children.

The reasoning in this argument is most vulnerable to criticism on the grounds that the argument

(A) discounts evidence indicating that not all mothers love their babies wholeheartedly

(B) fails to consider that many children thrive in day care

(C) belittles the fact that many women have to work to help support their families

(D) presupposes the truth of the conclusion it is attempting to establish

(E) suggests that fathers, grandparents, and other close relatives are inadequate caretakers

4. Researchers in Germany have discovered that dogs can understand human language quite well and that all are capable of comprehending a vocabulary no smaller than that understood by members of other intelligent animal species, such as chimpanzees, dolphins, and parrots. Many dogs, such as the border collie named Rico, can understand more than 200 words and are capable of learning new ones.

If all these statements are true, which one of the following must also be true?

(A) Many dog owners spell words that their dogs recognize, such as bath, instead of saying them out loud because they know their dogs will understand the words and overreact.

(B) Dogs can learn words only if their human trainers consistently use the same words for the same objects.

(C) Some chimpanzees are capable of understanding more than 200 words.

(D) Dogs in Germany understand more human words than dogs in other countries.

(E) A vocabulary training method effective with chimpanzees would also be effective with dogs.

5. The recipe says to bake this pie for 40 minutes at 250 degrees. I can bake it in half the time if I double the temperature, so I am going to bake it for 20 minutes at 500 degrees.

Which one of the following is most closely parallel in its flawed reasoning to the flawed reasoning in this argument?

(A) The label on the aspirin bottle says to take one aspirin every four hours. My headache is very bad, so I will take two aspirin every four hours.

(B) The directions on the bag of cat food say to give a 9-pound cat 1 cup of food every day. My cat weighs 13 pounds, so I will give her 1.5 cups of food every day.

(C) My neighbor wants me to give her plant a gallon of water every day. I will not have to water it as often if I give it more water each time, so I am going to give it 2 gallons of water every other day.

(D) The hair-highlighting kit says to leave the bleach on my hair for 20 minutes and then wash it out. I want my hair to be very blond, so I am going to leave the bleach on my hair for 40 minutes.

(E) The express train goes twice as fast as the local train but costs twice as much. I want to reach my destination quickly, so I will pay twice the price of the local train to ride the express.

6. Businessman: It makes absolutely no sense for businesses to engage in charitable giving or socially conscious activities. The whole purpose of a business is to maximize profits for its owners or shareholders.

The reasoning in this argument is most vulnerable to criticism because the argument fails to consider the possibility that

(A) the IRS allows businesses to deduct some of the money they spend on charitable contributions

(B) the goodwill and publicity generated by charitable giving can increase a business's sales significantly

(C) not every business owner believes that the single and entire purpose of the business is maximizing profits for owners and shareholders

(D) an increasing number of investors seek out socially conscious mutual funds

(E) some businesses that spend a good portion of their profits on charity still make a large profit overall

7. Nutritionist: The United States is currently facing an epidemic of obesity. Average weights have increased in all populations and at all ages. This is almost certainly due to the pervasiveness of fast food, which every citizen is consuming in larger quantities than two decades ago.

Which one of the following, if true, would most call into question the nutritionist's explanation of the obesity epidemic?

(A) Though average weights have increased, the weight gain has occurred exclusively among people who were already overweight; thin people have not gained weight, despite the fact that they, too, are consuming more fast food than was the case two decades ago.

(B) The increase in average weights has reached down into populations of children, resulting in incidences of type 2 diabetes, which formerly was considered an exclusively adult disease, occurring in people under the age of 14.

(C) Some nutritionists believe that some of the weight gain among Americans is due to the substitution of high-fructose corn syrup for sugar in the soft drinks served at fast food restaurants.

(D) Many school districts have ended physical education programs in recent years, citing lack of funding and the need to spend most school time on academic subjects rather than sports and exercise.

(E) At the same time the overall population has grown heavier, the ideal of beauty has grown thinner, with near-anorexic young women setting an impossible standard of attractiveness.

8. All human beings are primates. All primates are mammals. All mammals are vertebrates. Therefore, all human beings are both mammals and vertebrates.

Which one of the following arguments is most similar in its pattern of reasoning to this argument?

(A) All dogs are canines. All canines are mammals. All canines are vertebrates. Therefore, all dogs are both mammals and vertebrates.

(B) All flies are insects. All insects are arthropods. All arthropods are invertebrates. Therefore, all flies are both arthropods and invertebrates.

(C) All whales are cetaceans. All cetaceans are mammals. All mammals have mammary glands. Therefore, all whales have mammary glands.

(D) All snails are mollusks. All mollusks have shells. All oysters are bivalves. All bivalves have shells. Therefore, all creatures with shells are bivalves and mollusks.

(E) All gorillas are primates. All chimpanzees are primates. All primates are vertebrates. Therefore, all gorillas and chimpanzees are vertebrates.

9. Sergeant: Ordinarily, all soldiers must obey every order from their superiors. There is an exception, though; when a superior orders a soldier to commit an act that is against the law, then it is permissible for the soldier to refuse to carry out the order.

Which one of the following judgments conforms most closely to the principle stated by the sergeant?

(A) It is permissible for a soldier to refuse to obey an order to torture and abuse prisoners of war because that would violate national and international law.

(B) It is permissible for a solder to refuse to obey an order to fire on the enemy because the soldier believes that killing other humans is immoral.

(C) It is permissible for a soldier to refuse to obey an order stationing him in another country because he does not believe that the military should be in that country.

(D) It is permissible for a soldier to refuse to obey an order to imprison an enemy soldier because the soldier believes that such imprisonment should be against the law.

(E) It is permissible for a soldier to refuse to obey an order to bomb a town because the soldier knows that civilians would be among the casualties.

10. Legal theorist: It is impossible for the states to regulate obscenity without violating the constitutional guarantee of free speech. U.S. courts have struggled since the 1950s to define obscenity and have for the most part failed to come up with a consistent definition that works reliably. In 1964, Justice Stewart summed up the difficulty of this problem by declining to suggest a definition but stating that, for his part, "I know it when I see it." Clearly, coming up with a suitable definition of obscenity that does not encroach upon non-obscene speech is unachievable.

What is the main point of the legal theorist's argument?

(A) Because defining obscenity at the federal level is impossible, the states should create their own standards of decency tailored to local community preferences.

(B) It is impossible to pass laws prohibiting obscenity without violating the free speech rights of those producing the material.

(C) The difficulty of defining obscenity is proof of the fact that courts and legislatures shouldn't be involved in regulating speech of any kind.

(D) It will be impossible to formulate a legally suitable definition of obscenity.

(E) The problem of defining obscenity was most succinctly stated by Justice Stewart in a 1964 decision.

11. No employer wants to face the liability it would incur if a drug-using employee made a serious mistake on the job. The best way to avoid this situation is to require all employees to have their urine tested before hiring and then to perform urine tests on all employees at random times. These urine tests help employers determine which of their employees are regular users of serious drugs such as cocaine, methamphetamines, and heroin.

Each of the following, if true, would cast doubt on the author's reasoning EXCEPT:

(A) Testing a strand of hair is a much more reliable method of identifying those who use serious drugs regularly; residue of illicit drugs remains in hair for three months.

(B) Urine tests cannot spot cocaine, heroin, or methamphetamines that were taken more than one or two days previously, so weekend drug users can avoid detection fairly easily.

(C) Random drug testing costs the American workplace many millions every year and only catches a small percentage of those who have consumed drugs.

(D) Most consumers want to feel sure that the employees of businesses they patronize are not abusing serious drugs on the job.

(E) Employees can easily cheat on urine tests by purchasing urine from businesses that sell it specifically to help people pass workplace drug tests.

12. Albert, a careful shopper, bought a pair of shoes from a well-known catalog, choosing the catalog based on its guarantee. This guarantee states that the seller will take back any item of merchandise and provide the buyer with either a replacement item or a full refund at any time and for any reason. Over the next 20 years, Albert acquired seven pairs of shoes from the catalog by returning the shoes whenever they wore out and requesting a replacement pair. He never paid for a pair of shoes other than the original pair. When his wife criticized him for taking advantage of the catalog company, he replied that he had done nothing wrong.

Which one of the following principles, if established, most helps to justify Albert's position?

(A) A buyer and a seller enter into an unwritten contract when the seller offers an item for sale and the buyer agrees to purchase it for the seller's stated price.

(B) A customer should not take unfair advantage of a catalog's goodwill gesture and should understand that an unconditional guarantee is not meant to be identical to a lifetime guarantee.

(C) A seller should not make promises that it does not intend to keep because there will always be customers who try to get the maximum value of every dollar by abusing sellers if necessary.

GO ON TO NEXT PAGE

(D) It is the seller's responsibility to set prices for its merchandise that are sufficient to cover its expenses and generate a profit.

(E) A seller is obligated to observe the terms of the contract of sale, even if doing so works to the seller's own disadvantage.

13. Abelard: The city should provide more money for public schools. More money would allow the schools to hire more teachers and reduce class sizes from 30 to 25 children, which would result in a better education for all students.

    Heloise: I don't believe hiring more teachers and reducing class sizes will benefit students. Good teachers should be able to teach as many students as they are given. A class of 30 students isn't too large for a good teacher to handle.

    Which one of the following, if true, most undermines Heloise's objection to Abelard's analysis?

    (A) Schools in Japan typically have between 40 and 45 students per classroom, and the Japanese educational system is widely believed to be excellent.

    (B) A school district in another state reduced class sizes from 30 to 25 students; within a year, average test scores had increased by 25 percent.

    (C) Teachers like smaller classes better than larger ones because smaller classes are easier to manage.

    (D) Many taxpayers want to spend as little as possible on public schools.

    (E) Private schools often limit classes to 18 or fewer students.

14. In 2003, luggage belonging to 2.2 million passengers failed to arrive at the destination at the same time as the passenger. Travelers should never check their bags when they fly on commercial airlines.

    Which one of the following, if true, most weakens this argument?

    (A) Airlines advise passengers to pack a small carry-on bag containing essential medicines, eyeglasses or contact lenses, toiletries, and a change of clothes.

    (B) When a traveler loses her luggage, she must sometimes hastily buy clothes for business meetings, resulting in great expense.

    (C) Buying new clothes to replace those that were packed in lost luggage is not always possible; for example, passengers who arrive at their destination during a national holiday may have to wait a day or two for shops to open.

    (D) Many holiday travelers plan to shop at their destinations anyway, and losing luggage is a good excuse to buy new clothes.

    (E) Despite the large number of lost bags, airlines only lose the bags of 4 out of every 1,000 passengers, so the odds of arriving without checked luggage are very low.

15. LASIK, or Laser-Assisted in Situ Keratomileusis, is a surgical procedure used to correct vision problems such as nearsightedness. In the procedure, a surgeon cuts a flap from the surface of the patient's cornea, uses a laser to reshape the middle portion of the cornea, and then replaces the flap. In most cases, LASIK can correct a patient's vision to near 20/20, eliminating the need for corrective lenses. Patients should be warned, though, that no doctor can guarantee a good result, and they do run the risk of side effects, including loss of vision, severe dry eyes, glare or halos that impair night vision, and loss of depth perception.

    Which one of the following is most strongly supported by this information?

    (A) Some patients who undergo LASIK find that they can no longer drive a car at night.

    (B) A prospective LASIK patient must find a surgeon who is experienced in using the LASIK machinery.

    (C) Patients who need reading glasses before undergoing LASIK often still need them after the procedure.

    (D) Even if a patient achieves 20/20 vision after LASIK, his eyesight can still change with age, resulting in imperfect vision once again.

    (E) LASIK is usually successful at improving a patient's vision, but it does not always result in perfect uncorrected eyesight and can create new problems for the patient.

16. Brightly lit high-rise buildings kill approximately 1 billion birds every year. The birds, flying on their migratory paths, become captivated by the lights in the building and fly toward them; they then either crash into the glass, which is invisible to them when interior lights are on, or they fly around and around the source of light until they are exhausted and tumble to the ground. On some mornings, janitors of high-rise buildings must shovel piles of dead birds from the sidewalk. A simple solution is very effective at combating this problem: If a building's residents simply turn off all interior lights at night, no birds will be attracted to the building.

If all these statements are true, then which one of the following must be false?

(A) Turning on the lights inside a building makes it easier for birds to see the glass windows and avoid flying into them.

(B) Many tenants of high-rise office buildings habitually leave their interior lights and signs lit up all night.

(C) In Chicago, two years after most tenants of high-rises agreed to turn off their lights at night, bird mortality fell by 80 percent.

(D) Rare species such as Kirtland's warbler are vulnerable to running into lighted buildings, which will speed up the eventual extinction of the species.

(E) Birds running into buildings is only a problem during the birds' migrations between their northern and southern territories, just a few weeks out of the year.

17. Americans blame the outsourcing of jobs to foreign countries for high unemployment today, complaining that companies are taking jobs from U.S. citizens and sending them to other nations, where labor is less expensive. Statistics issued by the U.S. Department of Labor, however, indicate that only 9 percent of layoffs are due to outsourcing, and of that 9 percent, nearly three-quarters of the jobs are moved to other locations within the United States, not to foreign nations.

These statements, if true, most strongly support which one of the following?

(A) Americans who are laid off from their jobs are right to blame the government for encouraging businesses to look abroad for cheaper labor.

(B) American workers should not worry about losing their jobs to outsourcing.

(C) Outsourcing of jobs to foreign nations is an inevitable consequence of globalization, as are layoffs of American workers who do jobs that can be performed much more cheaply in other countries.

(D) Outsourcing to foreign countries is not nearly as important a cause of layoffs as many Americans mistakenly believe.

(E) Outsourcing of jobs to other locations within the United States does not disrupt the national economy but does benefit one local economy at the expense of another.

18. In many nations throughout the world, child labor is still prevalent. In some countries, more than half of the children under 14 work full time, often in dangerous conditions. This causes a cycle of poverty that is detrimental to the economic development of the countries; child labor is the result of poverty, but it also causes poverty to continue.

Which one of the following, if true, contributes most to this explanation of the cycle of poverty?

(A) Without a social safety net, poverty-stricken families have no alternative but to send their children to work in menial jobs.

(B) Many developing nations do not have enough schools to educate all the children born there, so parents choose to send their children to work instead.

(C) Girls who are forced to work as children tend to grow up with health problems that affect the health and prosperity of their own children.

(D) Children who work cannot go to school, and without an education, they cannot get high-paying jobs as adults, so their own children are forced to work instead of attending school.

(E) In some developing nations, the middle and upper class depend on a plentiful supply of cheap servants, usually in the form of young girls from poor families.

19. California has passed a law that will require car manufacturers to drastically reduce the fossil-fuel emissions from automobiles in the next five years. These requirements are far stricter than those imposed by the federal government. Seven other states on both coasts have also passed laws ordering reduced emissions, and several others have announced plans to follow suit. Environmentalists praise the new law, asserting that these states' efforts will slow global warming.

Which one of the following is an assumption required by the environmentalists in making their assertion?

(A) States on the coasts are more likely to be interested in environmental issues.

(B) Reducing fossil-fuel emissions will slow global warming.

(C) Car manufacturers could have reduced emissions long ago but did not because the law did not force them to.

(D) Individual states have environmental priorities that are different from those of the federal government.

(E) Environmentalists have lobbied car manufacturers to reduce emissions.

20. Philip: Hybrid cars are the best response to the impending energy crisis. They are powered by a combination of gasoline and electric power; the gasoline engine recharges the battery when it runs, resulting in an extremely efficient use of fuel. They get excellent mileage, have good power, and are very comfortable.

Ryan: Instead of developing hybrid cars, car manufacturers should have kept making small, light, fuel-efficient, gasoline-powered cars. Fuel-efficient cars from the 1970s got better gas mileage than today's hybrids and did not come with the added burden of a complex battery that will inevitably become a problem when it comes time to dispose of it.

Ryan responds to Philip by

(A) denying the severity of the problem Philip addresses

(B) using an analogy to reveal a situation that Philip has not considered

(C) challenging the validity of the information Philip provides in support of his solution

(D) arguing that an alternate solution would have better dealt with the problem Philip addresses

(E) providing a counterexample that calls Philip's reasoning into question

21. Legislator: Our state is deeply interested in maintaining the integrity of families. We believe families are the building blocks of our state, and we want to do everything we can to support them. To help families stay intact, we have designed a brochure that will be distributed to all new mothers and to girls and young women who seek birth control at publicly funded clinics. This brochure emphasizes the importance of the family and informs women that they should finish school, find a job, and get married before having children.

The legislator's reasoning is most vulnerable to criticism because it fails to recognize that

(A) many women do not want to be married

(B) that pamphlets may not be the best way to disseminate information

(C) the main problem facing single mothers is lack of financial support from the fathers of their children

(D) families may not consist of only females

(E) girls who are seeking birth control at publicly funded clinics are not the teenagers most likely to get pregnant

22. Stuart and Steve each drove from Yokohama to Tokyo, leaving at the same time. Stuart drove his car. Steve drove a small motor scooter that could not go more than 25 kph. They both drove the same route, which had a speed limit for cars of 60 kph. Yet, they both arrived at their destination at the same time.

Which one of the following, if true, most helps to explain why Stuart and Steve arrived in Tokyo at the same time?

(A) Steve did not drive faster than 25 kph, but he did sometimes drive on the shoulder to pass stopped cars.

(B) The traffic between Tokyo and Yokohama was so bad that Stuart could not go faster than 25 kph.

(C) Stuart drove the speed limit when he could.

(D) Stuart and Steve relied on the same navigational aids.

(E) Stuart had to stop at 74 red lights, and Steve had to stop at 68 red lights.

23. Judge: The defendant has admitted that he is prone to road rage, which is why he attacked the driver at the red light. In addition to a fine and community service, I am going to sentence the defendant to yoga classes, which will help him bring his anger under control.

Which one of the following is an assumption on which the judge's reasoning depends?

(A) Practitioners of yoga never attack fellow drivers.

(B) Fines and community service are not sufficient penalty for road rage.

(C) Uncontrolled anger is a cause of road rage.

(D) A punishment should be modeled on the crime.

(E) The defendant's road rage was justified but still inexcusable.

24. At least 29 million people used online matchmaking and dating services last year, and that number is expected to increase in the near future, but prospective users of such services should be careful. Far more men than women visit dating sites, which makes it easy for women to find partners but much harder for men. Users can easily lie and claim to be single when in fact they are not. The sites can't guarantee that no sexual predators will try to use the service. And because users must rely on the honesty of fellow participants in describing themselves, some hopeful daters receive unpleasant shocks when meeting their correspondents for the first time.

Which one of the following most accurately expresses the main conclusion of this argument?

(A) Women who use online dating services face much better odds than men of finding a partner.

(B) Online dating can be very dangerous because the dating services cannot effectively bar sexual predators from participating.

(C) Despite the popularity of online dating services, participants should realize that such services come with many potential pitfalls.

(D) Online dating services should insist that no one who is married or otherwise attached to a partner participate in their programs.

(E) In the next five years, millions of people will seek out online matchmaking services, type in their personal data, send in photographs of themselves, and peruse the vital statistics of other people using the same service.

GO ON TO NEXT PAGE

25. Art critic: Formalism is an interpretive method that emphasizes the form of an artwork as opposed to its content. Formalist criticism excludes external considerations such as symbolism, history, politics, economics, or authorship, focusing instead on the forms structuring a work of art. Beginning in the 1970s, formalism was often allied to structuralist modes of thinking that sought to understand the workings of an artwork based on its internal properties. The postmodern reaction against formalism in the 1980s largely condemned it on the basis of its disinterest in worldly affairs.

Which one of the following principles, if valid, most helps to justify the postmodern reaction to formalism?

(A) Everything necessary to comprehend a work of art is contained within that work of art.

(B) Art appreciation depends on the personal taste of the observer.

(C) A viewer's pleasure in a work of art emanates from the work of art itself rather than its subject matter.

(D) An artwork's meaning is dependent on contingent features of the artist's psyche and society rather than on any inherent quality of the work itself.

(E) Any attempt to deconstruct and subsequently explain an abstract work of art essentially strips it of its intrinsic value.

Writing Sample

Two sisters are planning a horseback-riding vacation in August between one sister's taking the MCAT and beginning the fall semester, which gives them two weeks to work with. They must choose between two trips, one in Ireland and one in the Dominican Republic. Write an essay in favor of choosing one destination over the other based on the following considerations:

>> The sisters want to spend as many days as possible riding horses.

>> The sisters want to improve their riding skills through instruction by qualified teachers.

The riding vacation in Ireland would place the sisters on fine, well-trained horses in the hands of excellent riding instructors. Every morning the sisters would spend two hours in the ring, working on equitation skills and jumping, and then every afternoon they would go for a trail ride through the countryside. They could expect their riding skills to improve a great deal, although they would not have much free time to simply ride around on their horses. Due to price constraints and the pre-med sister's schedule, if the sisters go to Ireland they will be able to spend only one week there.

If the sisters choose the vacation in the Dominican Republic, the favorable exchange rate and cheaper air fares would allow them to stay for two weeks. They would ride horses every day with an experienced guide, who would take them on trails in the mountains, through sugar cane fields, and on the beach. They would also be allowed to ride freely as much as they wanted. The guide in the Dominican Republic is not a qualified equitation teacher, and he would not instruct the sisters on riding technique beyond the basics of handling the horses safely.

Chapter 16

Practice Exam 1: Answers and Explanations

In this chapter, you find the answers and explanations to the test in Chapter 15. This chapter doesn't contain sample answers for the writing sample, mainly because there would be no point; you need to practice writing for yourself, and we don't want you to mistakenly think there's some "perfect" essay. Besides, it's not scored, anyway.

Take your time with these helpful explanations, but also know that you can find an abbreviated key at the end of this chapter if you need to score your test quickly. This chapter also includes information about computing your score.

Section I: Analytical Reasoning

<u>Questions 1–7</u>

As part of your pre-question preparation, set up your game board. Start by assigning your game pieces, designated by the abbreviation of all the guys' names to single letters (B, C, D, M, and T). If you'd like, create a board that lists potential volleyball games with room for two players each. The conditions don't specify the total number of games, so start with space for five, which you may have to modify as you read through the rules. The rules state that if B plays with M, B can't play with C. Record this rule and its contrapositive: that if B plays with C, B can't play with M. The next rule states that any person who plays with D once must play with M once. Designate "any person" with an X. Remember the contrapositive: that any person who doesn't play with M also doesn't play with D. Record these conditions along with the rules that T plays only once and D and M never play together.

Now, what can you deduce? It looks as though T could play with B, C, or M. But if T can play only one game, he never plays with D because that requires T to play another game with M. You can add this rule to your list.

Lo and behold, you've come up with a decent diagram that looks a little something like this:

B C D M T

1		2		3		4		5	

If BM → no BC

If BC → no BM

If XD → XM

If no XM → no XD

T = 1

No DM

No DT

You can continue to consider possible team combinations, such as T can only pair with B, C, or M, but it may be more efficient to save further combination considerations for when you answer each related question.

1. **C. Biff and Chas; Chas and Deke; Chas and Marc; Marc and Trip**

The first question in the set almost always asks for a complete and accurate list. These are the only questions for which you don't need to refer to a game board. Just look through the options for rule violations and eliminate wrong answers. Focus first on the easiest conditions. Based on the third rule, eliminate answers that have Trip playing more than once. Choice (D) is out. Next, based on the first rule, look for any answers that have Biff playing with both Marc and Chas; that knocks out Choice (A). Now, looking at the fourth rule, does an answer have Deke and Marc playing together? Yes, Choice (B) does, so cross it off. Last, looking at the second rule, does a choice have someone playing with Deke but not with Marc? Yep. Choice (E) has Trip playing with Deke but not with Marc (which, if it happened, would violate rule three). That leaves Choice (C); run through the answer to make sure it works. It has Biff playing with Chas but not with Marc, so that's fine. Trip plays once, with an allowable partner. Chas plays with both Deke and Marc. It all checks out, so Choice (C) is correct.

2. **C. five**

The multiplication principle tells you that, at most, only ten teams of two can be made up out of five players. The possibilities are BC, BD, BM, BT, CD, CM, CT, DM, DT, and MT.

The first condition states that you can't have both BC and BM, so you're left with nine possible teams.

From the fourth condition, you know DM isn't possible, so there are at most eight possible teams.

The third condition states that T plays on only one team, so you're down to a maximum of five possible teams: (BC or BM), BD, CD, CM, and (BT, CT, DT, or MT). You've deduced that DT isn't possible, which doesn't change the maximum possible team but eliminates DT from the mix. The second condition requires any player who teams up with D also play with M. You can satisfy this condition and maintain a maximum of five teams. To keep BD, you need to add BM by knocking out BC. That gives you at most these possible five combinations: BD, CD, CM, BM, and (BT, CT, or MT).

So the answer is Choice (C).

3. C. Biff and Trip play a game together, and neither Biff nor Trip plays with anyone else.

This question gives you no additional information to work with, so you need to assess each answer choice. Starting with Choice (A), if Biff and Chas play together and no one else, Deke can't play because your game board setup reveals that Deke can't play with Marc or Trip. Choice (A) can't be true. If Biff plays with Marc, then Chas could play with Trip, but that would once again leave no one to team with Deke. According to the second condition, Chas can't play with Deke without also playing with Marc, but the answer choice states that Marc plays with only Biff. Choice (B) is wrong. If Biff and Trip play together, as designated by Choice (C), Chas could play with Deke and Marc. That gives everyone at least one game and violates no rules. So Choice (C) could be true and is likely the correct answer. Check the last two options, though, just to make sure you haven't missed something. If Chas and Marc play together, you once again run up against the Deke rule. Because no one can play with Deke without also playing with Marc, Choice (D) is impossible. If Marc and Trip play together, that causes the same problem — anyone who plays with Deke must also play a game with Marc, so Choice (E) is wrong. Choice (C) is the correct answer.

4. B. Chas and Deke

This question offers another condition, that three players team up with Biff. Refer to your game board and note that B can't team up with both M and C, so the possible three teams created with B can be (BM or BC), BT, and BD. But whoever teams with D must team with M, so B must play with M, T, and D. That eliminates Choice (A). C can't play with B, but he must play. You can't pair him (or anyone else) with T, so Choices (C), (D), and (E) are out. The answer must be Choice (B), which is perfectly acceptable when you consider that the possible team combinations could be BM, BT, BD, CM, and CD.

5. C. Chas and Deke

Consider which player can pair up with all the others. You know it's not Trip; he plays only once. And it can't be Deke because he can't pair with Trip or Marc, which means it also can't be Marc. Biff can't pair with Chas and Marc, so it can't be Biff. That leaves Chas. When you pair Chas with all four players, you get CB, CD, CM, and CT. Eliminate answers that could be true or must be false. The only pair that must be teamed is Chas and Deke, Choice (C).

6. E. Deke and Trip

Remember that Trip can play only one game, and anyone who plays with Deke is committed to playing a game with Marc, too. So Trip can never play a game with Deke. The answer is Choice (E).

7. D. Marc plays exactly two games.

This question provides an additional rule, that Marc is the only player to team with Biff. Neither Marc nor Trip can pair with Deke, so Chas must play with Deke, and if Chas teams up with Deke, he must also play with Marc. Marc must play with both Chas and Biff, and Chas must play with both Marc and Deke. Either Chas or Marc could play with Trip. The teams that must result from the additional rule appear on the game board:

B C D M T

	1		2		3		4		5	
	B	M	C	D	C	M	T	C/M		

If BM no BC

If BC ⟶ no BM

If XD ⟶ XM

If no XM ⟶ no XD

T = 1

No DM

No DT

Chas and Marc must play more than one game, so Choices (A) and (B) are out. Deke can play only once, so Choice (C) isn't possible. Chas plays no more than three games, which make Choice (E) impossible. The only possible scenario is Choice (D).

Questions 8–12

Before answering the questions, take some time to set up your game board. The game pieces are 2P, 2G, and 2M for ponies, geldings, and mares. Write the six possible horses on the game board. Create six columns, numbered 1 to 6, to mark the positions of the horses as they walk in line. Write in what you know about their placement, marking the positions that must or must not contain particular horses.

Take a moment to consider additional rules. If the third horse can't be a pony, then it must be a gelding or a mare. If the sixth horse can't be a mare, it must be a gelding or a pony. Note these conditions on your chart. Now remember that the wrangler can't put two horses of the same type next to each other. So the first and second horses can't both be geldings, and positions 3 to 6 must contain one gelding. This rule affects all your computations; keep track of the restrictions on your diagram.

P P G G M M

	1	2	3	4	5	6
	G if no G in 2	G if no G in 1	̶P̶			̶M̶

G = 1 or 2

No GG, PP, MM

That's your permanent diagram. Be sure you give yourself a little room to jot down possibilities. You may be able to come up with a few other conditions, but moving on to the questions as quickly as you can is important. Before you do, note that having a gelding in the second position provides more restrictions than a gelding in the first position.

8. **E. The fifth horse is a pony.**

The question offers no additional rule, so you need to consider the possibilities set forth by each answer choice. The answer *cannot* be true, so eliminate choices that could or must be true. Write the possible orderings you come up with next to each answer choice; you may refer to them again. Try Choice (A). If the first horse is a pony, then the second one must be a gelding, and the third must be a mare; if the sixth horse is a gelding, then the fourth can be a pony and the fifth a mare: PGMPMG. That works. Now Choice (B). You can do that one: MGMPGP. You know Choice (C) works because the second horse is a gelding in the ordering you came up with in Choices (A) and (B). The same holds for Choice (D). The orderings you came up with for Choices (A) and (B) place a mare in the third position. That leaves Choice (E). It's likely correct, but try it out anyway just in case you've missed something. If the fifth horse is a pony, the last one must be a gelding because it can't be a mare. The fourth horse must be a mare because it's next to a pony, and you need your other gelding for one of the first two slots. Then you run into a problem: The third horse can't be a pony. It can't be a mare because that puts a mare next to another mare, and it can't be a gelding because the other gelding has to go in one of the first two spots. The game board with the lineups for each answer looks like this:

P P G G M M

	1	2	3	4	5	6
	G if no G in 2	G if no G in 1	~~P~~ G or M			~~M~~ P or G
A/C/D	P	G	M	G	M	P
B/C/D	M	G	M	P	G	P
E				M	P	G

G = 1 or 2

No GG, PP, MM

If G in 1, no G in 2 - G = 3, 4, 5, or 6

If G in 2, no G in 1 or 3 - G = 4, 5, or 6

Putting the pony in the fifth spot results in an impossible lineup, so Choice (E) is your answer.

9. **D. The fifth horse is a mare.**

Consider the new rule this question provides. If the third and fifth horses are the same type, what can't they be? They can't be ponies because the third horse can't be a pony. They can't be geldings because you have only one gelding to use in the last four spots. So they must be mares. Take a look at the answers. The correct choice for this "must be true" question has to be Choice (D). The other answers all could be true, but they don't have to be; work them out if you want.

10. **A. The first horse is a gelding.**

This question is easy, or it should be if your diagram looks right and you understand the rules. If the third horse is a gelding, then what happens to the lineup? You know the first must be a gelding because you can't place a gelding in the second position next to the other gelding, and you have to have a gelding in position 1 or 2. The correct answer has to be Choice (A). You can test the other answers if you want, but Choice (A) is the only one that must be true.

11. **E. the third and last horses**

You could plug the same horse into all those pairs and see what you get, but there's a faster way to work this one. Look at your diagram. You know the third horse can't be a pony, and you know the sixth horse can't be a mare. You also know they both can't be geldings because you need one gelding to occupy the first or second position. So the third and sixth horses can't be the same type. That's Choice (E).

If you want to test the possibilities, try this: Make both members of the pair designations in each answer choice the *same* kind of horse and see whether that works out. First Choice (A): You know from your answer to Question 10 that both the first and third horses can be geldings, so that's wrong. Try Choice (B). If you make the first and fourth horses geldings, you could have this perfectly legal lineup: GPMGMP. Now take a look at Choice (C). If you make both the second and fourth horses ponies, you get GPMPMG. That's fine. (You can also make them both geldings, but that would be overkill.) Try Choice (D). You could have MPGMPG, which is fine. Choice (E) has to be the right answer.

12. **D. fourth, sixth**

Don't you hate it when the rules change? Just think of the poor wrangler! Anyway, here's how to work this one. To accommodate three ponies and still keep each separated from the other (pony rivalry?), you have to put one in the middle, in position 3 or 4, but you can't put a pony third, so you have to put a pony fourth. Cross out Choice (A) because it doesn't list the fourth position. The two remaining ponies have to be at least one position away from fourth. Only one position to the right of fourth fulfills that requirement: the sixth. Eliminate Choices (B) and (C) because they don't include the sixth position. From the remaining Choices (D) and (E), you know that you need to evaluate just the second position. The third pony can be first or second as long as a gelding takes the other spot.

1	2	3	4	5	6
G if no G in 2	G if no G in 1	~~P~~ G or M			~~M~~ P or G
P/G	P/G	G/M	P	G/M	P

So the spots that must be occupied by ponies are the fourth and the sixth positions, Choice (D).

Questions 13–19

Creating the right diagram takes you far with seemingly complicated grouping problems like this one. In this case, you have seven players to place in one of three locations. Start with what you know. First, list the game pieces: B, C, M, R, S, Y, and Z. Your places are f, l, and o. (*Tip:* Make the places lowercase so you don't mix them up with people.) Then set up a quick chart of the three tournament locations and shortcuts for each of the rules.

You can start making some conclusions at this point. If twice as many people go to Fargo as go to Omaha, then there are two possibilities: Either one person goes to Omaha and two to Fargo, leaving four to go to Little Rock; or two people go to Omaha, four go to Fargo, and one goes to Little Rock. That's useful. Write that down in a little template, adding the useful permanent information about C always going to Fargo and Y never going to Fargo:

B C M R S Y Z

f	o	l
2 × o ~~Y~~ C	½ × f	

BR

No SY

No MZ

After you have this framework in place, plugging in possibilities is simple. You can make a few deductions just by looking at your game board. For example, if B and R must attend the same tournament, then their possible locations are quite limited. They can fit only into locations with at least two open slots, and even then you have to allow space for the people that have to be separated. So realistically, B and R can either attend the conference in Little Rock when it has four slots (it's the only one with two open spots in that first possibility) or the conference in Fargo when it has four slots. That's good to know. What about the two slots allocated to Omaha in the second scenario? B and R can't have them; you have two pairs of members that have to be split up — S and Y, and M and Z — and Little Rock has only one slot open, so you need an Omaha slot for one of those pairs. Update the game board with this info:

B C M R S Y Z

Option 1				Option 2		
f	o	1		f	o	1
̶Y̶				̶Y̶		
C		B	R	B R C		

No SY
No MZ

Now *that* is a diagram! And instead of an unlimited number of scenarios, you now have two discrete possibilities, each of which is nearly half complete.

13. **B. Maev attends the tournament in Fargo.**

Consider the new temporary rule provided by this question. How can Brunhild and Yorick attend the same tournament? According to your game board, they can attend together only if they both go to the tournament in Little Rock in the first option. That leaves one slot open in each of the cities to be occupied by Maev, Solomon, and Zilla. Now go through the answer choices and eliminate the one that must be false. Choice (A) is wrong because Brunhild must be in Little Rock. Choice (B) could be true; Maev could take the open slot in Fargo, leaving space for Zilla in Little Rock:

f	o	1			
̶Y̶					
C	M	S	B	R	Y	Z

Choice (C) is wrong because Roxanne is with Brunhild in Little Rock. Choice (D) is wrong because Solomon can't attend the same tournament as Yorick, and Yorick must be in Little Rock. Choice (E) is wrong because Yorick must be in Little Rock. That leaves Choice (B) as the only possible answer.

14. **B. Solomon is the only team member who attends the tournament in Omaha.**

You can eliminate several answers just by looking at your original game board. Choice (A) can't be true because Roxanne can't attend a tournament without Brunhild. Choice (C) is wrong because either two or four people must go to Fargo. Choices (D) and (E) are wrong because there's no way that either two people can go to Little Rock or three to Fargo. So could Choice (B) work? Yes, it's possible for the team to send only one member to Omaha, and there's no reason it can't be S. Choice (B) is correct.

15. A. Brunhild attends the tournament in Fargo.

This question tells you to use the second option on your original game board. When you know which option to use, you don't have to do much to figure out the answer. If one member goes to Little Rock, then four go to Fargo and two to Omaha. Who has to go to Fargo in that scenario? Cayenne, Brunhild, and Roxanne. Choice (A) looks like your answer. Skim the other choices anyway — they're all possible, but none of them is required by the rules. Choice (A) is correct.

16. A. Brunhild and Roxanne

Rephrase this exception question so that you remember to choose the answer with the members who *can't* go to Omaha. Choice (A) includes Brunhild, whose only options are Little Rock and Fargo and thus can never sample the delights of Nebraska's largest city. Look over the other choices to make sure no one else is prohibited from attending the Omaha tournament. They all look fine, and they're all pairs, which is certainly possible. (If any choice had three members, that would have been a dead giveaway right answer.) So Choice (A) is correct.

17. C. Brunhild, Solomon, and Zilla: the tournament in Little Rock

Eliminate Choices (A) or (B); Brunhild can't go to Omaha. Your game board's first option indicates that you could add Solomon and Zilla to Little Rock and maintain all conditions. Choice (C) doesn't obviously violate anything yet, so skip it for the moment to see whether Choices (D) and (E) have clear problems. Choice (D) does; Yorick can't go to Fargo. Choice (E) doesn't work either. When you refer to the second option on your game board, you see that space for only one more participate remains. Either Zilla or Solomon can participate in Fargo but not both. That leaves Choice (C) as the only legal possibility. Test it out completely just to be sure. If you put Brunhild, Roxanne, Solomon, and Zilla in Little Rock, then Yorick can go to Omaha, and Maev can go to Fargo, which separates the incompatible people and keeps Yorick away from Fargo.

f	o	l			
Y					
C	M	Y	B	R	S	Z

That works, so Choice (C) is right.

18. B. Cayenne, Yorick, and Zilla do not attend the same tournament.

Eliminate answers that could be true or must be false. Choice (A) is wrong because it could be true. In the second option, Brunhild and Cayenne can attend the same tournament in Fargo. Choice (B) must be true. Yorick and Cayenne can't be together because Cayenne must go to Fargo and Yorick never goes to Fargo. Check the other answers just to be sure. All are possible, but none of them must be true. You can put Maev and her various partners together, but you can also separate them. Choice (B) is correct.

19. **D. Maev, Solomon, Yorick**

Your game board indicates that either two people go to Fargo and five go elsewhere or four go to Fargo and three go elsewhere. That means any answer that doesn't have either three or five choices is wrong; eliminate Choices (A) and (B) immediately. Choices (C), (D), and (E) have three people listed, which means you're looking at the second option on your game board. In that option Cayenne, Brunhill, and Roxanne *must* go to Fargo. Choices (C) and (E) are both wrong because they both include Roxanne. That leaves Choice (D). Could Choice (D) work? Sure. Send Zilla to Fargo, send Solomon to Little Rock, and send Yorick and Maev to Omaha and you've observed all rules:

f				o		l
⊁						
B	R	C	Z	Y	M	S

Choice (D) is correct.

Questions 20–26

This kind of open grouping problem with ordering can be tricky. However, this problem is easier than you may think when you keep the rules in mind.

REMEMBER

Start with what you know. List the seven game pieces: C, C, C, V, V, V, and V. You have five cups in a row, and each cup contains one or two scoops. Create a game board with columns 1 through 5 and two spaces under each column. You don't really know where the row begins or ends; that means you can number just as well from right to left as from left to right. It's totally arbitrary. Add your topping possibilities: s, s, n, n, n, n, and n.

The rules don't give you any permanent homes for these ice creams or toppings. Either flavor of ice cream can get either topping. You must remember to account for every flavor and every topping. Every possible scenario must include four vanillas, three chocolates, two sprinkles, and five nuts. When you plug in data, you can account for both flavor and topping using a system of uppercase and lowercase (for example, vanilla with sprinkles would be Vs, and chocolate with nuts would be Cn). Write the conditions in shorthand underneath your chart so your game board looks something like this:

C C C V V V V
s s n n n n n

1		2		3		4		5	

No Vn|Cs

No Cs|Vn

No CV in one cup

Before you jump into the questions, think a little bit. You know every cup can hold up to two scoops. With only five cups and seven scoops, at least two cups will have two scoops. Does every cup need a scoop of ice cream in it? Not necessarily. You don't know how many teenagers are sharing this frozen monstrosity; maybe there are only four of them, and each one gets his or her choice in an individual cup, leaving one cup empty. Here's another thought: You can't mix flavors in one cup, but you can mix toppings. So you can put two scoops of vanilla in one cup, and top one with nuts and one with sprinkles.

20. **D. 1: nothing; 2: two scoops of vanilla with nuts; 3: two scoops of chocolate with nuts; 4: two scoops of vanilla with sprinkles; 5: one scoop of chocolate with nuts**

For questions that ask for the complete and accurate arrangement, you simply need to look for obvious rule violations. Check answers for ones that list more than two scoops per cup. Choice (A) has three scoops in cup 5, so it's no good. Look for answers that don't give you three chocolate and four vanilla. Choice (E) has four scoops of chocolate, which is too many. Consider the rule that there are two sprinkle toppings and five nuts. Choice (C) has three scoops with sprinkles, so it's wrong. The first condition specifies that no nut-topped scoop can sit next to a sprinkle-topped scoop. Choice (B) has a vanilla with nuts in cup 2 next to a chocolate with sprinkles in cup 3; that doesn't work. Choice (D) must be the answer. It maintains all conditions: You have four vanillas, three chocolates, five nuts, and two sprinkles, and you don't have either vanilla and chocolate intermingled in the same cup or vanilla with nuts next to chocolate with sprinkles. That looks good. Choice (D) is the answer.

21. **A. At least one cup contains exactly one scoop of chocolate ice cream.**

First, note that you're looking for something that can't be false, which is another way of saying that it must be true. Now consider the answers. Choice (A) looks like a good option right off the bat because it contains the fewest restrictions. If you have seven scoops of ice cream, and the most scoops you can put in the same cup is two, and three of those scoops are chocolate, and you can't put vanilla and chocolate in the same cup, then inevitably, at least one cup will contain nothing but one scoop of chocolate ice cream and its topping.

1		2		3		4		5	
V	V	C	C	V	V	C			

No CV in one cup

Choice (A) is obviously the correct answer, and you can save time by spotting it and moving on. Just for the sake of study, consider the other answers. Each of them is in fact possible but doesn't necessarily have to be the case. This ice cream sundae is pretty flexible. Remember, an answer that *could* be true but isn't necessarily true isn't good enough; it *must* be true to be correct. Choice (A) is correct.

22. **C. three**

You already know the answer can't be Choices (D) or (E). You run out of cups before distributing all seven scoops. Choice (C), three, looks like a good answer; test it to see whether it's possible. If you put two scoops of vanilla with nuts in cups 1 and 2, then a scoop of chocolate with nuts in cup 3, followed by single scoops of chocolate with sprinkles in cups 4 and 5, you have three cups each containing exactly one scoop of ice cream. You don't need to bother with Choices (A) and (B). Choice (C) is correct.

23. E. All the scoops of vanilla are in the second and fourth cups.

This question offers another temporary condition. If the third cup is empty, that leaves you only four cups to hold all seven scoops of ice cream. Because you have four scoops of vanilla, you'll have to have two cups that each contain two scoops of vanilla, which leaves one cup with one scoop of chocolate and one cup with two. To separate the two cups of vanilla, you have to put one on either side of cup 3 (either cup 1 or cup 2 will hold 2 scoops of vanilla, and cup 4 or cup 5 will hold the other two). The chocolate scoops occupy the cups not occupied by vanilla. You can't put sprinkles on a scoop of chocolate; you can't avoid putting chocolate and vanilla in adjacent cups, and some of the vanilla must have nuts on it. Here are a couple ways you could arrange the sundae:

C C C V V V
s s n n n n

1		2		3		4		5	
Vs	Vs	Cn				Cn	Cn	Vn	Vn
Cn		Vs	Vs			Vn	Vn	Cn	Cn

No Vn|Cs

No Cs|Vn

No CV in one cup

Now look at the answers. Eliminate choices that must be true or must be false. Choice (A) must be true; one cup contains one scoop of chocolate. Choice (B) must be true; you can't arrange this sundae in a way that puts scoops of chocolate in adjacent cups. Choice (C) must be true; you can't put sprinkles on any of the chocolate scoops because they all have to be in cups next to cups with scoops of vanilla. Choice (D) must be true. Choice (E) is the only answer that doesn't have to be true. The vanilla scoops could be in the second and fourth cups, but they could also be in the first and fifth, or the first and fourth, or the second and fifth. Choice (E) correct.

24. D. A scoop of chocolate with nuts is in the fifth cup.

Add the new temporary condition to your game board.

Notice that with two sprinkles accounted for, all the other scoops must have nuts on them. That means you still have to place a Cn, Vn, Vn, and Vn.

C n   V n   V n   V n

1		2		3		4		5	
		Vn				Cs	Cs		

No Vn|Cs

No Cs|Vn

No CV in one cup

Apply the possibilities to your game board and eliminate answers that violate the conditions. Try Choice (A). If you put chocolate with nuts in cup 1, then you have a problem because you have to put a vanilla with nuts in either cup 3 or cup 5, if not both, but both of them are adjacent to the chocolate with sprinkles in cup 4, so Choice (A) doesn't work. Choice (B) has to be wrong because vanilla is already in the second cup and you can't mix the flavors in the same cup. Choice (C) is also wrong because that puts three scoops in one cup. Now try Choice (D); could you put a scoop of chocolate with nuts in cup 5? Sure, and then you could fit two scoops of vanilla with nuts in both cups 1 and 2 and satisfy all the rules. Choice (D) looks like your answer, but check Choice (E) anyway. Could you put two scoops of ice cream in cup 5, like Choice (E) suggests? No. The two scoops would have to be vanilla because you only have one scoop of chocolate left. All the remaining vanilla scoops have nuts on them, and you can't put Vn next to Cs. Choice (E) must be false, and Choice (D) is correct.

25. C. the third cup

If each scoop of chocolate gets its own cup, then the four scoops of vanilla must occupy only two cups. The scoops of vanilla have nuts on them, which means two of the scoops of chocolate have sprinkles on them and therefore can't be next to vanilla. So, in no particular order, your cups will be: VnVn, VnVn, Cn, Cs, and Cs. To satisfy the first rule, you have only one way to ensure that vanilla with nuts doesn't get put next to chocolate with sprinkles: Separate them with the one remaining scoop of chocolate, which must have nuts on it. That scoop of chocolate with nuts has to go in the center cup, cup 3. Then you could put the vanilla in cups 1 and 2 and the chocolate with sprinkles in cups 4 and 5; or the vanilla could go in cups 4 and 5 and the chocolate with sprinkles could go in cups 1 and 2. Cup 3 is the only place vanilla can't go, so the answer is Choice (C). Here's the diagram:

1		2		3	4		5	
Cs		Cs		Cs	Vn	Vn	Vn	Vn
Vn	Vn	Vn	Vn	Cs	Cs		Cs	

No Vn|Cs

No Cs|Vn

No CV in one cup

26. E. 1: one scoop of vanilla with sprinkles; 2: empty

Test the answer choice possibilities on your game board and eliminate those that are possible. All you really have to do is sketch in the contents of the first two cups and then mentally see whether you can fill in the rest; you don't need to plot out the whole thing if you can see how to work it out easily. (Yes, we know we ordinarily say to diagram everything; in this case, though, running through the possibilities in your head is quicker, at least for most of the answers. If you get confused, though, by all means keep writing everything down. All we're suggesting is that if you can work part of a problem mentally without getting confused and without hurting your accuracy, doing so is okay and saves you time.) Try Choice (A). Choice (A) works fine. If you put the sprinkles on two of the remaining three scoops of vanilla, distributing the rest of the ice cream would be easy. Consider Choice (B), which puts all sprinkles on top of the vanilla scoops, so you don't run into pesky rules about neighboring scoops. Cross out Choice (B) and check Choice (C). You may want to draw this one out on your game board because the answer allocates only one scoop of ice cream. This scenario works fine if you allocate the scoops like this: 1: empty; 2: Cn; 3: VsVs; 4: CnCn; 5: VnVn.

1	2		3		4		5	
	Cn	Vs	Vs	Cn	Cn	Vn	Vn

No Vn|Cs
No Cs|Vn
No CV in one cup

Now try Choice (D): Sure, Choice (D) works. You don't have any chance of a chocolate with sprinkles being put next to a vanilla with nuts, so you can just distribute the rest of the scoops as you see fit. That leaves Choice (E), which looks like this:

C C C V V V
s n n n n n

1	2	3	4	5
Vs	X			

No Vn|Cs
No Cs|Vn
No CV in one cup

Uh-oh. You run into a problem here. The problem isn't the sprinkles; you could put them on another scoop of vanilla. The problem is that you have three scoops of vanilla, three scoops of chocolate, and only three cups to put them in. You can't place them without violating the condition against mixing flavors in one cup. Choice (E) is impossible and therefore is your answer.

Section II: Logical Reasoning

1. **D. Christie's states in its auction catalogs that all buyers should consult outside specialists before bidding on antiques, especially in the case of extremely valuable items.**

   You need to weaken the argument. Tempest claims that, based on expert opinion, her urns aren't 18th century, and therefore, Christie's advertised them falsely. To weaken this conclusion, look for evidence that would suggest Christie's catalog copy was not false advertising. Choice (A) actually strengthens Tempest's argument by bolstering her evidence that Christie's advertised the urns as 18th century. Choice (B) doesn't directly address the issue of whether Christie's advertised the urns falsely. The general difficulty in dating antiques doesn't help Tempest's case, but it also doesn't help exonerate Christie's in this particular case. Tempest's argument doesn't refer to scientists, so Choice (C) is unlikely to strengthen or weaken Tempest's argument, which is after all about Christie's truthfulness, not methods of dating urns. Choice (D) is a very good answer because it specifically addresses the Christie's advertisement. If Christie's told Tempest upfront that she shouldn't rely exclusively on the claims in its catalog, then she can't blame the auction house if she didn't have her urns assessed before purchasing them. Choice (E) isn't relevant because it regards the integrity of the experts but not the integrity of Christie's advertisement. Choice (D) is correct.

2. **C. Recent studies have shown that a large proportion of criminals sentenced to death are later shown to be innocent of their crimes.**

This is a "weaken" question. The argument's conclusion is that those convicted of heinous crimes by juries deserve the death penalty because such criminals are incorrigible and the families of victims need them to die for closure. Note, though, that the conclusion says "anyone whom a jury convicts," which isn't necessarily the same group of people that the evidence talks about — that is, those "who commit coldblooded, premeditated murders." What if someone is convicted wrongly? Choice (A) doesn't weaken the argument. The author uses family feelings as evidence to support the conclusion. Choice (B) is an advantage of using the death penalty and doesn't hurt the argument. Cost, by the way, doesn't enter into the argument at all. Choice (C) does weaken it. If large numbers of convicts are in fact innocent, then they're not incorrigible extreme criminals, and they don't deserve to be executed. Choice (D) is evidence of how pleasant the death penalty can be, and it doesn't hurt the argument. Choice (E) is not relevant because the author's argument isn't based on the actions of other states. Because the author concludes that the death penalty should continue because convicted murders deserve it, Choice (C) is the best answer.

3. **D. assumes that the only reason anyone would attend law school is to acquire a job at a top-ranking, high-paying law firm**

The problem with this argument is that it suggests that there's no point in attending any law school that's not in the top ten, because those are the only schools that lead to jobs in high-paying firms. But working for a top-ranking, high-paying law firm may not be the only reason to go to law school. Choice (A) is wrong because the argument doesn't promise anything. Choice (B) doesn't work because the argument doesn't address quality of education. Choice (C) is wrong because nothing in the argument implies that the author thinks top-firm recruiting practices are good or bad — there aren't any value judgments here, so you can't attack them. Choice (D) is your answer. Surely, some people can think of reasons to attend law school that go beyond finding a job in a top-ranking law firm. Choice (E) isn't relevant. You can't identify any misrepresentation based on the information contained in this argument. Choice (D) is correct.

4. **C. Birds are the only indicator species of West Nile virus for humans.**

The exterminator's conclusion is that there probably won't be an outbreak of West Nile virus in humans this summer is based on the fact that no one has found dead birds carrying the virus. That would be good evidence if the presence of the virus in birds is the sole indication that the West Nile virus has been eradicated, so that's the assumption you're looking for. If birds aren't susceptible to the West Nile virus, the lack of the virus in birds wouldn't be enough to state that humans aren't susceptible. Choice (A) isn't relevant because whether birds are more susceptible to death from the virus doesn't tell you anything about whether they're a predictor of human infection. The argument doesn't depend on the relative effectiveness of spraying this year compared to last, so Choice (B) is out. Choice (C) is a good answer. If birds are the only indicator species for humans, and the virus hasn't killed any birds yet, that would be good evidence that an outbreak among humans is unlikely. Choice (D) goes against what the exterminator assumes because it suggests that a human outbreak is actually possible, even though the birds show no evidence of the virus. Choice (E) is completely irrelevant. The effect of insecticide on birds has no bearing on whether a bird outbreak predicts a human outbreak. Choice (C) is the correct answer.

5. **A. Stem cell research should not be banned.**

Isolate the premises of the editorialist's argument to identify the conclusion he leads to. The editorialist presents the opposing view, states the reasoning behind the view, and declares that the reasoning is flawed. The premises of the argument are that some want to ban stem cell research because they say stem cells are embryos, but stem cells aren't embryos. The editorialist then adds another premise, a statement about the benefits of stem cell research. So, the argument goes something like this: (1) Some want to ban stem cell research based on a faulty premise. (2) They are wrong, and (3) stem cell research is beneficial. Therefore, stem cell research should not be banned. Choices (C) and (D) restate premises and can't be the overall conclusion. Choice (B) is a conclusion the editorialist makes on the way to reaching the overall conclusion, but it's not the conclusion as a whole. Because the argument is specifically about stem cell research and not research in general, Choice (E) is too broad to be the editorialist's conclusion. Choice (A) provides the overall message of the editorialist's argument.

6. **C. DNA samples taken from the heart in question and from hair cut from Marie Antoinette's head when she was a child indicate that the heart and hair sample came from people who were closely related.**

Some scientific evidence — DNA or something like that — proving conclusively that the heart was Louis XVII's would support the argument. Choice (A) doesn't necessarily help because what was "traditional" doesn't necessarily apply to every situation; an impostor's heart could have been removed and preserved to fool Louis's enemies in this exceptional case. Choice (B) is scientific evidence that tells you the age and sex of the heart's owner, but that information doesn't rule out an 8- to 12-year-old male commoner. Choice (C) supports the argument. If Louis's mother and the heart have similar DNA, that would be scientific proof of the heart's identity. Choice (D) is an interesting factoid but doesn't establish that the heart belonged to Louis. Choice (E) could be evidence that the heart belonged to a child who died in prison but doesn't help identify who that child was. Choice (C) is the best support for the conclusion.

7. **D. early specialization in a single sport is beneficial to children**

Emilio and Julienne disagree about whether early specialization in youth sports is beneficial or harmful to children. Only Julienne mentions teamwork, leadership, and enjoyment of sports, which eliminates Choices (A) and (B) as bones of contention. They both seem to think that kids should play sports, so Choice (C) is out, and they don't discuss an age below which kids should play sports at all, so Choice (E) is wrong. Choice (D) is the answer; Emilio thinks early specialization is good, and Julienne thinks it's bad.

8. **A. Most home freezers can store food for no more than three months.**

Okay, if food at 0 degrees lasts a year, food at 5 degrees should last six months, and food at 10 degrees should last three months. That looks like Choice (A). Choice (B) doesn't necessarily follow from the statements because they say nothing about homeowners' knowledge. The statements don't address safety, only flavor, so Choice (C) doesn't have to be true. Choice (D) isn't a necessary implication of the statements because they say nothing about commercial freezers. Likewise, the statements provide no information about how long homeowners actually store their frozen food, so Choice (E) isn't relevant. Choice (A) is best.

9. **E. A botanist finds a new kind of cactus in the driest part of the desert. All plants that live in the dry desert are extremely efficient at collecting and retaining water. Therefore, this new cactus must be extremely efficient at collecting and retaining water.**

The pattern goes like this: mollusk = deep; all deep = predator; therefore mollusk = predator. You can rewrite that as A = B; all B = C; therefore A = C. Choice (A) goes like this: enthusiast (A) finds studio (B); studio (B) = experienced instructors (C); therefore enthusiast (A) finds good instructors (D). "Experienced and highly trained" isn't necessarily the same as "good," so Choice (A) isn't quite right. Choice (B) goes as follows: player (A) = Croatia (B); most

Croatian players (B) = tall and hardworking (C); player (A) = tall and hardworking (C). The original argument qualifies the second premise as "all" B = C, but the answer choice qualifiers the second premise as "most" B = C. This is not a match. Choice (C) goes like this: tomato (A) = garden (B); all tomato (A) = nightshade (C); therefore tomato (A) = nightshade (C). That's not much of a conclusion. To match the given argument, the second statement would have to say something about all things found in the garden. Choice (D) reasons as follows: A = perfect sapphire; all sapphire (A) = hard and durable (B); therefore perfect sapphire (A) = hard and durable (B). This answer doesn't provide you with a "C" element in the argument. Check out the reasoning in Choice (E): cactus (A) = desert (B); all desert (B) = efficient with water (C); therefore cactus (A) = efficient with water (C). That duplicates the pattern stated in the argument, so Choice (E) is correct.

10. **B. A wife wants her husband to wash the dishes, take out the garbage, and make the bed in the morning, but she knows he won't do all three. She most dislikes taking out the garbage herself, so she makes a point of asking him to do that many times and ignores the dishes and bed.**

Look for an answer that involves someone who chooses one battle that matters the most to him out of several possible less important ones. Choice (A) is no good because the sister isn't prioritizing one battle out of many; the scenario addresses no battle other than the gas tank scuffle. Choice (B) looks like a good choice. The wife chooses to ask her husband to complete the one task that she cares most about out of several tasks she'd like to see done. Choice (C) illustrates the dangers of trying to fight two battles at once, so it's wrong. Choice (D) is an example of someone not fighting a battle at all but running away instead. Choice (E) doesn't fit because it doesn't present a choice of battles, only different paths to the same goal. Choice (B) is the best answer.

11. **D. The cheap foods that make up the majority of the diets of poor people are full of calories but devoid of essential nutrients.**

Look for an answer that shows why people who spend little on food still get fat. Make sure there's a connection between money and food. Choice (A) explains nothing about the surprising paradox that some people who live in poverty experience both malnutrition and obesity. Choice (B) is a possibility but doesn't really explain why obesity is the result of this lack of nutritional knowledge instead of, say, starvation. Choice (C) doesn't focus on impoverished people, so it doesn't explain why they in particular are malnourished and obese. Choice (D) does resolve the paradox. If affordable food is full of calories, it makes people fat, and if it's devoid of nutrients, it can result in malnutrition. Choice (E) doesn't address poor people specifically, so like Choices (A) and (C), it doesn't resolve the paradox surrounding their particular obesity and malnutrition. Choice (D) is the answer.

12. **C. Most people use Windows computers. Therefore, software producers should not bother to make any software for Macintosh computers.**

The reasoning goes like this: most players = male; manufacturers shouldn't bother with females (non-males). Choice (A) reasons that most cyclists = male, so manufacturers should concentrate on males. That's close but not right because it states what manufacturers should do with males rather than what they should not do with females. Choice (B) states that most Americans = cellphones, so most Americans shouldn't bother with landlines. This argument gets that something should not be done, but it states what consumers shouldn't do rather than what manufacturers shouldn't do. Choice (C) reasons that most users = Windows, so software producers shouldn't bother with Macintosh. That follows the original line of reasoning. Choice (D) goes most lawyers = glasses, so optometrists should target lawyers. The original argument concludes with what an industry should *not* do for its less common customers rather than with what it should do. Choice (E) states that Labs = easy to train, so a person who wants an obedient dog should consider Labs. There's no parallel at all here to a situation about manufacturers and their various customers. Choice (C) is correct.

13. **D. Because drivers talking on cellphones are distracted, they are more prone to get into accidents.**

You're looking for an assumption. Assumptions connect the premises to the conclusion. The conclusion is that if drivers can't talk on cellphones, the roads will be safer, based on the evidence that drivers on phones are distracted. That means the author assumes that distracted drivers are unsafe drivers. (Yes, that's obvious, but the author doesn't explicitly say what the connection is, so it's an assumption.) Choice (A) is tricky and could be a possible answer if you were asked to support the legislator's argument, but information about the results of a specific cellphone use study is way too specific to be the legislator's assumption. Assumptions are rarely based on particular statistical data. See whether you can find a better answer. Choice (B) is wrong; the author probably does assume that this is the legislature's job, but this assumption isn't necessary to the specific argument connecting distraction and road safety. Choice (C) doesn't work; the author isn't concerned with distinctions among types of cellphones users. Choice (D) is something the author assumes — it explains the connection between cellphones and distracted drivers and dangerous roads. Choice (E) contains mostly irrelevant details about other behaviors, and to the extent it addresses drivers on cellphones, it just reiterates evidence the argument already explicitly states. Choice (D) is the right answer.

14. **A. equates time spent on a job with quality, without examining the products to verify the quality**

The partner draws a direct correlation between time spent on a task and quality of work, which isn't in fact a foregone conclusion. Choice (A) looks like a good answer. The partner's reasoning is flawed because he assumes the work that took longer is better without even reading the briefs to compare them. Choice (B) isn't the flaw. He's not criticizing Attorney B and, if anything, is happy with her performance. Choice (C) doesn't work because the partner does explain why he thinks Attorney B's brief is better. Choice (D) doesn't quite work because the argument never recommends keeping track of time as a general practice. Choice (E) is irrelevant. Therefore, Choice (A) is correct.

15. **E. assumes incorrectly that a characteristic found in the majority of a group must also be found in the majority of each subgroup within that group**

The student faultily assumes that because most insects have wings, most ants also must have wings to qualify as insects. But in fact, there's nothing inconsistent about most insects having wings and very few (or even no) ants having wings. There are so many other winged insect types out there to make up the difference and maintain the truth of the teacher's definition ("in most cases wings"). Choice (A) is wrong because the student actually does consider this possibility. Choice (B) is wrong because the student's conclusion takes into account his reliance on his teacher's accuracy. Choice (C) is an irrelevant criticism. The student's argument is merely that ants aren't insects; making this argument doesn't require him to say what they are instead. Choice (D) is both inaccurate and irrelevant. The student says nothing about the significance of wings, and it wouldn't matter anyway. You're only interested in the presence or absence of wings, not in their uses. Choice (E), on the other hand, points out the student's reasoning error clearly. It's just a bit tricky because it states the problem in general terms, without referring specifically to ants or insects, but that doesn't make it any less correct as a statement of the student's flaw. Choice (E) is the best answer.

16. **C. It fails to realize that spending money on discounted items is still spending money and will result in no savings at all.**

Ah, the more you spend the more you save, or maybe the more you spend the more you spend. Spending money, even at a discount, is spending, not saving. Choice (A) is wrong.

All the merchandise is 25 percent off, so the speaker isn't wrong about that. Choice (B) is wrong because the author doesn't make any claims about the actual dollar prices of anything. Choice (C) is an area in which he is vulnerable to criticism; he doesn't save anything if he spends money. (He may get better prices on items he would have bought anyway, thereby paying less than he might have, but he's still spending, not saving.) Choices (D) and (E) don't work because the reasons for the sale aren't relevant. Choice (C) is correct.

17. **B. The high deductibles of consumer-driven health insurance plans will lead to higher healthcare costs.**

Christina thinks that the high deductibles of consumer-driven health plans save money by minimizing the use of doctors, and Guthrie disagrees, arguing that they may actually cost more in the long run because untreated conditions could get much worse. Christina doesn't address the topic of Choice (A), so it can't be a point of disagreement. Choice (B) looks like a good possibility; they do disagree on whether raising deductibles will lower (Christina) or raise (Guthrie) costs in the long run. Choice (C) can't work because neither discusses the relationship of business size to health insurance affordability. Choice (D) presents an area where the two agree rather than disagree; they both think high deductibles will keep people away from the doctor. Choice (E) refers to a minor aspect of only Christina's argument, on which Guthrie has nothing to say, so it can't be their area of disagreement. Choice (B) is correct.

18. **B. Even well-known and widely available information, provided in an unexpected context, can be misleading.**

The argument concludes that meaning of language often derives from context and that people may not recognize simple concepts when they encounter them in a new or unusual situation. Choice (A), though possibly true, isn't the conclusion. The Internet discussion board is offered only as an example of the importance of context. Choice (B) mirrors the summary of the conclusion, so it's likely the correct answer. Choice (C) is too general. You know that because of the inclusion of the word "always." Additionally, the speaker's primary objective is to comment on a phenomenon rather than give advice on how to deal with it. Choice (D) is wrong because the participants obviously do know about the popular movie. More to the point, the main conclusion is about context in general, not about movies, perfumes, or the Internet, which are only part of an example in support of that conclusion. The same for choice (E); perfume names are only part of the author's example. Choice (B) must be correct.

19. **A. The higher concentration of oxygen in nitrox becomes toxic when it is compressed at increasing depths.**

On the one hand, nitrox is safer than air. On the other, it's more dangerous than air. What's the difference? Note the last sentence, in which the divemaster describes nitrox's hazards. He says nitrox is dangerous "at greater depths that are safe for divers using air." So the apparent discrepancy must be due to nitrox's behavior at depths, and something about going deep makes it dangerous. Choice (A) looks like a good explanation for this phenomenon. If oxygen gets dangerous when compressed, that explains why nitrox is hazardous at depths that don't make air especially dangerous. The divemaster never mentions anything about different behaviors exhibited by nitrox divers, so you can't assume Choices (B) or (C) offer an explanation for the apparent paradox. Choice (D) sounds like a real hazard, but it's not connected with the seeming discrepancy surrounding nitrox's safety because all divers face this bacteria risk. Choice (E) would, if anything, make nitrox sound even safer and doesn't begin to explain why it's more dangerous than air in some circumstances. Choice (A) is correct.

20. **E. It is a statement of fact about which the author goes on to make an opinion.**

The claim in the question is a statement of fact in the first sentence that the speaker explores more thoroughly, concluding with the statement that it's a mistake. She's not suggesting that it's a good thing, so Choices (A) and (D) are wrong. It's not evidence, so Choice (B) is wrong. Her actual conclusion is that not taking vacation is a mistake, so Choice (C) is wrong. It's a statement of fact that provides the background information for the author's opinion about what Americans should do with their vacation time, so Choice (E) is correct.

21. **D. A class taught by a PhD, even in a lecture format with hundreds of students, is a better learning environment than a smaller class taught by an instructor without a PhD.**

The author concludes that having classes taught by PhDs instead of instructors improves students' learning experience, so he must assume that PhDs, even in very large classes, are somehow better at teaching than instructors in smaller ones. Choice (A) isn't his assumption; in fact, the reference to increased class sizes suggests that the university won't be hiring more faculty. Choice (B) contradicts the author's conclusion, assuming that student participation is a good thing. Choice (C) is interesting information but isn't essential to the conclusion about the practices of the particular Southern state university, especially because it doesn't mention students' learning experiences. Choice (D) looks like the right answer. The author does seem to think that a class taught by a PhD is somehow superior, which explains why he thinks the change would benefit students. Choice (E) explains why the university may want to increase classes taught by PhDs, but it doesn't explain how that would benefit students. Choice (D) is correct.

22. **E. the opinion of the international community is important to the United States**

Griselda cares what other countries think of the United States; Theodore doesn't. They both suggest that other countries could disapprove of the United States' actions: Griselda mentions alienating other nations, and Theodore suggests that countries disapprove of sending troops. So Choice (A) is wrong. Choice (B) makes a general statement about military responses to foreign threats and isn't specific to the actions of the United States in light of foreign opinion. Choice (C) is wrong. Theodore and Griselda appear to agree that the United States should act in its best interest. Theodore states the point outright, and Griselda suggests it when she says that the United States should act in a way that assures national security. Choice (D) is also wrong. Griselda doesn't mention the United Nations, so you can't assume what she thinks about its role in all matters. Choice (E) is correct because while Griselda thinks the United States should consider how its actions affect other nations, Theodore says that foreign opinion is irrelevant.

23. **A. assumes that consuming any amount of alcohol during pregnancy will cause birth defects and intellectual disability**

The obstetrician draws a connection between all alcohol consumption and pregnancy that may not be entirely justified by the facts. Heavy drinking may always be bad, but he provides no additional information to show that light drinking is equally bad or will definitely cause birth defects. Choice (A) looks like a good answer. The obstetrician is assuming that any amount of alcohol is equally deleterious, when in fact his evidence has only connected birth defects with heavy drinking. Choice (B) isn't as good. The doctor doesn't mention prevention or suggest that women be forcibly stopped from drinking, merely that they should choose not to drink during pregnancy. Choice (C) doesn't work because the doctor doesn't mention the state or its interest in children's health. Choice (D) isn't really a flaw. The argument doesn't suffer from lack of proof; it is the unwarrantedly broad conclusion the obstetrician draws from the evidence he does provide that's the problem. Choice (E) would be a bad thing to do, but the obstetrician doesn't do it; he never suggests that drinking is the only way a child may end up with birth defects. Choice (A) is the best answer.

24. **D. A university that licensed a low-cost online workshop on proper citation techniques for its incoming students found itself needing to commit significantly fewer valuable staff hours to handle incidents of unintentional plagiarism.**

Look for an answer in which someone's preparation saves money by avoiding a more expensive problem that otherwise would have occurred. Choice (A) doesn't work because the homeowner isn't preventing a problem. Choice (B) doesn't work because it doesn't mention that measles were prevented via this measure. Choice (C) is an example of preparation, not prevention. Choice (D) does conform to the principle; the little amount of money spent on the workshop prevents the waste of valuable staff resources later. Choice (E) doesn't work quite as well. The problem wasn't headed off in the first place; it actually occurred. Choice (D) is the best answer.

25. **C. A large number of studies have confirmed that the more anxious a patient is, the more protracted his or her recovery from a medical condition is.**

The psychologist claims that patients do better when they like their doctors; the premises are three factors that result from liking your doctor. To support this argument, you need to find statements that link those factors with health improvements. Choice (A) doesn't help. It illustrates the danger of people not liking their doctors but doesn't prove the psychologist's point that patients who like their doctors are healthier. Choice (B) provides evidence of how the average doctor doesn't have a good relationship with patients, but it doesn't show the results of good doctor-patient rapport. Choice (C) does support the conclusion by linking one effect of liking a doctor (less anxiety) to a greater improvement in health. Choice (D) may suggest that improving doctor-patient communication is desirable, but it doesn't specifically link improved communication to improved patient health. Choice (E) presents a reason for poor doctor-patient communication but doesn't show how that affects patient health. Choice (C) is correct.

Section III: Reading Comprehension

1. **D. Recumbent bicycles, which were banned from competition in the 1930s and thus neglected for much of the 20th century, offer many advantages over upright bicycles and come in many designs.**

Think what this whole passage is about. You know that it describes a kind of bicycle called a *recumbent* that's designed differently from a regular bicycle, which the passage refers to as an "upright" bicycle. It mentions a bit about the history of recumbents and why they were banned from competition, describes the advantages of recumbents, spends a paragraph on different recumbent designs, and then concludes with a paragraph on how to improve recumbent hill-climbing. It's mostly informative, but the author definitely has an agenda — notice how she dwells on the advantages of recumbents.

Choice (A) is definitely wrong. The UCI's decision is only a minor part of the entire passage, not the main idea. Choice (B) isn't the main idea, either. Although the author does mention that recumbents have surged in popularity, which has generated new design interest, that's not the main idea of the whole passage; instead, it's kind of the main idea of the third paragraph. Choice (C) is true and is one of the author's points, but it's not her main idea, which has to apply to the entire passage. Choice (D) looks like the right answer. It sums up the gist of the entire passage pretty well and doesn't add anything that the passage doesn't say.

Choice (E) is true and is also one of the author's points, but it doesn't sum up the main idea of the entire passage. Choice (D) is correct.

2. **A. The seating position places the cyclist in a permanent aerodynamic tuck, with arms and legs contained within the rider's torso profile, thereby creating less wind resistance than an upright rider faces.**

The passage makes it clear that aerodynamic efficiency is the reason for recumbent bicycles' speed. Look for an answer that emphasizes the aerodynamic advantages of recumbents. Choice (A) looks good, but check the others. Choice (B) is wrong because the author explicitly says that most recumbents are made of steel, *not* of lighter materials. Choice (C) is a bit tricky because recumbents do maximize aerodynamics, and fairings and seat position do play a role in aerodynamics, but the main way that recumbents maximize aerodynamics is through an aerodynamic tuck. The author clearly states that fairings are optional, so you can't assume that fairings are responsible for the aerodynamic improvement. Choice (D) doesn't really work because you know that bicycle manufacturers neglected recumbents for most of the 20th century. Choice (E) doesn't work either; it's not specifically steering that makes recumbents faster, and one steering configuration is known to be faster than the other. Choice (A) is the right answer.

3. **E. After a second-rate cyclist won a race and broke several records on a recumbent, the UCI decided that recumbents offered too much mechanical advantage and that, in order for races to reflect actual ability, all riders should use the same kind of bicycle.**

The UCI (incidentally, *Union Cycliste Internationale* is a French name, though all the words resemble English; the English version is International Cycling Union) banned recumbents after a lousy cyclist won a race on one, proving that his bike was faster than the other bikes because he himself wouldn't have won on an upright bike. Choice (A) is wrong because the passage says nothing about other cyclists petitioning anyone. Choice (B) is totally wrong because the author never mentions anyone setting records on upright bikes. Choice (C) isn't in the passage. Choice (D) starts off promising with the mention of the second-rate cyclist but then veers into nonsense about press attention, so that's no good. That leaves Choice (E), which is the correct answer.

4. **B. Recumbent bicycles are lighter than upright bicycles, which gives them an advantage at hill climbing.**

Find the answer to this one by the process of elimination. If you prefer, highlight the passage where you find answer choices that do appear. Choice (A) is mentioned; the author mentions comfort several times. Choice (B) looks wrong. The author says that recumbents are heavier than uprights, not lighter, so this answer certainly isn't one of the advantages she lists. Choice (C) is in the passage as an advantage; so are Choices (D) and (E). Choice (B) is correct.

5. **A. to argue that, contrary to what they may expect, cyclists can climb hills well on recumbent bicycles, and to suggest ways to improve climbing performance**

Before predicting the right answer, you may want to quickly skim this paragraph. Now, in your own words, why did the author write this paragraph? The last paragraph contains the author's discussion of climbing on recumbents. She mentions that some cyclists believe that recumbents are slow at climbing, claims that they aren't, and offers a suggestion or two of ways recumbent cyclists can improve their climbing prowess. Choice (A) matches up with that description quite well. Choice (B) is wrong, though it may be a bit confusing; the author does say that recumbent cyclists can climb hills well, but she isn't proving anything, just making a statement that she could back up with evidence if she chose to, though she doesn't. Choice (C) isn't exactly right. The author does discuss cadence, but that's not her primary purpose in writing the paragraph. Choice (D) doesn't work because, although the author does dispute the contention that recumbents can't climb, she doesn't offer anecdotal evidence; the claim that "most experienced recumbent riders" climb well isn't anecdotal evidence — you need some actual examples of fast riders for this answer to be right. Choice (E) is wrong; the author does recommend weight lifting, but that isn't the main point of the paragraph. Choice (A) is correct.

6. **C. Recumbent bicycles could be improved by being produced with carbon fiber frames.**

This question doesn't direct you to any particular part of the passage, so check the answers to determine where to focus. Choice (A) refers to wheelbase length and steering location. The third paragraph discusses the different wheelbase lengths and steering positions of recumbent bikes, so start there. The paragraph states that a short wheelbase is faster than a long wheelbase, and above-seat steering is more aerodynamic than below-seat steering. The passage indicates that recumbent bicycles are more aerodynamically efficient, so Choice (A) is looking good so far. Keep reading. For Choice (A) to be correct, you have to be able to justify that the recumbent bike is faster in *all* conditions. The last paragraph discusses using recumbents on hills and states that experienced riders can equal the performance of upright bikes on grades up to 12 percent. But what about inexperienced or weaker riders and grades steeper than 12 percent? The recumbent bike isn't faster than an upright in every condition. Eliminate Choice (A). Choice (B) seems promising. The third paragraph says that the popularity of recumbent bikes has surged and that their new designs make them comfortable, but the passage doesn't necessarily link their popularity to their comfort, so Choice (B) is likely incorrect. The carbon fiber mentioned in Choice (C) is discussed at the end of the third paragraph, where the author mentions that a few high-end recumbents have replaced heavy steel with lightweight carbon fiber. The suggestion is that these lightweight models are superior to the heavier versions, so Choice (C) seems like a good option. Choice (D) is easy to eliminate. The passage doesn't indicate that adding a fairing to an upright bike is even possible, and the reference to a 15-percent speed increase is too specific to justify. Choice (E) is also out for some of the reasons mentioned in the discussion of Choice (A). Building body strength and adjusting shifting techniques may allow recumbent riders to attain equal efficiency on grades up to 12 percent, but likely not on grades steeper than 12 percent. The most easily justified answer is Choice (C).

7. **E. A cyclist who wants to maximize speed and comfort and is not interested in racing should choose a recumbent over an upright bicycle.**

You can't predict the answers to this one, so just read through the choices and see which one jibes with what the author seems to believe. Choice (A) doesn't really work because the author probably wouldn't make such a blanket statement. She's precise in her numbers and not likely to generalize like that, with no consideration for different riders. Choice (B) is wrong because, although the author mentions that recumbents have become more popular, nowhere does she mention absolute numbers of recumbent cyclists as compared to upright cyclists. For all you know, recumbent cyclists comprise a mere 1 percent of the cycling population. Because she hasn't mentioned this topic, you can't assume she'd agree. Choice (C) is wrong. A fairing would make a recumbent faster but by improving aerodynamics, not by reducing weight; if anything, the fairing would increase weight. Choice (D) is wrong. Even if the author conceded that a tucked position on an upright bike is as efficient as the normal position on a recumbent, she would never agree that it was as comfortable as sitting back in a recumbent seat. Choice (E) is correct; the author's points are that recumbents offer both speed and comfort, though it's true that you can't enter them in most bike races.

8. **C. The diagnosis of PTSD is highly controversial.**

Both authors overtly state that PTSD and the research and theories surrounding it are highly controversial. Choice (A) is mentioned only by the author of Passage B, and because you're only assessing the information found directly in the passage, you can't assume that the author of Passage B would necessarily agree. Same goes for Choice (E). Similarly, Choice (B) is mentioned by the author of Passage A but not by the author of Passage B. If you picked Choice (D), you may have missed the fact that the idea that trauma was limited to catastrophic events was referred to as a belief of the past, and more specifically, from the late '70s and early '80s.

Note: The two passages provide information about the diagnosis of PTSD as a medical disorder. Although both are relatively objective in purpose, Passage A seems more concerned with discussing the controversy surrounding whether PTSD is a legitimate diagnosis, and Passage B primarily describes the nature of PTSD symptoms.

9. **A. PTSD: A Brief History of a Modern Controversy**

Both passages begin with descriptions of how PTSD came to be recognized and then later cite how controversial the concept is, making Choice (A) the best of those listed. Though both note that some of the material on PTSD in the *Diagnostic and Statistical Manual of Mental Disorders* is indeed controversial, neither comes out and directly calls it false. Eliminate Choice (D) for the same reason — neither author implies that PTSD is a straight-up work of fiction. Choice (C) is pretty out of left field, so you can go ahead and knock that one out of contention. As for Choice (D), though the author of Passage B *does* note some common traits of PTSD sufferers, a "case study" implies a thorough analysis of a particular individual, and that is not present in either passage.

10. **E. Sufferers of PTSD experience a lack of interest in day-to-day activities they used to find enjoyable.**

Choice (A) is an argument made by the author of Passage A, when he says the concept of a *traumatic stressor* has broadened to such an extent that, today, the vast majority of American adults have been exposed to PTSD-qualifying events. Choice (B) is made by the author of Passage (B), when he states that "People with PTSD are consumed by concerns about personal safety." Choice (C) is also described in the first paragraph of Passage B. Choice (D) is mentioned by the author of Passage A as one of two concerns of the past that have "again resurfaced in contemporary debates. . . ." As for Choice (E), remember that you need to cast aside anything you may personally know about PTSD and instead focus only on the material in the passage. Though Choice (E) may well be true, it isn't stated in either passage and therefore is the best choice of those available.

11. **A. The author of Passage A suggests that PTSD may be an invalid diagnosis, while the author of Passage B indicates that PTSD is a valid disorder with recognizable symptoms.**

In discussing the controversy over whether PTSD should be a medical diagnosis, Passage A uses diminishing terminology such as "merely" to describe the way that many symptoms have been combined to create the diagnosis of PTSD. This diminution implies that the diagnosis may not be a real medical condition but instead the invention of social and political activists. This recognition allows you to eliminate Choices (C) and (E). Passage B appears to accept that PTSD is a valid diagnosis and focuses on its symptoms. So you can cross out Choice (D). That leaves you with Choices (A) and (B). Passage B doesn't indicate that no other disorder exhibits PTSD's symptoms and in fact implies that two other disorders (ASD and AD) may have similar symptoms. Choice (B) must be wrong. Choice (A) is a better answer.

12. **E. to categorize the primary symptom of PTSD as a problem with the manner in which its sufferers respond to their environment**

Passage B begins with an assertion of the generally accepted cause of PTSD and links a stressor to its symptoms. It then goes into more detail about how the stressor contributes to PTSD symptoms and stresses the importance of the reaction of the PTSD sufferer to real or imagined dangers. You can eliminate answer choices that don't relate to why PTSD symptoms occur. Choice (B) regards an aspect of Passage A rather than Passage B. Choice (C) suggests that Passage B is about traumatic stress disorders in general instead of PTSD in particular. The passage doesn't compare PTSD suffers to trauma survivors who don't have PTSD, so Choice (A) isn't correct. Between Choices (D) and (E), Choice (E) is a better answer because the passage doesn't list causes or mention more than one general cause of PTSD symptoms. Choice (E) correctly summarizes Passage B's focus on the primary cause of PTSD symptoms, which is the way that sufferers react to stressful events.

14. **C. the controversy over whether PTSD is a medical diagnosis is complicated by the motivations of the movement behind PTSD**

Refer to the line reference and consider the context of the quoted words. The author of Passage A asserts that PTSD as a disorder is controversial and mentions the political and social construct to explain that some believe that PTSD as a disorder may have been created by psychiatrists who were against the Vietnam War and, therefore, PTSD isn't a medical disorder at all. You may be tempted by Choice (A) because it addresses the influence of antiwar psychiatrists, but you don't have enough information in the passage to assess the actual motives of the creators of the diagnosis. You don't know specifically from the passage that they were concerned with getting medical treatment for veterans. Choice (B) provides an opposing idea to the information in Passage A, and you know it's wrong because it suggests that something should be done. Descriptive passages are rarely calls for action. Choice (D) may sound good at first because it uses language straight from the passage, but Passage A doesn't talk about those who suffer from medical diseases from natural events. You know that Choice (E) is off base; Passage A doesn't focus on the controversy over PTSD's causes. The best answer is Choice (C). It notes that the context of the words in question relate to the controversy over whether PTSD is a real medical condition or a constructed one, and it indicates that its origination by a movement by antiwar psychiatrists calls into question its validity as a medical diagnosis.

14. **C. Authority is a kind of power that does not explicitly depend on persuasion or coercion for its effect.**

This passage is tough. A bit of strategy: You will of course have read the questions before tackling the reading, and you'll have noticed that this passage only has five questions. In this situation, you may be well served by postponing this reading until the end. It's not worth as many points as the others, and it's harder to understand. Often, it doesn't matter whether you work the passages in order, but readings like this can really bog you down.

For a clue as to its topic, read the last sentence of the first paragraph, a common place to put a thesis: it's about "the particular manifestation of power that we call authority." This is an excerpt from a much longer piece on Alexander the Great, which is why Alexander appears in this passage, but Alexander isn't actually the focus of the passage; authority as a subcategory of power is.

Now, what's the central idea? The author is arguing that authority is a kind of power that relies for its effect on the speaker's ability to command and get people to obey him and doesn't depend on coercion or persuasion. Read through the answer choices and see whether you can find one that fits. Choice (A) doesn't work; the author has said that authority is a kind of power, which means they can't be the same thing. Choice (B) is backward — authority is a kind of power. You don't need to bother with the rest of the answer, which is also wrong. Choice (C) looks good. The author has said that "authority is a kind of power" and "for us to see authority in action, both coercion and persuasion must remain in the background," which adds up to Choice (C). Choice (D) doesn't work; though the author mentions Alexander, he's really incidental to this discussion and even more so is his general,

Antipater. Choice (E) is wrong, too. In the last paragraph, the author describes Alexander's exercise of authority but not of power. Choice (C) is correct.

15. **B. explore aspects of the concept of authority and its uneasy association with coercive and discursive power**

The second paragraph contains a discussion of authority and the relationship implied in any situation in which one person has authority over another. Choice (A) is wrong. Alexander doesn't appear in this paragraph. Choice (B) looks good — the author does mention "coercive power" and uses the word "uneasy" to describe relationships in which one person has authority over another. Choice (C) isn't right. The author may in fact suggest that coercive power is essential to authority, but that's not the point of the entire paragraph and is never really directly stated. Choice (D) is wrong. The author doesn't mention other scholars or their interpretations anywhere. Choice (E) is a statement that appears in the third paragraph, not the second, and it isn't the point there, either. Choice (B) is the best answer.

16. **C. is mostly conveyed through spoken communication**

In the second paragraph, the author correlates discursive function with authority's being a matter of speaking. Eliminate Choice (B) because it doesn't regard speaking, and later in the paragraph, the author states that demonstrations of coercive and persuasive power don't necessarily suggest a position of authority. It therefore follows that Choices (A) and (E) are also incorrect because the author suggests that authority stems from more than just commanding speech in the third paragraph, and indicates that persuasion should be hidden in the fourth paragraph. The author's statement in the third paragraph, that authority falters when the listener demands a reason for a command or asks about consequences, eliminates Choice (D). Choice (C) states the author's idea that authoritative actions are really authoritative speech.

17. **B. Power is a generic term for the ability to make someone do something; authority is a particular form of power, the ability to command without explicit persuasion or coercion.**

The definition of power appears in the first paragraph, and the definition of authority appears in the second. Note the author's use of the word "generic" to describe "power." Skimming the answers, Choices (B) and (E) look like possibilities. Choice (B) looks right and Choice (E) looks wrong; the author says that authority is a kind of power and that it should-n't depend on outright coercion or persuasion. Choice (A) is wrong because both authority and power can involve persuasion and coercion. Choice (C) doesn't work because nowhere does the author suggest that authority goes with politics and power goes with the military. Choice (D) is likewise wrong. Choice (B) is the best answer.

18. **A. The speaker's authority becomes weaker, whereupon that speaker can resort to persuasion or force, or reassert authority by invoking a privileged position.**

Here's what the author says: "If the listener demands a reason for a command or asks about the consequences of disobedience, the speaker's authority falters. At this point, authority may give way to persuasion or naked force, or it may be reasserted by invoking the privileged, authoritative position of the speaker." Choice (A) looks like it matches up pretty well with that. Choice (B) is wrong because the speaker doesn't necessarily lose power but may lose authority. In addition, you should automatically be suspicious of extreme wording such as "loses all power." Choice (C) is just plain wrong. Choice (D) isn't right either, because the speaker could also use persuasion or reinvoke his authority. Choice (E) definitely isn't right. Choice (A) is the best answer.

19. **E. The Panama Canal, built as a result of military strategists worried about transporting Navy ships from one ocean to another, not only expedited military transport but also made moving cargo between the oceans easier, opening a wealth of economic opportunities.**

This passage is a short history lesson on the Panama Canal — the events that preceded its construction and the worries they caused, and then the effects on the world after it was operational. Choice (A) isn't the main point, though it is a factoid you can figure out from the passage. Choice (B) isn't the main point, either; the passage isn't only about the U.S. Navy's use of the canal during World War I. Choice (C) sums up the first half of the passage but doesn't do justice to the whole thing. Choice (D) is a conclusion that the author doesn't state. Choice (E) is the best answer; it sums up the passage nicely.

20. **D. Without the canal, the only way to transport boats from the Atlantic to the Pacific was to sail them around the entire continent of South America, which took more than two months.**

Why did the United States decide it needed the Panama Canal? The only way to get ships from the Atlantic to the Pacific or vice versa was to sail around the entire continent of South America. The narrow Isthmus of Panama (an *isthmus* is a little strip of land with ocean on either side of it) was an obvious place to construct a passage to shorten the trip. Choice (A) isn't right; the Navy had no desire to build two complete fleets. Choice (B) is true, but the passage gives the impression that the impetus behind the construction was military, not commercial. Choice (C) is misleading because it's the event that starts off the passage, but you're looking for a logistical problem, and having a ship blown up doesn't fit that category. Choice (D) looks right. The problem was indeed that it took too long to move ships from one ocean to another. Choice (E) is similar to Choice (C) in that it mentions the event that begins the passage and led to worry by military strategists, but the single instance of lacking a ship wasn't the logistical problem that led to the digging of a major canal. Choice (D) is correct.

21. **B. The U.S. Navy was unable to use all its ships in the same conflicts because it took far too long to sail ships from the Atlantic to the Pacific and vice versa.**

Here's what the passage says: "The impossibility of sailing north of North America, and the distance of the voyage around South America, effectively divided the U.S. Naval forces into two fleets. Such a division was costly, inefficient, and ultimately less powerful than a fleet that could unify on demand." What that phrase means, then, is that without a shortcut between oceans, the Navy essentially had to keep one fleet in the Pacific and one fleet in the Atlantic; ships couldn't necessarily sail to help one another because the trip took so long. Choice (A) is wrong. Naval commanders certainly wished they could mobilize their entire fleet in the same place at the same time. Choice (B) looks correct. Choice (C) doesn't work; the USS *Oregon* did in fact make it to Cuba in time to play a pivotal role. The problem was that the Navy couldn't count on this happening in the future, but the trip wasn't impossible. Choice (D) isn't right; it describes one incident that exemplified the two-fleet problem but doesn't sum up the phrase in question. Choice (E) doesn't work either because the author never mentions air power. Choice (B) is right.

22. **C. Spain could have won the fight for Cuba.**

After the USS *Maine* blew up, the Navy wanted to send its brand spanking new battleship to Cuba, but the author points out that the Navy had to wait 67 days for it to get there, with naval officers undoubtedly biting their nails the whole time. Why were they nervous? Spain and the United States were fighting over Cuba. The author doesn't say exactly what was going on, but you can assume that if the USS *Oregon* hadn't arrived on time, Spain would have taken Cuba. (In fact, Cuba had started a war for independence from Spain, and the United States sent the *Maine* to assist the Cubans. After the war, Cuba was independent. But you don't need to know that to answer the question.) Skim the answers; Choice (C) looks exactly right. Choice (A) may be true, but the author doesn't imply it. Choice (B) is wrong because, although the loss of more ships would have been undesirable, that wasn't the nation's primary concern. Choice (D) is irrelevant. You don't have any reason to assume San Francisco needed defense. Choice (E) may also work, but that's hardly what the passage suggests the Navy was worried about (surely the Navy would have found another opportunity to use the *Oregon*). Choice (C) is the best answer.

23. **A. It has transformed Panama into a major player in world trade.**

Read through the passage and mark off the answer choices that you find. Choices (B), (C), (D), and (E) are all in there, mostly in the last paragraph. Conspicuously absent from the author's discussion of the canal's impact is its effect on its home nation, Panama. Choice (A) is the answer.

24. **E. describe the drawbacks of sending ships around South America and the reasoning that led to the decision to build the Panama Canal**

In the second paragraph, the author discusses the concerns and desires the Navy had that led to the construction of the Panama Canal. Choice (A) is wrong because, even though the thinking of military strategists on the subject of the Spanish-American War does appear, that's just a piece of evidence that backs up the main point of the paragraph. Choice (B) is misleading because the paragraph starts off with the *Oregon*'s contribution, but the battleship never appears again in that paragraph, so it's not the primary purpose. Choice (C) is wrong. The action in the second paragraph occurs before the canal was built, so it can't mention the costs and benefits of traveling through it. Choice (D) is wrong. There weren't any effective alternatives to the canal. Choice (E) is correct. The military couldn't help but notice that South America was awfully big and time-consuming to sail around and reasoned that a canal through Panama would speed things up nicely.

25. **B. to describe the history behind the construction of the Panama Canal and the canal's importance to world trade and the U.S. military**

This is an analytical history passage, describing events and interpreting the forces behind the decisions of the time. Choice (A) isn't right. The author doesn't really get into the business of justifying U.S. actions in building the canal. Choice (B) looks good. Choice (C) is wrong because the passage never mentions imperialism. Choice (D) is wrong because the author doesn't get into discussing the construction of the canal. The passage skips from military strategists worrying in the late 1800s to the use of the canal in World War I, and you never find out about the details of construction. Choice (E) is wrong, too, because explosion of the *Maine* is just incidental to the story, not the author's primary concern. Notice that you don't see anything about the *Maine* after the first paragraph. Choice (B) is the best answer.

Section IV: Logical Reasoning

1. **B. People who don't have children attending public schools cannot benefit in any way from the existence of public schools.**

The curmudgeon assumes that the only way a person can benefit from public schools is by having children who attend them. Choice (A) is wrong. Although Choice (A) presents a possible benefit from public education, it goes too far to be the curmudgeon's basic assumption. Remember to stay close to the text — an assumption is the most basic piece of evidence that bridges the stated evidence to the conclusion. Choice (A) goes a step beyond the assumption and makes another assumption — that education is necessary to vote intelligently — but the curmudgeon never mentions voting or democracy in her argument. Choice (B) looks like the right answer; she does believe a childless person can't benefit from public schools, and that belief links the premise of the curmudgeon's argument to her conclusion that public schools don't benefit her. Choice (C) is probably something the curmudgeon would agree with, but it's not the assumption that ties together the premise to the conclusion. She mentions nothing about other people getting undeserved benefits. Choice (D) is totally wrong because it has nothing to do with the argument. Choice (E) is a point that someone arguing with the curmudgeon may bring up, but it's not the curmudgeon's assumption. Choice (B) is the only correct answer.

2. **D. misinterprets the results of the research by failing to note that the sleep technique suggested by scientists requires the sleeper to remove the socks before trying to sleep**

Focus on the actual conclusion: Insomniacs should try wearing socks to bed. Choice (B) isn't the flaw; the magazine suggests only that insomniacs *try* wearing socks, not that sock-wearing provides an absolute cure for sleeplessness. Choice (A) is wrong because the magazine justifies the technique with reference to scientific research. Choice (C) isn't a flaw in reasoning; on the LSAT, a reference to scientific research is usually sufficient documentation for a claim. Choice (E) is wrong because the magazine doesn't criticize insomniacs. However, the conclusion leaves off the crucial step of removing the socks before bed to allow the feet to cool off — that's its mistake. The magazine misinterprets the study's results and should have added that, for the technique to work properly, the feet must first be warmed and then be allowed to cool off, such as by removing socks. Choice (D) looks like the best answer.

3. **D. presupposes the truth of the conclusion it is attempting to establish**

This argument is created through circular reasoning. The conclusion that mothers should stay home to care for their children is based on the similar premise that mothers are the ones who should raise their children. Choice (A) is wrong because the speaker offers no evidence to specifically discount. Choice (B), if true, may be something to bring up in an opposing argument, but this kind of real-world rebuttal isn't a flaw in the internal logic of the author's argument (and in any case, "many" would be too weak to do much damage). Choice (C) is wrong; the argument doesn't talk about women in the workplace. Choice (D) looks right. The author makes a generalization that *all* mothers should stay home and offers only another generalization (that everyone knows mothers love their babies) and a restatement of the conclusion (mothers should raise their children) to support it. Choice (E) reaches beyond the score of the argument. The author doesn't specify potential caregivers other than mothers. Choice (D) is the best answer.

4. **C. Some chimpanzees are capable of understanding more than 200 words.**

Did you take a good look at the question before you started reading the statements? You're looking for something that *must* be true. Underline that word so that you know what the right answer will look like. Now that you know what you're looking for, do some quick thinking before going on to the answer choices. What *must* be true? You may think something like, if dogs can understand as many words as chimps, dolphins, and parrots, and dogs can understand 200 words, then chimps, dolphins, and parrots can understand at least 200 words. Choice (A) may be true, but it doesn't have to be true based on the information contained in the argument. You can't get to Choice (B) from the argument, which doesn't address training techniques. Choice (C) looks like a logical conclusion and a good answer. If many dogs can understand more than 200 words, and intelligent animals (chimpanzees in this case) are capable of understanding no fewer words than dogs, you can indeed deduce that at least some chimpanzees are capable of understanding more than 200 words. Choice (D) misses the point. The researchers may have been in Germany, but the animals could be from anywhere. Choice (E) isn't a conclusion you can make because the author never mentions training methods, only results. Choice (C) is right.

5. **C. My neighbor wants me to give her plant a gallon of water every day. I will not have to water it as often if I give it more water each time, so I am going to give it 2 gallons of water every other day.**

Yikes — burnt pie. The reasoning in the argument goes like this: 40 minutes at 250 = 20 minutes at 500. You want to find an answer that results in more or less an identical flaw: the author mistakenly assuming that a time-sensitive process can be halved in duration simply by doing it twice as intensively. Choice (A) goes like this: one aspirin every four hours; I'll do two aspirin every four hours. That's not a match. Choice (B) states that 9 pounds gets 1 cup; 13 pounds gets 1.5 cups. That reasoning seems sensible and not flawed. You're looking for a flawed argument, so Choice (B) won't work. This answer may look attractive to you because it manipulates the proportions in the directions in a similar way to that in the argument, but remember that the argument messes up that manipulation; the cat-feeder here presents the same flawed calculation as the original. Choice (C) reasons that 1 gallon every day = 2 gallons every other day. That's very close to the reasoning in the argument, which doubled the temperature and halved the time. Choice (D) is like this: bleach for 20 minutes; I'll do bleach for 40 minutes. The quantity of bleach isn't affected, so that argument isn't flawed in the same way (but that doesn't mean you should apply that reasoning to your own hair!). Choice (E) figures that twice as fast is worth twice the cost, which isn't necessarily flawed reasoning. Choice (C) is the best answer.

6. **B. the goodwill and publicity generated by charitable giving can increase a business's sales significantly**

This author assumes that there's no possible connection between charitable giving and profit-making, so you're looking for an answer choice that suggests such a link that's been overlooked in reaching the extreme conclusion on hand here. Choice (A) is attractive but wrong because, for all you know, "some" deductions could be quite minor. Choice (B) is correct because it suggests a direct link between charity and profits and thus calls into question the businessman's assumption that charitable giving makes no sense. Choice (C) is irrelevant. A flaw in the businessman's reasoning will be an unjustified conclusion based on the evidence he's given; statements that quibble with that evidence aren't flaws in his logic. Choice (D) may be nice, but the argument isn't about investors and mutual funds. Choice (E) also conveys an altruistic sentiment, but it's not clear that the charitable giving at these "some businesses" is driving their profits or detracting from it. Choice (B) is the best answer.

7. **A. Though average weights have increased, the weight gain has occurred exclusively among people who were already overweight; thin people have not gained weight, despite the fact that they, too, are consuming more fast food than was the case two decades ago.**

The nutritionist blames fast food for the obesity epidemic. Any evidence disproving a connection between fast food and obesity would weaken the argument. Choice (A) looks like it may do that; if everyone is eating more fast food than before but only certain people are getting fatter, then eating fast food alone can't be the cause. Choice (D) provides another possible reason for childhood obesity but doesn't speak to the rise in obesity in the population overall. Choice (C) actually reinforces the argument that fast food is the culprit. Neither Choice (B) nor Choice (E) addresses the fast food–obesity connection, so Choice (A) must be the answer.

8. **B. All flies are insects. All insects are arthropods. All arthropods are invertebrates. Therefore, all flies are both arthropods and invertebrates.**

This argument lends itself to being written as an equation: H = P; P = M; M = V; H = M and V. Try writing the answers as equations to see whether one comes out the same. Choice (A) goes like this: D = C; C = M; C = V; D = M and V. That's so close but not quite there; canines appear twice at the beginning of a sentence, which ruins this one. Choice (B) states that F = I; I = A; A = I; F = A and I. That looks identical to the argument, so it's a good answer. Choice (C) reasons that W = C; C = M; M have mammary glands; W have mammary glands. Nope. Choice (D) goes like this: S = M; M have shells; O = bivalves; bivalves have shells; creatures with shells = bivalves and mollusks. Totally wrong. Choice (E) indicates that G = P; C = P; P = V; G and C = V. That's not it. Choice (B) is correct.

9. **A. It is permissible for a soldier to refuse to obey an order to torture and abuse prisoners of war because that would violate national and international law.**

Look for an answer in which a soldier refuses to carry out an order he knows is against the law. Choice (A) looks right. Torture violates the law, so a soldier can legitimately refuse to carry out torture orders. Choice (B) isn't right. Soldiers aren't allowed to refuse orders that are simply against their own consciences. Choice (C) is wrong. A soldier's belief that the military shouldn't be involved in a particular conflict isn't the same as violating an actual law. Choice (D) is wrong for the same reason. Choice (E) is also wrong. For the answer to be right, it has to say that the action is against the law, not simply against an individual's conscience or moral beliefs. Choice (A) is the right answer.

10. **B. It is impossible to pass laws prohibiting obscenity without violating the free speech rights of those producing the material.**

Your job for questions that ask for the main point is to pick out the conclusion in the argument. The commentary's conclusion is that defining obscenity without violating free speech guarantees is impossible. That's actually stated in the first sentence. On the LSAT there's no reason why an argument can't begin with the conclusion (its "main point") and then provide support for it. Choice (A) isn't the theorist's point; she doesn't mention the different roles of federal and state governments. Choice (B) works because it states exactly the end point of the theorist's reasoning, her main point. Choice (C) is wrong. The theorist doesn't suggest that courts and legislatures ignore all speech, just obscenity. Choice (D) is the final premise of the theorist's evidence, so it's not the main point. Remember, just because a statement occurs at the end of an LSAT argument doesn't mean it's automatically the conclusion. Choice (E) doesn't work because it's simply another piece of evidence; the main point builds on this premise to reach its conclusion. Choice (B) is correct.

11. **D. Most consumers want to feel sure that the employees of businesses they patronize are not abusing serious drugs on the job.**

Make sure you know what you're looking for: Look for the one answer that doesn't hurt the argument. It doesn't necessarily have to strengthen the conclusion, but it can't weaken it. What's the conclusion? That the best method to avoid drug-using employees from making mistakes on the job is to administer random urine tests. And this is based on the fact that these tests can detect certain drugs. Just go down the list and eliminate any answer choice that does weaken the link from this premise to conclusion. The last choice standing is right! Choice (A) weakens the argument that urine tests are the best method by suggesting hair tests are better. Choice (B) weakens the argument by suggesting that urine tests can't spot drugs taken more than a couple of days ago. Choice (C) weakens the argument by suggesting that random drug tests are mostly useless and thus unlikely to be the best method (the part about their cost, by the way, is irrelevant to this argument). Choice (D) doesn't weaken the argument. What consumers want is irrelevant to the success of urine tests in best detecting employee drug use. Choice (E) weakens the argument. If it's easy to cheat on urine tests, they can't be very effective. Choice (D) is the best answer.

12. **E. A seller is obligated to observe the terms of the contract of sale, even if doing so works to the seller's own disadvantage.**

Albert would argue that he was acting as the catalog told him he could act and therefore isn't taking unfair advantage of the seller. In other words, he is abiding by the terms of the agreement, as is the seller, so he isn't taking advantage of the company. Choice (A) states only that buyers and sellers enter unwritten contracts during transactions, but that doesn't justify Albert's actions, at least not completely; look for something better. Choice (B) is wrong. Albert takes advantage of the seller's goodwill by all evidence with the seller's consent. Choice (C) doesn't work because it doesn't bolster Albert's rationale to his wife; if anything, it undercuts it by calling it an abuse. Choice (D) doesn't justify Albert's position, though it's a reasonable warning to merchants. Choice (E) is the best answer. When Albert bought the shoes, the sale contract stated that he could have them replaced at any time, so he's only observing the contract's terms, as in fact the seller is. Choice (E) is the best answer.

13. **B. A school district in another state reduced class sizes from 30 to 25 students; within a year, average test scores had increased by 25 percent.**

Heloise doesn't believe that reducing class size makes any difference. See whether you can find an answer providing evidence that it does. Choice (A) actually helps Heloise make her point. If the Japanese thrive on very large classes, size may not be a problem. Choice (B) provides statistical evidence that does undermine Heloise's position. If reducing class sizes made a sizable difference in a short time, maybe it's valuable. Choice (C) doesn't really undermine her point. Teachers may like small classes better, but that doesn't mean they're better for students. Choice (D) would, if anything, help her point, though it's really irrelevant to the issue of student performance. Choice (E) could undermine her point if it went further, but the mere fact that private schools limit class size tells you nothing about the performance of the students in the smaller classes (and what you think you may know about private school students' performance in the real world wouldn't ever matter on the LSAT). Choice (B) is the best answer.

14. **E. Despite the large number of lost bags, airlines only lose the bags of 4 out of every 1,000 passengers, so the odds of arriving without checked luggage are very low.**

That's a lot of lost luggage, but maybe the problem isn't as serious as the numbers make it seem. Choice (A) doesn't weaken the argument; if anything, it strengthens it. If airlines warn passengers to pack carry-ons, they must expect luggage to get lost. Choice (B) also strengthens the argument because it suggests that lost checked luggage can be expensive and inconvenient. Choice (C) doesn't weaken the argument for the same reason. Choice (D) doesn't really weaken the argument; although some travelers may not mind having to go shopping, many do, and luggage can contain more than just clothes. Choice (E) does weaken the argument that travelers shouldn't check their bags. If the odds of losing luggage are that low, then checking bags is fairly safe. Choice (E) is correct.

15. **E. LASIK is usually successful at improving a patient's vision, but it does not always result in perfect uncorrected eyesight and can create new problems for the patient.**

The information is about the benefits and risks of LASIK. Choice (A), while attractive, isn't a conclusion you can safely draw from the facts; though the passage says night vision can be impaired, the information says nothing about it being so bad as to prevent driving. Choice (B) doesn't work; the passage doesn't address the differences in doctors. In fact, the passage says the risks apply to all doctors. Choice (C) isn't supported by the passage. The passage tells you nothing about reading glasses, and in fact suggests that most patients need no glasses afterward. Choice (D) isn't in the passage either; the paragraph doesn't address aging. Choice (E) makes the most sense. According to the passage, LASIK has many benefits but some real risks. That actually makes a pretty good conclusion, summing up the information rather nicely. Choice (E) is the right answer.

16. **A. Turning on the lights inside a building makes it easier for birds to see the glass windows and avoid flying into them.**

You can't predict this answer, so dive in and find the one that outright contradicts ("must be false") the information in the passage. Choice (A) looks like the right answer; the passage tells you that birds can't see glass when lights are on inside. Choice (B) is probably true if birds are running into buildings in record numbers. Choice (C) could be true based on the information in the passage. Nothing in the passage indicates whether Choice (D) could be true or false. Choice (E)'s statement is possible; the passage says the bird–building problem occurs during migration. Choice (A) is the only necessarily false statement and is therefore correct.

17. **D. Outsourcing to foreign countries is not nearly as important a cause of layoffs as many Americans mistakenly believe.**

The statements suggest that outsourcing to foreign countries isn't nearly the problem many Americans think it is. Choice (A) is wrong. The author doesn't think anyone should blame the government for letting jobs go overseas; instead, she suggests that foreign outsourcing is a fairly small factor in unemployment. Choice (B) sounds like it may work, but continue to check the remaining answers. Choice (C) is wrong. Although this fact about outsourcing may be true, it's not substantiated by information in the passage. Choice (D) looks right; that's exactly what the statements suggest, and it's more specific than Choice (B) because it mentions foreign outsourcing specifically. According to the passage, about three-quarters of 9 percent of laid-off workers lost their jobs to local outsourcing, so outsourcing is a possible, albeit remote, concern. Choice (E) may be a true statement, but nothing in the argument would require it to be true. Choice (D) is the best answer.

18. **D. Children who work cannot go to school, and without an education, they cannot get high-paying jobs as adults, so their own children are forced to work instead of attending school.**

First, be sure of what the question is asking. You're looking for an explanation of a phenomenon. If child labor is both a problem of poverty and a cause of poverty, there must be some sort of vicious cycle going on, probably caused by the fact that people are working as children and passing their disadvantages on to their own children. Choice (A) is only a partial answer, and introducing the social safety net is irrelevant. Choice (B) doesn't make sense. It sounds as though parents have a choice of whether to send their kids to school or work. Look for something better. Choice (C) may be true, but it doesn't totally explain how child labor and poverty feed on each other without filling in several more steps from health to poverty. You want a tighter explanation. Choice (D) explains the phenomenon best; that's a real circular problem. When uneducated children are unable to earn much, the situation forces their own children to be uneducated child laborers. Choice (E) doesn't really explain the cycle of poverty. Choice (D) is the best answer.

19. **B. Reducing fossil-fuel emissions will slow global warming.**

The environmentalists like the emissions-reduction laws because they think such laws will slow global warming; clearly they're assuming there's a connection between the two. Although this connection may seem obvious, the passage never explicitly makes the link, so it's an unstated assumption. Choice (A) is wrong because the author says nothing about coastal states being environmentally conscious. Choice (B) looks exactly right. Choice (C) doesn't come up. Choice (D) is interesting, and the author does touch on environmental priorities, but it's not the assumption that leads from premises to conclusion. Choice (E) isn't something you can conclude from the information given. Choice (B) is correct.

20. **D. arguing that an alternate solution would have better dealt with the problem Philip addresses**

Philip thinks hybrids are the greatest thing since sliced bread, but Ryan's not so impressed. He thinks older technology was a better solution than heavy, complicated hybrids and their weird batteries. Look for an answer choice that states Ryan's response. Choice (A) is wrong because Ryan, if anything, also seeks a solution to the problem of inefficient cars. Choice (B) is wrong because Ryan doesn't offer an analogy; he sticks with the issue of cars. Choice (C) is wrong because Ryan doesn't question Philip's facts about hybrids; he just offers different facts about older cars that he thinks are more pertinent. Choice (D) gets right to Ryan's approach of offering a better solution. Choice (E) is wrong because Ryan's response doesn't contain a counterexample to disprove Philip's reasoning. Choice (D) is the best answer.

21. **D. families may not consist of only females**

Pro-family brochures distributed only to women? Though many women may not want to get married, that's not the main flaw in the reasoning, so Choice (A) is wrong. Choice (B) may be true but not because of flawed reasoning. Choice (C) may also be true, but the legislator isn't thinking only of single mothers. Choice (D) does name a flaw; any efforts to improve the family need to recognize that women aren't the only people in them. Choice (E) may well be true, but it's not the main reason the thinking is flawed. Choice (D) is the best answer here.

22. **B. The traffic between Tokyo and Yokohama was so bad that Stuart could not go faster than 25 kph.**

The best explanation for this otherwise surprising result would be something that suggests that Stuart's car couldn't get close to the allowed maximum speed of 60 kph. Choice (A) explains how Steve kept moving but doesn't account for Stuart's slow performance. Choice (B) could well offer an explanation; if the traffic was terrible, Stuart couldn't go any faster than Steve. Choice (C) doesn't help explain matters. If Stuart was driving 60 kph, he should have arrived sooner, unless he couldn't achieve that speed often, but the answer doesn't tell you how often he could go 60kph. Choice (D) doesn't help either because, all things being equal, Stuart should have arrived much earlier. Choice (E) had to be frustrating for the two drivers but still doesn't answer the question. Stuart stopped more, but he should have been able to drive faster when he was moving. Choice (B) makes the most sense.

23. **C. Uncontrolled anger is a cause of road rage.**

This judge must be assuming that there's some connection between controlling anger and eliminating road rage. It seems pretty obvious but isn't explicitly stated, so it counts as an assumption. Choice (A) is too extreme. The judge says that yoga can help control anger but doesn't suggest that yoga practitioners *never* lose control. Choice (B) isn't the reason for the sentence of yoga. The judge is trying to improve the man's behavior, not just impose a more serious sentence. Choice (C) looks like a good answer because the judge clearly assumes that yoga, which apparently helps control anger, is an apt punishment for a road rage defendant. Choice (D) may be tempting, but yoga isn't offered as a fitting payback for road ragers; it's offered as an attempted cure. Choice (E) is wrong. The judge doesn't give the impression that road rage is justified in this case. Choice (C) is the best answer.

24. **C. Despite the popularity of online dating services, participants should realize that such services come with many potential pitfalls.**

To predict the conclusion, think about where the evidence is leading you. Try to compose a sentence that would follow the last sentence in the argument, beginning with the word "therefore." The argument's natural conclusion is that online dating must be approached with caution. Choice (A) isn't the conclusion but a piece of evidence the author mentions. Choice (B) is too specific to be the conclusion, though the author does suggest that sexual predation may be a danger. Choice (B) expresses a detail instead of the general conclusion of the entire prompt. Choice (C) looks like a good answer; it summarizes the author's argument pretty well. Choice (D) isn't the author's point; he's not recommending that online dating services take any specific actions. Choice (E) is a prediction about the future of online dating that can't be inferred from anything in this passage, so it isn't its main conclusion. Choice (C) is right.

25. **D. An artwork's meaning is dependent on contingent features of the artist's psyche and society rather than on any inherent quality of the work itself.**

To best approach this question, notice that the postmodern reaction is *against* formalism, which the art critic defines as an emphasis on an artwork's form rather than its content or subject matter. So eliminate principles that justify form over content. Choices (A) and (C) emphasize the form of an artwork rather than its content, so those principles undermine rather than justify the reaction against formalism. Neither the formalist view nor the postmodern reaction mentions how personal taste relates to art evaluation, so Choice (B) is irrelevant. The remaining answers, Choices (D) and (E), appear to contradict each other. Choice (E) suggests that art loses its inherent (inner) value when people attempt to explain it or give it external meaning, and Choice (D) asserts that art's message comes from the artist's social and psychological experiences, which suggests that the artist intends a piece of art to mean something beyond its form. The principle that an artist projects meaning through artwork is more consistent with the postmodernist view that art should convey an interest in worldly affairs. Therefore, Choice (D) most justifies the postmodern reaction against formalism.

Answer Key for Practice Exam 1

Section I: Analytical Reasoning

1.	C	8.	E	15.	A	22.	C
2.	C	9.	D	16.	A	23.	E
3.	C	10.	A	17.	C	24.	D
4.	B	11.	E	18.	B	25.	C
5.	C	12.	D	19.	D	26.	E
6.	E	13.	B	20.	D		
7.	D	14.	B	21.	A		

Section II: Logical Reasoning

1.	D	8.	A	15.	E	22.	E
2.	C	9.	E	16.	C	23.	A
3.	D	10.	B	17.	B	24.	D
4.	C	11.	D	18.	B	25.	C
5.	A	12.	C	19.	A		
6.	C	13.	D	20.	E		
7.	D	14.	A	21.	D		

Section III: Reading Comprehension

1.	D	8.	C	15.	B	22.	C
2.	A	9.	A	16.	C	23.	A
3.	E	10.	E	17.	B	24.	E
4.	B	11.	A	18.	A	25.	B
5.	A	12.	E	19.	E		
6.	C	13.	C	20.	D		
7.	E	14.	C	21.	B		

Section IV: Logical Reasoning

1.	B	8.	B	15.	E	22.	B
2.	D	9.	A	16.	A	23.	C
3.	D	10.	B	17.	D	24.	C
4.	C	11.	D	18.	D	25.	D
5.	C	12.	E	19.	B		
6.	B	13.	B	20.	D		
7.	A	14.	E	21.	D		

Computing Your Score

Add up the total number of correct answers from each section; if you got everything right, you should have a raw score of 101.

Section I ___

Section II ___

Section III ___

Section IV ___

Now compare your raw score to the following chart. That would be your LSAT score if this were a real LSAT. It's not, so whatever you get on this test should just give you an idea of your abilities.

Raw Score	LSAT Score	Raw Score	LSAT Score	Raw Score	LSAT Score	Raw Score	LSAT Score
98–101	180	97	179	96	178	95	177
94	176	93	175	92	174	91	173
90	172	89	171	88	170	87	169
86	168	84–85	167	83	166	82	165
80–81	164	79	163	77–78	162	75–76	161
74	160	72–73	159	71	158	69–70	157
67–68	156	66	155	64–65	154	62–63	153
60–61	152	59	151	57–58	150	55–56	149
54	148	52–53	147	50–51	146	48–49	145
47	144	45–46	143	44	142	42–43	141
40–41	140	39	139	37–38	138	36	137
34–35	136	33	135	31–32	134	30	133
29	132	27–28	131	26	130	25	129
23–24	128	22	127	21	126	20	125
18–19	124	17	123	16	122	15	121
0–14	120						

REMEMBER

The real LSAT has an extra experimental multiple-choice section thrown in the mix, but you can't identify it. It looks just like the rest, and it doesn't count toward your final score.

TIP

Wrong answers don't subtract from your raw score on the LSAT. So, if you run out of time, make sure you bubble in an answer for each question. You may get some right just by sheer luck!

Chapter **17**

Perfecting with Practice: LSAT Practice Exam 2

Ready for another practice test? Sure you are!

Like the previous practice exam in Chapter 15, we set this one up like a real LSAT. For best results, try to take this practice exam under simulated LSAT conditions.

1. **Find a quiet place to work, where nothing can distract or interrupt you.**

2. **Use the answer grid provided.**

   You'll mark answers directly next to the answer choices when you take the digital LSAT on a tablet. You may use blank scratch paper throughout the test for making notes.

3. **Set your watch or alarm clock for 35-minute intervals.**

4. **Don't go to the next section until the time allotted for the current section is up.**

5. **If you finish early, check your work for that section only.**

6. **Don't take a break during any one section.**

7. **Give yourself exactly one 10-minute break between sections III and IV.**

The answers and explanations to this test's questions are in Chapter 18. When you finish your test, check the accuracy of your responses using the answer key at the end of Chapter 18. Count the number of questions you answered correctly in each section; add those together to compute your raw score. Then read the explanations for the questions you missed to learn how to answer the question type correctly in the future. If you have time, read through the explanations to the questions you aced, too, to gain further insight into mastering the LSAT.

REMEMBER

Keep in mind that this practice exam isn't an official LSAT. Although it serves as good practice for your test-taking technique and has the advantage of detailed explanations of all answers in the following chapter, don't assume that your score on this test is exactly the score you can expect when you take a real LSAT. LSAT PrepTests are still the best practice for that, but even they can't duplicate the stress you'll feel on test day and, therefore, still can't tell you precisely what score you'll receive when you take the LSAT for real.

Answer Sheet for Practice Exam 2

Section I

1. Ⓐ Ⓑ Ⓒ Ⓓ Ⓔ
2. Ⓐ Ⓑ Ⓒ Ⓓ Ⓔ
3. Ⓐ Ⓑ Ⓒ Ⓓ Ⓔ
4. Ⓐ Ⓑ Ⓒ Ⓓ Ⓔ
5. Ⓐ Ⓑ Ⓒ Ⓓ Ⓔ
6. Ⓐ Ⓑ Ⓒ Ⓓ Ⓔ
7. Ⓐ Ⓑ Ⓒ Ⓓ Ⓔ
8. Ⓐ Ⓑ Ⓒ Ⓓ Ⓔ
9. Ⓐ Ⓑ Ⓒ Ⓓ Ⓔ
10. Ⓐ Ⓑ Ⓒ Ⓓ Ⓔ
11. Ⓐ Ⓑ Ⓒ Ⓓ Ⓔ
12. Ⓐ Ⓑ Ⓒ Ⓓ Ⓔ
13. Ⓐ Ⓑ Ⓒ Ⓓ Ⓔ
14. Ⓐ Ⓑ Ⓒ Ⓓ Ⓔ
15. Ⓐ Ⓑ Ⓒ Ⓓ Ⓔ
16. Ⓐ Ⓑ Ⓒ Ⓓ Ⓔ
17. Ⓐ Ⓑ Ⓒ Ⓓ Ⓔ
18. Ⓐ Ⓑ Ⓒ Ⓓ Ⓔ
19. Ⓐ Ⓑ Ⓒ Ⓓ Ⓔ
20. Ⓐ Ⓑ Ⓒ Ⓓ Ⓔ
21. Ⓐ Ⓑ Ⓒ Ⓓ Ⓔ
22. Ⓐ Ⓑ Ⓒ Ⓓ Ⓔ
23. Ⓐ Ⓑ Ⓒ Ⓓ Ⓔ
24. Ⓐ Ⓑ Ⓒ Ⓓ Ⓔ
25. Ⓐ Ⓑ Ⓒ Ⓓ Ⓔ
26. Ⓐ Ⓑ Ⓒ Ⓓ Ⓔ
27. Ⓐ Ⓑ Ⓒ Ⓓ Ⓔ
28. Ⓐ Ⓑ Ⓒ Ⓓ Ⓔ
29. Ⓐ Ⓑ Ⓒ Ⓓ Ⓔ
30. Ⓐ Ⓑ Ⓒ Ⓓ Ⓔ

Section II

1. Ⓐ Ⓑ Ⓒ Ⓓ Ⓔ
2. Ⓐ Ⓑ Ⓒ Ⓓ Ⓔ
3. Ⓐ Ⓑ Ⓒ Ⓓ Ⓔ
4. Ⓐ Ⓑ Ⓒ Ⓓ Ⓔ
5. Ⓐ Ⓑ Ⓒ Ⓓ Ⓔ
6. Ⓐ Ⓑ Ⓒ Ⓓ Ⓔ
7. Ⓐ Ⓑ Ⓒ Ⓓ Ⓔ
8. Ⓐ Ⓑ Ⓒ Ⓓ Ⓔ
9. Ⓐ Ⓑ Ⓒ Ⓓ Ⓔ
10. Ⓐ Ⓑ Ⓒ Ⓓ Ⓔ
11. Ⓐ Ⓑ Ⓒ Ⓓ Ⓔ
12. Ⓐ Ⓑ Ⓒ Ⓓ Ⓔ
13. Ⓐ Ⓑ Ⓒ Ⓓ Ⓔ
14. Ⓐ Ⓑ Ⓒ Ⓓ Ⓔ
15. Ⓐ Ⓑ Ⓒ Ⓓ Ⓔ
16. Ⓐ Ⓑ Ⓒ Ⓓ Ⓔ
17. Ⓐ Ⓑ Ⓒ Ⓓ Ⓔ
18. Ⓐ Ⓑ Ⓒ Ⓓ Ⓔ
19. Ⓐ Ⓑ Ⓒ Ⓓ Ⓔ
20. Ⓐ Ⓑ Ⓒ Ⓓ Ⓔ
21. Ⓐ Ⓑ Ⓒ Ⓓ Ⓔ
22. Ⓐ Ⓑ Ⓒ Ⓓ Ⓔ
23. Ⓐ Ⓑ Ⓒ Ⓓ Ⓔ
24. Ⓐ Ⓑ Ⓒ Ⓓ Ⓔ
25. Ⓐ Ⓑ Ⓒ Ⓓ Ⓔ
26. Ⓐ Ⓑ Ⓒ Ⓓ Ⓔ
27. Ⓐ Ⓑ Ⓒ Ⓓ Ⓔ
28. Ⓐ Ⓑ Ⓒ Ⓓ Ⓔ
29. Ⓐ Ⓑ Ⓒ Ⓓ Ⓔ
30. Ⓐ Ⓑ Ⓒ Ⓓ Ⓔ

Answer Sheet for Practice Exam 2

Section III

1. Ⓐ Ⓑ Ⓒ Ⓓ Ⓔ
2. Ⓐ Ⓑ Ⓒ Ⓓ Ⓔ
3. Ⓐ Ⓑ Ⓒ Ⓓ Ⓔ
4. Ⓐ Ⓑ Ⓒ Ⓓ Ⓔ
5. Ⓐ Ⓑ Ⓒ Ⓓ Ⓔ
6. Ⓐ Ⓑ Ⓒ Ⓓ Ⓔ
7. Ⓐ Ⓑ Ⓒ Ⓓ Ⓔ
8. Ⓐ Ⓑ Ⓒ Ⓓ Ⓔ
9. Ⓐ Ⓑ Ⓒ Ⓓ Ⓔ
10. Ⓐ Ⓑ Ⓒ Ⓓ Ⓔ
11. Ⓐ Ⓑ Ⓒ Ⓓ Ⓔ
12. Ⓐ Ⓑ Ⓒ Ⓓ Ⓔ
13. Ⓐ Ⓑ Ⓒ Ⓓ Ⓔ
14. Ⓐ Ⓑ Ⓒ Ⓓ Ⓔ
15. Ⓐ Ⓑ Ⓒ Ⓓ Ⓔ
16. Ⓐ Ⓑ Ⓒ Ⓓ Ⓔ
17. Ⓐ Ⓑ Ⓒ Ⓓ Ⓔ
18. Ⓐ Ⓑ Ⓒ Ⓓ Ⓔ
19. Ⓐ Ⓑ Ⓒ Ⓓ Ⓔ
20. Ⓐ Ⓑ Ⓒ Ⓓ Ⓔ
21. Ⓐ Ⓑ Ⓒ Ⓓ Ⓔ
22. Ⓐ Ⓑ Ⓒ Ⓓ Ⓔ
23. Ⓐ Ⓑ Ⓒ Ⓓ Ⓔ
24. Ⓐ Ⓑ Ⓒ Ⓓ Ⓔ
25. Ⓐ Ⓑ Ⓒ Ⓓ Ⓔ
26. Ⓐ Ⓑ Ⓒ Ⓓ Ⓔ
27. Ⓐ Ⓑ Ⓒ Ⓓ Ⓔ
28. Ⓐ Ⓑ Ⓒ Ⓓ Ⓔ
29. Ⓐ Ⓑ Ⓒ Ⓓ Ⓔ
30. Ⓐ Ⓑ Ⓒ Ⓓ Ⓔ

Section IV

1. Ⓐ Ⓑ Ⓒ Ⓓ Ⓔ
2. Ⓐ Ⓑ Ⓒ Ⓓ Ⓔ
3. Ⓐ Ⓑ Ⓒ Ⓓ Ⓔ
4. Ⓐ Ⓑ Ⓒ Ⓓ Ⓔ
5. Ⓐ Ⓑ Ⓒ Ⓓ Ⓔ
6. Ⓐ Ⓑ Ⓒ Ⓓ Ⓔ
7. Ⓐ Ⓑ Ⓒ Ⓓ Ⓔ
8. Ⓐ Ⓑ Ⓒ Ⓓ Ⓔ
9. Ⓐ Ⓑ Ⓒ Ⓓ Ⓔ
10. Ⓐ Ⓑ Ⓒ Ⓓ Ⓔ
11. Ⓐ Ⓑ Ⓒ Ⓓ Ⓔ
12. Ⓐ Ⓑ Ⓒ Ⓓ Ⓔ
13. Ⓐ Ⓑ Ⓒ Ⓓ Ⓔ
14. Ⓐ Ⓑ Ⓒ Ⓓ Ⓔ
15. Ⓐ Ⓑ Ⓒ Ⓓ Ⓔ
16. Ⓐ Ⓑ Ⓒ Ⓓ Ⓔ
17. Ⓐ Ⓑ Ⓒ Ⓓ Ⓔ
18. Ⓐ Ⓑ Ⓒ Ⓓ Ⓔ
19. Ⓐ Ⓑ Ⓒ Ⓓ Ⓔ
20. Ⓐ Ⓑ Ⓒ Ⓓ Ⓔ
21. Ⓐ Ⓑ Ⓒ Ⓓ Ⓔ
22. Ⓐ Ⓑ Ⓒ Ⓓ Ⓔ
23. Ⓐ Ⓑ Ⓒ Ⓓ Ⓔ
24. Ⓐ Ⓑ Ⓒ Ⓓ Ⓔ
25. Ⓐ Ⓑ Ⓒ Ⓓ Ⓔ
26. Ⓐ Ⓑ Ⓒ Ⓓ Ⓔ
27. Ⓐ Ⓑ Ⓒ Ⓓ Ⓔ
28. Ⓐ Ⓑ Ⓒ Ⓓ Ⓔ
29. Ⓐ Ⓑ Ⓒ Ⓓ Ⓔ
30. Ⓐ Ⓑ Ⓒ Ⓓ Ⓔ

Section I
Logical Reasoning

TIME: 35 minutes for 24 questions

DIRECTIONS: Read the passage and choose the best answer. Some questions may have more than one answer that looks right. Select the one that answers the question most completely. Don't assume anything that isn't directly stated, and don't let your imagination run wild; all the information you need is in the arguments and the answer choices.

1. Consumer review: This mail-order catalog claims that its customers save money by buying clothing through it, but the economy it promises is illusory because it only occasionally marks down its normal prices.

   Which one of the following is an assumption on which the consumer review's argument depends?

   (A) This catalog's competitors mark down their normal prices more frequently and by greater amounts.

   (B) This catalog is economical only when its normal prices are marked down more than occasionally.

   (C) This catalog marks its normal prices down by smaller amounts than do its competitors.

   (D) The competitors have lower normal prices.

   (E) Consumers should make purchases by mail order only when the normal prices are marked down.

2. The archaeological findings at level IVa of a bronze-age settlement in Turkey show how the settlement met its end. The village was surrounded by a thick, defensive wall. The findings include a large number of clay vessels sunk in the ground, as though for long-term storage of food during a siege. A number of bronze arrowheads were found, and at least one of the structures seems to have suffered a fire. Therefore, this settlement was clearly destroyed in war, either with its neighbors or with foreign invaders.

   Which one of the following most accurately describes a flaw in the argument?

   (A) The argument is circular, with the premises taking for granted the truth of the conclusion.

   (B) The evidence is varied, but the conclusion is unified and therefore suspect.

   (C) The argument depends on intermediate conclusions, which make the final conclusion invalid.

   (D) The argument makes a historical conclusion but does not give specific dates to support it.

   (E) None of the pieces of evidence point directly to the conclusion, and all of them could lead to different conclusions.

3. Oceanographer: The size of oceanic waves is a function of the velocity of the wind and of *fetch*, the length of the surface of the water subject to those winds. The impact of waves against a coastline is a function of the size of the waves and the shape of the sea bottom. The degree of erosion to which a coastline is subject is a function of the average impact of waves and the geologic composition of the coastline.

   If the oceanographer's statements are true, which one of the following must also be true?

   (A) The fetch of winds is related to the shape of the sea bottom.

   (B) The size of oceanic waves will not fluctuate far from an average for any given stretch of ocean.

   (C) The degree of erosion to which a coastline is subject is related to the shape of the sea bottom.

   (D) The size of oceanic waves is related to the shape of the sea bottom.

   (E) The average velocity of the wind in an area plays no role in the degree of erosion to which a coastline is subject.

GO ON TO NEXT PAGE ➤

4. Historian: For a historian to assert that one historical event or circumstance caused another is nearly impossible. Given any coherent historical narrative, the sequence of events makes the notion of causation a tempting trap; a subsequent event can seem a necessary outcome of those that preceded it. But this is a mere consequence of the backward-looking perspective of the historian's art. That one event did in fact happen, and that other events did in fact happen prior to it does not make the subsequent event inevitable or a direct outcome of those that went before.

The claim that "this is a mere consequence of the backward-looking perspective of the historian's art" plays which one of the following roles in the historian's argument?

(A) It is used to identify the theoretical imperative that is the argument's concern.

(B) It is an illustration of a premise that is used to support the argument's conclusion.

(C) It is used to indirectly support a claim that the argument in turn uses to directly support the conclusion.

(D) It is used to explain a consideration that may be taken to undermine the argument's conclusion.

(E) It is the conclusion that the argument aims to support.

5. Despite five consecutive years in which global consumption of grain has been greater than global production, it is unlikely that the world is facing a near-term crisis in the food supply. The average shortfalls have been mainly due to reduced output from farms in China, which is moving from a policy of central control over agricultural production to a more market-driven model. Therefore, if demand for grain continues to fall short of supply, Chinese production of grain should increase dramatically.

Which one of the following principles most helps to justify this reasoning?

(A) Global markets respond more slowly than regional markets, so local rates of production usually change more rapidly than the global average.

(B) When agricultural production is centrally controlled, it is unable to respond to changing demand by adjusting rates of supply.

(C) Average shortfalls are most readily remedied by local increases in production.

(D) When agricultural production is market-driven, it is likely to respond to rising demand by increasing production.

(E) Centrally controlled agricultural production has been shown to be more inefficient than market-driven models.

6. Economist: Health insurers are largely immune to the factors that are limiting profit in many sectors of the healthcare economy. Consumers have shown a willingness to pay almost any price for health insurance premiums. Capital demands, which are the responsibility of doctors and hospitals, are increasing dramatically, even as cost-containment measures, largely encouraged by the insurers and their friends in government, have forced new levels of fiscal discipline upon hospitals and doctors. Patients still need MRIs and buildings to put them in, but hospitals are limited in how much they can charge patients for the use of these facilities.

Which one of the following most accurately describes the role that the statement "patients still need MRIs and buildings to put them in" plays in the economist's argument?

(A) It is a specific example of a general condition described in the course of the argument.

(B) It is used to counter a consideration that may be taken to undermine the argument.

(C) It is used to indirectly support the claim made by the argument.

(D) It describes a social side effect of the benefit with which the argument is concerned.

(E) It introduces the conclusion that the argument intends to support.

7. As peer-to-peer (PTP) file-sharing networks flourished, the ability of consumers to download music without paying seriously damaged the prosperity of the recording industry. The numbers speak for themselves. During this time, revenues from sales of CDs in the United States fell by tens of millions of dollars a year, despite the fact that prices for individual CDs kept pace with inflation. Clearly, then, PTP file-sharing was killing the recording industry.

The argument depends on assuming which one of the following?

(A) that all sharing from PTP networks violates copyright

(B) that no other explanations exist for the decreasing revenues from CD sales

(C) that the musicians and producers have a right to profit from the distribution of music

(D) that people who download music would otherwise have purchased it on CD

(E) that a complex relationship exists between file-sharing and the market in music, both online and on CD

8. Engineer: In any complex machine on which human life depends, critical systems must have many layers of built-in redundancy. So in designing airplanes, whose control surfaces depend on hydraulic systems for their movement, engineers must include multiple independent redundant systems of hydraulic lines, each capable of giving the pilot control of the airplane's control surfaces. More redundancy is always better than less, so if an airplane design is deemed relatively safe with three redundant hydraulic systems, it must be deemed safer with four, and safer still with five.

The engineer's argument is most vulnerable to criticism on the grounds that it

(A) assumes that redundant systems will not be subject to simultaneous failure

(B) fails to take into account any practical factors that may limit the number of redundant systems or practical trade-offs involved in increasing levels of redundancy

(C) focuses on one area — movement of the control surfaces — without taking into account other important considerations of safety

(D) is limited to a single kind of engineering project and may not be applicable as a general rule

(E) gives no comprehensive criteria for judging relative levels of safety, according to which you could evaluate its claim that increasing redundancy yields increasing safety

9. Forcing businesses to furnish employees with paid leave for family concerns, such as paternity leave or leave to care for a sick child, is a terrible idea. If a business allows employees to take this time off, the workers will take advantage of the privilege and come to work as little as possible. This will destroy productivity and workplace morale.

Which one of the following, if true, most seriously weakens the argument?

(A) European countries guarantee employees generous family leave and paid vacation time, but the European standard of living is slightly below that of the United States.

(B) Most male workers refuse to take paternity leave even though it is allowed under federal law and their employers encourage it; they fear they may anger co-workers and harm their chances for promotion if they take time off for what is still seen as a frivolous reason.

(C) The FMLA requires employers to grant employees 12 weeks a year of unpaid leave for family purposes; although employers save money because the leave is unpaid, they often must spend money to find a replacement for the employee who takes time off.

(D) In some workplaces, the loss of a single employee at a busy time of year can be devastating, even if that employee plans to return after a few weeks; allowing family leave can overwhelm the employees who stay on the job.

(E) Allowing employees to take leave for family matters reduces absenteeism, improves morale, and surprisingly increases productivity because the employees who are granted leave tend to work much harder and more efficiently when they come back to work.

GO ON TO NEXT PAGE

10. Casino gambling tends to be detrimental to individuals who live in the county where the casino is located, but paradoxically, it benefits businesses in those same counties. Individual bankruptcy rates in counties with casinos are more than double the national average. Bankruptcy rates for businesses in the same counties are 35 percent lower than the national average.

Which one of the following, if true, most helps to explain this apparent paradox?

(A) Businesses profit from casino gambling because they take in money from local and visiting gamblers, whereas local individuals have more opportunities to lose money gambling.

(B) Casinos are known to take advantage of gamblers by setting odds in such a way that the casino always makes a profit.

(C) Counties with casinos have many business opportunities for entrepreneurs who want to open hotels, restaurants, and other service businesses.

(D) Gambling functions as an addictive disease in many people; they find themselves unable to stop gambling even when they're seriously in debt and must borrow money to continue.

(E) Counties that vote to allow casinos to open generally are poor counties with high unemployment and low levels of education.

11. Social services worker: We approve of the government's new policy on food stamps. Instead of issuing actual stamps, the government now provides recipients with debit cards that they can use to buy groceries. Each month their accounts are electronically credited with their allowance, and they can spend the money just as if it were in a bank account but only on specific approved items. This method eliminates the inconvenience and embarrassment associated with food stamps, increases the number of qualified recipients who actually buy food with their allowance, and prevents the type of fraud that was a problem associated with the paper coupons.

All of the following, if true, help to support the position of the social services worker EXCEPT:

(A) In communities that use the food stamp debit cards, participation in food stamp programs has increased 74 percent since changing to cards from coupons.

(B) Paper food stamp coupons have long been abused by people who trade them for drugs or weapons at several cents on the dollar.

(C) The food stamp program is meant to improve nutrition among people with low incomes, and the government has long wanted to make sure program funds are used to buy food.

(D) People used to have to pick up their paper coupons at a government office once a month, which proved too inconvenient for many people who lacked transportation or free time.

(E) Some food stamp recipients say they prefer the paper coupons because they can't tell how much money they have in their debit card accounts.

12. Primatologist: We have discovered a new kind of primate in Madagascar, the fat-tailed lemur. These lemurs hibernate, sleeping in holes in trees for up to seven months out of the year. Winter temperatures in Madagascar rarely drop below 86 degrees, so these lemurs do not hibernate to escape the cold but perhaps to conserve energy during the dry season, when food is scarce. This is the first time anyone has found an animal that hibernates during hot weather, disproving the common belief that only animals in cold climates hibernate.

Which one of the following most accurately describes the role played in the primatologist's argument by the assertion that this is the first time anyone has found an animal that hibernates during hot weather?

(A) It challenges the long-held belief that primates never hibernate.

(B) It accuses scientists who have studied hibernation in the past of wrongfully assuming that hibernation only occurs in cold weather.

(C) It highlights the importance of this discovery because it disproves a long-held theory about hibernation.

(D) It calls into question the assumption that this behavior is true hibernation and suggests that it may be something else.

(E) It sets up a rival theory so that the primatologist can disprove it.

13. Director: I've decided to cast the famous American actor Burt Lancaster as the prince in my epic film of the Sicilian classic novel *The Leopard*. I want him for his star appeal and his massive dignity. The film will be in Italian, but Lancaster can't speak Italian, so I'll let him speak his lines in English and then have an Italian actor dub them in Italian. The result will be a seamless Italian film with a famous actor to help sales.

Which one of the following is an assumption on which the director's argument depends?

(A) Italian audiences will refuse to see a film of an Italian classic that does not use an Italian actor in the title role.

(B) The other actors in the film may object to playing their scenes with a character who cannot speak their language.

(C) To increase sales, having a famous actor in the title role of a film is more important than having an actor who can speak the film's language.

(D) Teaching Lancaster enough Italian to allow him to deliver his lines in the correct language would be impossible.

(E) Lancaster would feel uncomfortable working with a director and crew who did not speak English.

14. Alberto: We should eradicate mosquitoes from the earth. Mosquitoes cause a great deal of harm to humans, transmitting serious diseases such as malaria, dengue fever, and encephalitis, and they don't do anything desirable. Ecologists have found that the loss of a single species from an ecosystem doesn't usually harm the rest of the ecosystem, so eradicating mosquitoes wouldn't harm the environment, which of course would be undesirable.

Which one of the following, if true, would most weaken Alberto's argument?

(A) Mosquito-borne diseases such as malaria are responsible for millions of deaths and millions of dollars of lost productivity every year.

(B) One inevitable consequence of restoring wetlands to their original state is an increase in mosquito populations.

(C) Mosquitoes have historically kept human and other animal populations down by spreading disease among them.

(D) Many animals eat mosquitoes and other flying insects.

(E) The only substances that could eradicate all mosquitoes would also kill off many birds and beneficial insects.

15. Public parks are intended for use by all citizens equally. But when groups such as schools or churches use a park for parties or other organized events, they bring large numbers of people to the park at one time. Therefore, there should be strict rules against large groups using public parks.

The argument's reasoning is vulnerable to criticism on the grounds that the argument takes for granted that

(A) large groups of people may be noisy or become violent

(B) individuals have complained about large groups of people using public parks

(C) public parks are designed with use by organized groups in mind

(D) members of organized groups, like other individuals, pay taxes that support public parks

(E) large numbers of people coming to a park prevent individuals from enjoying use of the park

16. Employers have recently begun to offer their employees the opportunity to save money for future healthcare or family care expenses in flexible spending accounts, or FSAs. These accounts allow employees to set aside pretax salary income for specific expenses, which can result in a substantial savings on income tax. Surprisingly, though, very few employees have taken advantage of FSAs.

Which one of the following, if true, contributes most to an explanation of why few employees have chosen to save money in FSAs?

(A) Insurance companies have started to offer employees debit cards to go with FSAs, which makes it much easier to spend FSA funds.

(B) Not all employers offer FSAs to their employees.

(C) Employees can use funds saved in FSAs to pay for over-the-counter drugs and other healthcare costs that are not covered by insurance.

(D) Funds saved in FSAs must be spent during the plan year or forfeited.

(E) Employers who move to consumer-driven healthcare plans with high deductibles are finding that more of their employees choose to open FSAs.

17. Many Latin American countries established democratic governments in the past decade. Recently, however, six elected heads of state have been ousted during violent revolutions. A majority of people in those countries, dissatisfied with continuing poverty, have stated that they would install a dictator if he promised to improve economic conditions.

These statements, if true, most strongly support which one of the following conclusions?

(A) Some 220 million Latin Americans, nearly half the population of the region, live in grinding poverty without many of the basic necessities of life.

(B) The governments of these six Latin American countries, though democratically elected, are plagued by corruption and graft.

(C) A majority of residents of these six Latin American countries do not believe that democracy is necessarily the best form of government for them.

(D) Weak governments in Latin America are one of the reasons drug trafficking and illegal immigration to the United States have increased in the last decade.

(E) Some citizens of Latin American countries have expressed the opinion that rule by organized crime is preferable to democratically elected leadership.

18. Years ago people enjoyed homemade eggnog and cookie dough made with raw eggs without fear, but today raw eggs are spoken of as a biohazard, a potential hotbed of salmonella waiting to cause disease and death with the slightest contact. In previous decades, salmonella was generally found on the outside of eggshells, mainly from the eggs having come in contact with the waste products of the chickens who laid them. More recently, however, a growing number of chickens are themselves infected with salmonella, thus allowing the bacterium to be present inside the egg itself. So where once simply washing uncracked eggs protected diners from illness — usually some form of gastrointestinal distress, only rarely fatal — now only cooking eggs thoroughly can guarantee a safe dining experience.

Which one of the following most accurately expresses the main conclusion of the argument?

(A) Salmonella poisoning is on the increase but is rarely fatal.

(B) The relationship between salmonella and eggs has in fact changed over the years, justifying the recent caution with which people regard raw eggs.

(C) Some caution is merited when handling raw eggs, although the facts behind salmonella and eggs do not merit extreme levels of caution.

(D) The risk of food poisoning from eating raw eggs is related to the conditions under which the eggs are produced, which have changed over time.

(E) The caution with which people regard their food is related to a better understanding of the science behind food poisoning.

19. Software engineers know that a poorly written application can consume more memory than it should and that running out of memory can cause an application to crash. However, if a crashing application causes the whole operating system to crash, the fault lies with the operating system.

Which one of the following, if true, is least helpful in establishing that this conclusion is properly drawn?

(A) Operating systems with generous amounts of memory are less susceptible to crashing, even when applications are poorly written.

(B) Operating systems can isolate the memory used by individual applications, even when an application uses a large amount of memory.

(C) An operating system can monitor an application's consumption of memory and take action when that gets too high.

(D) Techniques for programming operating systems to catch and handle memory errors are well-defined and well-known among programmers.

(E) Because many applications can run simultaneously under a single operating system, the operating system should have a well-defined method of managing memory consumption.

20. The document was published under a license that allows others to copy it and disseminate it as long as they do so for noncommercial purposes only. Company A included copies of the document in a training manual that it marketed and sold, arguing that the license was invalid. However, even if the license were proved invalid, the copyright was still valid, leaving Company A with no rights to use the document in any way at all.

Which one of the following situations best demonstrates the principle illustrated by this argument?

(A) The warranty on the laptop computer claimed to be rendered void if the user opened the case. But the manual that came with the laptop included instructions for opening the case to upgrade the computer's memory. Consumers successfully argued that those instructions constituted an endorsement of users' opening the case and that, therefore, the warranty was not void.

(B) When the 13-year-olds were caught trying to enter an NC-17 movie at a multiplex, they argued that the cashier at the ticket counter had sold them tickets for that movie. The manager explained that the cashier's error did not change the rules of age limits and movie ratings.

(C) A restaurant was fined by the Alcoholic Beverage Commission for serving distilled liquors when its license covered only beer and wine. The restaurant's manager argued that he had applied for the proper license and expected to receive it within days. The ABC countered that a license was valid only from the moment the restaurant posted it on the premises.

(D) Ted's parents have stated that he cannot drive the station wagon unless it is to Alice's house. When his mother saw the station wagon parked at the mall, some miles away, Ted argued that Alice was not at home. Ted's mom pointed out that he ought, upon discovering that fact, to have driven straight home.

(E) The celebrity sued the magazine for publishing photographs of him sunning himself in his backyard, which was enclosed by a high fence. The magazine claimed that he was a public figure and did not, therefore, have the same rights to privacy as normal citizens. The celebrity claimed that the extensive fence around his yard justified his privacy rights when behind it, despite his prominent stature in the eyes of the public.

21. Scholar: Greek epic poetry emerged as an art form before any of it was ever written down. Singers developed a specialized vocabulary that allowed them to compose poems about the heroes of the Trojan War as they sang them. These poems were neither made up from scratch as the singer sang nor fixed texts that were memorized and repeated verbatim. Even after written texts were created that captured these orally composed poems, the tradition continued to evolve, with written texts of the same poem differing from place to place and from time to time, according to the circumstances of their production and the interests of their creators and their intended audiences.

If the scholar's statements are true, which one of the following must be true?

(A) Each written edition derived from the first written version of an orally composed epic.

(B) No single written edition of a Greek epic can claim to represent the "original" version.

(C) The poems inevitably grew longer and more narratologically complex over the centuries.

(D) The tradition of composing epics orally died away as the poems came to be written down.

(E) The older editions of the poems were less likely to have been influenced by local politics than subsequent editions.

22. Curator: This museum does not grant people the right to use images of items in its collection in online publications. We are obliged to do everything in our power to ensure the continued appeal of visiting our collection in person.

The curator's argument depends on assuming which one of the following?

(A) Taking photographs of art objects, especially using a flash, can damage the objects by accelerating the fading of paint.

(B) The museum sells pictures of its collection in its gift shop, which is an important source of income for the museum.

(C) Images placed online are easily copied and reused by other people.

(D) The quality of most electronic images, especially those online, falls short of the professional standards of the museum.

(E) If people see online images of items in the museum's collection, they will no longer be interested in seeing the collection with their own eyes.

23. Career counselor: Many large international companies have changed their practices regarding international assignments. They are placing much more emphasis on helping spouses of expatriate employees to adjust to the foreign environment. This has reduced premature returns by 67 percent.

Which one of the following is an assumption upon which the career counselor's argument depends?

(A) Spousal and marital difficulties were formerly responsible for a large number of premature returns from foreign assignments.

(B) When an employee is placed in a foreign assignment for a year or less, his or her family sees the assignment as an adventure.

(C) Expatriate employees work long hours and travel a great deal, and their children make new friends at school, but spouses often have no friends and no work to support them while they're abroad.

(D) The majority of international assignments today last for less than a year, but ten years ago, 70 percent of them lasted much longer than one year.

(E) Many companies now offer expatriate spouses language training, career guidance, and assistance in finding homes and schools.

24. Traveler: When I flew to Boston on Tuesday, I checked my suitcase but carried my computer on the plane. When I arrived at Logan Airport, none of the checked bags from the flight had arrived. The baggage office clerk was very helpful with my polite questions but punished the other passengers who were so rude by making them wait for her assistance.

Which one of the following principles is best illustrated by the traveler's reasoning?

(A) A stitch in time saves nine.

(B) Do not price an unborn calf.

(C) Do not put all your eggs in one basket.

(D) Neither a borrower nor a lender be.

(E) You catch more flies with honey than you do with vinegar.

DO NOT TURN THE PAGE UNTIL TOLD TO DO SO **STOP** DO NOT RETURN TO A PREVIOUS TEST

Section II
Reading Comprehension

TIME: 35 minutes for 26 questions

DIRECTIONS: Read each passage and answer the questions that follow it. Some questions may have more than one answer that looks correct. In that case, pick the one that answers the question most completely and correctly. Don't assume anything that isn't stated in the passage or the questions. All the information you need to answer the questions is contained in the passage, questions, and answer choices.

Questions 1–6 refer to the following passage.

Black Apollo, by Kenneth Manning, describes the life of Ernest Everett Just, one of the first black scientists in America. Manning recounts Just's impoverished origins in South Carolina, his adaptations to a white educational system, and his professional careers as a zoology professor at Howard University and as an embryologist at Marine Biological Laboratory. Despite countless difficulties imposed upon him by a world in which a black person was not supposed to practice science, Just became an internationally esteemed biologist. His story is one of courage, determination, and dedication to science. But Manning's goals are more far-reaching than to simply tell a story or describe one man's life. After all, though Just was a brilliant biologist, he was not ultimately pivotal to the development of either science or race relations in the 20th century. The issues brought out in his story, however, are pivotal. A comprehensive appreciation of the conditions that Just faced in his daily work offers a powerful lens through which to examine the development of science and racial boundaries in America.

Manning wrote Just's story as a biography. In some respects, biography does not seem to be a promising medium for great historical work. Biographies simply tell a story. Most students receive their introductions to the history of science in the worshipful biographies of past scientific giants. Benjamin Franklin and Albert Einstein offer excellent examples to young students of how scientists contribute to society. Biographies are popular for children's reading lists (and bestseller lists) because they have simple subjects, can present clear

moral statements, and manage to teach a little history at the same time. This simplicity of form, however, does not preclude the biography from being a powerful medium for historical work and social commentary.

The biography yields *particular* rewards for the historian of science. One of the central principles of the history of science, indeed a central reason for the discipline, is to show that science is a product of social forces. This principle implies that historians and sociologists have insights on the practice of science that scientists, to whom the subject would otherwise fall, are less likely to produce. Moreover, if society does influence science, then it behooves historians to explain how such an important process works. The human orientation of the biography makes it an excellent medium in which historians can do this work. Were a researcher to investigate the development of scientific theory solely by reading the accounts written of a laboratory's experiments — by looking only at the "science" — the researcher would likely see a science moved by apparently rational forces toward a discernible goal. But this picture is incomplete and artificial. If that researcher examines science through the people who generated it, a richer mosaic of actors emerges. The science biography has the potential to reveal both the person through the science and the science through the person. From these perspectives, the forces of politics, emotions, and economics, each of which can direct science as much as rational thought, are more easily brought to light. *Black Apollo* is a riveting example of what a historian can accomplish with a skillful and directed use of biography.

1. Which one of the following most accurately states the main point of the passage?

(A) Ernest Everett Just was an extremely important biologist during the 20th century, both because of his contributions to the field of embryology and because of his race.

(B) Scientists tend to ignore the social, historical, and political forces that surround all scientific research and discovery, which makes their interpretations of scientific events incomplete.

(C) Biographies are a popular genre for children's books because they can tell discrete stories in an accessible fashion, incorporating scientific knowledge into a person's life and thereby making it more interesting to readers.

(D) Manning's work exemplifies how biography can be a powerful tool for a historian of science, who can use the genre to explore the effects of politics, economics, and emotions on the direction of scientific development.

(E) Kenneth Manning wrote *Black Apollo* to criticize racial prejudices and to prove that Ernest Everett Just could have been much more successful if he had not been the victim of discrimination.

2. According to the passage, the main goal of the discipline called *history of science* is to

(A) illuminate the effects of social forces on scientists in a way that scientists themselves are unlikely to do

(B) explain scientific discoveries in a manner that is easily understood by non-scientists

(C) write biographies of important scientific figures that portray their work against a social and political background

(D) influence scientific research by identifying the most important scientific contributions in history

(E) provide an academic discipline that allows people without science training to study scientific concepts

3. What is the primary purpose of the second paragraph?

(A) to describe the many things Ernest Everett Just accomplished despite the racial prejudice he faced

(B) to suggest that biography is really too simple a historical form for the historian of science to use to convey complex ideas

(C) to explain why biography is both a popular historical genre and a powerful medium for explaining the significance of scientific discoveries

(D) to argue against using biographies to teach children about scientific figures from the past

(E) to advocate increased teaching of the sciences in schools and universities

4. The author of the passage would be most likely to agree with which one of the following statements?

(A) One of the best ways to come to an understanding of the realities of race relations and scientific development in the 20th century is to read an in-depth account of the life of one of the people who lived and worked in that world.

(B) The goal of a historian of science is to glorify the accomplishments of his historical subjects, embellishing them if need be.

(C) A scientific historian should pay close attention to the social and literary aspects of a scientific biography and play down the actual science, because readers can turn to scientific reports to get that information.

(D) Ernest Everett Just was likely the most important black biologist, and in fact one of the most important biologists, of the 20th century.

(E) Biography is too limited a genre to allow a historian of science to do justice to a topic, but it is useful occasionally because most readers find biographies more accessible than other historical formats.

GO ON TO NEXT PAGE

5. According to the passage, why is Ernest Everett Just significant enough to warrant a biography?

   (A) Just was one of the first professional black scientists in the United States.

   (B) Just grew up in poverty but overcame this initial adversity to attend Howard University and then become a professional scientist.

   (C) Just was a biologist whose work was known and respected internationally.

   (D) Just's daily experiences illuminate the conditions characterized by both scientific research and racial relations during his lifetime.

   (E) Just became a college professor and an embryologist at Marine Biological Laboratory.

6. When the author mentions "simplicity of form" at the end of the second paragraph, this most nearly refers to

   (A) the simple language common to historical biographies intended for children

   (B) the idea that a biography can serve as the primary introduction to scientific history

   (C) the aspect of biographies that makes them insufficient for significant historical pedagogy

   (D) the powerful social commentary that a heroic life story can provide

   (E) the story aspect of biographies that may in some ways make them seem incapable of providing meaningful social commentary

Questions 7–13 refer to the following passage.

Sodium lauryl sulfate (SLS) is an emulsifier and surfactant that produces lather and foam that can dissolve oil and dirt on skin and hair. SLS and another similar detergent, sodium laureth sulfate (SLES), are commonly used as foaming agents in cleaners, shampoos, and toothpaste. Both of these substances are derived from coconut oil. They make liquid and paste cleansers more effective at cleansing because they allow the cleanser to disperse more readily over the object being cleaned and make it easier to rinse the cleanser away. SLS and SLES have been used for years in numerous products sold to consumers. Other foaming agents are available, but SLS and SLES have remained popular because of their low cost, effectiveness, lack of taste and odor, and long history of safe use.

The use of SLS and SLES comes with a few minor risks. The substances burn human eyes, a phenomenon well-known to anyone who has ever gotten a drop of shampoo in her eye. A high enough concentration of SLS will burn skin if it remains in contact with the skin for a long time, though normally this is not a problem because the products containing SLES or SLS are diluted with water and quickly rinsed away. SLS in toothpaste can cause diarrhea in someone who swallows a large quantity of it, but it is not known to be toxic if ingested in small quantities.

Many people have become afraid of SLS and SLES in recent years, largely as a result of widespread rumors circulated on the Internet that blame SLS and SLES for causing numerous ailments in humans, including hair loss, dry skin, liver and kidney disease, blindness in children, and cancer. SLS has been called "one of the most dangerous substances used in cosmetic products." Rumors warn that SLS and SLES can react with other ingredients in products to form nitrates, which are potential carcinogens. Detractors of SLS and SLES point out that these substances are used in cleansers intended for the floors of garages and bathrooms and in engine degreasers. This is true; it is also true that household and garage cleaners are not sold for cosmetic use, come with warnings of possible skin and eye irritation, and are perfectly safe to use for their intended purposes.

These Internet warnings of the dangers of SLS and SLES are absurd and unsubstantiated. The U.S. Food and Drug Administration (FDA) has approved the use of SLS and SLES in a number of personal care products. The Occupational Safety and Health Administration (OSHA), the International Agency for Research on Cancer, and the American Cancer Society have all done extensive research on SLS and SLES and concluded that they do not cause cancer.

7. Which one of the following best summarizes the main idea of the passage?

(A) A few minor risks are associated with the use of SLS and SLES, but consumers should feel safe in using products containing these substances because the FDA has approved them for use in personal care products.

(B) Manufacturers of shampoos and toothpastes include the artificial chemicals SLS and SLES in their products because they are cheap and effective surfactants, despite the known dangers associated with them.

(C) SLS and SLES are detergents that are commonly used in personal care products because they are effective and safe, despite unsubstantiated rumors to the contrary.

(D) Widespread rumors circulated on the Internet blame SLS and SLES for numerous ailments in humans, including hair loss, dry skin, liver and kidney disease, blindness in children, and cancer.

(E) It is entirely possible to use SLS and SLES in both personal care products such as shampoos and industrial products such as engine degreasers because, at lower concentrations, the substances are perfectly safe to use on human skin.

8. The author's reasoning in the third paragraph to argue that the use of SLS and SLES is safe is most like which of the following arguments?

(A) The FDA warning that the pesticides used in conventional farming are carcinogenic is unwarranted. This is not true. People have been consuming produce grown on conventional farms for decades.

(B) This set of baking pans perfectly browns breads, cakes, and other baked goods when they are used as intended in a conventional oven. The results are not ideal when the same set of pans is used to cook items in the microwave; foods are cooked unevenly, burned in some areas, and raw in others.

(C) It is true that those who oppose legislation that would bring about universal health care are entities such as insurance companies and medical providers whose economic bottom lines would be adversely affected should such legislation come to pass. It is also true that these entities could possibly benefit from the proposed changes to health care.

(D) The rumors that a certain celebrity has been accused of shoplifting are untrue. The report has been exposed as a tabloid publicity stunt.

(E) While it is true that the playpen manufactured by ToyCo has defects that may make it unsafe for use by children over six months old, it is also true that a playpen manufactured by ChildCo is said to be unsafe.

9. The author mentions the FDA in the last paragraph most likely to

(A) point out that the FDA has approved the use of SLS and SLES in personal care products

(B) suggest that the FDA has the best interests of consumers at heart

(C) imply that the FDA's opinion that SLS and SLES are safe for use in personal care products excuses manufacturers from testing their personal care products for safety

(D) protest the FDA's approval of the use of SLS and SLES in personal care products

(E) refute claims that SLS and SLES are dangerous

10. Which of the following questions is directly answered by the passage?

(A) What other foaming agents are available instead of SLS and SLES?

(B) What are the effects of ingesting SLS in small quantities of toothpaste?

(C) Which personal care products containing SLS and SLES has the FDA approved?

(D) Why do some products contain emulsifiers?

(E) What causes SLS and SLES to create a burning sensation in the eyes and on the skin?

GO ON TO NEXT PAGE

11. Which one of the following best describes the organization of the passage?

    (A) a list of known risks of exposure to SLS and SLES; a list of unsubstantiated risks of exposure to SLS and SLES; a conclusion stating that SLS and SLES are perfectly safe

    (B) a description of several common surfactants and the way in which they work; several anecdotal accounts of injuries and illnesses allegedly caused by SLS and SLES; a call for the government to ban the use of SLS and SLES in consumer care products

    (C) a description of the chemical composition of SLS and SLES; a list of evidence against the use of SLS and SLES in personal care products; a proposal to manufacturers suggesting that they use only naturally occurring substances in their products

    (D) an overview of the many uses of SLS and SLES; an explanation of why manufacturers use these substances in both consumer care and household cleaning products; a criticism against people who spread rumors over the Internet; praise for the FDA

    (E) a description of SLS and SLES and their uses; known risks of SLS and SLES; criticisms aimed at SLS and SLES by detractors on the Internet; evidence that SLS and SLES are safe and the rumors unfounded

12. The primary purpose of the third paragraph is

    (A) to criticize makers of personal cleansing products for including harsh chemicals in their shampoos, toothpastes, and other offerings

    (B) to describe the way SLS and SLES work and explain why they are commonly used in various foaming products

    (C) to warn readers of the dangers associated with exposure to SLS and SLES, which include cancer, skin irritation, blindness, and kidney and liver ailments

    (D) to propose other naturally occurring substances that manufacturers could substitute for SLS and SLES in their products

    (E) to explain why some people fear SLS and SLES and to list the diseases that Internet rumors have linked to the substances

13. It can be inferred from the passage that the author would be most likely to agree with which one of the following statements?

    (A) It is unreasonable for people to be afraid of substances that have been deemed safe by the FDA and several other major organizations, and that have a long history of safe use, simply on the basis of unsubstantiated rumors.

    (B) Consumers can trust the FDA to make sure that all consumer products are safe because the FDA is funded by tax dollars and takes seriously its mission to ensure the health of American citizens.

    (C) The Internet is not a very reliable source of information on health topics unless that information has been posted by government agencies or major advocacy groups.

    (D) SLS and SLES are cheap and effective surfactants and emulsifiers, but they aren't especially safe to use in products intended for direct physical contact with human skin.

    (E) If enough concerned consumers protest the inclusion of SLS and SLES in personal care products, they can persuade manufacturers to use all-natural ingredients, but there's no reason for them to do this because SLS and SLES are safe.

Questions 14–19 refer to the following two passages. The first is adapted from Forensic Psychology and Law, by Ronald Roesch, Patricia A. Zapf, and Stephen D. Hart (John Wiley & Sons, Inc.). The second is adapted from Forensic Psychology: Crime, Justice, Law, Interventions, 2nd Edition, edited by Graham Davies and Anthony Beech (John Wiley & Sons, Inc.).

Passage A

There are many factors that may account for mistaken eyewitness identification. Wells distinguished between system variables and estimator variables. *System variables* affect the accuracy of eyewitness testimony that the criminal justice system has some control over. For example, the way a question is worded or the way a lineup is constructed may impact the accuracy of eyewitness identification. In these instances, the justice system has some control over these variables. *Estimator variables,* on the other hand, are those that may affect the accuracy of eyewitness testimony but that the criminal justice system does not have any control over. These variables have to do with the characteristics of the eyewitness or the circumstances surrounding the event witnessed. For example, the amount of attention that an eyewitness paid to a perpetrator, how long an eyewitness viewed a perpetrator, or the lighting conditions under which a perpetrator was viewed would be examples of estimator variables. The vast majority of the research on eyewitness identifications deals with system variables since they are under the control of the justice system and thus can be modified accordingly to improve the accuracy of eyewitness identifications and testimony.

Much research has shown that asking an eyewitness misleading questions will influence his or her subsequent reports of a prior observed event. Some theorists contend that the misleading questions serve to alter the original memory trace.

Race, gender, and age are three characteristics that have been examined to determine the extent to which they impact eyewitness accuracy. Each is an estimator variable and, therefore, out of the control of the justice system. With respect to age, the majority of the research has examined the differences between adults and children in terms of eyewitness testimony.

Research on gender differences in eyewitness identification indicates that there is no evidence that females are any better or worse than males. Similarly, there is no evidence that members of one race are better or worse at eyewitness identification than members of another race. However, there is evidence to suggest that people are better at recognizing the faces of members of their own race than they are at recognizing the faces of members of other races.

Passage B

Human cognitive abilities are incredible. Consider the task faced by an eyewitness who is present during a street crime. The cognitive system allows the witness to transform characteristics of the light reflected towards her eyes into visual information and characteristics of perturbations in the air made by the culprit's vocal system into auditory information. The person synchronizes these sources of information (and sometimes smells, tastes, and tactile information) with a highly functional knowledge base of past experiences. At later points in time, the witness is able to use this continually adapting knowledge base to bring that distant information into the present. As amazing as these cognitive abilities are, they are not perfect. Information is forgotten and distorted, and the past century of memory research has revealed some systematic patterns for these deficits.

To understand how findings from memory research can be applied to a forensic context, it is necessary to understand how memory science works. Within a criminal context, eyewitness memory is a tool that, if reliable, should be diagnostic of guilt or innocence. By this we mean that presenting eyewitness evidence should usually make guilty people seem more likely to be guilty, and innocent people seem more likely to be innocent. In the U.S. Supreme Court's *Daubert* (1993) ruling, the court argued that, for scientific evidence to be presented, there should be a known error rate. The courts do not state what the maximum error rate (or the minimum reliability) should be to allow evidence to be presented in court because this threshold would likely depend on the type of evidence and could depend on peculiarities of an individual case.

One of the main goals for eyewitness researchers is to estimate this error rate and show how it varies by different factors. Ultimately, to estimate the reliability of any forensic tool as complex and context-dependent as eyewitness memory, it is necessary to understand how the system works.

14. Which of the following statements best describes the relationship between the two passages?

(A) Passage A presents an opinion about the accuracy of eyewitness testimony that Passage B calls into question.

(B) Passage A relies on research to prove the validity of a statement, while Passage B primarily supports its statements with anecdotal evidence.

(C) Passage A provides a general definition of a term that Passage B defines more specifically.

(D) Passage A evaluates some of the circumstances that may contribute to a particular phenomenon; Passage B elaborates on that analysis.

(E) Passage A focuses on the psychological and sociological implications of a finding, while Passage B concentrates on the legal applications.

GO ON TO NEXT PAGE

15. Which one of the following statements is most strongly supported by both passages?

(A) Eyewitness testimony is highly accurate considering the complexity of human memory.

(B) Eyewitness testimony is often flawed because it is influenced by a variety of factors.

(C) The human memory follows an arc pattern over one's lifetime, strengthening through adulthood and then weakening as one enters old age.

(D) Little if any evidence supports the fact that males provide more accurate eyewitness testimony than females.

(E) Determining a known error rate for eyewitness testimony involves a complex integration of many variables.

16. Which one of the following claims about eyewitness testimony is not suggested by Passage A?

(A) How the lighting in a particular event affects the reliability of eyewitness identification is a variable that warrants a good amount of study.

(B) The accuracy of eyewitness identification can be negatively affected by the eyewitness's race.

(C) The many factors that can lead to mistaken eyewitness identification can be grouped into two main categories.

(D) Much research has been done to assess how the order of a lineup may affect eyewitness identification.

(E) Asking misleading questions is one of the variables that affect the accuracy of eyewitness testimony over which the judicial system has at least some measure of control.

17. The passages have which of the following aims in common?

(A) to express the need for researchers to come up with a calculable error rate to determine whether eyewitness evidence may be admissible in court

(B) to define episodic memory and explain how it may come into play in judicial proceedings

(C) to identify the differences between system and estimator variables

(D) to determine how race, age, and gender can affect the accuracy of eyewitness testimony

(E) to understand how memory and human cognitive abilities are affected by a variety of different factors

18. Which of the following statements most accurately characterizes a difference between the two passages?

(A) Passage A discusses how misleading questions can affect the accuracy of eyewitness testimony, whereas Passage B dismisses the importance of how a witness is questioned.

(B) Passage A emphasizes the importance of forensic research; Passage B is primarily concerned with the way that same research influences how system variables, such as controlling lineups, are manipulated by judicial proceedings.

(C) Passage A discusses the role that gender plays in eyewitness testimony while Passage B dismisses the idea that gender influences eyewitness accounts.

(D) Passage A focuses on controlling the variables in eyewitness testimony, and Passage B concentrates on understanding the science behind human recollection.

(E) Passage B focuses on how research can improve the reliability of eyewitness testimony; Passage A does not.

19. Which of the following statements is not supported by one or both of the passages?

   (A) Human memory sometimes fails to recollect events exactly how they happened.

   (B) The cognitive system is remarkable because it is able to match sensory stimuli with previous experience.

   (C) Testimony based on a witness's memory ideally should provide confirmation of a culprit's guilt.

   (D) The 1993 *Daubert* ruling involved a court argument surrounding the need for a known error rate in regards to eyewitness testimony.

   (E) Lighting issues and the length of time someone witnessed an event are examples of system variables.

Questions 20–26 refer to the following passage.

Public education as it is currently known was a creation of a German government worried about the dangers of workers' uprisings that was then transformed by Enlightenment and Romantic educational theories into an institution genuinely concerned with developing human minds. Before the 1700s, Europe had no public education. Parents who wanted their children to be educated paid for private schools or private tutors. The rest of the children in Europe worked. Many of them worked alongside their parents in spinning factories, producing thread for Germany's burgeoning textile industry. The textile mill owners blatantly exploited their workers, which led to increasing levels of unrest on the part of the peasants. During the 1750s, King Frederick II asked his minister of Silesia, Ernst Wilhelm von Schlabrendorff, to find a way to channel the energy of restless peasants into something that would be less dangerous to the throne than riots.

Schlabrendorff suggested that the king could mold a compliant citizenry if he created a system of state-run schools. These schools could teach the children of the peasantry that their lot was ordained by God, that they should not try to improve it, that the government was good to them, and that they should not question authority, along with teaching reading, writing, and arithmetic. School would be compulsory, and children who did not attend could be punished by truant officers.

This would shift children's primary loyalty from their parents and families to the state; their parents would be powerless against the truant officers and thus would be forced to send their children to school whether they wanted to or not. Aristocrats liked this idea. They liked the thought of schools making peasants more docile and patriotic, and they appreciated the way state-run schools would teach children of lower social classes to accept their position in life. In 1763, Frederick gave Schlabrendorff the go-ahead to start opening schools, and soon every child in Silesia between the ages of 7 and 15 was attending school. These earliest schools, called *Spinnschulen*, combined work with education. Children took classes in the mornings and spun thread in the afternoons.

By the 1800s, the Spinnschulen had metamorphosed into full-day schools with state-certified teachers who taught a state-approved curriculum, and Germany became a hotbed of educational theory, much of it influenced by 19th-century Romanticism that directly contradicted the principles that had led to the foundation of public schools in the 1700s. Johann Bernhard Basedow used the work of Enlightenment scholars to argue that education should be a holistic pursuit, incorporating physical movement, manual training, realistic teaching, and the study of nature. Friedrich Froebel invented kindergarten in the mid-1800s, creating a "children's garden" based on the belief that children are naturally creative and productive, and he developed special toys designed to teach specific skills and motions. Wilhelm von Humboldt specialized in secondary and university educational theory, insisting that advanced students should pursue independent research and prizing above all three educational principles: self-government by teachers, unity of teaching, and academic freedom.

GO ON TO NEXT PAGE

20. The passage is primarily concerned with discussing which one of the following?

(A) the use of public schools to disseminate political messages, as exemplified by German public schools in the 18th and 19th centuries

(B) the exploitation of the working class by German aristocracy in the 18th century and the use of public education to justify this practice

(C) the philosophical origins of public schools in 18th century Germany and the transformation in educational thinking in the 19th century

(D) the thinking of German educational theorists and their influence on modern educational practices

(E) the role of Frederick II's minister of Silesia and the German aristocracy in the creation of public schools in Germany

21. The passage suggests which one of the following about the owners of textile mills in the 1700s?

(A) They wanted their child workers to have the benefit of an education, so they opened schools within their factories and required all young workers to attend classes.

(B) Because they could pay children less than adults, they preferred to hire young workers whenever they could.

(C) They were indifferent to the well-being and needs of their workers.

(D) They were all aristocrats who believed their authority was divinely ordained and that, as a result of this divinely ordained position, they had a duty to care for the less fortunate people in their communities by providing work and education for them.

(E) They were uniformly patriotic and supported the authority of their king without question, and they advocated for the opening of Spinnschulen because this would allow peasants to be taught the same patriotic ideals they held so dear.

22. According to the passage, how did 19th-entury schools differ from 18th-century schools?

(A) Eighteenth-century schools were intended to make textile mills run more efficiently by making workers become more skilled at their jobs; 19th-century schools were no longer attached to textile factories.

(B) Eighteenth-century schools were concerned primarily with teaching working-class children to accept their fate and love their ruler; 19th-century schools began to focus on developing the full human potential of students.

(C) Eighteenth-century schools were open only to children of the aristocracy whose parents could pay their tuition. By the 19th century, schools were open to all free of charge, but poorer students had to pay their way by working in spinning factories in the afternoons.

(D) Eighteenth-century schools were designed to instill patriotic ideals in the peasantry and make them docile and compliant; 19th-century schools instead tried to develop all children into free thinkers.

(E) Eighteenth-century schools were not appealing to parents, who often tried to keep their children out of school and as a result were punished by truant officers; 19th-century schools, on the other hand, were appealing to both parents and children because educational philosophers believed a more pleasant environment was more conducive to education.

23. What does the author mean by the phrase "increasing levels of unrest" in the first paragraph?

(A) riots and other forms of violence against the owners of textile factories by peasants unhappy at their treatment

(B) political speeches and demonstrations by politicians trying to earn the working-class vote

(C) aggression from neighboring countries looking to invade Germany

(D) religious turmoil between Catholics and Protestants

(E) juvenile delinquency and vandalism by unemployed and uneducated young men

24. According to the passage, what did German aristocrats think about the idea of creating public schools?

(A) They feared that educating the working classes would make them less docile and accepting of their position in life and more likely to rise up and overthrow the nobles.

(B) They disliked the idea of paying taxes to support public schools and resented the king and Schlabrendorff for forcing this expense on them.

(C) They appreciated Schlabrendorff's brilliance in concocting an idea that would both make the peasantry more compliant and simultaneously produce more workers for the spinning factories.

(D) They approved of disseminating religious education to the masses because this would make the citizenry more compliant and less likely to engage in workers' rebellions.

(E) They liked the idea because it would make the peasantry more complacent and accepting of their fate, which would help keep the aristocracy safe in their prosperity.

25. According to the passage, what was the purpose of using truant officers to keep children in school?

(A) to ensure that all children received the full education that was their right, even if their parents wished instead to keep them working at home

(B) to take away the authority of parents and replace it with state power over children and citizens

(C) to assist parents in making sure that their children attended school as required by catching and punishing children who failed to attend

(D) to indoctrinate children and their parents with political messages designed to help the aristocracy

(E) to assist the king and his administration in molding a compliant citizenry through voluntary participation in state-run schools

26. Which one of the following best summarizes the views of 19th-century educational thinkers?

(A) The function of state-run schools is to instill obedience, patriotism, and docility in the working classes; wealthy children whose parents can afford to pay can have a more liberal education provided by private tutors.

(B) The most important subject for children to learn is religion, which is why schools should be run by the Church and should include all aspects of worship and theology.

(C) Most people cannot adequately educate their children on their own, but the state has an interest in an educated citizenry, so it is the government's job to provide public education and see that people send their children to school.

(D) People learn best in an environment that respects their individuality, affords them freedom, and incorporates a variety of aspects of learning, such as physical movement, manual skills, and independent exploration.

(E) A child's best and first teacher is his or her mother, so mothers should be encouraged to teach their children at home; this produces better results than public schools and is much cheaper for the state.

DO NOT TURN THE PAGE UNTIL TOLD TO DO SO STOP DO NOT RETURN TO A PREVIOUS TEST

Section III

Logical Reasoning

TIME: 35 minutes for 25 questions

DIRECTIONS: Read the passage and choose the best answer. Some questions may have more than one answer that looks right. Select the one that answers the question most completely. Don't assume anything that isn't directly stated, and don't let your imagination run wild. All the information you need is in the arguments and the answer choices.

1. Economist: On average, the more a person donates to a religious group, the less likely that person is to participate in religious activities, including weekly or daily religious services. Therefore, we can conclude that the wealthiest people attend the fewest services.

   Which one of the following statements, if true, most seriously weakens the economist's argument?

   (A) People with average incomes tend to donate more to religious groups than wealthier individuals.

   (B) Many wealthy people claim that they feel more comfortable skipping services if they give more money to their churches.

   (C) Conservative Protestants tend to continue attending services even when they donate large amounts.

   (D) One of the causes of the Protestant Reformation in the 1500s was the Church's practice of granting indulgences to parishioners who donated money.

   (E) The bigger a check a parishioner writes, the more likely he is to skip services the following weekend.

2. Geneticist: The odds of having a child born with Down syndrome increase dramatically when a woman reaches the age of 35. By the age of 49, a woman has a one in four chance of conceiving a child with such abnormalities. Yet the vast majority of Down syndrome children are born to mothers under the age of 35.

   Which one of the following, if true, most helps to reconcile the geneticist's two claims?

   (A) The number of women having babies in their forties has increased in the last decade.

   (B) Down syndrome is one of the most common birth defects.

   (C) Many mothers decide to abort fetuses that are diagnosed with chromosomal abnormalities in prenatal tests.

   (D) New tests can now identify fetuses affected with Down syndrome in the first trimester.

   (E) Most babies are born to mothers under the age of 35.

3. Shoe company: Our shoes are masterpieces of podiatric design. We use wide toe boxes to give toes room to spread naturally. Our foot beds support the entire foot, toe, arch, and heel. Slightly raised heels and a curved sole alleviate fatigue and facilitate walking. The materials we use in soles are excellent shock absorbers. We guarantee that your feet will love our shoes or your money back.

   The claim that "we guarantee that your feet will love our shoes or your money back" plays which one of the following roles?

   (A) It infers from the information preceding it that advanced podiatric design is essential to comfortable shoes.

   (B) It implies that if a consumer purchases these shoes and they hurt her feet, the company will refund her purchase price.

   (C) It suggests that all customers who buy these shoes are satisfied with their purchases.

   (D) It criticizes the design of most mass-produced shoes, which are much more likely to cause foot problems.

   (E) It argues that only shoes designed by certified podiatrists can guarantee healthy and pain-free feet.

4. The administration has issued new regulations restricting travel to Cuba and limiting the amount of time visitors can spend there. Only Cuban-Americans are allowed to visit Cuba. They can visit only once every three years for 14 days, they may bring only $300 in cash to the country, and they may not bring back to the United States any merchandise purchased in Cuba. These regulations should hasten the fall of Cuba's repressive dictatorship, which should benefit all Cuban people.

Which one of the following, if true, most weakens the argument?

(A) Many Cubans avoid financial hardship because they rely on cash and goods brought to them by relatives who previously could visit once a year and bring in a maximum of $3,000.

(B) United States citizens who are not Cuban-American will not be allowed to visit Cuba at all.

(C) Cuba's government is led by a communist dictator, who has been in control of the island nation since the 1950s.

(D) Critics of the law have accused the administration of pandering to the demands of the powerful Cuban-American lobby in Florida.

(E) The Treasury Department believes that Cuba's regime receives a great deal of financial support from infusions of cash brought into the country by Cuban-Americans.

5. Airline representative: We have reduced the number of award seats available to customers wanting to exchange 25,000 frequent-flier miles. However, we have significantly increased the number of flights on which any seat can be exchanged for 50,000 miles, giving travelers much greater scheduling flexibility. We believe customers will appreciate this change.

The reasoning in the airline representative's argument is most vulnerable to criticism on the grounds that the argument

(A) suggests that customers with more frequent-flier miles deserve more access to seats than those with fewer frequent-flier miles

(B) criticizes customers who use frequent-flier miles to purchase seats for their inflexibility

(C) neglects to mention that airlines dislike awarding frequent-flier seats because they cut into profit margins

(D) assumes without offering evidence that customers value scheduling flexibility enough to pay double the frequent-flier miles for it

(E) disingenuously encourages people to use their frequent-flier miles to upgrade to first-class instead of purchasing coach class tickets

6. Sociologist: Women tend to marry up; that is, they marry men who are at least their equals in education and income. This trend is not as apparent among women with the most education and the highest incomes, who are more likely to marry men of equal status, but it is perceptible among women with less education and lower incomes. Thus it seems likely that many men, especially poverty-stricken ones, will never manage to find wives.

The conclusion drawn by the sociologist follows logically if which one of the following is assumed?

(A) Highly educated women are most likely to marry educated men.

(B) Wealthy men are more physically attractive to women than are poor men.

(C) Across all income levels, women have on average higher educational attainments than men.

(D) Highly educated men still make more money than their female counterparts.

(E) Low-income women are more interested in education than their male counterparts.

GO ON TO NEXT PAGE ▶

7. Bullying bosses are a common fixture of the workplace. They usually abuse subordinates simply because they enjoy exerting power for its own sake. Subordinates who are abused by their bosses typically perform their jobs as usual and almost never lodge formal complaints, preferring to complain in sessions with co-workers during which they discuss their bosses' misdeeds.

Which one of the following best illustrates this proposition?

(A) Boss Maureen blames subordinate Skylar for all her mistakes, informing clients that she would have gotten work done on time but for his incompetence. Skylar files a complaint with the Equal Employment Opportunity Commission and receives a right-to-sue letter for national origin discrimination.

(B) Boss Frank makes subordinate David stay late every afternoon, making him do work that he could have done in the morning if he had known about it. David tolerates this for a few months and then accepts a job at a rival company.

(C) Boss Belinda makes fun of the way subordinate Casey dresses, telling her that no one will ever take her seriously with her budget wardrobe. Casey informs her company's human resources manager of Belinda's comments and is transferred to another department.

(D) Boss Bill requires that subordinate Paul bill a certain number of hours but often fails to provide Paul with enough work. Paul comes to the office every day and pretends to work without accomplishing very much, spending much of his time complaining about Bill to his secretary.

(E) Boss Stephanie constantly criticizes subordinate Kim's work, correcting it one way one day and then correcting it back to its original state the next. Kim meekly accepts the criticisms but spends every Thursday evening at a bar with co-workers making fun of Stephanie.

8. To earn a graduate equivalency diploma, a student must pass tests on subjects taught in high schools, proving that he or she has mastered them to the degree assumed of a high school graduate. It makes sense for a student to drop out of high school and earn a GED. A GED takes much less time to earn than a high school diploma and provides evidence that the student has learned everything he or she would have learned in high school.

Which one of the following, if true, most seriously weakens the argument?

(A) Some GED-prep programs incorporate enrichment activities into their test preparation, such as taking students to art exhibits and theatrical performances.

(B) Most colleges and universities consider a GED equivalent to a high school degree for admission purposes.

(C) Many successful businesspeople dropped out of high school and earned a GED.

(D) Employers assume that high school graduates generally have a much higher level of mastery of academic subjects than those who earn GEDs.

(E) Many GED students are slightly older than high school students, and they often hold jobs in addition to studying to pass the GED tests.

9. The legislature should ban over-the-counter sales to minors of cold medications containing dextromethorphan, commonly known as DXM. Teenagers have been taking overdoses of these medications to induce a cheap high and hallucinations, but high doses of this drug can cause comas or death. Emergency room visits involving this substance have increased recently, as teens research DXM on the Internet. A ban is the best way to protect our young people.

Which one of the following, if true, most strongly supports this argument?

(A) Effects of DXM overdoses include high fever, seizures, comas, and death.

(B) DXM is not an addictive substance and will not induce chemical dependency in regular users.

(C) The standard dose of DXM for treating colds is 15 milligrams; teenagers commonly take 100 milligram doses to induce hallucinations and a feeling of unreality.

(D) A ban on over-the-counter sales of cough medicines containing codeine reduced incidences of codeine overdoses by 50 percent in two years' time.

(E) Between 2000 and 2003, the number of calls to poison control centers about overdoses of DXM more than doubled.

10. Hurricanes start over the ocean and must remain over water to keep their powerful winds moving. They almost always form in the tropics in the late summer and early autumn, when the water is warmest. They lose strength when they move onto land and eventually dwindle and die away.

If these statements are true, which one of the following must also be true based upon them?

(A) A city on the coast is more vulnerable to being struck by a hurricane than an inland city.

(B) Hurricanes can never strike coastal areas in the northern part of the United States because the water there is too cold.

(C) Most hurricanes begin in the eastern Atlantic and travel westward toward the Americas.

(D) It would be impossible for a hurricane to do much damage more than a few miles from the coast.

(E) Hurricanes that form in the early fall tend to be stronger than hurricanes in the late summer.

11. Parent: I'm not going to have my child vaccinated against common childhood diseases. I fear the side effects of the vaccines. In any case, because other children are vaccinated, I won't have to fear my child catching the diseases the vaccines are designed to prevent.

A reasoning flaw in the parent's argument is that the argument

(A) criticizes parents who do have their children vaccinated

(B) makes an emotional plea against forcing children to undergo injections

(C) attacks government leaders who have insisted on a national vaccination program

(D) implies that other parents are not as knowledgeable about the side effects of vaccines

(E) assumes that no other parents will take the same stance against vaccination

GO ON TO NEXT PAGE

12. The phrase "under God" in the Pledge of Allegiance is not unconstitutional because, throughout our nation's history, various presidents and political leaders have invoked God in inaugural addresses, Thanksgiving speeches, and other public statements of national unity. Therefore, requiring public school teachers to lead their students in the pledge every day does not force religious beliefs on anyone.

The argument is most vulnerable to criticism on the grounds that it

(A) ignores evidence that many politicians do not invoke God in public addresses because they believe it would be an improper exercise of religion

(B) fails to acknowledge that the majority of U.S. citizens approve of including the phrase "under God" in the pledge

(C) equates freedom of expression by national leaders with proof that requiring students to mention God in the pledge is not an unjust imposition of religious beliefs

(D) praises teachers who lead their classes in the Pledge of Allegiance for performing an act of patriotism that deserves no reward

(E) assumes that all U.S. citizens believe in the same deity and wish to invoke that deity's protection of the nation and its people

13. Barsad: Europeans work far fewer hours on average than Americans do. Full-time workers in Europe rarely work more than 35 hours a week and take off between four and six weeks every year. This more humane work pattern is directly tied to the higher income taxes imposed on Europeans; high taxes reduce the take-home profit of working long hours, which takes away any incentive workers may have to put in more time than necessary to achieve a comfortable standard of living.

Preston: Within Europe, no consistent correlation exists between higher income taxes and shorter working hours. In Ireland, for example, taxes have hardly risen at all in the last 30 years, but the country's workers have nevertheless decreased their average working hours by 25 percent.

This dialogue lends the most support to the claim that Barsad and Preston disagree with each other about which one of the following statements?

(A) Europeans value leisure much more than Americans do, as evidenced by their shorter workweeks and much more generous vacation policies.

(B) Europeans work shorter hours than Americans because higher income taxes remove any incentive they may feel to increase their take-home pay by working longer hours.

(C) Higher income taxes in the United States would inspire Americans to cut back on the hours that they work, which would benefit families and equalize wealth in the nation.

(D) Despite the fewer hours they spend at work, Europeans have a standard of living that is no more than 25 percent lower than that enjoyed by Americans.

(E) Some studies have found a correlation between higher taxes and shorter hours, but those studies also found that the taxes accounted for only one-third of the difference in hours between Americans and Europeans.

14. History has shown that people will reduce their consumption of fuel only if they have a financial incentive to do so. For example, in the energy crisis of the 1970s, people drastically lowered their consumption of gasoline. When California suffered its own statewide energy crisis in 2001, the state promised a 20 percent discount on power bills to consumers who reduced their power consumption, and a majority of citizens managed this feat. The government should therefore implement financial incentives to reduce energy consumption, such as taxes on gasoline or rewards for reduced consumption.

Which one of the following is an assumption required by the argument?

(A) The government should not interfere with energy policies and should instead let the market guide consumption.

(B) In some cases, citizens have reduced their power consumption even without incentives.

(C) Policies created during the energy crisis of the 1970s should serve as a model of policies that could address the current energy crisis.

(D) Getting citizens to use less energy than they currently do is desirable.

(E) The federal government should follow California's lead in setting energy policy.

15. Requiring public school students to adhere to dress codes or wear uniforms has many benefits. It cuts down on disciplinary problems, reduces theft, and makes it difficult for wealthy students to make fun of poorer ones because of their clothes. Dress codes do reduce individual expression, but a public school doesn't need to be a training ground for nonconformists. A dress code can work, though, only if all students are required to follow it.

Which one of the following is most strongly supported by the information above?

(A) Public schools should be a forum for individual expression.

(B) Enforcing conformity on public school students is justifiable.

(C) The only way to implement a dress code is to assign students an official uniform.

(D) Most parents of public-school students like dress codes because dressing their children for school is easier and cheaper.

(E) Dress codes reduce theft and other disciplinary problems without necessarily harming individual expression.

16. I bought a pair of glasses from an optometrist. One of the lenses regularly pops out of the frame. Therefore, this optometrist does not know how to make a good pair of glasses.

The reasoning in the argument is most vulnerable to criticism on the grounds that the argument

(A) does not allow the optometrist a chance to defend himself

(B) does not consider the possibility that other optometrists also make defective frames

(C) criticizes the optometrist's use of a particular technique when making glasses

(D) jumps to the conclusion that the defect in the glasses must be due to the optometrist's lack of skill

(E) accuses the optometrist of deliberately sabotaging the glasses

17. If Person A promises to do something on the condition that Person B perform a specific action, and Person B performs that action, then Person A is obligated to do whatever he or she promised to do.

Which one of the following most closely conforms to this principle?

(A) A man promises a woman that he will give her an engagement ring as soon as he returns from his military deployment. When he returns, he gives her an engagement ring.

(B) A boss promises his workers a party if they reach a sales goal by the end of the month. They reach their sales goal, but the boss decides the party would be too expensive and buys pizza instead.

(C) A seal trainer gives her seals fish as a reward whenever they perform their tricks correctly. The seals perform perfectly, and the trainer gives them fish.

(D) A mother promises to take away her son's toy airplane if he throws a tantrum that afternoon. He throws a tantrum that afternoon, so she takes his toy airplane.

(E) A professor promises a student that he will write a good recommendation for her if she does well in the class. She does poorly, so he writes her a bad recommendation.

18. Zoologist: I have discovered a gene that controls whether an individual is monogamous. I took a gene from the monogamous prairie vole and implanted it into its more promiscuous relative, the meadow vole. Thereafter, the meadow voles with the new gene became monogamous.

Which one of the following, if true, would provide the most support for the zoologist's argument?

(A) Studies on humans and other mammals have shown that receptors for the hormone vasopressin play a role in autism, drug addiction, and the formation of romantic attachments.

(B) Prairie voles typically form lifelong partnerships, which scientists have linked to an increased number of receptors for the hormone vasopressin.

(C) Meadow voles live in a harsher environment than prairie voles and cannot afford to pass up opportunities to mate as often as possible.

(D) The zoologist used a harmless virus to capture the gene and transfer it into the meadow voles.

(E) The meadow voles that had the prairie vole gene implanted in them were released into and observed in the same habitat in which they had previously lived.

19. An art museum has bought a bronze statue that it believes is a sculpture of the god Apollo by the famous ancient Greek sculptor Praxiteles. Only a few sculptures known to be by Praxiteles still exist today, and many sculptures once thought to be by him were actually copies of his originals made by ancient Romans. Dating ancient sculpture accurately is difficult for scholars, but they have found several features of this statue that make it likely that it dates from the era of Praxiteles, and it certainly conforms to the sculptor's style.

Which one of the following is most strongly supported by this information?

(A) The art museum cannot be confident that this statue was made by Praxiteles.

(B) In some cases, museums have purchased sculptures that they believed were ancient works and later discovered that they were made by modern forgers.

(C) After extensive research and investigation, scholars will be able to state conclusively whether this statue was made by Praxiteles.

(D) The statue is certainly an original Greek bronze statue dating from the late fourth century BC or the early third century BC.

(E) Praxiteles's style is so distinctive that it is readily apparent when a statue is one of his originals as opposed to a copy.

20. Psychologist A: Psychologists should not refer to the people who participate in their experiments as *subjects,* which is an extremely impersonal term that could apply as well to rodents. They should instead call them *participants,* which implies willing consent, except in the case of infants, who of course cannot consent and should be called *individuals.* This concept has been included in the new guidelines for psychologists who conduct research.

Psychologist B: I wish the psychologists' governing body had never decided to change the guidelines. The term *subject* worked for years, and my colleagues and I never felt that the word denied the humanity of the people we studied. We now never know what to call the people we use in our studies, and we fear criticism if we inadvertently use the wrong term.

Psychologist A and Psychologist B disagree about whether

(A) those who take part in psychological experiments prefer to be called *participants*

(B) the psychologists' governing body has the authority to change guidelines on terminology used by researchers

(C) the new terminology guidelines were a valuable and necessary update to the field of psychological research

(D) some older children are capable of consenting to participation in research studies

(E) the word *subject* implies a passive participant, and the word *participant* implies an active one who has given her consent

21. Gynecologist: Scottish researchers have developed a test that allows them to predict at what age a woman will experience menopause. The scientists use a model that compares a woman's ovaries to "average" ovaries to see whether her ovaries are aging faster or more slowly than average. They have discovered that the size of ovaries is directly related to the number of eggs they contain, which in turn is directly related to fertility. This discovery will significantly influence women's decisions on when to have children.

The gynecologist's conclusion follows logically if which one of the following is assumed?

(A) Women with smaller ovaries tend to have less success with assisted reproduction techniques, such as in vitro fertilization.

(B) Most women experience menopause around the age of 50, but their fertility starts to decline at the age of 37.

(C) Any discovery that allows women to predict when they will experience menopause will influence their decisions on when to have children.

(D) The test cannot tell women how likely they are to conceive in the years just prior to menopause.

(E) Every woman is born with several million eggs in her ovaries, which formed while she was a fetus; the number of eggs dwindles over her lifetime, until at menopause she has 1,000 or fewer.

22. School board member: A school in a wealthy suburb and a school in a poverty-stricken part of the inner city received exactly the same funding and got completely different results. The school in the suburb sent all its graduates to college, but the school in the city sent only 10 percent to college and suffered a 25 percent dropout rate before graduation. Clearly, the inner-city school is wasting its money, whereas the suburban school puts its money to good use.

The reasoning in the school board member's argument is flawed because the argument

(A) mistakenly finds a correlation between levels of funding and graduation rates

(B) assumes that most of the inner-city school students are unprepared for college

(C) fails to consider that funding levels are not the only factors influencing school performance

(D) unfairly criticizes the administrators of the inner-city school for their students' failures

(E) jumps to the conclusion that students in the suburbs are more intelligent and harder working than students in the inner city

GO ON TO NEXT PAGE

23. Motorcyclists are told always to wear helmets when they ride their motorcycles. But helmets only protect riders when they have wrecks, and wrecks occur only once out of every 1,000 rides. Therefore, a motorcyclist would be perfectly safe if he wore his helmet only once out of every 1,000 rides.

Which one of the following employs a flawed argumentative strategy that is most closely parallel to the flawed argumentative strategy in this statement?

(A) My European client calls once a week, always in the evening, after everyone has left the office. I will be sure to get his messages if I turn on my telephone's answering machine once a week.

(B) This sunscreen allows me to stay in the sun 15 times longer than I could without sunscreen. If I apply two coats of it, it will allow me to stay in the sun 30 times longer.

(C) The odds are 1,000 to 1 against winning the big jackpot on this slot machine. If I play the slot machine 1,000 times, I am sure to win the big jackpot.

(D) Seat belts protect passengers in automobile accidents, but accidents only occur in one out of every 2,000 car trips. Because drivers are in the car the most, they should wear their seat belts most often.

(E) Top law schools accept one out of every 20 applicants. Therefore, someone who wants to get into a top law school should apply to 20 of them.

24. During the 20th century, the introduction of widespread indoor plumbing and electricity and the invention of machines such as washing machines and dishwashers made it much easier for women to accomplish their daily housekeeping chores. Ironically, by the 1950s, women actually spent *more* time doing housework than they had 40 years earlier, before these innovations.

Which one of the following, if true, most helps to resolve the apparent discrepancy in this passage?

(A) By the 1950s, people expected cleaner clothes and surroundings and more elaborate meals than they had earlier in the 20th century.

(B) Women who had gone to work outside the home in the 1940s subsequently found housekeeping a poor substitute, which led directly to the feminist movement of the 1960s.

(C) The 1950s were the height of the postwar baby boom, and women had to spend a great deal of their time caring for their children.

(D) Husbands of the 1950s were highly unlikely to help their wives with housework or cooking, though they did typically care for the car and the yard.

(E) In the 1950s, many young families moved to newly built suburbs, where wives often found themselves isolated during the day while their husbands went to work and their children went to school.

25. European Union: To reduce consumer confusion, we have issued new rules regulating the use of regional names on food products. Under these rules, actual geographical origin will take precedence over traditional usage, so a product such as Parmesan cheese can no longer be called that unless it was produced in Parma, Italy.

American Food Manufacturers Union: This ban is outrageous and unfair to food manufacturers and distributors. Certain regional names have been in common use for centuries and have taken on a generic meaning; all consumers know that the term *Parmesan* refers to a type of cheese, not to the geographical region in which the cheese was manufactured.

Based on this conversation, the European Union and the American Food Manufacturers Union disagree on which one of the following points?

(A) whether a product originating in one region can be produced with the same level of quality when made in another region

(B) whether the European Union should allow American food products bearing names of European regions to be imported into Europe

(C) whether Americans of European ancestry can still appreciate the nuances in taste that result from manufacturing food products in specific regions famous for them

(D) whether consumers think that geographical food names are generic

(E) whether it is possible to have an intellectual property right in a geographical name

Section IV
Analytical Reasoning

TIME: 35 minutes for 25 questions

DIRECTIONS: Each group of questions in this section is based on a set of conditions. In answering some of the questions, it may be useful to draw a rough diagram. Choose the response that most accurately and completely answers each question and blacken the corresponding space on your answer sheet.

Questions 1–5 refer to the following scenario.

It is 1848, and a number of women and men are attending the first United States convention in support of women's rights in Seneca Falls, New York. Six prominent feminists and abolitionists will speak at this meeting: Susan B. Anthony, Frederick Douglass, Jane Hunt, Lucretia Mott, Elizabeth Cady Stanton, and Martha Wright. Each of them will speak once and only once, and only one person speaks at a time. One person speaks per hour; the first speaker begins at 2 and the last one at 7. The following rules determine the order in which they speak:

Neither Frederick Douglass nor Lucretia Mott may speak at 6.

Elizabeth Cady Stanton speaks before either Frederick Douglass or Lucretia Mott but not before both.

If Jane Hunt speaks at 2, then Susan B. Anthony must speak after Martha Wright.

If Elizabeth Cady Stanton speaks at 4, then Martha Wright speaks at 7.

1. Which one of the following could be an accurate order of speakers?

(A) Frederick Douglass, Jane Hunt, Elizabeth Cady Stanton, Lucretia Mott, Martha Wright, Susan B. Anthony

(B) Frederick Douglass, Elizabeth Cady Stanton, Susan B. Anthony, Martha Wright, Lucretia Mott, Jane Hunt

(C) Jane Hunt, Lucretia Mott, Susan B. Anthony, Elizabeth Cady Stanton, Martha Wright, Frederick Douglass

(D) Jane Hunt, Martha Wright, Frederick Douglass, Elizabeth Cady Stanton, Susan B. Anthony, Lucretia Mott

(E) Martha Wright, Elizabeth Cady Stanton, Jane Hunt, Frederick Douglass, Susan B. Anthony, Lucretia Mott

2. If Jane Hunt speaks at 2, then which one of the following must be false?

(A) Susan B. Anthony speaks at 5.

(B) Frederick Douglass speaks at 3.

(C) Lucretia Mott speaks at 3.

(D) Martha Wright speaks at 4.

(E) Martha Wright speaks at 5.

3. If Martha Wright speaks at 7, then which one of the following must be true?

(A) Jane Hunt speaks at 4.

(B) Elizabeth Cady Stanton speaks at 4.

(C) Lucretia Mott speaks at 5.

(D) At least one person speaks before Jane Hunt speaks.

(E) At least two people speak before Frederick Douglass speaks.

4. All of the following speakers can speak at 2 EXCEPT:

(A) Susan B. Anthony

(B) Frederick Douglass

(C) Lucretia Mott

(D) Elizabeth Cady Stanton

(E) Martha Wright

5. Which one of the following could be an accurate partial schedule of speakers?

(A) Susan B. Anthony at 3; Elizabeth Cady Stanton at 6

(B) Jane Hunt at 2; Elizabeth Cady Stanton at 3

(C) Jane Hunt at 2; Martha Wright at 7

(D) Martha Wright at 3; Elizabeth Cady Stanton at 4

(E) Elizabeth Cady Stanton at 5; Susan B. Anthony at 7

A ballroom dance club has seven members: four women — Madeleine, Natasha, Olivia, and Phoebe — and three men — Antonio, Bertrand, and Christophe. They have entered a ballroom competition that has five events performed in this order: foxtrot, paso doble, rumba, tango, and waltz. Each member of the club competes in exactly one event. They compete either in pairs of one man and one woman or as solo performers. The following rules determine who dances with whom and in which event:

Antonio competes as a solo performer.

Natasha competes as part of a pair.

Olivia competes in the rumba.

Bertrand cannot compete in an event immediately before or immediately after the event in which Christophe competes.

6. If Phoebe is the only member who competes in the foxtrot, and Bertrand competes in the rumba, then which one of the following must be true?

(A) Antonio competes in the paso doble.

(B) Antonio competes in the waltz.

(C) Madeleine competes in the paso doble.

(D) Natasha competes in the tango.

(E) Natasha competes in the waltz.

7. If Antonio chooses his event first, what is the maximum number of the remaining events from which Natasha can choose her own event?

(A) one

(B) two

(C) three

(D) four

(E) five

8. If solo women compete in the foxtrot and the paso doble, then which of the following members must compete in the tango?

(A) Antonio

(B) Madeleine

(C) Natasha

(D) Natasha and Christophe

(E) Phoebe and Bertrand

9. Which one of the following is a complete and accurate list of the members who CANNOT dance solo?

(A) Bertrand, Natasha, and Phoebe

(B) Christophe, Bertrand, and Natasha

(C) Madeleine and Natasha

(D) Madeleine, Natasha, and Phoebe

(E) Natasha and Olivia

10. Which of the following is a complete and accurate list of the women who could compete solo?

(A) Madeleine

(B) Phoebe

(C) Madeleine and Olivia

(D) Madeleine and Phoebe

(E) Madeleine, Olivia, and Phoebe

11. If the four women compete in four consecutive events, and Natasha competes in the waltz, then which of the following is a complete and accurate list of the events in which members must compete as solo performers?

(A) foxtrot and paso doble

(B) foxtrot and tango

(C) paso doble

(D) foxtrot, paso doble, rumba, and tango

(E) tango

12. If the three men compete in the first three events, then which one of the following must be true?

(A) Bertrand competes in the foxtrot.

(B) Bertrand and Madeleine compete in the same event.

(C) Bertrand and Natasha compete in the same event.

(D) Christophe competes in the rumba.

(E) Natasha competes in the foxtrot.

GO ON TO NEXT PAGE

Seven famous chefs — Andrea, Berthe, Emilio, Jacques, Kimiko, Marthe, and Nigel — have volunteered their services for a presidential dinner. It consists of five courses, served in the following order: hors d'oeuvres, consommé, entrée, salade, and dessert. The dinner begins at 7 and ends at 10. One or two courses are served each hour, at 7, 8, and 9. The chefs refuse to work with one another, so each course is prepared by exactly one chef. No chef can prepare more than one course per hour. The following chefs have offered to prepare the following courses:

Hors d'oeuvres: Berthe and Marthe

Consommé: Andrea and Kimiko

Entrée: Andrea and Nigel

Salade: Berthe, Emilio, and Jacques

Dessert: Emilio, Kimiko, and Marthe

13. What is the minimum number of chefs who could prepare the entire meal?

(A) two

(B) three

(C) four

(D) five

(E) six

14. If the salade is served at 9, which one of the following could be a complete list of chefs who prepare a course served at 8?

(A) Andrea and Kimiko

(B) Berthe

(C) Emilio and Nigel

(D) Kimiko

(E) Marthe

15. Which one of the following CANNOT be a complete and accurate list of the chefs who prepare the meal?

(A) Andrea, Berthe, Jacques, and Kimiko

(B) Andrea, Berthe, Kimiko, and Marthe

(C) Andrea, Emilio, Marthe, and Nigel

(D) Andrea, Jacques, Kimiko, and Marthe

(E) Berthe, Emilio, Jacques, and Marthe

16. Which one of the following pairs of chefs could each prepare two courses served during the same two time slots?

(A) Andrea and Berthe

(B) Andrea and Kimiko

(C) Andrea and Marthe

(D) Berthe and Emilio

(E) Kimiko and Nigel

17. Which one of the following pairs of chefs could each prepare a course served at 7 and a course served at 9?

(A) Andrea and Kimiko

(B) Andrea and Marthe

(C) Berthe and Kimiko

(D) Berthe and Marthe

(E) Emilio and Marthe

18. Which one of the following could be a complete and accurate list of the chefs who prepare the meal?

(A) Andrea, Berthe, Emilio, and Nigel

(B) Andrea, Emilio, Jacques, Kimiko, and Nigel

(C) Berthe, Emilio, Kimiko, and Marthe

(D) Berthe, Emilio, Marthe, and Nigel

(E) Emilio, Jacques, Kimiko, and Marthe

On a Friday afternoon, an English literature student rents from the local library five film versions of literary classics — *Emma, Great Expectations, Ivanhoe, Middlemarch,* and *Wuthering Heights* — to help him prepare for an exam the following Friday morning. Three of the films are on disc and two are on videotape. The student can watch no more than one film per evening, and Thursday is the last night he can watch a film. The student must schedule his film viewing under the following conditions:

Emma is on videotape. *Wuthering Heights* is on disc.

The student must watch *Wuthering Heights* before he watches *Emma.*

The student must watch *Middlemarch* and *Ivanhoe* after he watches *Great Expectations.*

The student must watch *Emma* on Monday.

The student cannot watch any two videotapes on consecutive days or any two discs on consecutive days.

The student must watch a film on disc on Saturday.

19. Which one of the following could be an accurate schedule of the student's viewing of the films?

   (A) Friday: *Great Expectations*; Saturday: *Wuthering Heights*; Sunday: *Emma*; Tuesday: *Middlemarch*; Wednesday: *Ivanhoe*

   (B) Friday: *Great Expectations*; Saturday: *Wuthering Heights*; Monday: *Emma*; Tuesday: *Middlemarch*; Wednesday: *Ivanhoe*

   (C) Friday: *Great Expectations*; Saturday: *Wuthering Heights*; Monday: *Emma*; Tuesday: *Middlemarch*; Thursday: *Ivanhoe*

   (D) Friday: *Wuthering Heights*; Sunday: *Great Expectations*; Monday: *Emma*; Tuesday: *Ivanhoe*; Wednesday: *Middlemarch*

   (E) Saturday: *Wuthering Heights*; Monday: *Emma*; Tuesday: *Middlemarch*; Wednesday: *Great Expectations*; Thursday: *Ivanhoe*

20. If the student watches *Great Expectations* before he watches *Emma*, then which one of the following statements CANNOT be true?

   (A) *Great Expectations* is on disc.

   (B) *Ivanhoe* is on disc.

   (C) *Middlemarch* is on disc.

   (D) The student does not watch a film on Sunday.

   (E) The student does not watch a film on Wednesday.

21. If *Middlemarch* is on videotape, then which one of the following statements could be true?

   (A) *Ivanhoe* is on videotape.

   (B) The student watches *Emma* exactly three days before watching *Middlemarch*.

   (C) The student watches *Great Expectations* exactly one day before watching *Middlemarch*.

   (D) The student watches *Ivanhoe* on Wednesday.

   (E) The student watches *Middlemarch* on Thursday.

22. Which one of the following statements must be false?

   (A) The student watches films on both Friday and Monday.

   (B) The student watches films on both Monday and Wednesday.

   (C) The student does not watch a film on either Friday or Sunday.

   (D) The student does not watch a film on either Sunday or Wednesday.

   (E) The student does not watch a film on either Tuesday or Thursday.

23. If the student watches *Great Expectations* after he watches *Wuthering Heights*, then which one of the following statements must be false?

   (A) The student does not watch a film on Friday.

   (B) The student watches *Ivanhoe* before he watches *Middlemarch*.

   (C) The student watches *Great Expectations* before he watches *Emma*.

   (D) *Great Expectations* is on disc.

   (E) *Ivanhoe* is on disc.

24. If the student does not watch a film on Wednesday, then which one of the following statements must be true?

   (A) The student watches *Great Expectations* on Friday.

   (B) The student watches *Great Expectations* on Tuesday.

   (C) The student watches *Ivanhoe* on Tuesday.

   (D) The student watches *Ivanhoe* on Thursday.

   (E) The student watches *Middlemarch* on Tuesday.

25. If the student watches *Ivanhoe* before he watches *Middlemarch*, then how many different ways could he schedule his list of films to view them all during the week?

   (A) one

   (B) two

   (C) three

   (D) four

   (E) five

Writing Sample

A third-year law student has just received two job offers, one from a small boutique firm and the other from a large firm. Write an essay in favor of choosing one law firm over the other based on the following considerations:

>> The student wants to work for a firm that will allow him to explore many different areas of practice.

>> The student wants to work for a firm that will give him early responsibility and client contact and possibly advance him rapidly.

The small boutique firm limits its practice to estate planning, tax law, and bankruptcy work. Because the firm has only four attorneys, the student would immediately receive his own clients and his own files. The hiring partner has promised him that the firm will help the student gain proficiency, and if he learns quickly and gets along with his co-workers, he could become a partner in three or four years.

The large firm has teams who handle a wide variety of practice areas, including insurance defense, corporate, employment law, workers' compensation, construction litigation, real estate, and healthcare. The firm typically rotates its new associates through all these areas, allowing them to spend six months to a year working with a particular team before moving to another. By the fifth year, most associates have become permanent members of a team; this prepares them for partnership, which is never offered before an associate has worked for the firm for at least seven years.

Chapter 18

Practice Exam 2: Answers and Explanations

This chapter has answers and explanations to the multiple-choice sections in Chapter 17, as well as an abbreviated key at the end of the chapter if you need to score your test quickly. It doesn't contain sample answers for the writing sample because no correct answer exists for an essay response. The LSAT doesn't score your essay, but law schools may read it. Respond in a well-organized and legible manner to adequately satisfy the assignment.

Section I: Logical Reasoning

1. **B. This catalog is economical only when its normal prices are marked down more than occasionally.**

   The review must be assuming that it's impossible that the prices in this catalog can save customers money without being specially marked down. Choice (A) is wrong because the argument doesn't depend on the behavior of the catalog's competitors. Choice (B) looks correct. The review must assume this catalog's prices are cheap only when marked down. Choice (C) isn't right. When the catalog does mark down its prices, customers evidently save money. Choice (D) is wrong because this argument isn't about the catalog's competitors. Choice (E) doesn't work because the argument doesn't address mail-order purchasing as a whole, nor does it propose what the customers *should* do. Choice (B) is correct.

2. **E. None of the pieces of evidence point directly to the conclusion, and all of them could lead to different conclusions.**

   The conclusion is that the settlement was destroyed in war. The evidence, though, doesn't seem that clear. It's not a circular argument, because the author doesn't state upfront that he thinks the settlement perished in war, so Choice (A) is wrong. Choice (B) doesn't work. Yes, the evidence is varied and the conclusion is unified, but that's what conclusions are supposed to do — bring together varied evidence into a single conclusion. Choice (C) is wrong because the argument doesn't contain any intermediate conclusions. Choice (D) is wrong because the argument doesn't make any historical conclusions. Choice (E) is the best answer; it's by no means certain that these bits of evidence point to one single conclusion.

3. **C. The degree of erosion to which a coastline is subject is related to the shape of the sea bottom.**

Choice (A) doesn't look right. If fetch is the length of the surface of the water, it shouldn't be related to the shape of the sea bottom. Choice (B) definitely seems wrong because the statements only state the factors (wind velocity and fetch) that influence wave size; there's nothing to suggest that wave size stays close to an average. Choice (C) does make sense because the impact of waves is related to the shape of the sea bottom, and the coast's erosion is related to the impact of waves. Choice (D) is wrong because the size of waves comes from wind and fetch, not the shape of the bottom. Choice (E) looks wrong, too. Wind velocity creates size of waves, size of waves affects impact, and impact affects erosion, so average velocity of wind playing no role in erosion doesn't make sense. Choice (C) is the best answer.

4. **D. It is used to explain a consideration that may be taken to undermine the argument's conclusion.**

The historian is arguing that for historians, seeing one event as an inevitable consequence of another is a mistake. The phrase in question explains that the historians' position of looking back on events results in their erroneous belief that, because one event precedes another, a prior event necessarily causes the later event. Choice (A) is wrong; a "theoretical imperative" sounds like a requirement, and this statement is an explanation. Choice (B) isn't an illustration of the premise, which would be an example of a historian making this kind of mistaken attribution of causation. The statement doesn't support any claim, so Choice (C) is wrong. Choice (D) seems to make sense. The historian is explaining that, although historians sometimes see events as inevitable consequences of other events, that's just an occupational hazard of the historical profession and not justified. Choice (E) is wrong. The conclusion is that historians can't in fact assert that events follow one another inevitably. Choice (D) is the best answer.

5. **D. When agricultural production is market-driven, it is likely to respond to rising demand by increasing production.**

The speaker concludes that Chinese production will rise if demand requires it based on the premise that Chinese production is now market-driven. Clearly the author connects market-driven methods with matching supply and demand. Choice (A) isn't right because it isn't actually about the difference between global and regional markets but about China's transformation to a market economy. Choice (B) doesn't justify the conclusion but explains how things worked under China's older system. Choice (C) is wrong because the speaker isn't talking about local production. Choice (D) looks like the right answer. The speaker bases his conclusion on the principle that a market economy will respond to increased demand with increased production. Choice (E) isn't right. The speaker doesn't mention inefficiency or even compare a market-driven system to a centrally regulated one; he's only interested in the effects of China's transition between the two. Choice (D) is the best answer.

6. **A. It is a specific example of a general condition described in the course of the argument.**

The economist argues that, because patients need medical care and hospitals, regardless of what those services cost, hospitals and doctors rather than insurers bear the brunt of cost-containment measures; the MRI statement provides an example. Choice (A) is a good answer; the statement is a specific example of capital demands (MRIs and buildings) of the general condition of fiscal discipline described in the argument. Choice (B) doesn't work because the MRI statement doesn't counter an attack. Choice (C) isn't as good an answer as Choice (A). The author's claim or conclusion is that health insurers are still profiting from healthcare while doctors, hospitals, and patients are being increasingly squeezed, but the MRI statement doesn't indirectly support that claim. Choice (D) doesn't work. Patients' needing treatment isn't a social side effect but a normal event that remains consistent, regardless of changing circumstances. Choice (E) is wrong; the MRI statement doesn't introduce the conclusion about the immunity of health insurers. Choice (A) is correct.

7. **B. that no other explanations exist for the decreasing revenues from CD sales**

To make her conclusion, the author must assume that PTP file-sharing was entirely or largely responsible for the drop in sales of CDs. She doesn't mention copyright issues, so Choice (A) is wrong. Choice (B) looks like the right answer. Choice (C) isn't at issue; the argument doesn't address the rights of musicians or producers to profit. Choice (D) is a possibility, but it's not as good as Choice (B). It's not obvious that the author specifically assumes that people who download music would purchase it on CD if they couldn't download it. People may have downloaded far more pieces of music than they would have purchased on CDs. Choice (E) doesn't really fit with the argument, which isn't about complex relationships in the music market but about how file-sharing has killed the record industry. Choice (B) is best.

8. **B. fails to take into account any practical factors that may limit the number of redundant systems or practical trade-offs involved in increasing levels of redundancy**

The engineer believes that the more redundant control systems an airplane has, the safer it will be. But what if having so many control systems causes problems of its own, such as increasing the possibility of pilot confusion or eliminating space for other safety systems? Choice (A) is wrong; the engineer does think that simultaneous failure can occur, which is why he believes multiple systems are necessary. Choice (B) looks like it could be the answer because it addresses problems involved with redundancy itself. Choice (C) is wrong. The engineer is discussing control surfaces, so he's not obligated to consider other safety considerations. Choice (D) is wrong. The engineer discusses airplane safety and isn't obligated to apply these concepts to other projects. Choice (E) is also wrong because the argument doesn't depend on being able to evaluate relative levels of safety. Choice (B) is correct.

9. **E. Allowing employees to take leave for family matters reduces absenteeism, improves morale, and surprisingly increases productivity because the employees who are granted leave tend to work much harder and more efficiently when they come back to work.**

To weaken the argument, look for an answer showing that allowing family leave doesn't hurt productivity or perhaps even helps it. Choice (A) doesn't affect the argument because standard of living isn't an issue, and it doesn't mention workplace productivity. Choice (B) could arguably weaken the argument because it provides evidence that workers may not abuse the privilege of leave — fathers aren't taking family leave at all, which weakens the conclusion that workers would work less if they had leave. On the other hand, if taking paternity leave angers co-workers, that strengthens the conclusion that family leave hurts workplace morale, so this isn't the best answer. Choice (C) strengthens the argument by showing that FMLA leave costs the employer money. Choice (D) also strengthens the argument by illustrating the destruction caused by one employee leaving for a while. Choice (E) weakens the argument. If employers are worried about productivity and morale, this choice says that allowing leave actually increases productivity and morale. Choice (E) is the right answer.

10. **A. Businesses profit from casino gambling because they take in money from local and visiting gamblers, whereas local individuals have more opportunities to lose money gambling.**

Look for an answer that may explain why counties with casinos have thriving businesses but bankrupt individuals. Choice (A) looks right. Businesses take in money from gamblers (who aren't all local), and locals give their money to casinos. Choice (B) doesn't help. Casino odds may explain why gamblers would go bankrupt but not why businesses would profit. Choice (C) explains why businesses thrive but not why individuals suffer. Choice (D) explains gamblers' losses but not businesses' gains. Choice (E) may help explain why individual bankruptcy rates are so high in areas with casinos but does nothing to explain the profitability of businesses in those areas. Choice (A) is the best explanation.

11. **E. Some food stamp recipients say they prefer the paper coupons because they can't tell how much money they have in their debit card accounts.**

Eliminate answers that support the position that debit cards are better than paper coupons. Choice (A) supports the argument by showing how the new debit cards increase participation. Choice (B) supports it by showing how paper coupons were often used for fraud. Choice (C) supports the worker's position because the debit cards can be used only for approved items. Choice (D) supports it because it shows how the cards are much more convenient, which will increase participation. Choice (E) is the only answer that doesn't support the social worker's position; it presents a disadvantage of the debit cards. Choice (E) is correct.

12. **C. It highlights the importance of this discovery because it disproves a long-held theory about hibernation.**

This discovery of an animal that hibernates in hot weather may be groundbreaking, especially if previous scientific wisdom held that hibernation only happens in cold weather. Choice (A) is wrong because the belief being challenged isn't that primates never hibernate but that animals never hibernate in the heat. Choice (B) isn't right because the assertion isn't an accusation of any kind. Choice (C) makes the most sense because it's an important discovery. Choice (D) is wrong. The primatologist never disputes the conclusion that the behavior is in fact hibernation. Choice (E) doesn't work because the primatologist isn't setting up a rival theory in a deliberate ploy to attack it. Choice (C) is right.

13. **C. To increase sales, having a famous actor in the title role of a film is more important than having an actor who can speak the film's language.**

Wow, that's a gamble, casting an English-speaking actor in an Italian movie and letting him speak his part in English while everyone else speaks Italian. But the director must have his reasons; he clearly thinks that Lancaster's fame is a more valuable commodity for sales than an ability to speak Italian would be. He must not think that Italian audiences would refuse to see the film with Lancaster or he would never cast him, so Choice (A) is wrong. Choice (B) may be true, but actors' objections don't seem to be the director's concern. Choice (C) is right — the director obviously believes fame is more important to box-office success than Italian ability. Choice (D) is beside the point. The director doesn't think coaching Lancaster in Italian is necessary. Choice (E) is also beside the point; maybe Lancaster would feel uncomfortable, but the director isn't concerned about that here. Choice (C) is correct.

14. **E. The only substances that could eradicate all mosquitoes would also kill off many birds and beneficial insects.**

Alberto suggests that, because losing a single species won't hurt an ecosystem, eradicating mosquitoes will cause no environmental problems. Look for an answer that disproves this.

Choice (A) is a reason in favor of eradicating mosquitoes. Choice (B) doesn't strengthen or weaken the argument because it concentrates on the effect of restoring wetlands on the mosquito population rather than the effect that eradicating the mosquito population would have on wetlands. Choice (C) provides another strike against mosquitoes and may strengthen the argument. Choice (D) may suggest that mosquitoes do play a role in the ecosystem, but by itself it doesn't really hurt Alberto's argument. The answer could weaken the argument if it were more specific, such as providing evidence that mosquitoes are the only thing some birds eat. Choice (E) does weaken Alberto's conclusion. If the only way to eradicate mosquitoes would inevitably devastate birds and other insects, then Alberto can't suggest that his proposal would have no environmental costs. Choice (E) is right.

15. **E. large numbers of people coming to a park prevent individuals from enjoying use of the park**

The author assumes that large groups in parks are bad, but she gives no reasons for this claim; she just assumes that they're bad and shouldn't be in the park. She implies but doesn't directly state that large groups somehow interfere with all citizens' equal rights to the park. Choice (A) is wrong because the author doesn't suggest that large groups are noisy or violent. She mentions no complaints, so Choice (B) is wrong. Choice (C) goes against her argument, so it's wrong. Choice (D) likewise weakens her argument, so it's wrong. Choice (E) is the only answer that makes sense. If she's assuming that large groups interfere with individual citizens' enjoyment of the park, then the groups would be a problem. Choice (E) is correct.

16. **D. Funds saved in FSAs must be spent during the plan year or forfeited.**

Choice (A) looks like a reason why employees should use FSAs. Choice (B) offers an explanation of why there may not be widespread employer participation in FSAs, but it doesn't explain why many of those employees who have the opportunity to participate in FSAs choose not to. Cross out Choice (C) because it's another clear benefit of FSAs. Choice (D) is a drawback of FSAs and may well explain why few employees use them. Choice (E) describes a trend toward FSA participation and therefore doesn't explain why so few employees currently use FSAs. Choice (D) is the best answer.

17. **C. A majority of residents of these six Latin American countries do not believe that democracy is necessarily the best form of government for them.**

It appears from this argument that many Latin American people don't like their democratic governments. Choice (A) provides additional support for the argument but doesn't draw a conclusion from the statements provided. Choice (B) offers an explanation for the residents' dissatisfaction with their governments but doesn't sum up the argument. Choice (C) makes sense as a conclusion; if the people are willing to substitute democratically elected leaders with a dictator, they must not be impressed with their leadership. Choice (D) introduces a side issue and is too specific to be a conclusion. Choice (E) supplies evidence that would support the conclusion but isn't itself a conclusion. Choice (C) is the best answer.

18. **B. The relationship between salmonella and eggs has in fact changed over the years, justifying the recent caution with which people regard raw eggs.**

The argument is about the changed risk of salmonella. In the past salmonella was only on the outside of eggs, but now it's inside the eggs themselves. Choice (A) can't conclude the argument because the author doesn't specifically state that salmonella has increased, only that its means of transmission has changed. Choice (B) makes sense as the conclusion; it sums up the argument's premise that changes in the way salmonella presents itself in eggs has altered the way people must handle eggs as food. Choice (C) isn't right. The author isn't suggesting that salmonella can't be serious, only that it's rarely fatal. Choice (D) doesn't quite work, because the author doesn't describe any change in egg production, only a change in the chickens producing them. Additionally, it doesn't address the egg preparation changes people have had to make. Choice (E) isn't right either. People in the past ate raw eggs safely because the eggs were uncontaminated, not because people were blissfully ignorant that the eggs contained salmonella. Choice (B) is best.

19. **A. Operating systems with generous amounts of memory are less susceptible to crashing, even when applications are poorly written.**

Okay, you want to find the four answers indicating that operating systems are responsible for the smooth functioning of applications and are able to somehow manage their memory problems. The best way to do this is by process of elimination. If you can find four answers that show the operating system handling applications' memory issues, then the answer that's left over should be correct. Choice (B) helps the conclusion because it shows that operating systems are responsible for handling the memory used by individual applications. Choice (C) helps because it shows that operating systems can spot overuse of memory and stop it. Choice (D) helps because it tells you that programmers should know how to program an operating system that can prevent memory errors, which means all operating systems should be able to do this. Choice (E) helps the conclusion because it describes what an efficient operating system should be able to do. Choice (A) is the only answer that doesn't put responsibility for memory management on the operating system; adding memory to the computer evidently can let the operating system off the hook. Choice (A) is the right answer.

20. **D. Ted's parents have stated that he cannot drive the station wagon unless it is to Alice's house. When his mother saw the station wagon parked at the mall, some miles away, Ted argued that Alice was not at home. Ted's mom pointed out that he ought, upon discovering that fact, to have driven straight home.**

This question is a tough one, requiring lots of reading and thinking. Company A has a limited license to use a product but violates the license, claiming it's invalid. But there's another rule beyond the license that makes Company A's actions wrong, even if the license is invalid. So General Rule (GR) states an action can't be taken; Limited Rule (LR) provides an exception to GR in certain circumstances. Party A violates LR by taking action and says it's okay because LR is invalid. Party A is still wrong because action violates GR. Whew! Look for an answer that follows this pattern. Choice (A)'s scenario provides GR (warranty). Party A (consumers) took an action that appeared to be endorsed by another document. Party A successfully proved it didn't violate GR. Because Party A prevails, the pattern can't be the same. Choice (B) provides GR (no 13-year-olds are allowed into NC-17 movies). The ticket seller made a mistake, which isn't the same as authorizing an LR exception, so the pattern breaks down in this scenario. Choice (C) portrays the attempt of Party A (the manager) to create a LR for the GR of the distilled liquor license. The authority states that the LR doesn't exist. This situation isn't the same as the original. Evaluate Choice (D). The GR is that Party A (Ted) can't drive the station wagon. The LR is that he may drive it to Alice's house. Party A violates LR but says it's okay because LR wasn't available. The authority (Mom) says Party A is still wrong because he violated GR. Even though Ted's situation is very different in subject matter from the original, it follows the same rule pattern. Choice (D) is likely the best answer. Choice (E) doesn't establish an LR for Party A to violate. The celebrity didn't grant permission to the magazine to photograph him in any circumstances, so the pattern is different. Choice (D) is correct.

21. **B. No single written edition of a Greek epic can claim to represent the "original" version.**

The author's conclusion is that texts of poems differed from place to place because of the changes in oral transmission of the same stories. Choice (A) is clearly wrong because the scholar isn't suggesting that each classical epic had one original text. Choice (B) looks right because the scholar argues that there can't be any "original" text but instead many written versions of the same epics. Choice (C) doesn't make sense. The scholar doesn't mention narratological complexity. Choice (D) doesn't work, either, because the scholar doesn't imply that people stopped transmitting epics orally after the poems were written down but in fact suggests the opposite — that they continued to compose even after they began transcribing. Choice (E) is totally wrong; the scholar gives no suggestion of political influence in the argument. Choice (B) is correct.

22. **E. If people see online images of items in the museum's collection, they will no longer be interested in seeing the collection with their own eyes.**

The curator seems to assume that if people see the images online, they won't have any interest in visiting in person. Choice (A) isn't the point because the curator isn't worried about damaging the images. Choice (B) doesn't work because the curator doesn't mention a concern for decreased revenue. Choice (C) likely isn't the curator's concern. He isn't specifically worried about the extent of online distribution but rather its effect. Check the remaining answers to see whether you have a better option. Choice (D) isn't his concern, either, because he doesn't mention quality issues. Choice (E) is the best answer. The curator is worried that online publication of the images will remove the incentive to visit the actual museum in person. Choice (E) is best.

23. **A. Spousal and marital difficulties were formerly responsible for a large number of premature returns from foreign assignments.**

If helping spouses has improved expatriate retention by such a huge amount, then unhappy spouses must have previously been responsible for lots of premature returns. Choice (A) looks like a good answer. If unhappy spouses contributed to employees' leaving international assignments, helping spouses adjust would improve the situation. Choice (B) is wrong. If spouses are already thrilled with the international experience, their dissatisfaction is unlikely to contribute to employees' leaving their overseas posts. Choice (C) would support the argument, but it's too specific to be a necessary assumption on which the conclusion depends (there could well be other reasons why spouses are dissatisfied). Choice (D) doesn't explain why helping spouses has improved retention. Choice (E) provides an example of what companies are doing to help spouses but isn't the assumption that links the argument's premises to the conclusion. Choice (A) is the best answer.

24. **E. You catch more flies with honey than you do with vinegar.**

Now, this is a nice little question — a story and some proverbs. You have to decide which proverb — principle — matches the traveler's experience. A stitch in time saves nine means that early correction of problems prevents them from getting bigger; that doesn't really fit here, so Choice (A) is wrong. Don't price an unborn calf means you shouldn't depend on an event that hasn't yet occurred; that's not right, so Choice (B) is wrong. Choice (C) may work because the traveler does carry his computer with him, but it doesn't explain the comparative reaction of the clerk. Choice (D) is wrong because the traveler isn't borrowing or lending anything. Choice (E) is the best answer; because he was nice (honey) to the clerk (the fly), she was nice to him and punished the rude (vinegar) travelers by dawdling.

Section II: Reading Comprehension

1. **D. Manning's work exemplifies how biography can be a powerful tool for a historian of science, who can use the genre to explore the effects of politics, economics, and emotions on the direction of scientific development.**

   This passage is mainly about the effectiveness of biography as a genre for exploring the history of science and the importance of analyzing scientific discoveries from a historical perspective. The business about *Black Apollo* is just an example the author uses to illustrate his point. So Choice (A) is wrong because the passage's main point isn't the importance of Ernest Everett Just. Choice (B) is a point the author makes in the last paragraph, but it's not the entire passage's main point. Choice (C) appears in the second paragraph, but once again, it doesn't cover the whole passage. Choice (D) looks like the right answer; it sums up the overarching theme of the passage. Choice (E) is wrong because, like Choice (A), it focuses too much on *Black Apollo*. Choice (D) is correct.

2. **A. illuminate the effects of social forces on scientists in a way that scientists themselves are unlikely to do**

   According to the author, "One of the central principles of the history of science, indeed a central reason for the discipline, is to show that science is a product of social forces." That makes Choice (A) look like a very good answer. Choice (B) isn't exactly right. The author says people can learn scientific theories by reading the work of the scientists themselves. The drawback is that the picture given by scientists is incomplete because it ignores historical context. Choice (C) is also imprecise. Historians of science do write biographies, but biographies are just one way to accomplish their main goal of revealing the social forces behind scientific discovery. Choice (D) is wrong because the author never suggests that historians of science want to influence scientific research. Choice (E) is likewise wrong. History of science exists to analyze science as a part of society, not to make science palatable to non-scientists. Choice (A) is right.

3. **C. to explain why biography is both a popular historical genre and a powerful medium for explaining the significance of scientific discoveries**

   The second paragraph contains a discussion of biography as a historical genre and lists its many advantages. Choice (A) isn't at all the main point. It just barely appears in the paragraph. Choice (B) is wrong; the author does believe biography is a good historical form for the historian of science. Choice (C) looks like a good answer. Choice (D) is incorrect; the author says that biographies are very good for teaching children. Choice (E) never appears anywhere. Choice (C) is right.

4. **A. One of the best ways to come to an understanding of the realities of race relations and scientific development in the 20th century is to read an in-depth account of the life of one of the people who lived and worked in that world.**

   Choice (A) looks pretty good; this is in fact what the author has been saying about the history of science. Choice (B) is wrong. The author doesn't think historians should glorify their subjects and notes that Manning doesn't glorify Just. Choice (C) is also wrong. The author doesn't imply that a scientific history should downplay science simply because it's "history." Choice (D) isn't right. The author explicitly says that Just wasn't the most significant scientist of his time. Choice (E) contradicts what the author says in the second paragraph. Choice (A) is the best answer.

5. **D. Just's daily experiences illuminate the conditions characterized by both scientific research and racial relations during his lifetime.**

Here's what the passage says: "A comprehensive appreciation of the conditions that Just faced in his daily work offers a powerful lens through which to examine the development of science and racial boundaries in America." Choice (D) looks like the answer that matches best with this statement. The other answers are all true, but they're also incidental, facts that add up to a bigger picture but by themselves aren't enough to create a significant history.

6. **E. the story aspect of biographies that may in some ways make them seem incapable of providing meaningful social commentary**

The second paragraph largely discusses the capability of biographies to convey history. The author says, "Biographies simply tell a story," so the simple form the author refers to is likely the story format. The phrase "simplicity of form" doesn't limit the discussion of biographies to just those intended for children, so Choice (A) is wrong. The author doesn't single out just scientific biographies, so Choice (B) is wrong. Choice C initially seems attractive; the author states at the beginning of the paragraph that a biography doesn't seem to be a promising medium for a great historical work, but by the end of the paragraph, the author concludes that the simple story form doesn't preclude a biography from being a powerful work both historically and socially. Choice (C) fails to convey the author's ultimate message. Choice (D) is wrong because the author suggests that a biography's power to comment on social issues exists despite its simplicity. Choice (E) paraphrases the author's statement at the beginning of the paragraph about a biography's story format, and the mention of the simplicity of form refers to this organization. Choice (E) is correct.

7. **C. SLS and SLES are detergents that are commonly used in personal care products because they are effective and safe, despite unsubstantiated rumors to the contrary.**

This passage introduces the reader to a couple of detergents commonly used in numerous household products. It describes how they work and mentions a few hazards associated with them. The reason the author mentions those hazards in the second paragraph is to get the facts in ahead of the risks that are solely based on rumor, because her point in the last paragraph is that many of the things people fear about SLS and SLES aren't based on fact. She obviously thinks SLS and SLES are safe as they're commonly used and believes that approval by the FDA and other scientific organizations is sufficient proof of this safety.

Choice (A) is a possible answer, but it ignores the discussion of Internet detractors, so it doesn't cover the entire passage. Look for something with a more global application. Choice (B) is wrong. The presence of "despite" suggests that the author thinks incorporating SLS or SLES into personal care products is irresponsible or dangerous, which isn't justified by the passage. Choice (C) looks like a better answer than Choice (A) because it incorporates more of the passage's information. Choice (D) is wrong because this passage isn't about the Internet rumors but about counteracting them. Choice (E) is wrong. It's true that the author doesn't have a problem with using SLS in both shampoo and engine degreasers, but that's not the main point of the passage. Choice (C) is the best answer.

8. **B. This set of baking pans perfectly browns breads, cakes, and other baked goods when they are used as intended in a conventional oven. The results are not ideal when the same set of pans is used to cook items in the microwave; foods are cooked unevenly, burned in some areas, and raw in others.**

The author's reasoning in the third paragraph is that SLS and SLES are perfectly safe when they are used for their intended purposes. The answer that most resembles that reasoning is Choice (B), which states that the baking pans work perfectly when they're used for their intended purpose of cooking baked goods in a conventional oven. Choice (A) may be tempting because its topic is similar to the one in the passage, but it doesn't address the intended purpose of pesticides, so the reasoning is different. Choice (C) mimics the "it is true" and "it is also true" wording in the original argument, but the health-care position doesn't rely on the intended purpose of the legislation. Choice (D) is wrong because although it mentions rumor, it doesn't refer to intended product use at all. Choice (E) argues its case by implying that it's okay for a product to be unsafe because another comparable product is also unsafe. This doesn't follow the intended-purpose argument provided in the second paragraph. Choice (B) is correct.

9. **E. refute claims that SLS and SLES are dangerous**

The author says that the rumors about SLS and SLES are absurd and unsubstantiated and "the FDA has approved the use of SLS and SLES in a number of personal care products." That means she's using FDA approval as evidence of the substances' safety. Choice (A) looks like a possible answer, though it doesn't mention the author's suggestion that the FDA approval implies safety, so it misses the reason why the author brings up the FDA. Choice (B) is wrong because even though the author thinks that the FDA has the best interests of consumers in mind, that isn't the reason why the author mentions the FDA. The purpose of mentioning the FDA is to provide evidence debunking the Internet myths. Choice (C) doesn't work because the author isn't in fact suggesting that FDA approval of putting SLS and SLES in personal care products means that manufacturers don't have to test these products for safety. Choice (D) is wrong; the author isn't criticizing the FDA in any way — quite the contrary. Choice (E) works the best because the author mentions the FDA to achieve the larger goal of debunking the Internet rumors. Choice (E) is correct.

10. **D. Why do some products contain emulsifiers?**

You're seeking the question answered directly by the passage, so you need to eliminate answers that contain questions the passage doesn't answer or that the passage only implies an answer to. Choice (A) is wrong because although the passage says there are alternative foaming agents, it doesn't list those other agents. Choice (B) is out. The passage states the results of ingesting large amounts of toothpaste but doesn't state the effects of taking in small amounts. You know the effects aren't toxic, but you don't know exactly what they are. Choice (C) is wrong. Although you may infer that the FDA has approved SLS and SLES in toothpastes, cleansers, and shampoos because these products are on the market, you can't know that for sure from reading the passage. The correct answer must result from direct information in the passage. Because the passage doesn't appear to be about emulsifiers, you may be tempted to dismiss Choice (D). But the first sentence clearly states that SLS is an emulsifier. It goes on to explain the purpose of this emulsifier to dissolve oil and dirt on skin and hair, and mentions the products that contain SLS. Choice (E) is wrong. The second paragraph tells you that SLS and SLES cause burning, but it doesn't tell you how. Choice (D) is the best answer.

11. **E. a description of SLS and SLES and their uses; known risks of SLS and SLES; criticisms aimed at SLS and SLES by detractors on the Internet; evidence that SLS and SLES are safe and the rumors unfounded**

Look for an answer that could function as an accurate ordering of all paragraphs in the passage. Choice (A) isn't quite right because it leaves off the subject of the first paragraph. Choice (B) is wrong. The passage doesn't contain any anecdotal accounts of SLS injuries. Choice (C) doesn't work because the first paragraph doesn't describe the chemical composition of SLS and SLES. Choice (D) isn't quite right because it doesn't mention the known and unsubstantiated risks associated with the substances. Choice (E) is the best answer because it follows the structure of the passage closely.

12. **E. to explain why some people fear SLS and SLES and to list the diseases that Internet rumors have linked to the substances**

The third paragraph discusses the Internet rumors that hold SLS and SLES responsible for a host of ailments without providing proof. The author obviously wants to discredit these rumors; that's what the last sentence is all about. She's not criticizing, so Choice (A) is out. She's not describing the substances — that's in the first paragraph — so Choice (B) is out. She doesn't believe these risks are real, so she's not warning anyone of anything, and Choice (C) is out. She makes no proposals of alternate substances, so Choice (D) is out. Choice (E) is the best answer here.

13. **A. It is unreasonable for people to be afraid of substances that have been deemed safe by the FDA and several other major organizations, and that have a long history of safe use, simply on the basis of unsubstantiated rumors.**

Choice (A) looks like a good possibility. The author does seem to think it's silly to believe rumors about substances that people have been using safely for years. Choice (B) doesn't quite work. The author does trust the FDA but makes no mention of its sources of funding or mission. Choice (C) is wrong. While the author clearly thinks that some Internet information isn't trustworthy, the passage doesn't provide sufficient information for you to infer how she feels about information available about other health topics. For example, she could easily think that the Internet supplies good information on heart disease. Choice (D) doesn't work. The author does think SLS and SLES are cheap and effective surfactants and emulsifiers, but she doesn't think that they're unsafe to use in products that contact human skin. Choice (E) is wrong. The author probably wouldn't want to prevent manufacturers from using SLS and SLES in their personal care products, but there's no reason to believe that she thinks enough protests could stop this inclusion. She doesn't mention protests anywhere in the passage. Choice (A) is the best answer.

14. **D. Passage A evaluates some of the circumstances that may contribute to a particular phenomenon; Passage B elaborates on that analysis.**

You can answer comparison questions more efficiently by eliminating answers based on what's true for one passage and then for the other. For this question, you can start by examining each of the statements pertaining to Passage A. Choice (A) is wrong. Passage A presents facts regarding the factors that contribute to the inaccuracy of eyewitness identification; it isn't a persuasive piece intended to argue an opinion. Choice (B) may be true for Passage A; the passage does present research to support its statements. You could keep this option open. Choice (C) is wrong. Passage A presents a series of factors; it doesn't define one specific term. Choice (D) is true for Passage A. It discusses the circumstances (factors) behind a phenomenon (faulty eyewitness accounts). Choice (E) may be possible for Passage A; the passage addresses some sociological and psychological factors. To make the final determination among Choices (B), (D), and (E), examine the options in light of Passage B. Choice (B) doesn't work; Passage B doesn't rely on personal stories. Choice (D) still works; Passage B expands the analysis of what factors contribute to inconsistencies in eyewitness accounts. Upon further examination, Choice (E) is wrong. While it's true that Passage B is concerned with legal matters, it isn't more focused on legal applications than Passage A is. Choice (D) is the best answer to define what's true for both passages.

15. **B. Eyewitness testimony is often flawed because it is influenced by a variety of factors.**

The best answer incorporates a point suggested by both passages. Eliminate answers that can be supported by only one of the passages. Passage A makes the statement that there's no difference between the accuracy of male and female testimony, but Passage B doesn't discuss the role of gender, so Choice (D) is supported by only one passage and can't be right. Although both passages mention that eyewitness testimony is affected by a number of variables, only Passage B discusses the importance of determining an error rate. Passage A doesn't mention the establishment of an error rate for testimony, so you can't assume Passage A supports Choice (E). Neither passage discusses how memory improves or declines over time, so Choice (C) is out of contention. That leaves Choices (A) and (B). Choice (A) doesn't seem likely. The first line of Passage A states that "there are many factors that may account for mistaken eyewitness identification" and then goes on to describe the research of these factors, which implies that mistaken eyewitness identification occurs frequently enough to warrant significant study. Passage B stresses the science of memory and human cognitive abilities and states that they're "not perfect." In the third paragraph, the author of Passage B points out that establishing an error rate involves an awareness of the many factors that affect eyewitness accounts. Neither passage suggests that eyewitness testimony is "highly" accurate, but both imply that accounts may be flawed by the influence of several factors or variables. Because it's a better answer than Choice (A), Choice (B) is correct.

16. **A. How the lighting in a particular event affects the reliability of eyewitness identification is a variable that warrants a good amount of study.**

Your job is to eliminate reasonable implications of Passage A. The passage tells you that one's race can affect how well one recognizes someone's face, so it implies that one's race may adversely affect the reliability of an identification. Cross out Choice (B). The passage justifies the statement in Choice (C). It categorizes the factors as system variables and estimator variables. So Choice (C) is wrong. The passage states that the majority of research has gone into studying system variables, and the makeup of a lineup is a system variable. So you can reasonably infer Choice (D) from the statements in Passage A. The passage tells you that the way questions are worded is a system variable, and the judicial system has control over system variables. Therefore, the author of Passage A must think that the judicial system has control over whether a witness is asked misleading questions. Because Choice (E) is wrong, Choice (A) must be the answer. Passage A states that lighting can affect an eyewitness identification, but because lighting is an estimator variable over which the judicial system has little control, it's unlikely to receive much research. The passage states that system variables receive the majority of study. The best answer is Choice (A).

17. **E. to understand how memory and human cognitive abilities are affected by a variety of different factors**

Both passages discuss memory and how it's affected by different factors; what differs is the factors they discuss. Passage A covers variables that include the age, race, and gender of eyewitnesses and the wording of the questions they're asked. Passage B emphasizes the complexity of memory and cognitive abilities. Rule out choices that pertain to one passage but not the other. Choice (A) is a concern of Passage B but isn't mentioned in Passage A, so it's wrong. Choices (C) and (D) are important to Passage A but not to Passage B. Choice (B) isn't a goal of either passage. Though Passage B does indeed mention episodic memory, aside from defining the term, the passage doesn't show how the concept contributes to judicial proceedings. By process of elimination, the best answer is Choice (E). Both passages deal with the complex factors that affect cognitive ability and memory as they relate to the accuracy of eyewitness testimony.

18. **D. Passage A focuses on controlling the variables in eyewitness testimony, and Passage B concentrates on understanding the science behind human recollection.**

You can eliminate some answers quickly because they aren't true. Choice (A) is wrong because Passage B doesn't discuss witness questioning and therefore doesn't dismiss its importance. Choice (B) isn't right because how the judicial system controls certain variables is a concern of Passage A, not Passage B. Eliminate Choice (E) because both passages deal with how research can improve eyewitness accuracy: through research of system variables for Passage A and the establishment of an error rate in Passage B. Choice (C) may be tempting because Passage A mentions the effect of gender on eyewitness identification, but because Passage B doesn't discuss the relevance of gender on eyewitness testimony, Choice (C) is incorrect. Choice (D) is the only option that appropriately defines a noticeable difference between the content of the two passages. The primary focus of Passage A is the variables that affect the accuracy of eyewitness identification. Passage B is more concerned with the workings of the human mind and how this knowledge can be used to establish an error rate for witness testimony. Choice (D) is best.

19. **E. Lighting issues and the length of time someone witnessed an event are examples of system variables.**

This question asks you for the statement that isn't supported by either passage. Eliminate answers that appear in either of the two passages. The second paragraph of Passage B states that the *Daubert* case argued for the need of an established error rate, so Choice (D) is easy to eliminate. Choice (A) is a premise of both passages; they both state that human memory doesn't get it right every time. Passage B says that eyewitness memory should make "guilty people seem more likely to be guilty," and Choice (C) seems to paraphrase that statement. Passage B's first paragraph states that cognitive abilities are incredible and supports that statement with the assertion that visual, auditory, olfactory, tactile, and taste information synchronizes with past information to bring that information into the present, so the statement in Choice (B) is supported by Passage B. If you thought Choice (E) was supported by Passage A, you confused system variables with estimator variables. Lighting issues and the length of time someone witnessed an event are actually examples of *estimator* variables. Choice (E) is the answer that neither passage supports.

20. **C. the philosophical origins of public schools in 18th century Germany and the transformation in educational thinking in the 19th century**

This passage is about the origins of public education and the changes that occurred in educational philosophy in the first century of public schools; the whole thing is set in Germany. Choice (A) doesn't cover the whole passage; the political message seems to apply only to the first half. Choice (B) also focuses on just the first half and so isn't the passage's primary point. The final paragraph doesn't focus on exploitation at all. Choice (C) conveys the passage's overarching theme. Choice (D) is wrong because the passage doesn't get into modern educational practices. Choice (E) doesn't cover the whole passage, just the first part of it. Choice (C) is correct.

21. **C. They were indifferent to the well-being and needs of their workers.**

The author tells you that textile mill owners exploited their workers badly enough to incite revolts and that they embraced the concept of schools in the hopes that it would make the workers more docile. Choice (A) is quite wrong. The first schools weren't created to help the students so much as to help the nobles. Choice (B) could well be true, but the passage doesn't discuss it. Remember, all correct answers must not stray too far from the text. Choice (C) fits well with what the passage says about the owners. It does appear that they were indifferent to the well-being of their workers. Choice (D) isn't quite right. The passage doesn't specifically tell you that they were all aristocrats. Although some of them may have believed their authority was divinely ordained, you can't assume that was true of them all, nor is there any reason for you to assume that they cared about nurturing their workers. Choice (E) is wrong. The passage doesn't contain anything about the factory owners being patriotic. Choice (C) is the best answer.

22. **B. Eighteenth-century schools were concerned primarily with teaching working-class children to accept their fate and love their ruler; 19th-century schools began to focus on developing the full human potential of students.**

The educational difference between the two centuries was philosophical. Schools in the 1700s were meant for workers and intended to instill patriotism and gratitude toward the government into their students, but schools in the 1800s aspired to develop children to their full potential. Choice (A) isn't right because 18th-century schools had nothing to do with efficient textile mills. Choice (B) looks like a very good answer. Choice (C) doesn't work because 18th-century schools were for the children of workers, not the aristocracy, and in the 19th century, no one had to spin anymore. Choice (D) is tricky because it's very close to being correct, but the passage doesn't tell you that 19th-century schools aspired to create free-thinking students in general (though academic freedom was prized for advanced students), so it's wrong. Choice (E) may actually be true — it sounds like some parents of Spinnschulen children didn't like the schools if truant officers were necessary — but that's not the main difference between the centuries, and the passage doesn't really address this point. Choice (B) is the right answer.

23. **A. riots and other forms of violence against the owners of textile factories by peasants unhappy at their treatment**

Look at the sentence after the one that mentions increasing levels of unrest. It says that the rulers wanted "to channel the energy of restless peasants into something that would be less dangerous to the throne than riots." So "unrest" must mean riots and other violent uprisings by workers who disliked their lot in life. That would be Choice (A). None of the other answers work. Choice (E) is tempting because it concerns young people, and this passage is about schools, but the statement doesn't restrict the violence to young men. Choice (A) is correct.

24. **E. They liked the idea because it would make the peasantry more complacent and accepting of their fate, which would help keep the aristocracy safe in their prosperity.**

According to the passage: "Aristocrats liked this idea. They liked the thought of schools making peasants more docile and patriotic, and they appreciated the way state-run schools would teach children of lower social classes to accept their position in life." Choice (A) is wrong because the schools were intended to do just the opposite; educating workers was supposed to make them more docile, not more violent. Choice (B) doesn't work because the passage never mentions aristocratic resentment of taxes. Choice (C) may be a true statement, but the passage doesn't directly come out and say it. You know nothing of the aristocratic opinions of Schlabrendorff himself. Choice (D) is wrong because the passage doesn't tell you that the education would be specifically religious. Teaching children that their "lot was ordained by god" doesn't mean that the entire curriculum was religious. Choice (E) is the most suitable answer to this question.

25. **B. to take away the authority of parents and replace it with state power over children and citizens**

The truant officers were meant to take away parental authority over children and replace it with state control. Choice (B) is the most accurate answer. The truant officers weren't there to make sure every child was educated, so Choice (A) is wrong. They didn't help or indoctrinate parents or children, nor did they recruit boys into the army, which nixes Choices (C) and (D). The passage statement that school was compulsory, so Choice (E)'s statement that participation in school was voluntary is incorrect. Choice (B) is best.

26. **D. People learn best in an environment that respects their individuality, affords them freedom, and incorporates a variety of aspects of learning, such as physical movement, manual skills, and independent exploration.**

Nineteenth-century educational theorists believed in nurturing innate abilities and using holistic techniques. That's not Choice (A). In fact, Choice (A) is just the opposite of what experts thought in the 1800s. Choice (B) is wrong because nothing in the passage mentions religion. Choice (C) isn't right. The passage never suggests that the state has an interest in an educated citizenry, just an interest in a docile and patriotic one, and that wasn't the prevailing view in the 19th century anyway. Choice (D) looks like a perfect answer to this question. Choice (E) isn't right because the passage never mentions that mothers were good teachers for their own children. That makes Choice (D) correct.

Section III: Logical Reasoning

1. **A. People with average incomes tend to donate more to religious groups than wealthier individuals.**

The economist reaches the conclusion by assuming that those who donate the most are the wealthiest people. Choice (A) calls into question this assumption and therefore weakens the argument. Choice (B) strengthens the argument. An answer that offers an exception to the rule (such as evidence of some people who donate a lot and still attend plenty of services) isn't sufficient to weaken the argument, so Choice (C) is wrong. Choice (D) is largely irrelevant. Choice (E) is a more detailed restatement of the argument. You can eliminate the other four options, so Choice (A) must be correct.

2. **E. Most babies are born to mothers under the age of 35.**

So the odds go up for older women, but the numbers are bigger for younger women. That must mean that the total number of children being born to the two groups must be very different. If younger women have more babies with Down syndrome despite lower odds, many more of them must be having babies. Choice (A) doesn't reconcile the discrepancy and, if anything, would lead you to expect more women in their forties would have babies with Down syndrome. Choice (B) doesn't affect the question. Choice (C) doesn't contain any info that would help with the apparent paradox because it doesn't report which age group the information about mothers' decisions applies to. Choice (D) doesn't work because testing only provides information about which fetuses are affected, not why younger women produce the most Down syndrome children. Choice (E) is the best answer. Knowing that the majority of babies are born to women under 35 would explain why they also have the majority of Down syndrome babies.

3. **B. It implies that if a consumer purchases these shoes and they hurt her feet, the company will refund her purchase price.**

Choice (A) is incorrect because you have no reason to assume from the argument that advanced podiatric design is in fact essential to comfort. Choice (B) looks like a good answer. The guarantee implies that customers can get a refund if they don't experience the claims made in the rest of the argument. Choice (C) is wrong. The argument never says that everyone loves the shoes. Be wary of answer choices that contain extreme language, such as "all customers." Choice (D) is wrong because neither the argument nor the key sentence criticizes other shoes. Choice (E) definitely doesn't apply to that sentence, which doesn't mention podiatrists. Choice (B) is right.

4. A. Many Cubans avoid financial hardship because they rely on cash and goods brought to them by relatives who previously could visit once a year and bring in a maximum of $3,000.

This argument's conclusion has two elements. To weaken the argument, look for an answer suggesting that these regulations either won't hasten the fall of Cuba's dictatorship or won't benefit all Cuban people. Choice (A) is an example of how the regulations could hurt Cubans, so Choice (A) looks like a good answer. Choice (B) merely restates one of the premises and doesn't weaken their link to the conclusion. Choice (C) describes Cuba's government but doesn't specifically weaken or strengthen the argument because it fails to mention the effect of the new restrictions. Choice (D) isn't a good answer because it doesn't show how the administration is wrong about the ban's effects (it could pander and still achieve its goals). Choice (E) may strengthen the argument — if Cuba's regime is benefiting from visitors, limiting them would hasten the dictator's demise. Choice (A) is correct.

5. D. assumes without offering evidence that customers value scheduling flexibility enough to pay double the frequent-flier miles for it

The argument assumes that customers will like this change because they want more flexibility. If they don't in fact want flexibility, the argument becomes weaker. Choice (A) doesn't work because the airline isn't trying to suggest that customers with more miles deserve more seats. Choice (B) is wrong because there's no criticism here. Choice (C) may be a true statement, but it doesn't relate to the conclusion about the way customers view the change rather than how airlines are affected by frequent-flier awards. Choice (D) looks like a good answer. The airline is simply assuming that customers will appreciate this change, when in fact many of them may prefer to get less flexible seats for fewer miles. Choice (E) doesn't work; the airline isn't encouraging upgrades. Choice (D) is the best answer.

6. C. Across all income levels, women have on average higher educational attainments than men.

Choice (A) isn't an assumption but is in fact stated in the argument. Choice (B) isn't necessarily true. The sociologist isn't suggesting that women are choosing wealthy, educated men for their physical attractiveness. The concept in Choice (C) plays an important role in the argument; if even the poorest women are generally better educated than their male peers, the marrying-equal or marrying-up practice will leave some of these men unmarried forever. Choice (D) may be true but isn't directly relevant to an argument about marriage. Choice (E) isn't something you can assume from what's stated in the argument and is irrelevant anyway. Choice (C) is the best answer.

7. E. Boss Stephanie constantly criticizes subordinate Kim's work, correcting it one way one day and then correcting it back to its original state the next. Kim meekly accepts the criticisms but spends every Thursday evening at a bar with co-workers making fun of Stephanie.

You're seeking an answer that shows someone who submits to abuse and then criticizes the boss in private. You can save time by reading the second half of the answer choices. The ones that match the subordinates' behavior are the only ones you need to read entirely. The only answers that describe employees who complain about their bosses in private are Choices (D) and (E). Choice (A) doesn't work because Skylar does take formal action against his boss. Choice (B) is no good because David quits. Choice (C) doesn't work because Casey takes action within her company. Choice (D) is close, but it's wrong because Bill doesn't appear to be abusing Paul arbitrarily. The problem here is an inconsistent or incompetent boss more than a bullying boss. Choice (E) is the best answer.

8. **D. Employers assume that high school graduates generally have a much higher level of mastery of academic subjects than those who earn GEDs.**

The argument suggests that a GED is just as good as a high school education; look for an answer that contradicts that. Choice (A) doesn't work. You don't want evidence showing the benefits of earning GEDs. Choice (B) doesn't pose a problem. If universities accept GEDs, that's more evidence that they're as good as diplomas. Choice (C) actually strengthens the argument. Choice (D) does weaken it. If a GED might put one at a disadvantage on the job market, that's a reason to stay in school. Choice (E) doesn't strengthen or weaken the argument. Choice (D) is right.

9. **D. A ban on over-the-counter sales of cough medicines containing codeine reduced incidences of codeine overdoses by 50 percent in two years' time.**

Look for an answer that supports the claim that a ban on over-the-counter DXM sales will protect young people. Choice (A) describes the bad effects of DXM, which bolsters the premises of this argument but doesn't prove that a ban on OTC sales will help curb over-doses. Choice (B) is irrelevant because the argument isn't about the addictive properties of DXM but rather its harmful effects when taken in large dosages. Choice (C) is just more information on how teenagers abuse DXM, not how a ban on selling it would help stop the abuse. Choice (D) supports the claim that banning OTC sales would help. It worked with codeine, so it should work with DXM. Choice (E) is evidence of why DXM is dangerous but not why banning OTC sales would work to prevent abuse. Choice (D) is correct.

10. **A. A city on the coast is more vulnerable to being struck by a hurricane than an inland city.**

Choice (A) looks like a very good answer. If hurricanes need to be over water to maintain their strength, inland cities must be safer from them than coastal cities. Choice (B) doesn't necessarily have to be true. Hurricanes form over tropical water, but the argument doesn't suggest that they can't go into colder water. Choice (C) happens to be true, but the statements don't mention anything about the Atlantic specifically, so you can't infer this. Choice (D) doesn't follow because the argument says hurricanes lose strength over land, but it never mentions how many miles inland a hurricane would have to move before it loses most of its power to do damage. Choice (E) may be tempting, but you can't assume it. The argument gives you no basis on which to make distinctions between the two seasons. Choice (A) is right.

11. **E. assumes that no other parents will take the same stance against vaccination**

This parent assumes his child will be safe from diseases because all other children are vaccinated against them. But what if they aren't? The parent doesn't criticize other parents, so Choice (A) is wrong. He isn't appealing to emotion or trying to persuade other parents, so Choice (B) can't be right. He doesn't mention the government, so Choice (C) is wrong. He doesn't mention the knowledge of other parents, so Choice (D) is wrong. But he does assume that everyone else will get his children vaccinated and is counting on that to protect his child. Choice (E) is the best answer.

12. **C. equates freedom of expression by national leaders with proof that requiring students to mention God in the pledge is not an unjust imposition of religious beliefs**

The speaker suggests that requiring teachers to lead students in the pledge with the words "under God" isn't an unconstitutional imposition of religious beliefs because national leaders mention God all the time. This comparison makes a mistake; the behavior of national leaders doesn't set standards for what is and isn't constitutional. Choice (A) is wrong — what other politicians do isn't the issue. Choice (B) doesn't work; the issue isn't public consensus but constitutionality. Choice (C) looks like a good answer; the real problem with this argument is that it confuses the acts of national leaders with proof that something isn't unconstitutional. Choice (D) is wrong because it's not true; the argument doesn't praise teachers. Choice (E) is wrong because it doesn't address the argument's logic. The argument isn't about what people believe but about the propriety of requiring everyone to make a statement of belief. Choice (C) is the best answer.

13. **B. Europeans work shorter hours than Americans because higher income taxes remove any incentive they may feel to increase their take-home pay by working longer hours.**

The speakers disagree about whether high income taxes are behind Europeans' shorter work schedules. Choice (A) is wrong because they're not debating Europeans' love of leisure. Choice (B) is the source of disagreement. Choice (C) is wrong. Neither one has suggested that the United States should raise income taxes. Choice (D) doesn't work. They're not comparing European and U.S. standards of living. Choice (E) may be tempting, but it's not the source of disagreement; it works better as supporting evidence for Preston's argument. Choice (B) is the best answer.

14. **D. Getting citizens to use less energy than they currently do is desirable.**

Choice (A) isn't the assumption. The argument suggests that the government should interfere with energy policies. Choice (B) doesn't work; the speaker advocates for the use of incentives, so he must think they're necessary. Choice (C) is wrong because the author never mentions 1970s policies, only that people in the 1970s managed to reduce their energy consumption in the face of a crisis. Choice (D) looks like an assumption the author makes; he would only suggest the use of incentives to reduce energy consumption if he thought reduced energy consumption was desirable. Choice (E) is wrong. The author mentions California as an example but doesn't suggest that the federal government should offer the exact same incentives as California did. Choice (D) is the best answer.

15. **B. Enforcing conformity on public school students is justifiable.**

The author of the statements obviously doesn't think public schools should be a forum for individual expression, so Choice (A) is wrong. The author clearly doesn't object to conformity, so Choice (B) may be right. Choice (C) isn't right because the information mentions dress codes in addition to uniforms. Choice (D) is wrong. The information doesn't contain any evidence about parents' opinions of dress codes. Choice (E) is wrong. The author of the statements admits dress codes and uniforms limit individual expression and apparently doesn't care. Choice (B) is the best answer.

16. **D. jumps to the conclusion that the defect in the glasses must be due to the optometrist's lack of skill**

The conclusion is that the optometrist is incompetent; the evidence is that one lens pops out regularly. But there's no evidence that that's because of the optometrist's lack of skill. Choice (A) is wrong. Although giving the optometrist a chance to defend himself would be nice, it's not a fault of the argument that the speaker doesn't provide one. Choice (B) is wrong because other potentially unskilled optometrists have no bearing on the skills of the one in question here. Choice (C) doesn't work. The author doesn't mention any particular techniques. Choice (D) may be the answer. The author does jump to a conclusion here without making a connection between the glasses and the optometrist's skill. Choice (E) is wrong because the author doesn't suggest that sabotage played a role in the bad glasses. Choice (D) is the best answer.

17. **D. A mother promises to take away her son's toy airplane if he throws a tantrum that afternoon. He throws a tantrum that afternoon, so she takes his toy airplane.**

Look for an instance of someone carrying out a promise upon the successful completion of the specific act upon which that promise was predicated. Choice (A) is wrong because the woman wasn't asked to perform anything to receive the ring. Choice (B) is wrong because the boss gives the workers something other than what he promised. Choice (C) is wrong because the seal trainer makes no promise to the seals. Choice (D) is correct. The mom promises to do something (take away a toy) if her son does a particular action (throws a tantrum); he does it, so she keeps her promise. Choice (E) is wrong because the professor didn't promise a bad recommendation for a bad performance. Choice (D) works the best.

18. E. The meadow voles that had the prairie vole gene implanted in them were released into and observed in the same habitat in which they had previously lived.

Look for information that supports the assumption that the meadow voles' change in behavior was caused by the implanted gene. Choice (A) is wrong. The choice doesn't relate the effects of the hormone to the gene that makes meadow voles monogamous. Choice (B) explains what's up with prairie voles but not with meadow voles, and neither's genes are mentioned. Choice (C) explains why meadow voles are typically promiscuous but says nothing about whether a gene plays a part in that. Choice (D) says nothing about whether the transferred gene is the cause of the monogamous behavior. Choice (E) provides the most support for the assertion that the scientist's work with genes was the factor that turned the formerly promiscuous meadow voles into models of monogamy because it rules out a possible other important factor that may have explained the change (different surroundings). Choice (E) is the correct answer.

19. A. The art museum cannot be confident that this statue was made by Praxiteles.

Choice (A) looks like a good answer. The museum doesn't know for sure that this statue is by Praxiteles even though it has some evidence to hope it is. Choice (B) doesn't work because the passage never mentions modern forgers, only ancient Roman copiers. Choice (C) is wrong. The passage says that dating ancient sculptures accurately is difficult, which means scholars may not ever be able to date this one conclusively. Choice (D) is too specific to be a proper conclusion drawn from the passage. Choice (E) is wrong. The passage tells you that plenty of Roman copies have been mistaken for originals. Choice (A) is the best answer.

20. C. the new terminology guidelines were a valuable and necessary update to the field of psychological research

Psychologist A likes the change in practices referring to research participants; Psychologist B doesn't because it makes his life complicated. Choice (A) is wrong because they're not arguing about the preferences of participants; neither psychologist takes participants' preferences into account. Choice (B) is wrong because both psychologists seem to agree that the governing body has the authority to make these changes. Choice (C) looks right. They do disagree about whether the changes were a good thing. Choice (D) isn't right. Psychologist A mentions children's ability to consent, but Psychologist B doesn't address that issue at all, so you can't say that they disagree about it. Choice (E) is wrong because Psychologist B doesn't address this claim, so you don't know what he thinks about it (he could actually agree that *participant* is a more active label and still prefer the simplicity of *subject*). Choice (C) is the best answer.

21. C. Any discovery that allows women to predict when they will experience menopause will influence their decisions on when to have children.

The conclusion is that predicting when menopause will occur will make a difference to women planning when to have children, which must mean that knowing when menopause will occur will makes it easier to plan. Choice (A) is wrong because it doesn't explain why predicting menopause will help anyone. Choice (B) just provides general information about menopause. Choice (C) may be right — it provides a connection between knowing about the onset and menopause and making choices about when to have children. Choice (D) isn't relevant because the argument is about how accurately predicting the onset of menopause affects childbearing decisions, not how likely a woman is to conceive in the years immediately prior to menopause. Choice (E) is just information about ovaries, not an explanation of how this test will help make family planning decisions. Choice (C) is the best answer.

22. **C. fails to consider that funding levels are not the only factors influencing school performance**

The school board member assumes that the inner-city school's poor results are due to it squandering its money, which isn't necessarily the right conclusion; other factors may be involved. Choice (A) is wrong. The member isn't suggesting that funding is tied to graduation rates, because both schools got the same funding. Choice (B) is wrong because you can't necessarily assume the school board member thinks that the 90 percent of inner-city students that don't go to college were necessarily unprepared for college. Choice (C) looks like a possible answer. The school board member assumes that having equal budgets should mean that the schools' students should perform equally and fails to consider other possibly relevant differences between the schools, such as their facilities, their teachers, their level of parental involvement, and so on. Choice (D) isn't quite right. He's not directing criticism specifically at the administrators. Choice (E) is wrong. He's blaming the inner-city schools, not the inner-city students. Choice (C) is correct.

23. **A. My European client calls once a week, always in the evening, after everyone has left the office. I'll be sure to get his messages if I turn on my telephone's answering machine once a week.**

The flaw in the argument is the mistaken belief that the odds of an event occurring can tell you how often you need to do a certain act. Odds of 1 in 1,000 don't mean that every 1,000th trip will realize a certain event. It means that an accident could happen in any trip out of 1,000, and you can't predict which one. The flawed reasoning in Choice (A) is similar to this; turning on the answering machine on just one particular day won't necessarily catch a weekly phone call because the call could come on any day of the week. Choice (B) is wrong. The conclusion is mistaken but in a different way from the original argument. It's about proportionality not probability. Choice (C) isn't exactly the same as the original argument because you're not trying to guess which one of the 1,000 games will result in the jackpot; instead you're covering them all. That's actually closer to wearing the helmet for all 1,000 rides on the assumption that one of them will involve a wreck. Choice (D) is totally wrong because the second sentence is nothing like the original argument's conclusion; it doesn't state how many times people in cars should wear seat belts based on seat belt statistics. Choice (E) is flawed but not in the same way as the original argument. The flaw would be more similar to the original argument if the law student applied to only one of 20 law schools because the odds are 1 in 20 of being chosen. Choice (A) is the closest and is correct.

24. **A. By the 1950s, people expected cleaner clothes and surroundings and more elaborate meals than they had earlier in the 20th century.**

Choice (A) looks like an ideal answer. If standards went up, women could well spend more time on housework even with their labor-saving devices. Choice (B) is irrelevant; it says nothing about how long women spent on housecleaning. Choice (C) looks at first like it may explain the discrepancy, but the argument doesn't mention childcare, only housework. Choice (D) would work if it suggested that prewar husbands had helped their wives, but it doesn't. Choice (E) is irrelevant. Choice (A) is the best answer.

25. **D. whether consumers think that geographical food names are generic**

The two unions disagree about the EU's ban on using regional names for non-regional products, with the AFMU claiming that some regional names now have generic, not regional, meaning associated with them. Choice (A) is wrong because the unions aren't arguing about quality. Choice (B) is wrong because the European Union has issued rules regarding naming products, which isn't necessarily the same as banning the import of those products. Choice (C) is completely off; they're not debating taste buds. Choice (D) summarizes the crux of the disagreement. It looks like the right answer. The EU thinks generic names breed confusion; the AMFU thinks they don't. Choice (E) isn't right because they're not really debating intellectual property law in theory as much as addressing one specific instance of it. Choice (D) is the best answer.

Section IV: Analytical Reasoning

Questions 1–5

You don't need a game board to answer the first question in this ordering set, but you do for the remaining questions. To create an accurate game board, first make a list of the initials of the participants' last names: A, D, H, M, S, and W. (This step is especially important in this problem because the participants all have such long names.) Write out the speaking times in a row with space under them for plugging in data; go ahead and note that the 6 o'clock time slot can't contain either D or M. Then write the other rules and their contrapositives in shorthand under your game board.

Make additional deductions based on the rules. You know that S must speak no later than 6 because she must speak before D or M. You also know that S can't speak first in the 2 slot because either D or M must speak before her. Your initial game board will therefore look something like this:

A D H M S W

2	3	4	5	6	7
~~S~~				~~M~~ ~~D~~	~~S~~

S before D or S before M
No S before D and M
If H = 2, W before A
If no W before A, H ≠ 2
If S = 4, W = 7
If W ≠ 7, S ≠ 4

At this point, you could stop and consider the effects of a couple of possible scenarios. If D speaks at 4 and M speaks at 7, S must speak at 5 or 6. That's mildly interesting. You also know that if H speaks at 2, then S can't speak at 4, because then W would have a conflict between speaking at 7 (the last slot) and speaking before A. The rules really are quite explicit, so get going on the questions.

Just be aware that the numbering *starts* at 2 p.m. Many hapless students forget that the person speaking at 2 speaks first!

1. **D. Jane Hunt, Martha Wright, Frederick Douglass, Elizabeth Cady Stanton, Susan B. Anthony, Lucretia Mott**

Eliminate answers that contain rule violations. The first rule specifies that Douglass and Mott don't speak at 6. Choice (B) puts Mott in the 6 spot, so it must be wrong. The second rule states that Stanton can't speak before both Douglass and Mott, so Choice (E) is out. The third rule applies when Hunt speaks first. Choices (C) and (D) put Hunt in the first spot, but Choice (C) fails to put Anthony after Wright. The last rule applies when Stanton speaks at 4. Only Choice (A) has Stanton speaking at 4, but Choice (A) doesn't place Wright in the last speaking time at 7, so the only answer that doesn't violate a rule has to be Choice (D).

2. **E. Martha Wright speaks at 5.**

Record the temporary condition provided by this question on your game board. If Hunt speaks at 2, Wright must speak before Anthony, which means Wright can't speak last at 7. If Wright isn't in the 7 slot, Stanton can't be in the 4 slot. Stanton can't speak at 3 because then she'd have to speak before both Douglass and Mott. So Stanton must speak at 5 or 6. With Stanton in the 5 slot, the 6 and 7 slots must contain Anthony and either Douglass or Mott. With Stanton in the 6 slot, you know that either Douglass or Mott must be in the 7 slot. Because Wright has to speak before Anthony, Wright can't be in the 5 slot and Anthony can't be in the 3 slot. You could write out the possibilities for this question like this:

A D H M S W

2	3	4	5	6	7
~~S~~				~~M~~ ~~D~~	~~S~~
	~~S~~ ~~A~~	~~S~~	~~W~~		~~W~~
H	W, M, or D	A, W, M, or D	A, M, or D	S	D or M
H	W, D, or M	W, D, or M	S	A	A, M, or D

S before D or S before M
No S before D & M
If H = 2, W before A
If W after A, H ≠ 2
If S = 4, W = 7
If W ≠ 7, S ≠ 4

Now you can see that Choices (A), (B), (C), and (D) could work, so cross them out. That leaves Choice (E), which has to be false because it doesn't allow for three time slots after Wright to fit in Anthony, Stanton, and either Mott or Douglass. Choice (E) is correct.

3. **D. At least one person speaks before Jane Hunt speaks.**

When you record the temporary condition that Wright speaks at 7 to your game board, what do you know? The contrapositive to the third rule reveals that Hunt can't speak at 2 when Wright doesn't speak before Anthony. Check the answers. If Hunt can't occupy the 2 slot, at least one other person must speak before Hunt. Choice (D) says just that; one person must speak before Hunt. When you consider the possible scenarios, you realize that the other answer choices are either false or merely possible:

A D H M S W

2	3	4	5	6	7
S̶				M̶ D̶	S̶
H̶H̶					
M, D, or A D or M	M, D, or A S	S M, D, H, or A	M, D, H, or A M, D, H, or A	H or A H or A	W W

S before D or S before M
No S before D & M
If H = 2, W before A
If W after A, H ≠ 2
If S = 4, W = 7
If W ≠ 7, S ≠ 4

So Choice (D) is the only choice that must be true.

4. **D. Elizabeth Cady Stanton**

You can answer this question with a quick look at your original game board. Who can't occupy the first slot? Stanton; she can never speak at 2. The answer is Choice (D).

5. **A. Susan B. Anthony at 3; Elizabeth Cady Stanton at 6**

This problem is another rule-violation question. Plug the speakers into the time slots suggested by each answer choice and see whether they work. Choices (B) and (C) place Hunt in slot 2. You know from your work on Question 2 that when Hunt speaks at 2, Stanton can't speak at 3 and Wright can't speak at 7. Cross out Choices (B) and (C). Check the other answer choices with known restrictions. Choice (D) places Stanton in the 4 slot. When Stanton speaks at 4, Wright has to speak at 7. Choice (D) doesn't work. Consider Choice (E). If Stanton speaks at 5 and Anthony at 7, no slot is available for either Douglass or Mott to speak after Stanton, because neither of them can speak at 6. What about Choice (A)? You can schedule the speakers in the following order: Wright, Anthony, Hunt, Douglass, Stanton, Mott. Choice (A) is the only possible scenario.

Questions 6–12

First, create a game board for this grouping set. Make a list of the game pieces: the initials of the four women — M, N, O, and P — and three men — A, B, and C. Then create a game board that orders the dance events.

Consider the rules. You know that every event must have one member and that no member competes more than once. Every event with a pair of dancers must include one man and one woman. A dances alone, so the maximum number of pairs is two, and two women must dance solo. What else? Well, if O competes in the rumba, then A can't. Because N must be part of a pair, she must dance with B or C. You also know that the two pair events can't be back-to-back because B and C can't dance in consecutive events.

Record that what you know: There are two pairs and three solos; N is paired, which means you only need one more pair! Your main diagram may look something like this:

f		p		r		t		w	
				O	~~A~~				

Women = M N O P

Men = A B C

1 W and 1 M or solo

A = solo

N = pair

No B right before C

No C right before B

Either NB or NC

2 pairs and 3 solos

6. **E. Natasha competes in the waltz.**

Record the temporary conditions imposed by this question on your game board. When Phoebe dances solo in the foxtrot and Bertrand provides a partner for Olivia, only one event is left for Christophe to compete in — the waltz. He can't do the paso doble or tango without being immediately before or immediately after Bertrand. Natasha must dance with Christophe because she needs a male partner, and he's the only one available. So Natasha must also dance the waltz. Chart what you know on the game board:

f		p		r		t		w	
				O	~~A~~				
P		M or A		O	B	M or A		N	C

The answer is Choice (E).

7. C. three

You're looking for the maximum number of events for Natasha, so start high and work your way down. Because Antonio dances alone, Natasha won't have five events to choose from. Eliminate Choice (E). Olivia's already in the rumba slot, so four isn't possible. Cross out Choice (D). Could it be three? Try Antonio in the foxtrot. That leaves the paso doble, tango, and waltz open. Natasha could feasibly compete in any of those, as long as she dances with Bertrand or Christophe. Choice (C) is the answer.

8. A. Antonio

If solo women compete in the foxtrot and paso doble, they must be Madeleine and Phoebe because Olivia is booked for the rumba and Natasha dances as part of a pair. The only dance left for Antonio is the tango because Olivia and either Christophe or Bertrand are competing in the rumba. The only spot left for the other member of the Christophe-Bertrand duo is the waltz with Natasha. Your game board for this question looks like this:

f		P		r		t	w	
				O	A̶			
P or M		M or P		O	B or C	A	N	B or C

The answer must be Choice (A).

9. B. Christophe, Bertrand, and Natasha

You know that both Bertrand and Christophe must dance with partners because you need two pairs with one man in each and Antonio dances solo. The only answer that contains both Christophe and Bertrand is Choice (B).

10. E. Madeleine, Olivia, and Phoebe

When you know that two women must dance solo, you know the answer can't be Choice (A) or Choice (B). Unfortunately, none of the other answers include Natasha, who would be a dead giveaway that the answer was wrong. You already know from Question 9 that both Madeleine and Phoebe can compete solo, so Choice (C) has to be wrong. To choose between Choices (D) and (E), ask yourself whether Olivia can compete solo. Sure — if, for example, Phoebe and Christophe dance the paso doble and Natasha and Bertrand compete in the waltz, Olivia is on her own for the rumba. So the correct answer is Choice (E).

11. B. foxtrot and tango

Add the temporary conditions to your game board. When Natasha dances the waltz and the females dance consecutively, the females must dance the paso doble, rumba, tango, and waltz. That puts Antonio alone in the foxtrot. You can eliminate any answer choice that doesn't include the foxtrot: Choices (C) and (E). Bertrand or Christophe must compete in the waltz with Natasha because Natasha needs a partner. The remaining Bertrand or Christophe can't dance the tango right before the waltz, so he must dance either the rumba with Olivia or the paso doble with Madeleine or Phoebe. That means a solo woman must perform the tango. Either the paso doble or the rumba will be the third solo, but you don't know which. Your game board reveals the two possible arrangements of the solo events:

f	p		r	t	w
		o	A̶		
A	P or M	o	B or C	P or M	N	B or C
A	P/M	B/C	o	P or M	N	B or C

So the foxtrot and the tango are the only events that must have solo performers, and the answer is Choice (B).

12. **E. Natasha competes in the foxtrot.**

Add the temporary rule that the three men dance the first three dances to your game board. Neither Bertrand nor Christophe can dance the paso doble because they can't dance consecutively. So Antonio dances the paso doble. You also know that Natasha must dance the foxtrot with either Bertrand or Christophe. Your diagram for this question looks like this:

f	p		r	t	w
		o	A̶		
N	B or C	A	o	B or C	P or M	P or M

Natasha must dance the foxtrot, so the answer is Choice (E).

Questions 13–18

Organizing this complicated ordering problem can be challenging. Consider that you have three categories of information:

Times the courses can be served

The courses themselves

The chefs who can prepare them

To solve the accompanying questions, first make a list of your game pieces. Use lowercase initials for courses (h, c, e, s, and d) and uppercase initials for chefs (A, B, E, J, K, M, and N). Two things remain consistent: the order of the five courses and the three serving hours of the dinner. The serving hours stay in one order, but you don't know how many courses will occur at each one (though you do know it'll be one or two, not zero or three). That means that at 7 the kitchen could serve just hors d'oeuvres or it could serve hors d'oeuvres and consommé (which are, by the way, appetizers and a kind of soup). At 8, the kitchen could serve consommé and the entrée, just the entrée, or the entrée and salade. (*Salade* is the fancy French word for salad, but you already figured that out.) At 9, the kitchen will serve either salade and dessert or just dessert. Which course happens when depends on the other information in the questions. Assume the kitchen has enough room for two chefs to prepare different courses at the same time without interfering with each other. You can also assume that if two courses occur in one hour, they're served one after the other, not simultaneously. That must be the case if the courses are to occur in order.

Remember to leave your preconceived notions at the door! You may know that salad almost never comes after the entrée in a 5-star restaurant, and of course dessert always comes last, but that's not important here. What's important is what the facts say.

Three scenarios are possible, so make your life easier and just draw a game board to illustrate all three:

7	8	9
h	ce	sd

7	8	9
hc	e	sd

7	8	9
hc	es	d

When you plug in your data, just write the initials of the chefs under the course they're preparing. Be sure you have enough room.

Now, remember that though the same chef can prepare more than one course, no chef can prepare two courses the same hour. So if both hors d'oeuvres and consommé are served at 7, the same chef can't prepare them both. For example, if both consommé and the entrée come out at 8, Andrea can't prepare them both, even though he's offered to. (And yes, in this case, Andrea is a guy — he's Italian.)

Make yourself another little set of notes with abbreviations of courses and chefs. Doing so makes reading the abbreviations easier than the text version. Draw this new chart off to the side of your game board for quick reference:

h: B, M

c: A, K

e: A, N

s: B, E, J

d: E, K, M

13. B. three

You already know you can't have more than five chefs because there are only five courses and no chef wants to share glory with another. So Choice (E) has to be wrong. You're looking for a minimum number, so start with the smallest choice. Can you schedule a dinner with just two chefs cooking every course? To do that you'd have to find one chef who can cook three courses. Skim through your list of courses and chefs to see whether you can find any chef whose initial appears three times. Nope. No single chef can cook all three courses, so two is impossible and Choice (A) is wrong. Can you produce the whole dinner with just three chefs? Take, for example, the scenario in which dessert is the only course served at 9. You could come up with a scenario in which Berthe and Andrea cook both courses at both 7 and 8, leaving dessert to a third chef; that scenario would look like this:

7	8	9
h, c	e, s	d
B, A	A, B	E

So you could do the entire dinner with just three chefs. The answer is Choice (B).

14. **A. Andrea and Kimiko**

Include on your game board the temporary conditions the question provides. When salade comes at 9, so does dessert, so at 8 just the entrée or both consommé and the entrée are served. The group of chefs who can prepare these courses include Andrea, Kimiko, and Nigel, which means you can eliminate Choices (B), (C), and (E). Is there any reason you can't serve two courses at 8? No, which means you can eliminate Choice (D). To verify that Choice (A) is the answer, consider the three ways the 8 o'clock course could be served:

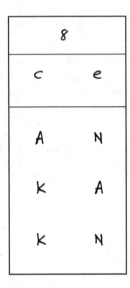

One of those choices, Andrea and Kimiko, happens to be the answer.

15. **E. Berthe, Emilio, Jacques, and Marthe**

Eliminate answers that are possible complete lists of chefs who could prepare the entire meal. Cross out Choice (A) because it could work. You could have

7	8	9
h	c e	s d
B	K A	J K

Here's one possibly for Choice (B):

7	8	9
h	c e	s d
B	K A	B M

You can arrange these chefs in a couple of other ways, but you need only one to eliminate Choice (B). To eliminate Choice (C), you can consider this possibility:

7	8		9	
h	c e		s d	
M	A	N	E	M

Here's a possibility for Choice (D):

7		8	9	
h	c	e	s	d
M	A	A	J	K

That leaves Choice (E). Does leaving out Andrea make such a difference? Yes. Without Andrea and without Kimiko, you have no one willing to make consommé. Nor do you have anyone to make the entrée; Andrea and Nigel are the guys for that, and neither of them is in the list. A superabundance of chefs to make hors d'oeuvres, salade, and dessert doesn't make for a lengthy or complete banquet. That means the answer that doesn't provide a complete and accurate list is Choice (E).

16. **A. Andrea and Berthe**

There are three ways this question could work; the two chefs can prepare the courses at 7 and 8, 8 and 9, or 7 and 9. Take a look at the answer choices; Andrea appears three times, so he's a good one to start with. The only way Andrea can prepare two courses is if he prepares consommé at 7 and the entrée at 8. Is there another cook who could prepare hors d'oeuvres at 7 and salade at 8? Yes. Berthe could do both, leaving dessert for someone else. This is the scenario you came up with in Question 13. That means the answer is Choice (A). (Try out the other possibilities yourself; you'll see that they don't work.)

17. **C. Berthe and Kimiko**

The only way for this question to work is to have hors d'oeuvres and consommé at 7 and salade and dessert at 9. Look at the list of courses with their corresponding chefs. Is there anyone who can make hors d'oeuvres and either salade or dessert? Yes. Berthe can do hors d'oeuvres and salade. Is there a chef who can do consommé and dessert? Yes, Kimiko. That's one of the possible answers: Choice (C).

7	8	9
h, c	e	s, d
B, k	?	B, k

None of the other pairs work; test them to see, but Choice (C) is the answer.

18. **A. Andrea, Berthe, Emilio, and Nigel**

This question is just like Question 15 — remember how much fun that was? This one, though, works the other way. Four of the answer choices are wrong and only one is correct; if one course is missing, then the answer is wrong. Try Choice (A). It looks like it should work. Try arranging the chefs like this:

7	8	9
h, c	e, s	d
B, A	N, E	E

Test the other four to make sure. Choice (B) doesn't work because no one on its list of five chefs can make hors d'oeuvres. Choice (C) has no one to make an entrée. Choice (D) has no one to make consommé. Choice (E) doesn't have anyone who can make an entrée. So Choice (A) is the only answer that works.

Questions 19–25

The first question in most logic game sets merely requires you to apply the rules to each answer. But coming up with a good, clear game board is the key to figuring out the solutions to the remaining questions in the set. First things first — set up the game pieces using uppercase initials for the movies (E, G, I, M, and W) and lowercase letters to mark film format (v for videotape and d for disc). You may also want to add two Xs to designate the two empty days. So, you designate *Emma* on videotape as Ev and *Wuthering Heights* on disc as Wd.

Draw a table on your game board with the nights of the week as column heads. Start on Friday and finish with Thursday. Note that there are seven nights and five films, so two nights are empty. Record the rules on your game board. The easiest rule to write down is Ev in the Monday column. The second rule states that the student watches Wd before Ev, so the student can't watch Wd on Tuesday, Wednesday, or Thursday nights. Because the student watches G before both M and I, he can't watch G on Wednesday or Thursday, nor can he watch M or I on Friday.

Consider the ramifications of the final rule. If the student can't watch any two videotapes or two DVDs next to each other, he can't watch any film on Sunday. Sunday must be an empty day. You also know that he must watch W on Saturday because that's the only way he can watch it before E without violating the final rule. You can draw a further conclusion: If the student watches a movie on Friday, it must be a videotape.

See whether you can come up with more information about the other films and nights. If the student views a film on Tuesday, it must be on disc. You also know that *Great Expectations* must come before both *Ivanhoe* and *Middlemarch*, but you don't know the order of *Ivanhoe* and *Middlemarch*. You can make that work in two ways — either *Great Expectations* is the video on Friday or it's a disc on Tuesday. If *Great Expectations* is a video scheduled for Friday, then *Ivanhoe* and *Middlemarch* are discs on Tuesday and Thursday. If instead *Great*

Expectations is a disc on Tuesday, then either *Ivanhoe* or *Middlemarch* is a videotape, and the other of the pair is a disc. In that case, the student would distribute *Ivanhoe* and *Middlemarch* in the proper order between Tuesday and Thursday. Note that the only possible film for Friday is *Great Expectations* on video (Gv), so if the student watches a film on Friday, that's the one. That means the two possible schedules look like this:

E G I M W X X
V v d d d

Fri	Sat	Sun	Mon	Tue	Wed	Thu
~~M~~ + V	Wd	X	Ev	~~Wd~~	~~G~~ ~~Wd~~	~~G~~ ~~Wd~~
Gv	Wd	X	Ev	Md or Id	X	Md or Id
X	Wd	X	Ev	Gd	Mv or Iv	Md or Id

Wd before Ev
G before M and I
No v v or d d

When you narrow down the possible schedules to these two, answering the questions is a piece of cake.

19. C. Friday: *Great Expectations*; Saturday: *Wuthering Heights*; Monday: *Emma*; Tuesday: *Middlemarch*; Thursday: *Ivanhoe*

You can usually answer the first question in the set by eliminating answer choices that violate the rules. The first condition states that the student watches *Wuthering Heights* before *Emma*. No choices violate this rule. The next condition specifies that the student watches *Middlemarch* and *Ivanhoe* after *Great Expectations*. Choice (E) violates the rule by scheduling *Middlemarch* before *Great Expectations*. Eliminate Choice (A) because it schedules *Emma* on Sunday. Choice (D) schedules *Wuthering Heights* on Friday and no film on Saturday, which violates the rule that the student watches a film on disc for Saturday. To determine whether Choice (B) or Choice (C) is correct, apply the fifth condition that a video and disc can't be watched on consecutive nights to both. Choice (B) schedules a disc (*Wuthering Heights*) on Saturday, which means that the film the student saw the night before (*Great Expectations*) must have been a video. *Emma* is also on video, so that takes care of the two films on videotape and means that the student views discs on two consecutive nights, Tuesday and Wednesday. That can't be. Choice (C) inserts an off day between the two films that must be on disc, so it's the only answer that doesn't violate a rule.

20. A. *Great Expectations* is on disc.

The only way the student can view *Great Expectations* before *Emma* is to watch it on Friday (the first schedule listed on your game board) because *Wuthering Heights* occupies Saturday and Sunday is off. The film on Friday must be on videotape; otherwise, it would violate the rule about putting films of the same format on days immediately before or after each other. So *Great Expectations* can't be on disc, and the answer is Choice (A). As for *Ivanhoe* and *Middlemarch*, either one of them could be on disc. You know there's no film on Sunday, and they could take place on Tuesday and Thursday, so the other four answers either must be or could be true.

Choice (A) is correct.

21. **C. The student watches *Great Expectations* exactly one day before watching *Middlemarch*.**

If *Middlemarch* is on videotape, the student must be watching the films according to the second schedule on your game board. So *Great Expectations* and *Ivanhoe* both must be on disc. In that case, *Great Expectations* must be on Tuesday, *Middlemarch* on Wednesday, and *Ivanhoe* on Thursday, with no film on Friday.

Of the answer choices, only Choice (C) is possible. Choice (A) is wrong because *Ivanhoe* is on disc. Choice (B) is wrong because the student must watch *Emma* two days before watching *Middlemarch*. Choice (D) is wrong because the student must watch *Ivanhoe* on Thursday. Choice (E) is wrong because the student must watch *Middlemarch* on Wednesday. But he must watch *Great Expectations* exactly one day before watching *Middlemarch*, so Choice (C) is correct.

22. **E. The student doesn't watch a film on either Tuesday or Thursday.**

Test the answers, checking them on your game board. Eliminate those that either must be or could be true. Try Choice (A). According to the first schedule, the student could watch G on Friday and E on Monday, so that could be true. Now take a look at Choice (B). He must watch a film on Monday, and Wednesday can go either way, so it could be true that he watches films on Monday and Wednesday. Try Choice (C). He could take Friday and Sunday off, so that could be true. Consider Choice (D). He definitely skips Sunday and could take Wednesday off if he watches *Great Expectations* on Friday, so it could be true that he doesn't watch on Sunday or Wednesday. That leaves Choice (E), and it's the only false statement. Every possible schedule on the game board requires the student to watch something on either Tuesday or Thursday. The answer is Choice (E).

23. **C. The student watches *Great Expectations* before he watches *Emma*.**

If the student watches *Great Expectations* after *Wuthering Heights*, he's watching films according to the second schedule on the game board. He must watch *Great Expectations* on disc on Tuesday, and *Middlemarch* and *Ivanhoe* must fall on Wednesday and Thursday, with the Thursday film on disc and the Wednesday film on videotape. Remember, either *Ivanhoe* and *Middlemarch* can be viewed on Wednesday or Thursday. The student can't watch anything on Friday, so Choice (A) must be true. Choice (B) could be true if *Ivanhoe* is on videotape, which would put it on Wednesday. Choice (C) must be false because *Emma* must be on Monday and *Great Expectations* must be on Tuesday; that looks like the answer. Choice (D) must be true because *Great Expectations* must be on disc. Choice (E) could be true because *Ivanhoe* could be on disc. Choice (C) is correct.

24. **A. The student watches *Great Expectations* on Friday.**

With five movies and seven nights to watch them, the student can take only two nights off. One of those is Sunday; the other could be Friday or Wednesday. If he takes Wednesday off, then the first schedule on your game board applies, and he has to watch a film on Friday. The only film he can watch on Friday is the videotape of *Great Expectations*. That means Choice (A) must be true, and Choice (B) is false. Choices (C), (D), and (E) are all possible but not necessarily true.

Choice (A) is the answer.

25. B. two

The schedule for Saturday, Sunday, and Monday is the same for every schedule on your game board. The day the student sees *Ivanhoe* depends on when he sees *Great Expectations*. If he watches *Great Expectations* on Friday, then *Great Expectations* is a videotape and *Ivanhoe* and *Middlemarch* are both discs. To watch *Ivanhoe* before *Middlemarch* and avoid viewing two discs on consecutive days, the student must watch *Ivanhoe* on Tuesday and *Middlemarch* on Thursday. If, on the other hand, he watches *Great Expectations* on Tuesday, *Great Expectations* must be on disc, and his Thursday movie must also be on disc. His Wednesday film — in this case, *Ivanhoe* — must be on videotape.

So the answer is Choice (B).

Answer Key for Practice Exam 2

Section I: Logical Reasoning

1.	B	8.	B	15.	E	22.	E
2.	E	9.	E	16.	D	23.	A
3.	C	10.	A	17.	C	24.	E
4.	D	11.	E	18.	B		
5.	D	12.	C	19.	A		
6.	A	13.	C	20.	D		
7.	B	14.	E	21.	B		

Section II: Reading Comprehension

1.	D	8.	B	15.	B	22.	B
2.	A	9.	E	16.	A	23.	A
3.	C	10.	D	17.	E	24.	E
4.	A	11.	E	18.	D	25.	B
5.	D	12.	E	19.	E	26.	D
6.	E	13.	A	20.	C		
7.	C	14.	D	21.	C		

Section III: Logical Reasoning

1.	A	8.	D	15.	B	22.	C
2.	E	9.	D	16.	D	23.	A
3.	B	10.	A	17.	D	24.	A
4.	A	11.	E	18.	E	25.	D
5.	D	12.	C	19.	A		
6.	C	13.	B	20.	C		
7.	E	14.	D	21.	C		

Section IV: Analytical Reasoning

1.	D	8.	A	15.	E	22.	E
2.	E	9.	B	16.	A	23.	C
3.	D	10.	E	17.	C	24.	A
4.	D	11.	B	18.	A	25.	B
5.	A	12.	E	19.	C		
6.	E	13.	B	20.	A		
7.	C	14.	A	21.	C		

Refer to Chapter 16 for tips on computing your score.

TIP

Chapter 19

Even More "Fun": LSAT Practice Exam 3

The best way to prepare for the LSAT is with practice, so here's another opportunity to sharpen your skills on a full-length exam.

You'll get the most benefit from this exercise if you try to duplicate the testing environment of the real thing. So before you begin, keep these test-taking tips in mind:

1. **Find a quiet place to work, where nothing can distract or interrupt you.**

2. **Use the answer grid provided.**

   You'll mark answers directly next to the answer choices when you take the digital LSAT on a tablet. You may use blank scratch paper throughout the test for making notes.

3. **Set your watch or alarm clock for 35-minute intervals.**

4. **Don't go to the next section until the time allotted for the current section is up.**

5. **If you finish early, check your work for that section only.**

6. **Don't take a break during any one section.**

7. **Give yourself exactly one 10-minute break between sections III and IV.**

When you're through, you can do a swift check of your success by consulting the answer key at the end of Chapter 20. After you calculate the number of questions you answered correctly in all sections, be sure to read the rest of that chapter to benefit from thorough explanations of how to approach each question on this exam.

TIP

Although this test is a lot like the real thing, it isn't a substitute for exposure to real LSAT questions. Ordering print or digital LSAT PrepTests from www.lsac.org allows you to apply what you've learned from reading this book to an actual LSAT.

Answer Sheet for Practice Exam 3

Section I

1. Ⓐ Ⓑ Ⓒ Ⓓ Ⓔ
2. Ⓐ Ⓑ Ⓒ Ⓓ Ⓔ
3. Ⓐ Ⓑ Ⓒ Ⓓ Ⓔ
4. Ⓐ Ⓑ Ⓒ Ⓓ Ⓔ
5. Ⓐ Ⓑ Ⓒ Ⓓ Ⓔ
6. Ⓐ Ⓑ Ⓒ Ⓓ Ⓔ
7. Ⓐ Ⓑ Ⓒ Ⓓ Ⓔ
8. Ⓐ Ⓑ Ⓒ Ⓓ Ⓔ
9. Ⓐ Ⓑ Ⓒ Ⓓ Ⓔ
10. Ⓐ Ⓑ Ⓒ Ⓓ Ⓔ
11. Ⓐ Ⓑ Ⓒ Ⓓ Ⓔ
12. Ⓐ Ⓑ Ⓒ Ⓓ Ⓔ
13. Ⓐ Ⓑ Ⓒ Ⓓ Ⓔ
14. Ⓐ Ⓑ Ⓒ Ⓓ Ⓔ
15. Ⓐ Ⓑ Ⓒ Ⓓ Ⓔ
16. Ⓐ Ⓑ Ⓒ Ⓓ Ⓔ
17. Ⓐ Ⓑ Ⓒ Ⓓ Ⓔ
18. Ⓐ Ⓑ Ⓒ Ⓓ Ⓔ
19. Ⓐ Ⓑ Ⓒ Ⓓ Ⓔ
20. Ⓐ Ⓑ Ⓒ Ⓓ Ⓔ
21. Ⓐ Ⓑ Ⓒ Ⓓ Ⓔ
22. Ⓐ Ⓑ Ⓒ Ⓓ Ⓔ
23. Ⓐ Ⓑ Ⓒ Ⓓ Ⓔ
24. Ⓐ Ⓑ Ⓒ Ⓓ Ⓔ
25. Ⓐ Ⓑ Ⓒ Ⓓ Ⓔ
26. Ⓐ Ⓑ Ⓒ Ⓓ Ⓔ
27. Ⓐ Ⓑ Ⓒ Ⓓ Ⓔ
28. Ⓐ Ⓑ Ⓒ Ⓓ Ⓔ
29. Ⓐ Ⓑ Ⓒ Ⓓ Ⓔ
30. Ⓐ Ⓑ Ⓒ Ⓓ Ⓔ

Section II

1. Ⓐ Ⓑ Ⓒ Ⓓ Ⓔ
2. Ⓐ Ⓑ Ⓒ Ⓓ Ⓔ
3. Ⓐ Ⓑ Ⓒ Ⓓ Ⓔ
4. Ⓐ Ⓑ Ⓒ Ⓓ Ⓔ
5. Ⓐ Ⓑ Ⓒ Ⓓ Ⓔ
6. Ⓐ Ⓑ Ⓒ Ⓓ Ⓔ
7. Ⓐ Ⓑ Ⓒ Ⓓ Ⓔ
8. Ⓐ Ⓑ Ⓒ Ⓓ Ⓔ
9. Ⓐ Ⓑ Ⓒ Ⓓ Ⓔ
10. Ⓐ Ⓑ Ⓒ Ⓓ Ⓔ
11. Ⓐ Ⓑ Ⓒ Ⓓ Ⓔ
12. Ⓐ Ⓑ Ⓒ Ⓓ Ⓔ
13. Ⓐ Ⓑ Ⓒ Ⓓ Ⓔ
14. Ⓐ Ⓑ Ⓒ Ⓓ Ⓔ
15. Ⓐ Ⓑ Ⓒ Ⓓ Ⓔ
16. Ⓐ Ⓑ Ⓒ Ⓓ Ⓔ
17. Ⓐ Ⓑ Ⓒ Ⓓ Ⓔ
18. Ⓐ Ⓑ Ⓒ Ⓓ Ⓔ
19. Ⓐ Ⓑ Ⓒ Ⓓ Ⓔ
20. Ⓐ Ⓑ Ⓒ Ⓓ Ⓔ
21. Ⓐ Ⓑ Ⓒ Ⓓ Ⓔ
22. Ⓐ Ⓑ Ⓒ Ⓓ Ⓔ
23. Ⓐ Ⓑ Ⓒ Ⓓ Ⓔ
24. Ⓐ Ⓑ Ⓒ Ⓓ Ⓔ
25. Ⓐ Ⓑ Ⓒ Ⓓ Ⓔ
26. Ⓐ Ⓑ Ⓒ Ⓓ Ⓔ
27. Ⓐ Ⓑ Ⓒ Ⓓ Ⓔ
28. Ⓐ Ⓑ Ⓒ Ⓓ Ⓔ
29. Ⓐ Ⓑ Ⓒ Ⓓ Ⓔ
30. Ⓐ Ⓑ Ⓒ Ⓓ Ⓔ

Answer Sheet for Practice Exam 3

Section III

1. Ⓐ Ⓑ Ⓒ Ⓓ Ⓔ
2. Ⓐ Ⓑ Ⓒ Ⓓ Ⓔ
3. Ⓐ Ⓑ Ⓒ Ⓓ Ⓔ
4. Ⓐ Ⓑ Ⓒ Ⓓ Ⓔ
5. Ⓐ Ⓑ Ⓒ Ⓓ Ⓔ
6. Ⓐ Ⓑ Ⓒ Ⓓ Ⓔ
7. Ⓐ Ⓑ Ⓒ Ⓓ Ⓔ
8. Ⓐ Ⓑ Ⓒ Ⓓ Ⓔ
9. Ⓐ Ⓑ Ⓒ Ⓓ Ⓔ
10. Ⓐ Ⓑ Ⓒ Ⓓ Ⓔ
11. Ⓐ Ⓑ Ⓒ Ⓓ Ⓔ
12. Ⓐ Ⓑ Ⓒ Ⓓ Ⓔ
13. Ⓐ Ⓑ Ⓒ Ⓓ Ⓔ
14. Ⓐ Ⓑ Ⓒ Ⓓ Ⓔ
15. Ⓐ Ⓑ Ⓒ Ⓓ Ⓔ
16. Ⓐ Ⓑ Ⓒ Ⓓ Ⓔ
17. Ⓐ Ⓑ Ⓒ Ⓓ Ⓔ
18. Ⓐ Ⓑ Ⓒ Ⓓ Ⓔ
19. Ⓐ Ⓑ Ⓒ Ⓓ Ⓔ
20. Ⓐ Ⓑ Ⓒ Ⓓ Ⓔ
21. Ⓐ Ⓑ Ⓒ Ⓓ Ⓔ
22. Ⓐ Ⓑ Ⓒ Ⓓ Ⓔ
23. Ⓐ Ⓑ Ⓒ Ⓓ Ⓔ
24. Ⓐ Ⓑ Ⓒ Ⓓ Ⓔ
25. Ⓐ Ⓑ Ⓒ Ⓓ Ⓔ
26. Ⓐ Ⓑ Ⓒ Ⓓ Ⓔ
27. Ⓐ Ⓑ Ⓒ Ⓓ Ⓔ
28. Ⓐ Ⓑ Ⓒ Ⓓ Ⓔ
29. Ⓐ Ⓑ Ⓒ Ⓓ Ⓔ
30. Ⓐ Ⓑ Ⓒ Ⓓ Ⓔ

Section IV

1. Ⓐ Ⓑ Ⓒ Ⓓ Ⓔ
2. Ⓐ Ⓑ Ⓒ Ⓓ Ⓔ
3. Ⓐ Ⓑ Ⓒ Ⓓ Ⓔ
4. Ⓐ Ⓑ Ⓒ Ⓓ Ⓔ
5. Ⓐ Ⓑ Ⓒ Ⓓ Ⓔ
6. Ⓐ Ⓑ Ⓒ Ⓓ Ⓔ
7. Ⓐ Ⓑ Ⓒ Ⓓ Ⓔ
8. Ⓐ Ⓑ Ⓒ Ⓓ Ⓔ
9. Ⓐ Ⓑ Ⓒ Ⓓ Ⓔ
10. Ⓐ Ⓑ Ⓒ Ⓓ Ⓔ
11. Ⓐ Ⓑ Ⓒ Ⓓ Ⓔ
12. Ⓐ Ⓑ Ⓒ Ⓓ Ⓔ
13. Ⓐ Ⓑ Ⓒ Ⓓ Ⓔ
14. Ⓐ Ⓑ Ⓒ Ⓓ Ⓔ
15. Ⓐ Ⓑ Ⓒ Ⓓ Ⓔ
16. Ⓐ Ⓑ Ⓒ Ⓓ Ⓔ
17. Ⓐ Ⓑ Ⓒ Ⓓ Ⓔ
18. Ⓐ Ⓑ Ⓒ Ⓓ Ⓔ
19. Ⓐ Ⓑ Ⓒ Ⓓ Ⓔ
20. Ⓐ Ⓑ Ⓒ Ⓓ Ⓔ
21. Ⓐ Ⓑ Ⓒ Ⓓ Ⓔ
22. Ⓐ Ⓑ Ⓒ Ⓓ Ⓔ
23. Ⓐ Ⓑ Ⓒ Ⓓ Ⓔ
24. Ⓐ Ⓑ Ⓒ Ⓓ Ⓔ
25. Ⓐ Ⓑ Ⓒ Ⓓ Ⓔ
26. Ⓐ Ⓑ Ⓒ Ⓓ Ⓔ
27. Ⓐ Ⓑ Ⓒ Ⓓ Ⓔ
28. Ⓐ Ⓑ Ⓒ Ⓓ Ⓔ
29. Ⓐ Ⓑ Ⓒ Ⓓ Ⓔ
30. Ⓐ Ⓑ Ⓒ Ⓓ Ⓔ

Section I
Logical Reasoning

1. The ivory-billed woodpecker has been considered extinct for the past several decades. Recently, researchers claim to have found a pair of ivory-billed woodpeckers in Arkansas. Their best evidence is a video that shows a large woodpecker flying away from the camera. The bird has the characteristic large white patches on the trailing edge of the wings. This is one of the factors that distinguishes ivory-billeds from the closely related pileated woodpecker. However, skeptics of the discovery argue that some abnormal pileateds can have extra white on the wing and that the bird in the video is most likely an abnormal pileated. They conclude that the ivory-billed has not been found and is still extinct.

Which of the following, if true, most strengthens the skeptics' reasoning that the ivory-billed woodpecker is still extinct?

(A) Before this discovery, the last reported ivory-billed woodpeckers were seen in Louisiana.

(B) The first person to discover the ivory-billed woodpeckers was not a specialist, but professional ornithologists were soon brought in to confirm the identification.

(C) In the same area where the video was shot, researchers also heard the distinctive double-tap used by ivory-billed woodpeckers.

(D) Of the five key field marks that identify ivory-billed woodpeckers, only the extra white on the wings has been seen, and this is also the only feature that occurs on abnormal pileated woodpeckers.

(E) The bird in the video is clearly seen using the shallow wing beats of the ivory-billed woodpecker rather than the deeper wing beats of the abnormal pileated woodpecker.

2. A cosmetics company did a study of hair colors involving 100 women, all of whom dyed their hair with the same product. Half of them then washed their hair with special shampoo made for color-treated hair, and half of them washed their hair with ordinary shampoo. After two months, there was no difference in color fading between the two groups. Therefore, shampoo for color-treated hair is valueless.

Which one of the following statements, if true, most seriously weakens the argument?

(A) Most shampoos contain the same basic ingredients, such as sodium lauryl sulfate or sodium laureth sulfate.

(B) Most hair experts recommend touching up hair color every four to six weeks.

(C) Both groups had equal numbers of women in their 30s, 40s, and 50s, with comparable natural hair colors.

(D) The women who had used shampoo for color-treated hair had softer and shinier hair than the women who used ordinary shampoo.

(E) Hair color technology has improved tremendously in the last ten years, making it possible for all women to successfully color their hair at home.

3. Snakes exist on every continent except for Antarctica, which is inhospitable to all cold-blooded animals. The continent of Australia is home to many of the deadliest snakes in the world. However, the nearby island nation of New Zealand has no snakes at all. Scientists estimate that snakes originated about 100 million years ago when the continents were joined and the snakes stayed on the main land masses of the continents when they split apart. Thus snakes are absent from New Zealand because they are unable to swim and therefore could not make the journey.

Which of the following, if true, would most strengthen this argument?

(A) Snakes are found on many other islands of the Pacific Ocean.

(B) Snakes are found in South America at latitudes farther south than New Zealand.

(C) Islands like Hawaii and New Zealand are very aggressive about preventing an accidental introduction of snakes.

(D) Sea snakes can swim and are present in the warmer oceans of the world.

(E) Snakes are also absent from other major islands, such as Hawaii, Ireland, and Greenland.

4. Dermatologist: Many people believe that they can prevent acne by using clay masks to draw impurities from pores and applying toner, which they think will close pores and prevent dirt from getting into them. If this were true, then acne would be very easy to treat with topical measures. In fact, acne blemishes develop within the skin itself and are affected by internal factors such as hormones and sebum. Therefore, using external measures such as masks and toners is useless.

The dermatologist's conclusion requires the assumption that

(A) clay masks can dry out the skin

(B) some people like the sensation of toners on their skin

(C) dirt on the skin does not cause acne

(D) doctors have successfully treated acne with oral antibiotics

(E) most dermatologists recommend that patients clean their faces with gentle soap instead of harsh cleansers

5. American citizens believe that they live in a democracy. In presidential elections, though, citizens do not get to vote for president. They can only choose electors who cast votes for president on behalf of entire states. Therefore, Americans do not actually live in a democracy.

Which one of the following exhibits a pattern of reasoning most similar to the one in the argument presented here?

(A) Most colleges have student government. All students are allowed to vote in student government elections. In fact, though, very few students vote or take any interest in student government affairs. Therefore, student government serves no useful purpose.

(B) All cities have local law enforcement programs. Usually, the police handle crime in the city, the sheriff's department handles county matters, and the state police handle matters that affect the entire state. Therefore, most cities have too much duplication of law enforcement jobs.

(C) The United States is said to have a free market economy. In fact, though, the U.S. economy is heavily regulated by the government, which gives many advantages to large businesses and punishes small companies and the self-employed. Therefore, the United States does not really have a free market economy.

(D) Most teachers believe that education courses are valuable. Many colleges and universities, on the other hand, look down on education degrees. Therefore, future teachers should not major in education.

(E) Most health insurers claim to offer their customers a variety of choices in health care. Doctors, however, do not post a menu of prices for customers to peruse before accepting treatment, and patients in hospitals do not get to choose the doctors who treat them. Therefore, health insurers are dishonest.

6. People usually meet expectations. Thus, if Person A informs Person B that he or she is expected to perform a particular duty and Person B accepts that duty, generally, Person B will perform the duty as expected.

Which one of the following best illustrates this proposition?

(A) A teacher informs a girl that she is responsible for feeding the class hamster every morning, and the girl agrees to do this. After this, the girl feeds the hamster every morning without the teacher telling her to.

(B) A partner asks an associate to write a memo on a legal issue. Because the associate is inexperienced, the partner supervises his work closely and helps him write several drafts of the memo.

(C) Country A has agreed to be Country B's military ally. Country A then elects a new president who disagrees with Country B's policies, and when Country B goes to war, Country A refuses to help.

(D) A coach teaches his players a particular strategy. The first time they use it in a game, they win. Thereafter, they go on to win the league championship.

(E) A psychologist tells a patient that behavior modification will help her quit smoking. The patient follows the program designed by the psychologist and quits smoking successfully.

7. Since the late 19th century, German schools have used a series of aptitude tests to shunt students into various tracks, some leading to the university, some to two-year clerical colleges, and some straight to technical jobs. The German educational system is currently plagued with discipline problems and underperforming students. Therefore, aptitude tests are valueless for sorting students.

All of the following, if true, weaken this argument EXCEPT:

(A) Disciplinary and other problems are most profound at technical schools with large immigrant populations, where students feel that society will not give them opportunities for self-improvement.

(B) Schools that attempt to teach the same subjects to students of all abilities are the most likely to suffer from discipline problems and failure because the work is too easy for bright students and too hard for slower ones.

(C) Sorting students by ability allows schools to gear curricula to individual needs, which results in better overall results.

(D) Until the early 1990s, the German school system was one of the best in the world, with excellent test results and virtually no disciplinary problems.

(E) Students who graduate from German technical schools are usually prepared to perform highly skilled jobs that pay them well.

8. All worker bees are female and have no sense of themselves as individuals. They instead live to further the welfare of the queen and her hive as a whole, helping her to lay eggs and raising her offspring. This means that workers spend their lives helping the queen to pass on her genetic traits and fail to pass on their own genes to offspring.

Which one of the following statements, if true, most seriously weakens this argument?

(A) All the bees in a hive are related to one another.; the workers are all sisters and the quen is their mother. There is no need for workers to pass on their own genes because they are furthering their mother's line.

(B) When a hive loses its queen, some workers develop the ability to lay eggs; these unfertilized eggs can hatch only into male drones.

(C) A bee colony has only one queen at a time. When a new queen hatches in a hive, she immediately seeks out all other queens and tries to kill them or drive them out.

(D) If a beekeeper can catch the queen from a swarm, he can install her in a beehive, and the entire swarm of worker bees will immediately move into the hive with her.

(E) Queen bees mate once in their lives and store sperm from this mating to fertilize all their worker eggs. Male drones hatch from unfertilized eggs.

GO ON TO NEXT PAGE ➤

9. Some scholars of mythology claim that myths exist to explain natural phenomena; for example, the myth of Zeus's casting lightning bolts from heaven helped the ancient Greeks explain an otherwise unexplainable event. Other scholars argue that myths are a way in which people explore psychological phenomena, such as a son's feelings toward his mother. If these various scholars are correct, then all myths can be interpreted both as explanations of natural events and explorations of psychology.

This argument is most vulnerable to criticism on the grounds that it

(A) draws a conclusion about myths that has already been discounted by experts in the field

(B) takes for granted that the myths of ancient people are relevant today

(C) imposes a modern, western sensibility on the myths of pre-modern people from a variety of cultures

(D) criticizes scholars who insist that one or the other interpretation of myths must be correct

(E) assumes that what is true of myths in general must also be true of each individual myth

10. Identifying the sex of parrotfish can be difficult. Juveniles of both sexes look alike. On the other hand, sexually mature males are large and brightly colored, with brilliantly colored scales that resemble those of colorful tropical parrots, whereas mature females are smaller than males and have more subdued coloration. In some species, males pass through an intermediate growth phase in which they continue to look identical to females before maturing into their full adult size and coloration.

If the statements in this argument are true, which one of the following would also have to be true?

(A) The sex of a non-juvenile parrotfish lacking brightly colored scales cannot always be easily determined.

(B) All male parrotfish are large and brightly colored.

(C) Female parrotfish use the bright colors of male parrotfish to judge which males are good mating prospects.

(D) Smaller size and subdued coloring help female parrotfish escape predators, to which mature male parrotfish are especially vulnerable.

(E) In all species of parrotfish, all males spend a part of their lives looking exactly like adult females.

11. Schools today have decreased funding and time for art, music, and drama classes, citing lack of money and a need to spend more time on academic subjects. This is tragic. Because of these decisions, the next generation of citizens will be a mass of automatons with heads stuffed full of facts and no appreciation of or talent for artistic pursuits.

The conclusion drawn in this argument follows logically if which one of the following is assumed?

(A) In the absence of school arts programs, many parents sign their children up for extracurricular classes in art and music.

(B) Schools with strong arts programs tend to produce students who also excel in academic subjects.

(C) Many people who never studied art, music, or drama in school nevertheless have gone on to become famous artists.

(D) If people are not exposed to the arts at school, they will never learn about them.

(E) The primary purpose of schools is to teach students the academic subjects they will need to flourish in the business world.

12. Columnist: Our town has lost its minor league baseball team. Another town in a different state offered to build a large, modern baseball stadium if the team would move there; our town has refused to update our stadium for years. This is a catastrophic loss to our town and will severely damage the local economy.

Which one of the following, if true, most strongly supports this argument?

(A) Building a new baseball stadium would have cost the town several million dollars that it would be unlikely to recoup through revenues generated by the baseball team.

(B) The baseball team's presence generated millions of dollars of revenue for the town every year by attracting out-of-town visitors who spent money on hotels, restaurants, and other goods and services.

(C) The current baseball stadium was already larger than necessary, and the bleachers were never more than half-full during home games.

(D) The baseball team would have gone to any city that was willing to grant its demands for new facilities, and it had no real loyalty to the town that had been its home for 20 years.

(E) In a local referendum, only a small minority of town citizens voted to spend the money necessary to build a new baseball stadium.

13. The President has proposed an initiative to help people stay married by teaching them skills needed to maintain relationships and raise healthy children. This initiative would focus on low-income unmarried people, who studies have shown are not likely to marry, even after they have children. We should support this initiative because it would be very beneficial to our most vulnerable citizens: the children of poor, unmarried women.

Which one of the following is an assumption required by this argument?

(A) If more poor people were married, society would be plagued by less drug dependency, crime, and teen pregnancy.

(B) People with higher incomes do not need as much help in maintaining their marriage and raising their children.

(C) Children raised by a mother and father who are married to one another are better off than children raised by a mother alone.

(D) The majority of welfare payments go to unmarried parents; encouraging marriage would reduce the number of people on welfare.

(E) Other governmental programs also designed to assist the family have been successful.

14. Isabel: The popular novels depicting the end of the world and the violent annihilation of all people who do not espouse a particular religion are dangerous. They encourage members of that religion to see all nonbelievers as evil people who deserve a horrific fate.

Ferdinand: I think you are overstating the significance of popular fiction. People read these books solely for entertainment purposes and do not allow them to affect their beliefs or actions.

The dialogue provides the most support for the claim that Isabel and Ferdinand disagree over whether

(A) popular novels depicting the end of the world are religious in nature

(B) plots involving the end of the world are suitable for popular novels

(C) books about the end of the world are popular

(D) popular fiction can affect people's beliefs and actions

(E) depiction of acts of violence are appropriate in a work of popular fiction

GO ON TO NEXT PAGE

15. Tia: Scientists and doctors have found that obesity is increasing rapidly in this country. Obesity causes many significant health problems. The government should therefore step in to regulate food manufacturing and advertising, which would help people consume fewer calories.

Muriel: It's true that obesity is increasing. The blame, however, lies with people who have made a personal choice to eat too much. Their weight is entirely in their control. Therefore, the government should not step in except perhaps to encourage people to eat more healthily and exercise occasionally.

This dialogue lends the most support to the claim that Tia and Muriel disagree with each other about which one of the following statements?

(A) Diet and exercise have proven effective at curing and preventing obesity in a large number of people.

(B) Government regulation is never the appropriate method for dealing with public health problems.

(C) Public schools can play an important role in teaching children the value of fruits, vegetables, and a balanced diet.

(D) Regulating modern food manufacturing and advertising would help prevent obesity.

(E) Private-sector approaches to problems are more successful than government programs.

16. Politician: Environmentalists claim that pollution is leading to global warming, which supposedly will raise the Earth's temperatures and lead to the melting of the polar ice caps, rising overall sea levels, and various other catastrophes. They must not have been paying attention to the winters lately; the last five years have seen record low temperatures in January and February. Therefore, global warming clearly is not happening.

The reasoning in the politician's argument is most vulnerable to criticism on the grounds that the argument

(A) relies on evidence that presupposes the truth of the conclusion that it seeks to support

(B) uses an emotional appeal instead of arguing based on facts

(C) seeks unethically to minimize the negative effects of a troubling phenomenon

(D) relies on evidence too partial to establish the conclusion drawn

(E) suggests unfairly that environmentalists are politically biased

17. People should not focus just on immediate payoffs when deciding on a course of action; many acts bring few immediate payoffs but result in much larger payoffs in the future.

Which one of the following most closely conforms to this principle?

(A) A college graduate with a lucrative job offer decides to decline it and instead borrow several thousand dollars to attend medical school in the hopes of receiving a much larger future income as a physician.

(B) Investing in the stock market is a wise choice for anyone with enough excess cash; the stock market has historically outperformed other forms of saving, though occasionally investors have lost all their money.

(C) Parents should encourage their children to attend religious services every week because people with strong religious faith tend to be more successful than those without faith.

(D) Building houses for Habitat for Humanity is a good activity, allowing poor people to become homeowners with all the pride of ownership and responsibility for paying for their own property.

(E) It makes sense to buy the best furniture one can afford; good pieces will last a long time, whereas cheaper furniture breaks quickly and must be replaced.

18. Studies have shown that women make at least half of all car-purchasing decisions. Women notice details that men do not; for example, women especially appreciate drink holders and a back seat that makes it easier for them to reach children in child seats. Women are also more likely than men to choose cars based on environmental friendliness. Only a few car models have been designed with women's tastes in mind, but these vehicles outsell all others by a huge margin.

Which one of the following is most strongly supported by the information in this passage?

(A) More car manufacturers should work to reduce emissions from their vehicles instead of building large, gas-guzzling, truck-like vehicles.

(B) Most purchasers of minivans are women who drive their children to school and extracurricular activities and thus appreciate the size, safety, and convenience of minivans.

(C) All car manufacturers should conduct careful market research to determine what their customers want in vehicles.

(D) Cars manufacturers that design cars according to female tastes can earn larger profits than those who do not.

(E) Because station wagons were very popular with women in the 1970s and 1980s, car manufacturers should make more station wagons to maximize profits.

19. Carter: A new study has shown that the more young children watch television, the more likely they are to develop attention deficit disorder. Television, for its part, has nothing to offer children. Because television offers no benefits and bears significant risks to development, children should never watch television.

Neri: The experts who ran that study believe that attention deficit disorder results from the extremely fast pace and disjointed nature of commercial television, not from the actual content of programs. Educational programs can actually stimulate brain development in young children; programs made by experts in child development can help them learn valuable lessons.

Carter and Neri disagree about whether

(A) violent programs on television teach children to behave more violently than they would if they did not watch such programs

(B) there is a difference in risk between children who watch less than one hour of television per day and those who watch more than three hours

(C) children can ever benefit from watching television

(D) the generation of people who grew up with educational programming have shown evidence of having benefited from their youthful television watching

(E) children who watch movies on videotape or DVD without commercials are as much at risk as children who watch commercial television

20. Park ranger: The National Park Service should pay close attention to naming its parks and monuments. Parks and monuments with attractive names bring in many more tourists than facilities with less inspiring names.

Which one of the following, if true, would provide the most support for the park ranger's assertion?

(A) Civil War buffs especially love Civil War battlefields, monuments, and state parks on which they can reenact historic battles.

(B) National parks in the western United States, which feature inspiring scenery, attract far more visitors than national parks in the eastern part of the country.

(C) The Sand Creek Massacre National Historic Site has a more appealing name than the Martin Van Buren National Historic Site.

(D) South Carolina's Congaree Swamp National Monument saw an increase in visitors after it changed its name to Congaree National Park.

(E) Yellowstone National Park brings in many visitors because it provides a variety of attractions, such as the Old Faithful geyser, petrified trees, and abundant wildlife.

GO ON TO NEXT PAGE

21. It is outrageous that the government has out-lawed smoking in so many public places. This is a question of civil liberties. Smokers know that smoking can make them sick, and if they choose to poison themselves, that should be their business. The government does not have the right to stop people from doing an activity that can only hurt the person engaging in it.

Which one of the following is an assumption required by the argument?

(A) The government does have the right to control activities that result in harm to others.

(B) The government should not outlaw smoking in private places.

(C) Smokers who know about the adverse effects of smoking are capable of quitting.

(D) The government does not have the authority to force drivers to wear seat belts.

(E) Exposure to secondhand smoke does not result in significant ill effects.

22. Actors tend to be extroverts who are perfectly comfortable appearing and speaking before a crowd of people. People who want to become more extroverted should therefore study drama and perform in plays.

The reasoning in the argument is most vulnerable to criticism on the grounds that the argument

(A) assumes that it is better to be extroverted than introverted

(B) presupposes that actors become extroverted because they study drama

(C) attributes a characteristic to actors without providing evidence to support that claim

(D) fails to adequately define the term "extrovert"

(E) ignores the other ways that people can improve their confidence in situations such as public speaking

23. Mathematician: In 1590, Sir Walter Raleigh discovered that the best way to store spherical objects such as cannonballs was stacked in a pyramid. Grocers who stock oranges also know intuitively that this principle makes

sense, because it allows the top objects to sink into the spaces between the lower ones, maximizing the number of objects that can fit into a given space. Raleigh created an equation to express this principle and the famous scientist Johannes Kepler agreed with him, but it was not until 2004 that mathematicians using computers came up with an acceptable proof of the concept. The proof requires far too many calculations to do by hand, and mathematicians have not double-checked them all; nevertheless, computers are extremely accurate at calculations and all portions of the proof that have been checked are correct, so the mathematical community can feel confident that the computer-created proof is valid.

Which of the following most accurately expresses the main conclusion of the mathematician's argument?

(A) Although a computer-created proof might be too complex to check by hand in the traditional manner, computers are reliable enough today that mathematicians should be willing to admit proofs done by computers into the body of accepted mathematical knowledge.

(B) Although stacking spheres in a pyramid is one of the most efficient ways of storing them, there is another method that is just as efficient: arranging them in a honeycomb shape. Because the proof does not acknowledge this, it should not be accepted as valid.

(C) Mathematicians have done proofs by hand for centuries. This is the accepted method for proving mathematical hypotheses. Computers have little place in the world of theoretical mathematics.

(D) The mathematical journal that published this proof noted that scholars have not checked the entire proof, although the portions they have checked have all been proven accurate. This level of accuracy is not high enough to justify publication of the proof.

(E) A rigorous mathematical proof follows a chain of logic that begins with stated assumptions and leads inexorably to an inescapable conclusion. It should include every step along the way. The sphere-stacking problem has far too many steps to prove by hand.

24. In 1995, the federal government gave states the right to set their own speed limits; several states immediately increased their speed limits to 70 miles per hour, and some even abolished limits entirely. In most cases, this has not been a problem; the overall percentage of accidents per drivers has not increased since the speed limits were raised. At the same time, however, highway accident fatalities have increased 6 percent.

Which one of the following, if true, most helps to resolve the apparent discrepancy described here?

(A) Teenage drivers are the most likely to exceed speed limits, and their driving skill is not yet equal to the task of avoiding high speed accidents.

(B) Accidents that occur at a higher speed are much more likely to be fatal than those at lower speeds.

(C) State governments are not as concerned with highway safety as the federal government was in the days of a federally mandated speed limit.

(D) In the 1970s, more people drove smaller, compact cars that got good gas mileage but were incapable of maintaining a high speed.

(E) Drivers today are often distracted by CD players, radios, cellphones, and other devices, which makes them more likely to get into accidents.

25. Consultant: It's always a good idea to start off a speech with a little joke. This relaxes the audience and makes them more willing to listen to what you have to say. Humor is a universal concept, so you should still start your speech with a joke even when speaking in a foreign country.

All of the following, if true, weaken this argument EXCEPT:

(A) It is very difficult to translate a joke into another language, and jokes from one country can be deeply offensive to people from other countries.

(B) In some societies, it is considered inappropriate for women to tell jokes.

(C) Many interpreters refuse to interpret jokes and simply inform the audience that the speaker has told a joke and request that the audience laugh.

(D) Studies have shown that audiences appreciate the opportunity to laugh while listening to a speech.

(E) Humor is a sign of aggression or dominance in some countries and can make an audience feel that the speaker is trying to exert power over them.

DO NOT TURN THE PAGE UNTIL TOLD TO DO SO **STOP** DO NOT RETURN TO A PREVIOUS TEST

Section II
Reading Comprehension

> **TIME:** 35 minutes for 27 questions
>
> **DIRECTIONS:** Read each passage and answer the questions that follow it. Some questions may have more than one answer that looks correct. In that case, pick the one that answers the question most completely and correctly. Don't assume anything that isn't stated in the passage or the questions. All the information you need to answer the questions is contained in the passage, questions, and answer choices.

Questions 1–7 refer to the following passage.

Junzaburou Nishiwaki, a 20th-century Japanese poet, scholar, and translator, spent his career working to introduce Japanese readers to European and American writing and to break his country out of its literary insularity. He was interested in European culture all his life. Born to a wealthy family in rural Niigata prefecture in 1894, Nishiwaki spent his youth aspiring to be a painter and traveled to Tokyo in 1911 to study the "White Horse" school of painting with the artist Seiki Kuroda; this painting style fused Japanese and European artistic traditions. After his father died in 1913, Nishiwaki studied economics at Keio University, but his real love was English literature. After graduating, he worked for several years as a reporter at the English-language *Japan Times* and as a teacher at Keio University.

Nishiwaki finally received the opportunity to concentrate on English literature in 1922, when Keio University sent him to Oxford University for three years. He spent this time reading literature in Old and Middle English and classical Greek and Latin. He became fluent in English, French, German, Latin, and Greek. While he was in England, Roaring Twenties modernism caught his eye, and the works of writers such as James Joyce, Ezra Pound, and T.S. Eliot were crucially important to his literary development. In 1925, Nishiwaki published his first book, *Spectrum*, a volume of poems written in English; he explained that English offered him much more freedom of expression than traditional Japanese poetic language.

Nishiwaki returned to Keio University in 1925 and became a professor of English literature, teaching linguistics, Old and Middle English, and the history of English literature. He remained active in modernist and avant-garde literary circles. In 1933 he published *Ambarvalia*, his first volume of poetry written in Japanese; this collection of surrealist verse ranged far and wide through European geography and history, and included Japanese translations of Catullus, Sophocles, and Shakespeare. Angered by the Japanese government's fascist policies, Nishiwaki refused to write poetry during the second world war. He spent the war years writing a dissertation on ancient Germanic literature.

After the war, Nishiwaki resumed his poetic pursuits and in 1947 published *Tabibito kaerazu,* in which he abandoned modernist language and returned to a classical Japanese poetic style, but with his own postmodernist touch, incorporating both Eastern and Western literary traditions. In 1953 Nishiwaki published *Kindai no guuwa,* which critics consider his most poetically mature work. He spent his last years producing works of criticism of English literature and Japanese translations of the work of such writers as D.H. Lawrence, James Joyce, T.S. Eliot, Stéphane Mallarmé, Shakespeare, and Chaucer. Nishiwaki retired from Keio University in 1962, though he continued to teach and write poetry. Before his death in 1982, he received numerous honors and awards; he was appointed to the Japanese Academy of Arts and Sciences, named a Person of Cultural Merit, and nominated for the Nobel Prize by Ezra Pound. Critics today consider Nishiwaki to have exercised more influence on younger poets than any other Japanese poet since 1945.

1. Which one of the following most accurately states the main idea of the passage?

   (A) Nishiwaki was a Japanese poet who rebelled against the strictures of his country's government and protested its policies toward Europe during World War II.

   (B) Nishiwaki was a Japanese poet and literary critic who embraced European literature as a way of rebelling against the constraints of his family and traditional Japanese culture.

   (C) Nishiwaki was a Japanese poet and professor who spent his life trying to convince young Japanese students that European literary forms were superior to Japanese poetic styles.

   (D) Nishiwaki was a Japanese poet and linguist who throughout his life chose to write in English rather than Japanese.

   (E) Nishiwaki was a Japanese poet and scholar who spent his life specializing in European literature, which proved tremendously influential to his own work.

2. The author's attitude toward Nishiwaki's life and career can be best described as

   (A) scholarly interest in the life and works of a significant literary figure

   (B) mild surprise at Nishiwaki's choosing to write poetry in a language foreign to him

   (C) open admiration for Nishiwaki's ability to function in several languages

   (D) skepticism toward Nishiwaki's motives in refusing to write poetry during the second world war

   (E) envy of Nishiwaki's success in publishing and academia

3. The primary function of the first paragraph is to

   (A) describe Nishiwaki's brief study of painting

   (B) introduce Nishiwaki and his lifelong interest in European culture

   (C) summarize Nishiwaki's contribution to Japanese literature

   (D) explain why a Japanese man chose to specialize in English literature

   (E) analyze European contributions to Japanese culture at the start of the 20th century

4. According to the passage, why did Nishiwaki stop writing poetry during World War II?

   (A) He was too busy with his contributions to the Japanese war effort.

   (B) The Japanese government rationed paper and ink, which made it impossible for him to write.

   (C) He disapproved of the Japanese government's policies and in protest refused to write poetry.

   (D) The Japanese government, fearing sedition, ordered him to stop writing poetry.

   (E) Work on his dissertation on German literature took up all his time.

5. The passage is primarily concerned with

   (A) comparing Nishiwaki's poetry to that of other Japanese poets of the 20th century

   (B) discussing the role of the avant-garde movement in Nishiwaki's writing

   (C) providing a brief biography of Nishiwaki that explains the significance of his work

   (D) explaining why writers can benefit from studying literature from other countries

   (E) describing the transformation in Japanese poetic style during the postwar period

GO ON TO NEXT PAGE

6. Which one of the following types of literature would the author suggest least interests Nishiwaki?

(A) Old English literature such as *Beowulf*

(B) modernist English verse such as *The Waste Land*

(C) Middle English literature such as *The Canterbury Tales*

(D) classical Greek works such as *Antigone*

(E) classical Japanese literature such as *The Tale of Genji*

7. Based on the passage, why did Nishiwaki choose to write his first published poems in English?

(A) He found that English allowed him to express a wider variety of thoughts and emotions than Japanese.

(B) He published the poems in London and believed that English readers would buy them if they were written in English.

(C) The poems were translations of Japanese poems into English.

(D) He believed that writing poetry in English would be a good way to improve his English language skills.

(E) The English literature department at Keio University required him to publish work in English before he could become a professor there.

Questions 8–14 refer to the following passage.

Biologists often fail to recognize the importance of a species to an ecosystem until that species is no longer present in the ecosystem. A case in point is that of the long-spined sea urchin, *Diadema antillarum*. Scientists and fishermen long considered the sea urchin a spiky pest that served no useful purpose; recreational divers would even feed sea urchins to fish just for fun. The last 20 years, however, have proven that the sea urchin does indeed play a valuable role in the marine environment.

Sea urchins are members of the phylum Echinodermata, the category of invertebrate animals with spiny exterior shells, which also includes starfish, brittle stars, and sand dollars. Sea urchins have a spherical body contained in a hard shell that is covered with long sharp spines. They walk around on shorter spines located on the underside of their bodies. A sea urchin's mouth is also located on its underside; this mouth is a five-toothed structure called Aristotle's Lantern, adapted to scraping algae and organic matter from rocks and corals. Sea urchins eat a vast amount of algae.

Exactly how much algae they consume has become clearer in the past two decades because urchins have virtually disappeared from many Atlantic environments. In 1983, a barge traveled from the Pacific to the Atlantic through the Panama Canal carrying a bacterium that proved devastating to the sea urchin population. Nearly all long-spined urchins in the tropical western Atlantic died as a result of this exposure. Without sea urchins to eat the algae, aquatic greenery grows out of control. It has completely covered some coral reefs. In Jamaica, before the sea urchins died off, algae covered just 1 percent of shallow reefs, but two years after the plague, it covered nearly 95 percent of shallow coral. Many reefs in the Bahamas have abruptly transformed from multicolored undersea wonderlands into monochromatic mossy-looking hillocks. Coral that is covered by algae quickly dies, unable to receive necessary sunlight and nutrients from the water. The algae cover also makes it difficult for both corals and sea urchins to breed, because their larvae cannot find a clean surface on which to anchor.

Scientists have completely changed their views of sea urchins from that of the early 1980s. Sea urchins are one of the first organisms to show signs of stress when water quality is bad, so the Environmental Protection Agency has begun monitoring sea urchins as an indicator of water conditions. Other scientists have taken on the task of redistributing the remaining sea urchins to endangered coral reefs. They hope that the sea urchins will clean off the reefs and make it possible for both coral and sea urchins to breed successfully and restore the marine environment to its healthy state.

8. Which one of the following most accurately expresses the main point of the passage?

(A) Events of the last two decades have shown that sea urchins play a vital role in the maintenance of the ecosystems in which they live, contrary to what many scientists formerly assumed.

(B) It is the duty of responsible scientists to manipulate environments to ensure that they remain in ecological balance, such as by transporting sea urchins to reefs that have become overgrown with algae.

(C) Members of the phylum Echinodermata are often underappreciated but are extremely important to the health of coral reefs.

(D) Excessive algae growth is a severe problem in the tropical western Atlantic, and if governments fail to take action in the very near future, all the coral reefs in that area could die.

(E) Governments should educate their citizenry on the importance of keeping ecosystems in balance because this will help prevent people from abusing natural resources or introducing foreign substances that might be dangerous to local plants and animals.

9. The primary purpose of the second paragraph is to

(A) support the claim that sea urchins are important to their ecosystems

(B) describe the appearance and eating habits of sea urchins

(C) argue that the loss of sea urchins is devastating to the overall ecosystem

(D) illustrate the attitude of scientists toward invertebrates

(E) suggest that other members of the phylum Echinodermata might also eat algae

10. Based on the passage, which one of the following best describes the relationship between sea urchins, starfish, brittle stars, and sand dollars?

(A) They are all invertebrates that eat algae.

(B) They were all devastated by the bacterium that entered the Atlantic in 1983.

(C) They are all members of the same phylum.

(D) They are all covered with long, sharp spines.

(E) They can all be divided into five segments that radiate out from a center point.

11. According to the passage, what happened to the sea urchin population in the tropical western Atlantic in the mid-1980s?

(A) Fishermen and water sports enthusiasts systematically killed them off, hoping to eradicate what they believed was a pest.

(B) A plague killed the coral, which became so covered with algae that sea urchins could no longer reproduce.

(C) A sudden increase in triggerfish, one of the main predators of sea urchins, resulted in most juvenile sea urchins being eaten before they could reach breeding age.

(D) A virus spread by other echinoderms caused sea urchins from the Bahamas to Jamaica to sicken and die.

(E) A bacterium carried by a ship entering the Atlantic from the Pacific spread throughout the population and killed nearly all sea urchins.

GO ON TO NEXT PAGE

12. Which one of the following, if true, best supports the author's claim that sea urchins are the key to removal of algae from coral reefs?

(A) Other animals, such as damselfish, also eat algae growing on coral reefs.

(B) The population of parrotfish, which eat coral, has increased in the years since the sea urchin population dropped.

(C) Coral reefs in regions that still have healthy sea urchin populations have almost no algae growing on them.

(D) Several different kinds of algae have grown on reefs in Jamaica and the Bahamas.

(E) New types of coral are beginning to predominate in areas that have lost sea urchin populations.

13. The author mentions the Environmental Protection Agency in the last paragraph primarily to

(A) point out the government's role in protecting marine habitats

(B) argue that the government should prevent shipping companies from transporting microbes from one marine environment to another

(C) provide an example of how the scientific community has altered its view of sea urchins

(D) illustrate how scientists since the early 1980s have failed to recognize the significance of sea urchins

(E) encourage voters to take a greater interest in environmental issues

14. Based on the passage, with which one of the following statements would the author be likely to agree?

(A) Humans can take an active role in assisting the recovery of ecosystems that have been harmed by human actions.

(B) It is a bad idea to remove sea urchins from successful breeding populations and introduce them into environments that might be hostile to them.

(C) Eradicating pests from the marine environment will make the waters of the tropical western Atlantic more pleasant for scuba divers and snorkelers.

(D) The Environmental Protection Agency should have fined the owner and pilot of the ship that carried the bacterium into the Atlantic in 1983.

(E) Animals other than sea urchins can adapt themselves to the ecological niche that sea urchins formerly occupied.

Questions 15–21 refer to the following two passages. The first is adapted from Managing Nonprofit Organizations, by Mary Tschirhart and Wolfgang Bielefeld (Wiley). The second is adapted from The Handbook of Nonprofit Governance, by BoardSource (Wiley).

Passage A

Leaders and managers of nonprofits face a variety of challenges. One of the most important is to keep the mission in mind in all decision making. Nonprofits must operate to fulfill their mission and are limited in their engagement in activities far afield from it. In addition they must keep in mind that the real owner of a nonprofit is the public. It is the public to whom they are ultimately accountable.

There are no designated shareholders or owners to please. Nonprofits are subject to the claims, and possible control, of many stakeholders, including donors, clients, board members, staff, volunteers, government at all levels, and community members. The expectations of these stakeholders can vary widely and leaders must balance competing demands.

Lester Salamon and others describe a number of additional challenges. Many nonprofits face fiscal difficulties, some starting with government cutbacks in the 1980s in areas where nonprofits were active. Government assistance has become more targeted and tied to stricter requirements. Not all nonprofits experiencing losses in government funding have been able to offset those losses with growth in private giving or earned income. There is growing competition as more for-profits move into areas traditionally served by nonprofits, such as health care, higher education, and employment training. The rise of B corporations, which are required to make decisions good for society, not just their shareholders, adds to the continuing erosion of sector boundaries. In addition nonprofits are under pressure from funders who are demanding more evidence that the nonprofits they fund are making a measurable positive impact, with some funders seeing themselves as investors with rights to influence strategic decisions.

Nonprofits are not immune from damage that can be caused by unscrupulous and fraudulent solicitors, financial improprieties, and executives and board members who care more about their own financial welfare than the mission of the organization.

Problems, when they do arise, are particularly disturbing because of the nature of nonprofits themselves — organizations created to provide some public benefit. Most people are familiar with the mechanisms that safeguard the integrity of government and business. Disenchanted voters can throw politicians out of office, and the branches of government view each other with watchful eyes. Businesses have shareholders or owners and are monitored by government agencies such as the Securities and Exchange Commission and the Occupational Safety and Health Administration. The media monitor both sectors and are quick to point out cases of corruption and poor performance.

Far fewer people understand how nonprofits are monitored and regulated. For much of its history, the nonprofit sector has operated outside the realm of harsh public scrutiny. No government agency exists exclusively to monitor the activities of nonprofits, most nonprofits aren't required to hold public meetings, and few journalists report on nonprofits with the same depth and focus devoted to business and government.

Nevertheless, nonprofits have many lines of defense against fraud and corruption. For example, all nonprofits are governed by a board of directors or trustees (there's no real difference) — a group of volunteers that is legally responsible for making sure the organization remains true to its mission, safeguards its assets, and operates in the public interest. The board is the first line of defense against fraud and abuse.

15. The authors of the two passages share a concern that

(A) for-profit business are moving in on areas traditionally served by nonprofit organizations

(B) no government or regulatory agency exists with the sole purpose of monitoring the activities of nonprofit organizations

(C) investors desire to see measurable results from the money they commit to nonprofit organizations

(D) nonprofits may face difficulties staying true to their overall mission

(E) nonprofit board members sometimes have their own financial interests at heart instead of those of the nonprofit

16. Which of the following titles would most appropriately fit both passages?

(A) Managing the Nonprofit Sector: An Overview

(B) The Funding Crisis within the Nonprofit Sector

(C) Balancing the Mission of a Nonprofit with the Mission of Funders

(D) The Board: A Nonprofit's First Line of Defense

(E) A Brief History of the Nonprofit Sector

17. Which of the following statements best describes the relationship between the two passages?

(A) The primary focus of both passages is how to overcome the challenges presented by the nature of their organizational structures.

(B) Passage A covers fiscal concerns faced by nonprofits, while Passage B establishes that nonprofits' biggest challenge is overcoming fraud and corruption.

(C) Passage A largely praises the management structure of an organization that Passage B mostly condemns.

(D) Passage A provides an overview of the types of challenges nonprofits face, and Passage B offers specific ways nonprofits can overcome these same challenges.

(E) Both passages suggest that the challenges nonprofits face are often exacerbated by the fact that they are organizations intended to serve the public good.

GO ON TO NEXT PAGE

18. Which of the following provides a statement with which the authors of both passages would agree?

(A) Nonprofits are dealing with an influx of for-profit agencies occupying roles once traditionally served by the nonprofit sector.

(B) Many nonprofits that have experienced a loss of government funding have been unable to offset those losses with earned income or private donations.

(C) Fiscal difficulties for many nonprofits stem from a period of heavy government cutbacks that took place in the 1980s.

(D) The public should hold managers, leaders, and boards of nonprofit organizations liable for their decisions.

(E) An organization's stakeholders include donors, clients, volunteers, and community members.

19. Passage B most clearly indicates which of the following?

(A) Due to their very nature, nonprofits are immune from any damage that could be inflicted by unscrupulous or fraudulent solicitors.

(B) The nonprofit sector does not benefit from oversight by a "watchdog" organization whose purpose is to promote integrity, as businesses and the government do.

(C) An influx of B corporations is a major contributor to the erosion of sector boundaries.

(D) Nonprofit organizations are largely limited from engaging in activities that do not directly contribute to the mission at hand.

(E) The media ultimately holds nonprofits accountable for their actions.

20. The authors of both passages are likely to agree with all the following EXCEPT:

(A) All nonprofits are governed by more than just one individual.

(B) Leaders and managers of nonprofits face a variety of challenges.

(C) Most people do not understand how nonprofit organizations are regulated and monitored.

(D) Nonprofits must always operate with the public's best interests at heart.

(E) Nonprofits are under pressure from stakeholders.

21. Both passages refer to the government in an attempt to

(A) show that the government plays no role in the oversight of nonprofits

(B) explain that the government is not a stakeholder in the management of nonprofits

(C) point out the extent that government funding cutbacks have affected the mission of most nonprofits

(D) describe how government agencies and nonprofits are similar

(E) indicate the role that government plays in the operation of nonprofits

Questions 22–27 refer to the following passage.

Since Dolly the cloned sheep arrived on the scene in 1997 and the Clinton administration banned cloning research that same year, cloning has spawned an ethical debate that is out of proportion to the procedure's reality. Cloning produces a plant or animal that is genetically identical to its "parent." To make a clone, scientists remove the DNA from an embryo and replace it with the DNA from another individual, presumably but not necessarily of the same species. Then they watch and wait for it to develop, either into a more mature embryo in a petri dish or a full-grown creature gestated in a female's womb.

Cloning could be used for many positive purposes. It could help in research on cancer, organ donation, contraception, and brain damage. Parents at risk of passing on genetic defects could have children without fear. Infertile couples wouldn't have to use the services of a sperm or egg donor; same-sex couples could reproduce together. The parents of a dead child could have a genetic copy of it made.

Critics of cloning raise issues that are more part of the debate on genetic engineering and science fiction, suggesting that nefarious scientists might use cloning to create a master race, presumably to carry out their abominable purposes. Some critics dislike the idea of manipulating human reproduction, preferring to believe that all humans are the result of entirely natural processes and ignoring the many cases of genetic engineering and assisted reproduction among humans, from in vitro fertilization to choosing to have children in an attempt to get offspring of a particular sex. Cloning does carry some legitimate risks — clones seem to age faster than normally conceived offspring, and carry a large number of genetic defects — but these are practical concerns outside the ethical points that cloning critics raise.

What many critics of cloning don't seem to realize is that creatures that are genetically identical to other creatures arise in nature all the time — identical twins are genetically identical to one another. A human being is only partly the product of his or her genes. A clone looks like the individual that donated its genes, but in all other ways it is unique. Critics worry that cloned children won't be treated naturally; but what does that mean? Parents might have unreasonable expectations of a cloned child, but that happens all the time with children conceived the usual way. Every child born enters the world to expectations and burdens, and no one says that the parents were therefore wrong to reproduce. Cloning is no more bizarre or artificial than other techniques of assisted reproduction. Every family has odd relationships; surely a cloned child could fit in as well as anyone. Reproduction is an intensely personal issue, and for that reason, the government doesn't interfere in most reproductive choices, including adoption and surrogacy. The creation of a family is always a fertile ground for dysfunction, unjustified expectations, and hurtful behavior. A cloned child, though conceived in an unusual way, would ultimately be just a child, and its parents just parents.

22. Which one of the following titles would best suit the contents of the passage?

(A) Cloning and the Death of the Family

(B) Dolly, Dr. Frankenstein, and DNA: The Dangers of Cloning

(C) The Mechanics of Cloning

(D) Cloning: Just Another Way of Making a Baby

(E) The Government's Role in Preventing Unethical Scientific Research

23. The author of the passage would most probably agree with which one of the following statements about critics of cloning?

(A) People who criticize cloning are deeply devoted to religion and use their faith to justify obstructing scientific research that could have many benefits.

(B) Critics of cloning are correct to worry about the potentially destructive aspects of cloning, such as the creation of a master race or the manipulation of children to meet the specific needs of their parents.

(C) Those who worry about human cloning also object to techniques commonly used today in assisted reproduction, such as in vitro fertilization or the use of surrogate mothers.

(D) Most critics of cloning are worried about aspects of cloning that are not substantially different from the potential problems associated with methods of reproduction already in common use.

(E) Critics of cloning are most concerned about the practical drawbacks of cloning, such as the fact that clones seem to age faster than individuals conceived the normal way, and that they contain a larger than usual number of defective genes.

GO ON TO NEXT PAGE

24. The primary purpose of the passage is to

(A) argue that most critics of cloning are focusing on drawbacks that are either outlandish or no different from the drawbacks of normal reproduction and that ethically cloning is not very different from normal reproduction

(B) explain the process of cloning and compare it to other techniques of genetic engineering and assisted reproduction, such as in vitro fertilization

(C) recommend that scientists and medical ethicists carefully consider the implications of allowing or banning research into cloning

(D) extol the many benefits of cloning, such as allowing same-sex couples to reproduce without having recourse to an external egg or sperm donor or allowing parents to make a clone of a dead child

(E) warn readers of the dangers of cloning, including both the ethical dilemmas of the odd family relationships cloning could create and the physical problems involved in the process of cloning

25. The author uses the words "nefarious" and "abominable" in the second paragraph to

(A) indicate that scientists who work with clones are morally bankrupt

(B) defend the Clinton administration's ban on research into human cloning

(C) describe the personalities of people who oppose cloning research

(D) criticize parents who want to use cloning to create particular children

(E) show that the worries of cloning critics are exaggerated and based more in fantasy than fact

26. The author would most probably agree with which one of the following statements about assisted reproduction?

(A) Children who are born as the result of fertility treatments tend to have emotional and health problems that are not as common in children conceived the traditional way.

(B) Governments should regulate scientific procedures and research according to what the citizen body believes is ethical and proper.

(C) Parents tend to treat children born through assisted reproduction differently from children conceived naturally because they value them more highly.

(D) In vitro fertilization is a sensible and positive use of technology to help people accomplish a natural human goal.

(E) Older parents and same-sex couples should not be allowed to use assisted reproduction to have children because that would violate the natural order.

27. The structure of the author's argument is best described as

(A) providing historical context for a controversial practice and then summarizing its benefits before concluding that its risks outweigh those benefits

(B) presenting the reasons why a particular scientific procedure was developed and then outlining the reasons why it was eventually banned

(C) introducing an ethical debate, presenting one side of that debate, then relying on the results of documented scientific research to argue for the reasonableness of adopting the debate's other position

(D) initially arguing in favor of one side of an ethical debate, finding fault with that position, and ultimately siding with the opposing viewpoint

(E) discussing the premises of two positions on a controversial issue and then dismissing the validity of one position because its argument relies on nonscientific considerations

Section III
Analytical Reasoning

TIME: 35 minutes for 25 questions

DIRECTIONS: Each group of questions in this section is based on a set of conditions. In answering some of the questions, it may be useful to draw a rough diagram. Choose the response that most accurately and completely answers each question and blacken the corresponding space on your answer sheet.

Questions 1–6 refer to the following scenario.

A yoga studio offers classes in three kinds of yoga: ashtanga, bikram, and iyengar. It has five instructors — Caroline, Janice, Marty, Suzanne, and Virginia — each of whom teaches at least one of and as many as three of these kinds of yoga. The following conditions apply:

Exactly two of the instructors teach classes in the same kind or kinds of yoga.

Marty and Suzanne both teach iyengar.

Caroline and Marty each teach fewer kinds of yoga than Janice.

Caroline does not teach any kind of yoga taught by Virginia.

Virginia does not teach any kind of yoga taught by Janice.

1. Which one of the following must be true?

   (A) Caroline teaches fewer kinds of yoga than Virginia does.

   (B) Marty teaches fewer kinds of yoga than Suzanne does.

   (C) Suzanne teaches fewer kinds of yoga than Janice does.

   (D) Virginia teaches fewer kinds of yoga than Janice does.

   (E) Virginia teaches fewer kinds of yoga than Suzanne does.

2. If Virginia does not teach iyengar, then which one of the following must be true?

   (A) Janice teaches bikram.

   (B) Janice teaches iyengar.

   (C) Marty teaches ashtanga.

   (D) Suzanne teaches ashtanga.

   (E) Virginia teaches bikram.

3. Which one of the following could be a complete and accurate list of the instructors who teach only bikram?

   (A) Caroline

   (B) Janice

   (C) Caroline, Virginia

   (D) Marty, Suzanne

   (E) Caroline, Suzanne, Virginia

4. Which one of the following could be a complete and accurate list of the instructors who teach iyengar?

   (A) Marty, Suzanne

   (B) Janice, Suzanne

   (C) Caroline, Janice, Suzanne

   (D) Caroline, Marty, Suzanne

   (E) Janice, Marty, Suzanne

5. How many instructors must teach only one kind of yoga?

   (A) one

   (B) two

   (C) three

   (D) four

   (E) five

6. If exactly three instructors teach ashtanga, which one of the following could be true?

   (A) Caroline teaches iyengar.

   (B) Janice does not teach ashtanga.

   (C) Marty teaches ashtanga.

   (D) Suzanne teaches bikram.

   (E) Suzanne does not teach ashtanga.

GO ON TO NEXT PAGE

Seven Roman noblemen — Antonius, Brutus, Cassius, Decimus, Octavius, Servilius, and Vipsanius — have to decide whether they support or oppose the rule of dictator Julius Caesar. Those who support Caesar call themselves Patriots; those who oppose Caesar call themselves Liberators. Each of the seven noblemen aligns himself with one of the two groups according to the following principles:

Octavius and Cassius do not join the same group.

Antonius and Decimus do not join the same group.

If Decimus decides to be a Patriot, so does Servilius.

If Brutus decides to be a Patriot, both Cassius and Vipsanius would be Liberators.

If Octavius decides to be a Patriot, Servilius would be a Liberator.

7. If Octavius joins the Liberators, which of the following must be true?

(A) Antonius joins the Liberators.

(B) Brutus joins the Liberators.

(C) Decimus joins the Patriots.

(D) Servilius joins the Patriots.

(E) Vipsanius joins the Patriots.

8. If Cassius and Vipsanius both join the Liberators, then which of the following must be false?

(A) Antonius joins the Patriots.

(B) Brutus joins the Liberators.

(C) Decimus joins the Liberators.

(D) Octavius joins the Patriots.

(E) Servilius joins the Patriots.

9. If Antonius and Vipsanius both join the Patriots, then which one of the following could be true?

(A) Brutus and Cassius both join the Liberators.

(B) Brutus and Octavius both join the Patriots.

(C) Cassius and Decimus both join the Patriots.

(D) Cassius and Octavius both join the Liberators.

(E) Decimus and Servilius both join the Patriots.

10. Which one of the following pairs of men cannot both be Liberators?

(A) Antonius and Octavius

(B) Antonius and Servilius

(C) Antonius and Vipsanius

(D) Cassius and Vipsanius

(E) Octavius and Servilius

11. What is the maximum number of noblemen who can be Patriots?

(A) one

(B) two

(C) three

(D) four

(E) five

12. Which one of the following could be an accurate and complete list of the Patriots?

(A) Antonius, Cassius, Vipsanius

(B) Antonius, Cassius, Decimus, Servilius

(C) Antonius, Octavius, Servilius, Vipsanius

(D) Brutus, Decimus, Octavius

(E) Decimus, Servilius, Vipsanius

Six plays are scheduled to be performed at the Dionysia, the annual theater festival in Athens. They are: *Antigone, Clouds, Electra, Frogs, Helen,* and *Orestes.* The plays will be performed on six consecutive days, beginning on Tuesday. In order to mix up comedy and tragedy, give the actors an occasional break, and accommodate the desires of the town fathers, the organizers must observe the following rules when arranging the schedule:

The performance of *Helen* is scheduled for Thursday.

Antigone must be performed on a day sometime after *Orestes.*

At least one of the plays is performed between the performance of *Antigone* and the performance of *Frogs.*

Exactly one of the plays is performed between the performances of *Clouds* and *Frogs.*

13. Which one of the following is an acceptable schedule for the festival, starting with the play performed on Tuesday?

(A) *Antigone, Electra, Helen, Frogs, Orestes, Clouds*

(B) *Electra, Orestes, Helen, Clouds, Antigone, Frogs*

(C) *Frogs, Clouds, Helen, Orestes, Antigone, Electra*

(D) *Orestes, Frogs, Helen, Clouds, Antigone, Electra*

(E) *Orestes, Antigone, Frogs, Helen, Clouds, Electra*

14. Which one of the following must be true?

(A) Either *Antigone* or *Orestes* is performed on Wednesday.

(B) Either *Antigone* or *Orestes* is performed on Friday.

(C) Either *Clouds* or *Frogs* is performed on Wednesday.

(D) Either *Clouds* or *Frogs* is performed on Friday.

(E) Either *Electra* or *Orestes* is performed on Saturday.

15. Which play CANNOT be performed on Sunday?

(A) *Antigone*

(B) *Clouds*

(C) *Electra*

(D) *Frogs*

(E) *Orestes*

16. Which one of the following must be false?

(A) *Antigone* and *Clouds* are performed on consecutive days, with no other play between them.

(B) Exactly one play is performed between *Antigone* and *Clouds*.

(C) *Electra* and *Orestes* are performed on consecutive days, with no other play between them.

(D) *Frogs* and *Orestes* are performed on consecutive days, with no other play between them.

(E) Exactly one play is performed between *Helen* and *Orestes*.

17. Which one of the following is a complete and accurate list of the days on which *Frogs* could be performed?

(A) Tuesday, Wednesday, Friday

(B) Wednesday, Thursday, Saturday

(C) Wednesday, Friday

(D) Wednesday, Friday, Sunday

(E) Wednesday, Friday, Saturday, Sunday

18. Which one of the following CANNOT be true?

(A) *Clouds* is performed on Wednesday.

(B) *Electra* is performed on Wednesday.

(C) *Frogs* is performed on Wednesday.

(D) *Orestes* is performed on Tuesday.

(E) *Orestes* is performed on Saturday.

Questions 19–25 refer to the following scenario.

A boutique law firm provides services in only four areas of law: employment, immigration, real estate, and tax. Four attorneys share the work; their names are Burton, Duway, Cheatham, and Howard. Each attorney specializes in at least one and at most three areas of law, according to the following specifications:

Duway specializes in any area of law that is also Cheatham's specialty.

Burton and Howard do not share any specialties with Cheatham.

Exactly one attorney specializes in tax.

Exactly two attorneys specialize in employment.

Exactly two attorneys specialize in real estate.

Exactly three attorneys specialize in immigration.

19. If Duway specializes in two and only two areas of law, which one of the following must be true?

(A) Burton does not specialize in tax law.

(B) Cheatham does not specialize in employment law.

(C) Duway does not specialize in tax law.

(D) Howard does not specialize in employment law.

(E) Howard does not specialize in tax law.

GO ON TO NEXT PAGE

20. Which one of the following must be true?

   (A) Burton specializes in more areas of law than Cheatham.

   (B) Howard specializes in more areas of law than Duway.

   (C) Duway specializes in more areas of law than Howard.

   (D) Duway specializes in more areas of law than Cheatham.

   (E) Burton specializes in more areas of law than Howard.

21. Each of the following could be a complete and accurate list of the attorneys who specialize in both employment and immigration EXCEPT:

   (A) Duway

   (B) Burton

   (C) Burton and Howard

   (D) Duway and Burton

   (E) Duway and Howard

22. If Cheatham specializes in exactly two areas of law, then each of the following must be false EXCEPT:

   (A) Duway specializes in tax law.

   (B) Duway specializes in exactly two areas of law.

   (C) Howard specializes in employment law.

   (D) Howard specializes in tax law.

   (E) Howard specializes in exactly three areas of law.

23. If Burton specializes in exactly three areas of law, which one of the following must be true?

   (A) Burton specializes in employment law.

   (B) Burton specializes in real estate law.

   (C) Burton specializes in tax law.

   (D) Howard specializes in employment law.

   (E) Howard specializes in tax law.

24. Which one of the following statements CANNOT be true of the attorney who specializes in tax?

   (A) The attorney also specializes in immigration but does not specialize in real estate.

   (B) The attorney also specializes in both immigration and real estate.

   (C) The attorney also specializes in real estate but not in immigration.

   (D) The attorney also specializes in employment but not in real estate.

   (E) The attorney specializes in neither employment nor real estate.

25. Each of the following must be false EXCEPT:

   (A) Burton specializes in three areas: employment, immigration, and real estate.

   (B) Burton specializes in three areas: employment, real estate, and tax.

   (C) Duway specializes in three areas: employment, immigration, and real estate.

   (D) Duway specializes in three areas: employment, real estate, and tax.

   (E) Howard specializes in three areas: employment, real estate, and tax.

Section IV

Logical Reasoning

TIME: 35 minutes for 25 questions

DIRECTIONS: Read the passage and choose the best answer. Some questions may have more than one answer that looks right. Select the one that answers the question most completely. Don't assume anything that isn't directly stated, and don't let your imagination run wild; all the information you need is in the arguments and the answer choices.

1. Manufacturer: Our child car seat is the safest on the market. We know it's safe because the most conscientious parents have bought it. We're sure they're the most conscientious customers because they bought the car seat that claimed to be the safest on the market.

   Which one of the following uses a pattern of reasoning that is most closely parallel to the flawed reasoning in the manufacturer's argument?

   (A) This soft drink is the best-tasting soft drink on the market. We know it's the best tasting because 8 out of 10 people who participated in taste tests said it was best.

   (B) Children who attend high-quality preschools tend to perform well when they enter elementary school. They perform well in elementary school because they attended high-quality preschools.

   (C) These soccer shoes must be the best because all the best soccer players use them, and the best players wear only the best shoes.

   (D) This web browser is the best on the market. The most technologically savvy people use this browser, and they can choose any browser they want.

   (E) This curl-enhancing lotion is the best styling product available. People with curly hair find that this lotion enhances their curls better than any similar product.

2. A current trend in home buying is the interest-only mortgage, where the borrower need only pay the interest on the loan. As a result, the principal, or amount borrowed, never decreases. Buyers frequently default because they never accumulate an ownership stake ("equity") in their homes, so these loans are bad for Americans and should therefore be eliminated entirely.

   Which one of the following is an assumption required by the argument?

   (A) Homeowners with interest-only mortgages will not accumulate equity based on the increasing value of their homes.

   (B) Some things that are bad for Americans should be eliminated entirely.

   (C) With an interest-only mortgage, the buyer does not need to pay back more than the interest.

   (D) Buyers with no equity in their homes frequently default on their loans.

   (E) Homeowners cannot afford to pay more than the interest on the loan.

GO ON TO NEXT PAGE

3. Normal, healthy human beings cannot tickle themselves because they anticipate the sensation and reduce their touch perception accordingly. By reducing the perception of completely predictable sensations, the brain is allowed to focus on crucial environmental changes not produced by one's own actions. A person who tried to tickle himself while also being tickled by someone else will have a heightened sense of the other person's touch in relation to his own. Healthy human beings also cannot mistake the sound of their own voice as that of another. Schizophrenics, however, might hear their own voices and, having not anticipated the sounds, be unable to recognize their voices as their own.

If the statements in this passage are accurate, which one of the following statements do they best support?

(A) Healthy human beings always anticipate the sounds of their own voices and differentiate them from other voices.

(B) Human beings cannot tickle themselves because they anticipate the sensation.

(C) Additional research in this area may lead to a more thorough understanding of why some people are more susceptible to tickling than others.

(D) A healthy human being that hears a tape of her own voice will not recognize it because she does not anticipate the sounds.

(E) Tickling yourself while someone else tickles you reduces your sensory perceptions, making you not react to the tickling.

4. Prosecutor: I have furnished evidence that the accused committed the crime in question. The defense agrees that the crime did occur. They say that the accused did not commit the crime, but they have not proven that someone else did. Therefore, the jury should find that the defendant is guilty.

The reasoning in the prosecutor's argument is flawed because the argument

(A) ignores evidence that the accused might be innocent

(B) criticizes the arguments by the defense without addressing their flaws

(C) confuses the defense's failure to prove that someone else committed the crime with proof that the accused is guilty

(D) implies that because the defense has admitted that the crime did occur, the defendant must be guilty

(E) fails to consider the possibility that someone else committed the crime

5. The interior western United States is sinking. The area of the U.S. between the Sierra Nevada Mountains and the Colorado Plateau is known as the *Basin and Range.* This area has been sinking for millions of years due to expansion of the Earth's crust. The lowest point in North America, Death Valley, California, is part of the Basin and Range. Because the southern portion of the region is sinking much faster than the northern portion, places like Phoenix, Arizona, at just over 1,100 feet of elevation, are very low, and places farther north, like Reno, Nevada, at almost 4,500 feet of elevation, are higher. The fact that the elevation of the southern part of the region is getting progressively lower allows more moisture from the Gulf of California to bypass places like Phoenix and penetrate farther into the northern part of the region.

If the statements in this argument are accurate, which one of the following is most supported by them?

(A) The southern portion of the Basin and Range region includes areas that are very dry and well below sea level.

(B) The region known as the Basin and Range will continue to expand into areas that are currently part of the Colorado Plateau.

(C) As the northern portion of the Basin and Range region continues to sink, the southern areas of the region will receive more moisture.

(D) The drier climate of places like Phoenix is attributable to the compression of the Earth's crust.

(E) As the Basin and Range area continues to sink, Phoenix, Arizona, will become drier, while areas to the north will receive more moisture.

6. Many names that people think of as Irish were actually brought to Ireland by the Anglo-Norman invasion of Ireland in the 12th century. These names, like Seamus, Patrick, and Sean are so widespread, because of the Catholic Church's requirements that Irish sons and daughters be named after saints. *Seamus* is the Gaelic version of *James,* and *Sean* is the Gaelic version of *John.* Criminal laws in Ireland from the 1500s to the 1900s forbade parents from giving their children traditional Irish names like Cathal, Aodh, and Brian. Now parents are free to give their children these long-forgotten, truly Irish names.

Which of the following inferences can be drawn from the statements above?

(A) Only Irish names used in Ireland before the 12th century are "traditional."

(B) Even after hundreds of years of use, names like Patrick, Seamus, and Sean are not "truly Irish."

(C) Parents in Ireland now give their children names like Cathal, Aodh, and Brian.

(D) Irish parents prefer to give their children names that are as traditionally Irish as possible.

(E) Criminal laws in Ireland are unnecessarily punitive.

7. The standard computer keyboard, called QWERTY because of the arrangement of the first six letters, is very inefficient. The letters were arranged in this odd but familiar manner when the first typewriters were being designed in the 1800s. When keys were arranged logically, typists could strike the keys very quickly. Early typewriters were so slow the fast typists caused mechanical problems in the machines. In order to slow down the typists, the keys were rearranged in a seemingly random order. If a manufacturer of computer keyboards were to arrange the keys in the most efficient manner, everyone would want to buy a new, improved keyboard.

Which of the following, if true, most undermines the reasoning in this argument?

(A) The human brain is incredibly flexible and can adapt to any arrangement of the keyboard, even if it is less efficient.

(B) Modern computer word-processing systems are much faster than the most accomplished typist, so there is no reason to use the slower keyboard.

(C) Computer keyboards include many keys that were not needed on manual or electric typewriters.

(D) Americans have universally adapted to the QWERTY keyboard and are not interested in learning an entirely new system.

(E) Discovering the most efficient arrangement of keys would require extensive tests on typists and nontypists alike.

8. Major airlines claim that the fares they charge have not increased in recent years. However, the various fees that used to be included in the quoted fare are now charged separately. The fees added to the quoted fare now include a security fee, a fuel surcharge, and an airport departure fee. The airlines are just following the example of other travel-related industries that have added on fees and taxes for years. The rental car and hotel industries usually quote a rate that is 20 percent less than the actual bill. In major cities, restaurants and bars usually have an additional tax rate that is included on the bill with the sales tax. Thus, there is not one aspect of traveling where the quoted price is the final price.

Which of the following, if true, most weakens the author's conclusion?

(A) The price of a gallon of gasoline that is quoted at the pump and on gas station signs includes all fuel taxes and fees.

(B) In countries other than the United States and Canada, the quoted price is often just a starting point for negotiations.

(C) Many items ordered through the mail include shipping and handling fees that are more than the cost of the actual item.

(D) The quoted price for travel on most cruise ships does not include excursion fees, beverages charges, and staff gratuities.

(E) The price quoted for a new car usually does not include the destination charge, which is the cost of getting the car to the dealership.

GO ON TO NEXT PAGE

9. During the last three years, a sizable drop in the number of cigarette smokers in America has occurred. The same period has also seen an increase in advertisements and warnings about the dangers associated with smoking, so the drop in the number of cigarette smokers must be a result of increased consumer awareness of smoking's hazardous effects.

The argument's reasoning is most vulnerable to which of the following criticisms?

(A) It relies on anecdotal evidence to draw its conclusion rather than scientific research.

(B) It makes a faulty analogy between occurrences three years ago and those of the present day.

(C) It cites experimental results that are unrelated to the conclusion.

(D) It confuses a correlation with causation.

(E) It fails to acknowledge that during the same three-year period, some smokers did not stop smoking.

10. Studies suggest that productivity in the workplace improves with a person's physical health. The firm of Claar & Carlisle, then, should enhance employee productivity by implementing mandatory fitness classes each morning before the workday begins.

Which of the following is an assumption required by this argument?

(A) The mandatory fitness classes will improve the physical health of Claar & Carlisle's employees.

(B) Fitness classes are better at promoting physical health than are nutrition classes.

(C) Many employees resent mandatory fitness programs and consider the decision of whether to work out to be a personal rather than work-related one.

(D) Mandatory fitness classes before work are more productive than fitness classes taken after work.

(E) Employees who work out regularly sleep more soundly than those who do not.

11. Rising Stars Dance Company has cemented its reputation as a premier children's dance school due in large part to major donations from former members who enjoy attending the annual statewide dance showcase. Although Rising Stars is widely regarded as being the best of its kind, the showcase was canceled this year; so Rising Stars will experience a resulting reduction in donations.

Which one of the following is an assumption on which this argument depends?

(A) Rising Stars' reputation as a premier children's dance school is enhanced by the amount of money it receives from donors.

(B) Rising Stars' annual showcase will likely be canceled next year as well.

(C) Some former members of Rising Stars contribute to the dance school because they enjoy attending the annual showcase.

(D) Former members of Rising Stars will have at least as much money to donate next year as they did this year.

(E) Contributions from former members are necessary for Rising Stars to be able to put on its annual showcase.

12. To lure customers away from competitors, Exploration Rent-A-Car has begun to offer fuel discounts to customers who spend more than $500 on any single rental. Exploration's executives claim that the discount program has been massively successful because single rentals of $500 or more are up 25 percent from before the program launched.

Which one of the following, if true, most undermines the reasoning made by Exploration's executives?

(A) Since the discount program began, most of the customers who spend $500 or more at Exploration are new customers.

(B) Most of the customers who used Exploration after the discount program launched spent more than $500 with every rental.

(C) The majority of the customers who have spent in excess of $500 on a single rental since the fuel discounts began are regular customers who now make lengthier but less frequent rental arrangements.

(D) Customers who generally spend less than $500 each time they rent from Exploration are unlikely to be persuaded to spend more by fuel discount incentives.

(E) Customers who took advantage of the fuel discounts at Exploration will continue to rent from there after the promotion ends.

13. The government should mandate that both men and women take, at minimum, two weeks of paid family leave following the birth of their child. That way, the child has the chance to develop meaningful relationships with both parents, and both parents can get a better idea of whether they would prefer to stay home with the child or return to the workplace.

Which one of the following, assuming all are true, does NOT offer a logical rebuttal to this argument?

(A) Parents who would prefer being in the workplace over staying home with a child may end up resenting the child, which may deter them from developing a meaningful relationship with their child.

(B) Parents can build meaningful personal relationships with their newborns after work hours.

(C) Deciding which parent stays home with a newborn after its birth is a decision for each set of parents to decide. A child's parents have a better sense of what is in the best interest of their family than the government does.

(D) Two weeks is not sufficient time for parents to decide whether they prefer to stay home with their child or return to the workplace.

(E) Parents who care for their child full time immediately after birth when the child is most vulnerable are likely to develop a stronger emotional connection with the child than parents who do not.

14. The cost of producing silk scarves in Taiwan is 35 percent less than it is in the United States. When you take into consideration taxes and shipping costs, it is therefore better for the company to produce the scarves in Taiwan than in the United States.

Which one of the following is an assumption on which the argument depends?

(A) Taxes on a scarf imported from Taiwan to the United States are less than 35 percent of the cost of manufacturing the scarf in the United States.

(B) The cost of transporting a scarf from Taiwan to the United States is more than 35 percent of the cost of manufacturing the scarf in the United States.

(C) Importing scarves from Taiwan to the United States will reduce manufacturing jobs in the United States by 35 percent.

(D) Manufacturing a scarf in Taiwan takes 35 percent less time than it does in the United States.

(E) Labor costs in Taiwan are 35 percent less than in the United States.

GO ON TO NEXT PAGE

15. Since the invention of digital downloads and MP3 music sharing, musicians have begun to focus more on making a profit and attracting fans who are technologically savvy and less on producing quality, meaningful music. As a result, music has lost much of its creativity and artistry.

Which one of the following is an assumption on which the argument depends?

(A) Technologically savvy fans prefer music that is not meaningful.

(B) Digital downloads and MP3 music sharing have made the music business more profitable.

(C) Some musicians sacrifice quality in a quest to make more money.

(D) Music must lack quality and artistry in order to be popular.

(E) Music is meaningful when it is creative and inventive.

16. A whistleblower at Goodman-Horning claims that the company discriminates against women, citing that of the 10 executives on staff only 1 is female and only 3 of the 50 subordinate staff members are female.

Which one of the following offers the strongest argument against the whistleblower's claims?

(A) Male and female executives at the company earn the same amount of money.

(B) The number of female job applicants that Goodman-Horning rejected is about the same as the number of female job applicants rejected by other similar companies.

(C) Male and female executives at the company are equally qualified.

(D) The long hours required of Goodman-Horning's executive staff members are less desirable for women.

(E) The ratio of male to female employees at Goodman-Horning is about the same as the ratio of male to female job applicants.

17. The federal government estimates that, per mile traveled, the ratio of the number of motorcycle deaths to automobile deaths is 37 to 1. Therefore, to protect the safety of their citizens, most states have implemented laws that mandate some sort of helmet use for motorcycle riders. Opponents of motorcycle helmet laws maintain that in a free country, people should have the right to engage in potentially dangerous behavior at their discretion as long as they are not harming others. They think it should be a matter of individual choice whether to wear a helmet when riding a motorcycle.

Which one of the following statements, if true, most weakens the helmet opponents' argument?

(A) Head injuries from motorcycle accidents exceed head injuries from auto accidents.

(B) Motorcycle insurance rates for all motorcycle owners have risen by 5 percent over the last decade to offset the medical costs associated with head injuries incurred by motorcycle riders who fail to wear helmets.

(C) Some states do not require motorcycle riders to wear helmets, leaving the decision of whether to wear a helmet up to the individual.

(D) Most states have laws that require bicycle riders under the age of 18 to wear helmets.

(E) More head injuries are reported by motorcycle riders who do not wear helmets than by those who do.

18. Executives of several large and small businesses have united in an effort to oppose proposed legislation that would prohibit them from requesting access to potential employees' social media accounts. Proponents of the new law state that requesting access to job applicants' social media pages is an egregious invasion of personal privacy and claim that what applicants post on their social media sites is no indication of how they would perform on the job.

Which one of the following, if true, adds the most support for the position of the group of executives?

(A) The level of discretion and common sense people exhibit when they use social media directly mirrors their use of the same in day-to-day personal and business interactions.

(B) Individuals who have a strong social media presence tend to be better informed than those who do not.

(C) Requesting and requiring access to another's social media page is a clear violation of First Amendment rights.

(D) Potential employers have the right to request access to anything they want from applicants, and the potential employee, in turn, has the right to deny access and pursue employment elsewhere.

(E) No level of privacy whatsoever can be assumed when it comes to the Internet.

19. Studies show that nearly one-third of women in America today give birth via Cesarean section, a far more expensive procedure than a vaginal birth. In 1965, fewer than 5 percent of all babies were born by using the Cesarean method. This proves that hospitals today are motivated primarily by money and do not have the best interests of their patients at heart.

The conclusion that hospitals do not consider the best interests of their patients is based on which of the following assumptions?

(A) The total number of births is higher today than in 1965.

(B) Women are not choosing elective Cesarean section deliveries for cosmetic and other personal reasons.

(C) Hospitals hire doctors based on their ability to generate income rather than on whether they exhibit concern for their patients.

(D) Statistics regarding medical procedures are far more accurate and readily available today than they were in 1965.

(E) There were as many surgeons trained in the Cesarean section procedure in 1965 as there are today.

20. As incidents of employee theft skyrocketed during the last decade, more and more businesses have implemented stiffer penalties and zero-tolerance policies. Yet most of these businesses are not seeing a decrease in the number of incidents of employee theft, so the stiffer penalties clearly are not working.

Which one of the following statements, if true, most weakens the argument?

(A) At the same time that businesses began imposing stiffer sanctions for employee theft, the average number of employees per business increased.

(B) Businesses have fewer employees now than they did ten years ago.

(C) In the last decade, most businesses have redefined their definition of theft.

(D) Businesses' theft prevention efforts in general have been reduced due to budget constraints.

(E) All new employees have been forced to undergo theft prevention training.

GO ON TO NEXT PAGE

21. In the 1970s, researchers on a small island nation conducted a study by using a sample of pregnant women who resided there. Of those sampled, 35 were daily smokers of marijuana and 35 had never smoked. The study indicated that the babies of the marijuana smokers were just as healthy as those of nonsmokers and concluded that smoking marijuana has little effect on the health of a woman's unborn child.

Which one of the following statements, if true, most weakens the conclusion of the researchers?

(A) The women in the study who smoked marijuana were from the same village, one whose residents were of a substantially higher socioeconomic status than the rest of the country, with better access to prenatal care.

(B) The women in the study who smoked daily reported less cramping and nausea throughout their pregnancies than those who did not smoke.

(C) The women in the study who smoked marijuana were from the same village, one that cultivated 85 percent of the country's supply of marijuana and whose residents used marijuana at a higher rate than residents of other villages.

(D) Marijuana has been shown to be far less damaging to an unborn fetus than tobacco is.

(E) The women in the study who smoked regularly were generally farther along in their pregnancies when the study began than those in the nonsmoking group.

22. Our state's students would benefit tremendously if the state government would allow for a school voucher system, where students are allotted a certain amount of money to spend for tuition at any school they like, public or private.

Which one of the following statements, if true, most weakens the argument?

(A) A school voucher program would increase competitiveness among schools and force underperforming schools to improve in order to attract enough students to stay afloat.

(B) Vouchers can help minimize the disparity between private and state education, a major divider in the current class system.

(C) Students in poorer neighborhoods cannot afford the transportation costs required to attend schools that are not located nearby.

(D) Educational historians agree that without outside incentives, schools are unlikely to change.

(E) Public schools tend to provide an overall better educational experience than private schools.

23. Serena: Anthropologists estimate that diseases brought to the Western Hemisphere by the first Europeans, including smallpox, hepatitis, typhus, and measles, killed 95 percent of the Native American population and allowed Europeans to begin their conquest of the continent. If the Native American population had been 20 times greater, only 4.75 percent of the population would have died, and the Europeans would never have been able to conquer North and South America.

Maeve: Those death rates are way too high. The average rate of death in Europe from the most virulent epidemic in recorded history, the Black Death of the 14th century, was only 33 percent. Even if the Native American populations were extremely vulnerable due to their never having been exposed to these diseases, the cumulative death rate of all the diseases should not have been more than 50 percent to 75 percent on average.

Serena's and Maeve's statements indicate that they disagree over the truth of which of the following?

(A) The Black Death of the 14th century was more virulent than the diseases that the Europeans introduced to the Native Americans.

(B) The Europeans introduced small pox, hepatitis, and other diseases to the Western Hemisphere.

(C) Anthropologists are incorrect in their estimation of the cumulative death rate due to diseases brought to the Western Hemisphere.

(D) The Europeans would not have conquered North and South America if the Native American population had been much larger.

(E) The Europeans infected 95 percent of the Native American population by introducing virulent diseases.

24. Employers lose millions of work hours from employees every year during the NCAA basketball tournament known as March Madness. The men's and women's tournaments are conducted simultaneously, and tens of millions of American workers enter contests where they pick the winner of each game. Because some early round games actually take place during work hours, many employees are constantly checking basketball scores instead of working. Even employees who do not watch basketball at any other time of the year get caught up in the excitement.

Which one of the following statements follows logically from the statements in this passage?

(A) Together, the men's and women's NCAA tournaments form the world's most popular sporting event.

(B) Many different strategies exist for predicting the tournament winners, such as using team names, mascots, or uniform colors.

(C) American businesses should make allowances for their employees' lack of productivity during these two special weeks of the year.

(D) The NCAA tournament is appropriately named because of the "madness" it creates among employees in March of every year.

(E) Employees should not be allowed to check sports scores during business hours.

25. Astronomers estimate that the next sunspot cycle will be 30 percent to 50 percent more active than the current cycle. Solar activity, including sunspots and solar flares, ejects huge quantities of charged particles into space. These particles are responsible for the phenomenon known as the *aurora borealis*, or "northern lights." The same particles also interfere with radio signals, disrupt satellite communications, and impede the transmission of power across high-voltage lines. Even though the next cycle of solar activity is predicted to be less intense than the peak cycle of a decade ago, the impacts will be felt by many more people around the world.

Which of the following statements, if true, would provide the strongest explanation for the paradox of the weaker solar activity's causing greater disruption?

(A) Fiber-optic cables that supply the Internet connections for tens of millions of Americans are not affected by solar activity the way that radio and satellite signals are.

(B) Radio signals have become stronger and less likely to be disrupted, but many people rely on a satellite signal for the music and news they hear on their radios.

(C) There are actually fewer high-voltage power lines in the Upper Midwest than there were a decade ago.

(D) The northern lights are usually seen only in the very highest latitudes, but during periods of intense activity, they can be seen as far south as Chicago.

(E) There has been an exponential increase in the number of people around the world with cellphones that could be disrupted by solar activity.

Writing Sample

Johnson, Stevens, & Kunam, a mid-sized advertising firm, is seeking a new manager for one of its oldest accounts, a snack food company. Using the following facts, write an essay in which you argue for hiring one of the following applicants over the other based on these two criteria:

>> The firm wants to hire someone who knows how to appeal to the client's ideal demographic — young adults who are technologically savvy.

>> The firm wants to hire someone with a significant amount of advertising experience.

Tyler is a recent graduate of a well-recognized journalism program, where he majored in digital media. He interned for six months with a large advertising firm that specializes in innovative campaigns that emphasize reaching college-age adults through social media, cellphone applications, and other innovative technologies. The glowing recommendation letter written by his internship supervisor confirms that Tyler is proficient in new technologies and has impressed clients with his creativity and innovation.

Miranda has worked as an advertising account executive for more than 30 years. She has managed successful campaigns for a variety of products, including comestibles, but she admittedly has little experience with digital media and new technologies. Her impressive portfolio contains a plethora of award-winning examples of print and TV advertisements.

Chapter 20

Practice Exam 3: Answers and Explanations

This chapter has answers and explanations for the multiple-choice sections in Chapter 19. Use the abbreviated key at the end of this chapter to score your test quickly, but be sure to read through the answer explanations for the questions you miss. For maximum benefit, read the explanations for all the questions. Your essay won't be scored, but examine your response through the eyes of a law school admissions officer. Does your essay provide a clear, well-supported position? Is it well-organized and free of glaring grammar, usage, and spelling errors? If you can answer yes to these questions, you've met the requirements of the exercise.

Section I: Logical Reasoning

1. **D. Of the five key field marks that identify ivory-billed woodpeckers, only the extra white on the wings has been seen, and this is also the only feature that occurs on abnormal pileated woodpeckers.**

   This question concerns the reported discovery of ivory-billed woodpeckers in Arkansas. The argument the skeptics challenge is that, because the sighted birds have large white patches on their wings and ivory-billed woodpeckers have large white patches, the sighted birds are ivory-billed woodpeckers. The skeptics argue that an abnormal pileated woodpecker may also have the distinctive white patches. You're asked to strengthen the skeptics' conclusion, so you need an answer choice that strengthens the idea that the white patches on the sighted birds are abnormalities of pileated woodpeckers.

   Choice (B) doesn't have much effect on the argument; the skeptics don't have an issue with the credentials of those who confirmed the identification. Choices (C) and (E) each weaken the skeptics' conclusion: Choice (C) indicates that researchers heard the audio sign of the ivory-billed — the distinctive double-tap — and Choice (E) indicates that the wing beats on the video are indicative of the ivory-billed rather than the pileated.

Make sure you remember which conclusion you're strengthening. The question requires you to support the skeptics' conclusion rather than the researchers' claim, so you can eliminate Choices (C) and (E), which support the idea that the bird may be an ivory-billed woodpecker.

You're left with Choices (A) and (D). You can eliminate Choice (A) because the fact that an ivory-billed was last seen in Louisiana doesn't necessarily mean one couldn't be in Arkansas. Choice (D) is the best answer of those available. The fact that the only sighted field mark of ivory-billed woodpeckers also happens to be the only one that's a feature of an abnormal pileated would support the skeptics' conclusion that the bird is more likely an abnormal pileated woodpecker than an ivory-billed variety.

2. **D. The women who had used shampoo for color-treated hair had softer and shinier hair than the women who used ordinary shampoo.**

The question wants you to weaken the argument. The argument concludes that shampoo for color-treated hair is valueless. The evidence for this claim is that colored hair washed with shampoo for color-treated hair faded as much as colored hair washed with normal shampoo. What weakens the claim that special color shampoo is valueless? Evidence of its value in some measure other than holding hair's color — so look for an answer that shows that this kind of shampoo does do something desirable that ordinary shampoo doesn't do.

Choice (A) is irrelevant to the argument; it's just a statement of ingredients and doesn't address the quality or performance of either kind of shampoo. Choices (B), (C), and (E) also have nothing to do with the relative performance of the two types of shampoos. Choice (D) is the only answer choice that addresses the possible value of shampoo for color-treated hair. If it makes hair softer and shinier than ordinary shampoo, then it does have some value, even if it doesn't preserve hair dye any better than ordinary shampoo. All you have to do is weaken the argument; you don't have to prove that it's wrong. Choice (D) is the best choice for that.

3. **E. Snakes are also absent from other major islands, such as Hawaii, Ireland, and Greenland.**

This question discusses the fact that no snakes live on the island nation of New Zealand. It asks you to strengthen the conclusion that the inability of snakes to swim is responsible for their absence. To strengthen the cause-and-effect argument, find an answer that promotes the lack of swimming as the primary cause of the lack of snakes. Choice (B) doesn't address the snake-swimming issue, so it doesn't strengthen the argument. There's no question of whether snakes exist in the areas around New Zealand. Choice (C) helps explain why snakes haven't been accidentally introduced in New Zealand, but it doesn't say anything about why they weren't on the island in the first place. Choice (D) discusses sea snakes, which are different from the land snakes the paragraph talks about, so their characteristics aren't applicable to the author's conclusion.

Choice (A) weakens the conclusion; if snakes appear on other islands, they must have gotten there somehow, regardless of whether they could swim. Choice (E) is the best answer of the five choices, because if snakes are absent from other large islands, the reason would seem to be that they can't swim. Don't allow your knowledge that snakes exist on islands like Hawaii stop you from choosing Choice (E). Remember that you're supposed to assume the answer choices are true regardless of whether you know otherwise.

4. **C. dirt on the skin does not cause acne**

The question asks you to find the assumption that the dermatologist must make in order to make the conclusion follow logically. The conclusion is that external treatments have no effect on acne. The evidence for this conclusion is that acne develops within the skin. The unstated assumption must be that nothing on or outside the skin's surface can cause that development within the skin; see if that's one of the answers.

Choice (A) is wrong because the dermatologist isn't critiquing the side effects of external acne treatments, just their effectiveness. Choice (B) is wrong because the sensation caused by toners has nothing to do with the causes of acne or the effectiveness of toners as a treatment. Choice (C) looks like the answer you want. If dirt on the skin doesn't cause acne, and it's only caused by internal sources, then Choice (C) justifies the doctor's claim that toners and masks that remove dirt or keep it out of pores don't work. Choice (D) seems to support the doctor's conclusion that acne is an internal problem; the success of oral antibiotics in treating acne doesn't necessarily rule out external factors (like dirt) in causing acne. Choice (E) may be true, but the dermatologist doesn't need to assume it to reach the conclusion. In fact, you could conceivably use Choice (E) as evidence against the conclusion. So the answer is Choice (C).

5. **C. The United States is said to have a free market economy. In fact, though, the U.S. economy is heavily regulated by the government, which gives many advantages to large businesses and punishes small companies and the self-employed. Therefore, the United States doesn't really have a free market economy.**

The question asks you to identify the pattern of reasoning and match it with an answer. The argument's pattern of reasoning goes like this: Although people think the United States is a democracy, citizens don't actually vote for president, so it's not a democracy. You can simplify the reasoning pattern: People think A, but here's an example of something that runs counter to A, so A isn't the case. Questions like this can be a bit time-consuming because you have to work out the thought pattern in all the answers. So forge ahead!

You could summarize Choice (A) like this: Most colleges have A, but few students participate, so A is useless; that's not the same. Choice (B) reasons that all cities have A, but so do counties and states, and that means A is needlessly duplicated. That's a different pattern. Choice (C) figures that the United States is said to be A, but here's an example of something that's not A, so A isn't really the case. That looks pretty close to the original argument's reasoning, so Choice (C) could be the answer. Choice (D) says that most teachers think A, but colleges disagree, so teachers shouldn't do A. That's not quite the same. Choice (E) goes like this: Most insurers claim A, but doctors and hospitals don't, so insurers are dishonest. That's way off. Choice (C) is by far the best choice, so it's your answer.

6. **A. A teacher informs a girl that she is responsible for feeding the class hamster every morning, and the girl agrees to do this. After this, the girl feeds the hamster every morning without the teacher telling her to.**

The question wants you to find an example that illustrates the proposition stated in the argument. That proposition is that people meet expectations. Look for an answer that shows someone receiving a task and performing it as expected. Choice (A) looks like a perfect choice: The teacher presents the girl with a task and expects her to do it, and the girl does. Choice (B) is wrong. In this case, the partner assigns the associate a duty but obviously doesn't expect the associate to be able to perform it and therefore supervises him closely. Choice (C) is an example of someone failing to meet expectations, so it's wrong. Choice (D) seems close to the proposition but doesn't fit it exactly because the original proposition regards doing one's assigned duty, not the success or failure of that duty. The players do learn the coach's strategy and execute it, but the scenario includes an additional result (they win) that isn't part of the original proposition; for this answer to fit the proposition, the players would instead merely execute the strategy as expected. Choice (E) doesn't involve anyone's expectations. The psychologist tells the patient something that may help her, and the patient follows the suggestion and succeeds. The psychologist's expectation is that the behavior modification technique, not the patient who follows it, will meet expectations, which is different from the original proposition. Choice (A) is the best answer.

7. **A. Disciplinary and other problems are most profound at technical schools with large immigrant populations, where students feel that society will not give them opportunities for self-improvement.**

The argument's conclusion is that aptitude tests have no value in sorting students. As evidence, it cites the problems that currently plague German schools, which have used these tests for more than a century. What weakens this argument? Well, if the argument blames aptitude-test-based sorting for the problems in German schools, anything that shows that the problems aren't due to the sorting or the tests weakens it. When you read the answers, look for four choices that do this. The correct answer doesn't. It doesn't necessarily strengthen the argument, but it doesn't weaken it.

Choice (A) doesn't obviously weaken the argument. If disciplinary problems are worst at technical schools and the cause is that students fear they won't ever receive the opportunity to improve, perhaps the sorting system is the root of the problem. You could argue that aptitude-test-sorting schemes are explicitly designed to restrict opportunities. The sorting can have benefits, but perhaps in this case, it also causes problems, such as resentment on the part of those students who get sorted into the lower echelons. Choice (B) weakens the argument by showing a reason why sorting students by ability is important, citing the problems that occur when students of mixed abilities end up in the same classroom. Choice (C) weakens the argument by claiming that schools that sort students by ability get better results. Choice (D) weakens the argument by claiming that the sorting system worked fine for more than 90 years. If the problems have only arisen in the last decade, perhaps some other cause is to blame. Choice (E) weakens the argument by stating that technical schools are actually very good at training the students who get sorted into them, suggesting a strength of the sorting method. Choice (A) is the only choice that doesn't weaken the argument, so it's the answer.

8. **B. When a hive loses its queen, some workers develop the ability to lay eggs; these unfertilized eggs can hatch only into male drones.**

The question asks for a statement that weakens the argument. The argument's conclusion is that worker bees never pass on their own genes. The evidence is that they put all their energy into nurturing the queen and her offspring. To weaken this argument, you need a statement that shows that despite their devotion to the queen, workers can pass on their own genetic traits. Choice (A) seems like it could be the answer because it suggests that workers are, in fact, furthering their genetic line by caring for the queen, who is, after all, related to them. But it doesn't quite work because it doesn't contradict the argument, which says that workers fail to pass on their own genes to offspring. See if a better choice is available. Choice (B) contradicts the argument's conclusion: If workers can, in fact, lay eggs, they do occasionally pass their genetic traits on to offspring, even if these offspring are exclusively male. Choice (C) doesn't weaken the argument, but it doesn't strengthen it, either. It's merely a statement of fact about queens. Choice (D) doesn't weaken the argument; if anything, it shows how workers subordinate their interests to the queens. Choice (E) is just more information about queens (and drones); it neither strengthens nor weakens the argument. Choice (B) is the best answer.

9. **E. assumes that what is true of myths in general must also be true of each individual myth**

The question asks you to find the argument's weak point. The argument concludes that all myths can fit into both categories (explanations of natural phenomena and explorations of psychological phenomena) based on the evidence that those are two general functions of myths. Choice (A) is wrong. You don't know if experts in the field have already discounted this conclusion because the argument doesn't say anything about them. Choice (B) is wrong because the argument says nothing about the relevance of myths in today's world. Choice (C) is wrong because the argument doesn't impose any sort of modern sensibility on myths; it doesn't mention pre-modern people or the difference between them and people today. Choice (D) is wrong because the argument doesn't criticize anyone. Choice (E) matches with the answer you hoped to find; the argument does indeed assume that all myths contain both natural and psychological phenomena and doesn't offer any proof that those general characteristics of myths are universal features of each and every myth. Choice (E) is the answer.

10. **A. The sex of a non-juvenile parrotfish lacking brightly colored scales cannot always be easily determined.**

The question asks you to find a statement that must be true if everything in the argument is true. The passage states that identifying the sex of parrotfish can be difficult, and it cites the various color patterns that male and female parrotfish display at different stages in their lives. You know enough information is available for you to infer more facts, but at this point, you don't know what, so why try speculating? You can't predict what the answer will be, so just read the statements carefully and get your head around the parrotfish facts. Then just read the answer choices one by one and see if one fits what you now know about these colorful fish.

Right off the bat, Choice (A) looks like a good choice. Because some post-juvenile but pre-sexually mature male parrotfish continue to look like females, it won't always be easy to identify the sex of a non-juvenile parrotfish; in the intermediate growth phase, a male and female can look alike. Check the other answers to make sure this one is the best. Choice (B) can't be right because the argument tells you that juvenile male parrotfish look like the smaller, less colorful females; only the sexually mature males are the ones who are large and brightly colored. Choice (C) may be true, but the argument isn't about female parrotfish mating behavior, so it isn't relevant. Choice (D) may also be true, but the argument says nothing about the importance of camouflage in avoiding predators. Choice (E) is wrong; the argument says that in *some* species, males at some time look like females, but you can't infer any information about all male parrotfish from this statement. Choice (A) is your answer.

11. **D. If people are not exposed to the arts at school, they will never learn about them.**

The question wants you to spot the assumption that the author makes in developing the conclusion. Based on the premise that schools devote less attention to teaching the arts, the argument concludes that the next generation of citizens won't appreciate art. The only way that could be the case is if schools are the only place where children get any arts education. That's the author's assumption.

Choice (A) is wrong. If the author assumed that, then she couldn't conclude that everyone would grow up ignorant of the arts. The author doesn't assume Choice (B), because she is interested in arts education for its own sake, not for the sake of academic subjects. Choice (C) is wrong; the author certainly isn't assuming that people become great artists independent of art education in school. Choice (D) is right. The author definitely assumes that if people don't learn art in school, they'll never learn it. Choice (E) is wrong; it serves as an argument in favor of ending arts programs in schools. Choice (D) is the right answer.

12. **B. The baseball team's presence generated millions of dollars of revenue for the town every year by attracting out-of-town visitors who spent money on hotels, restaurants, and other goods and services.**

The question wants you to find an answer that supports the argument's conclusion. The conclusion is that the loss of the baseball team will hurt the town, especially economically. To support this, look for an answer that shows how much money the team brought to the town.

Choice (A) doesn't support the conclusion. In fact, it supports the opposite conclusion that keeping the team would actually cost the town money instead of bringing in income. Choice (B) does support the conclusion; it shows how the team's presence brought in money by bringing visitors to the town. Choice (B) looks like a good answer. Choice (C) provides another reason why losing the team wouldn't hurt the town; no one attended the games anyway. Choice (D) criticizes the baseball team's loyalty and its demands, which does nothing to support the argument that the town would benefit by keeping it. Choice (E) is evidence of the town's apathy toward the team, not support for an argument that says losing the team would hurt the town. Choice (B) is the only answer that actually supports the conclusion, so it's the best one.

13. **C. Children raised by a mother and father who are married to one another are better off than children raised by a mother alone.**

The question informs you that the argument makes an assumption and asks you to identify it. The argument concludes that the president's initiative is worth supporting because it will help the children of poor, unmarried women based on the evidence that the program will help these women get married and stay that way. Clearly, the writer assumes that married mothers benefit these children; if kids don't benefit, then the argument falls apart. Look for an answer that says something about the benefits kids get from having married parents. Choice (A) is wrong because the author says nothing about drug dependency, crime, or teen pregnancy. This argument sticks to statements about relationships and healthy children. A reader might assume that drugs and crime are part of the equation, but the author of this argument doesn't. Choice (B) doesn't work. The author doesn't need to involve people with higher incomes in the conclusion about marriage and low-income people. Choice (C) is exactly what you want. If children raised by married moms and dads are better off than those raised by single mothers, it justifies the author's conclusion. Choice (D) may be another reason to encourage marriage, but in this argument the author is talking only about children, not welfare. Choice (E) is irrelevant; the author makes no mention of other governmental programs, successful or otherwise, and doesn't need this statement to make the argument hold together. Choice (C) is the correct answer.

14. **D. popular fiction can affect people's beliefs and actions**

The question asks you to find a statement upon which Isabel and Ferdinand disagree. Think for a moment about what's going on in the conversation. Isabel says that the novels in question are dangerous and explains why she thinks that. Ferdinand says he thinks she's wrong because she's exaggerating the influence the books have. So clearly they disagree about the impact these books have on their readers. See if one of the answers says this. Choice (A) is wrong. Ferdinand and Isabel don't argue about the religious nature of the books; Isabel mentions religion, but Ferdinand doesn't address that part of her contention. Choice (B) is definitely wrong. Isabel says nothing about the appropriateness of the end of the world as a topic for a novel; her focus is on the demonization of nonbelievers. Choice (C) is clearly wrong. Isabel and Ferdinand aren't arguing about whether the books are popular; they're arguing about whether popular fiction influences behavior. Choice (D) looks like a good choice. Isabel certainly does believe that popular fiction can affect people's behavior in a dangerous manner, and Ferdinand, on the contrary, states that people don't allow popular fiction to affect their beliefs and actions. Choice (E) is another wrong answer. Although Isabel suggests that some depictions of violence in novels are dangerous, Ferdinand doesn't address the issue of violence in popular fiction. That leaves Choice (D) as your best choice.

15. **D. Regulating modern food manufacturing and advertising would help prevent obesity.**

This question wants you to identify the source of Tia and Muriel's disagreement. Why are they arguing? Tia thinks the government should regulate food manufacturing and advertising, and Muriel thinks it shouldn't, not necessarily because that regulation wouldn't work but because she thinks individuals are in control of their own weight. They also disagree about the causes of obesity; Tia seems to place the blame squarely on modern food manufacturers and advertisers, while Muriel blames the obese individuals for their bad habits. Choice (A) is wrong because Tia and Muriel aren't debating the effectiveness of diet and exercise in weight control; they both may well agree with the statement. Choice (B) is tricky. Tia obviously thinks the government should intervene in public health problems, while Muriel seems to disapprove of such intervention. But Muriel does say that the government could take some limited action in encouraging diet and exercise and says nothing about other situations, so Choice (B) is too extreme. Choice (C) is wrong; neither speaker has mentioned public schools, so there's no telling what they think about school nutrition programs. Choice (D) looks pretty good. Tia obviously thinks that a lot of obesity comes from modern food, but Muriel thinks it comes from overeating. Choice (E) doesn't work because neither Muriel nor Tia has mentioned the difference between public- and private-sector efforts (just because Muriel doesn't want the government involved doesn't necessarily mean she wants the private sector involved). Choice (D) is the best answer here.

16. D. relies on evidence too partial to establish the conclusion drawn

The question asks you to find the point where the politician's argument is most vulnerable. The politician suggests that global warming isn't happening. As evidence, he mentions only that two months of recent winters have set record low temperatures, which ignores that average annual temperatures take into account data from all twelve months. See if one of the answers refutes the validity of the politician's evidence. Choice (A) is wrong; the premise and conclusion are different statements, so the reasoning isn't circular. Choice (B) is wrong because the politician isn't appealing to emotions at all. Choice (C) is wrong because the politician doesn't debate the potential effects of global warming but whether it's even occurring at all. Choice (D) is right because the politician assumes that a few months of record low temperatures can refute the claim that overall temperatures worldwide are increasing. Choice (E) is wrong because the politician doesn't mention the political leanings of environmentalists. Choice (D) is your best answer.

17. A. A college graduate with a lucrative job offer decides to decline it and instead borrow several thousand dollars to attend medical school in the hopes of receiving a much larger future income as a physician.

The question asks you to identify the answer that conforms to the principle stated in the argument. What is that principle? Basically, the argument suggests that investing for the future is better than taking immediate profits because the long-term profits from the investment will ultimately be larger. Look for an answer that shows someone postponing gratification or payoff in exchange for higher future profit. (This principle is familiar to anyone contemplating law school.) Choice (A) looks like a great choice. The student who turns down a job offer to pursue higher studies definitely exemplifies the principle in the argument. Choice (B) doesn't exactly fit the principle. It discusses the benefits of investing for the future but doesn't mention sacrificing immediate gratification here. Choice (C) is wrong. It recommends a particular action because there's a correlation between that action and future success, but attending church isn't an example of postponing immediate gratification to invest in the future (the author doesn't mention anything that one might be giving up by going to church). Choice (D) is wrong because, although Habitat for Humanity offers a great opportunity for poor people who want to own homes, neither the volunteer builders nor the new homeowners are declining a current opportunity to invest more heavily in an investment with a higher future payoff. Choice (E) may be sound advice, but it doesn't duplicate the argument's principle. In fact, if you buy good furniture now, you're not delaying anything. Choice (A) is the best answer.

18. D. Car manufacturers that design cars according to female tastes can earn larger profits than those who do not.

You want to find the answer best supported by the statements, which note that women buy half of all cars and like to buy vehicles that fulfill their needs and are less harmful to the environment. Look for the answer that incorporates all the statements: Plenty of women buy cars, women notice certain details, and cars designed with those details outsell cars that aren't designed with those details. Choice (A) is wrong because it doesn't mention what women want. You can almost certainly find a better choice than this. Choice (B) is wrong because nothing in the statements allows you to infer the particular type of car that women would like. Choice (C) may be true, but it doesn't address the statements regarding women's vehicle preferences. Choice (D) looks great. It relates women's vehicle preferences to how car manufactures should respond to those preferences, so it's a very good answer. Choice (E) is wrong. Although many people lament the passing of the station wagon, and it's entirely possible that car manufacturers may find that they still have a huge market for these vehicles, the argument isn't concerned with particular types of cars. Choice (D) is your answer.

19. **C. children can ever benefit from watching television**

The question wants you to identify the source of Carter and Neri's disagreement. Carter says that kids shouldn't watch TV because it gives them attention deficit disorder (ADD). Neri says that a blanket prohibition on children's TV watching isn't necessary because the disorder comes from watching a particular kind of program, and some programs are actually beneficial. Both speakers agree that TV can cause ADD; they disagree on whether TV can ever benefit children. Choice (A) is wrong. Carter and Neri haven't mentioned violence on TV, so you can't possibly know what they think about it. Choice (B) is wrong. Although Carter does mention the significance of spending more time watching TV, he doesn't mention specific durations. Neri doesn't address the amount of TV watching time at all, so you don't know whether they disagree about that. Choice (C) looks right; they definitely disagree about whether children can ever benefit from watching TV. Choice (D) is wrong. Neri does mention educational programs, but Carter doesn't specifically address them, and neither speaker discusses the past generation of TV watchers. Choice (E) is wrong because neither speaker addresses this issue. Choice (C) is correct.

20. **D. South Carolina's Congaree Swamp National Monument saw an increase in visitors after it changed its name to Congaree National Park.**

The question asks you to support the park ranger's assertion, which means you have to find an answer that provides evidence that the assertion is correct. The park ranger claims that parks and monuments with good names get the most visitors, so the National Park Service should give its parks and monuments appealing names. Look for an answer that shows how giving a park a good name attracts tourists. Choice (A) is totally wrong; it doesn't mention park names at all. Choice (B) is wrong because it attributes attractiveness of parks to location and scenery rather than name. Choice (C) may work because it does compare two parks with different names, but it doesn't say anything about how many people visit either park, so it's not a good choice. Choice (D) looks perfect; a park with more visitors after changing its name provides an example that supports the ranger's conclusion. Choice (E) is wrong. It claims that Yellowstone attracts visitors because people want to see its sights, not because they like the name "Yellowstone." Choice (D) is correct.

21. **E. Exposure to secondhand smoke does not result in significant ill effects.**

Focus on the conclusion. The argument expresses outrage that the government has outlawed public smoking based on the premise that the government doesn't have the right to force people to curtail activities that hurt only them. For the argument to reach the conclusion that the government's behavior is outrageous, the assumption must be that public smoking isn't harmful to other nonsmokers. Choice (E) conveys this answer. Choice (A) is wrong because it's an inference that could be drawn from the argument rather than an underlying assumption. Choice (B)'s statement about governing what happens in private spaces is likely one the author of the argument would agree with, but it's irrelevant to the argument about smoking in public spaces. Choice (C) is wrong because the argument doesn't address smokers' ability to control their behavior. Choice (D) is another conclusion the argument's author would likely agree with, but it isn't an assumption necessary to reach the original conclusion. Choice (E) is best.

22. **B. presupposes that actors become extroverted because they study drama**

The question asks you to determine where the argument is vulnerable. The argument claims that studying drama and performing can make a person more extroverted; the evidence for this conclusion is that actors are extroverted. The problem with this claim is that you don't know for sure whether actors are extroverted because they studied drama or people who are extroverted to begin with choose drama as a profession. If the latter is true, then studying drama won't make an introvert into an extrovert. Choice (A) is incorrect because the argument makes no judgments about the benefits of extroversion or introversion. Choice (B) looks correct; the argument assumes that acting makes people extroverted and ignores the idea that acting may attract extroverted people. Choice (C) isn't right. The argument doesn't supply much evidence of extroversion, but it does supply a little. However, a lack of evidence isn't the main problem. Choice (D) is wrong because the argument does define "extrovert" somewhat — as someone who is comfortable before a crowd of people. Even if it didn't define the term, that's not the argument's chief weakness. Choice (E) is wrong. The author never denies that there may be other ways for people to achieve extroversion and never suggests that acting is the only way. Choice (B) is right.

23. **A. Although a computer-created proof might be too complex to check by hand in the traditional manner, computers are reliable enough today that mathematicians should be willing to admit proofs done by computers into the body of accepted mathematical knowledge.**

The question asks you to identify the mathematician's conclusion. This is a long and complex argument on an esoteric topic, but don't let that bug you. Essentially, the mathematician is suggesting that the mathematical community should accept the computer-created proof of the orange-stacking concept; his reason is that computers are very accurate, and all the parts that have been hand-checked so far have been correct. So look for an answer that says this. The validity of the proof is the key. Choice (A) seems to be exactly what you want; the argument does conclude that computers are reliable enough to create acceptable mathematical proofs. Choice (B) is wrong because the mathematician isn't concerned with alternate methods of stacking oranges. He doesn't mention them at all, so they can't be part of his conclusion. Choice (C) is wrong because it's the exact opposite of the mathematician's conclusion; he thinks computers *do* have a place in the world of theoretical mathematics. Choice (E) is wrong because it describes the process of proving a mathematical theorem, not the mathematician's actual conclusion. Choice (A) is correct.

24. **B. Accidents that occur at a higher speed are much more likely to be fatal than those at lower speeds.**

The question asks you to resolve the discrepancy that the overall percentage of accidents per drivers hasn't increased since states raised their speed limits, but total accident fatalities have increased. So even though the number of accidents hasn't increased, the accidents that do occur have become more deadly, which is entirely possible. Look for an answer that connects cause (higher speeds) with effect (more fatal accidents despite fewer total accidents). Choice (A) doesn't explain the rise in fatalities because the argument doesn't mention illegal speeding, just higher legal speeds. Choice (B) looks correct. If higher speeds make accidents more deadly, then it makes sense for fatalities to rise even if total accident numbers don't. Choice (C) is wrong because the author isn't interested in resolving a statistical paradox rather than providing suggestions for state regulation. Choice (D) is wrong because it doesn't connect the lower speed limit with fewer fatalities. Perhaps slower cars caused fewer deaths, but the answer doesn't say that. Choice (E) is wrong because it attributes accidents to distractions rather than speed, and it doesn't distinguish between fatal and nonfatal accidents. Choice (B) is the best answer.

25. **D. Studies have shown that audiences appreciate the opportunity to laugh while listening to a speech.**

You need to find the answer that doesn't weaken the argument; that means eliminating the four answers that do weaken it. The argument's conclusion is that speakers should always start their speeches with a joke, even in foreign countries, because audiences in general like jokes. What would weaken this claim? Anything that disproves the contention that jokes work for foreign audiences. Choice (A) definitely weakens it; speakers shouldn't tell jokes if they'll offend their audiences. Choice (B) weakens the argument, at least as far as female speakers are concerned. Choice (C) weakens the argument; the last thing a speaker needs is for an interpreter to refuse to translate the speech. Choice (D) actually doesn't weaken the argument; if audiences like to relax by laughing, then telling a joke is a good idea. Choice (E) weakens the argument; no speaker wants to inadvertently commit an act of aggression. Choice (D) is the best answer.

Section II: Reading Comprehension

1. **E. Nishiwaki was a Japanese poet and scholar who spent his life specializing in European literature, which proved tremendously influential to his own work.**

This passage is biographical, telling the life story and listing significant contributions of a major Japanese literary figure. The author is fairly objective and doesn't seem to have much of an agenda beyond emphasizing Nishiwaki's embrace of European literature and culture. (Note, though, that this *is* an agenda. The author had to choose which details of Nishiwaki's life most interested him and chose to focus on Nishiwaki's interest in Europe. He didn't have to do this; for example, he could have emphasized Nishiwaki's participation in the avant-garde circles of the time or spent more time describing Nishiwaki's work and less on his life story. No text is a foregone conclusion before the author begins to write it.) Choice (A) is wrong. Nishiwaki did protest his government's policies, but rebellion against the government certainly isn't the passage's main point; the author mentions it in only one place. Choice (B) isn't exactly the main idea. Nowhere does the author suggest that Nishiwaki's family disapproved of his studying European literature; in fact, his father was still alive when he went to study a European-influenced style of painting, and you have no reason to assume he objected. He did choose to write in English to give himself more freedom than Japanese allowed, but that wasn't explicitly rebellion. Choice (C) isn't right, either; nowhere does the author say that Nishiwaki tried to convince his students that European literature was better than Japanese literature. Choice (D) is wrong, too; as far as you know, Nishiwaki only chose to write his first work in English and then wrote many others in Japanese. Choice (E) is correct, pretty well summing up the passage.

2. **A. scholarly interest in the life and works of a significant literary figure**

Skim the first words of the answers, which can help you eliminate a few right away. Choices (D) and (E) are certainly wrong; the passage doesn't include any skepticism or envy. Choice (B) is wrong, too. The author doesn't express surprise at Nishiwaki's use of a foreign language; nor does he seem particularly admiring, which eliminates Choice (C). Choice (A) looks like the best choice because this passage is objective; it's definitely scholarly, with all the author's emphasis on literary movements and descriptions of literary works.

3. B. introduce Nishiwaki and his lifelong interest in European culture

The first paragraph informs you that Nishiwaki was a major literary figure who was deeply interested in European culture, and it describes Nishiwaki's early years and education. So look for an answer that says something like that. Choice (A) isn't right. Although the author does mention Nishiwaki's brief study of painting, that doesn't explain the function the paragraph plays within the passage as a whole. Choice (B) looks like the right answer; the first paragraph does introduce Nishiwaki and sets up the reader to expect him to have more contact with European literature. Choice (C) is wrong. Aside from the first sentence, the paragraph doesn't actually say much about Nishiwaki's contribution to Japanese literature. Choice (D) isn't right, and in fact, nowhere in the passage does the author attempt to explain Nishiwaki's choice beyond noting that Nishiwaki found European literature interesting. Choice (E) is clearly wrong; this paragraph has nothing to do with European contributions to Japanese culture. Choice (B) is correct.

4. C. He disapproved of the Japanese government's policies and in protest refused to write poetry.

The relevant sentence reads, "Angered by the Japanese government's fascist policies, Nishiwaki refused to write poetry during the second world war." That makes Choices (A), (B), and (D) obviously wrong. Choice (C) rephrases that sentence, which makes it look like a good answer. Choice (E) may confuse you because the following sentence does tell you that Nishiwaki spent the war years writing a dissertation on German literature, but the way the two sentences are phrased makes it clear that the dissertation was simply how Nishiwaki chose to fill his time because he had already made the decision not to write poetry. So Choice (C) is correct.

5. C. providing a brief biography of Nishiwaki that explains the significance of his work

This is a main idea question. What's the main idea of this passage? To provide a biography of a Japanese writer, explaining why his work is important. Skim the answer choices and see if one of them matches. Sure enough, Choice (C) looks like a good answer. Check the others just in case. Choice (A) is wrong because the author doesn't mention the work of other Japanese poets. Choice (B) is wrong because although the avant-garde movement did influence Nishiwaki's writing, the author's discussion of it takes up only a small part of the entire passage. Choice (D) is wrong because the author doesn't mention the benefits of studying foreign literature. Choice (E) is wrong because the passage doesn't discuss changes in overall Japanese poetic style after the war. Choice (C) is the best answer.

6. E. classical Japanese literature such as _The Tale of Genji_

You know that Nishiwaki studied Old and Middle English, classical Greek and Latin, and a smattering of modernist English works at Oxford. That covers Choices (A) through (D) and leaves only Choice (E). You also know that Nishiwaki didn't especially love traditional Japanese poetic forms, of which _The Tale of Genji_ is an example. That makes Choice (E) the best answer. (Yes, Nishiwaki did have _some_ interest in Japanese literature, and he may well have appreciated _The Tale of Genji_, but the passage provides no basis for thinking that he actively pursued an interest in classical Japanese literature.)

7. A. He found that English allowed him to express a wider variety of thoughts and emotions than Japanese.

Here's the relevant sentence: "In 1925, Nishiwaki published his first book, _Spectrum_, a volume of poems written in English; he explained that English offered him much more freedom of expression than traditional Japanese poetic language." That makes Choice (A) the only sensible answer. The rest of them are just plain wrong.

8. **A. Events of the last two decades have shown that sea urchins play a vital role in the maintenance of the ecosystems in which they live, contrary to what many scientists formerly assumed.**

   This passage is about the importance of sea urchins to the marine environment, which has come as a surprise to many people who formerly discounted the significance of the spiny creatures. Choice (A) sums this up pretty well; it looks like a good answer. Choice (B) isn't really the main point; the author mentions a project to relocate sea urchins in the last paragraph, but that doesn't play a major role in the passage as a whole. Choice (C) isn't the main point, though it may be true; more important, the passage is about sea urchins, not all echinoderms. Choice (D) is also true, but it's not the main point either. The author uses information about excessive algae growth to prove her point that sea urchins are now recognized as important to the ecosystem. Choice (E) is just plain wrong; nowhere does the author mention the government's duty to educate people about the environment. Choice (A) is the correct answer.

9. **B. describe the appearance and eating habits of sea urchins**

   The second paragraph is a concise description of urchins and their activities. Skim the first words of the answer choices to see if one of them uses a word like "describe." Choice (B) does, and it looks like a good answer. Quickly check the others to make sure Choice (B) is best. Choice (A) is wrong because the second paragraph doesn't claim that urchins are important to the ecosystem; that claim is elsewhere. Choice (C) is wrong because its claim is also in another part of the passage, not in the second paragraph. Choice (D) is wrong because that information is in the first and last paragraphs. Choice (E) is wrong because the author doesn't mention the diets of other echinoderms. So Choice (B) really is the best answer.

10. **C. They are all members of the same phylum.**

    The second paragraph says: "Sea urchins are members of the phylum Echinodermata, the category of invertebrate animals with spiny exterior shells, which also includes starfish, brittle stars, and sand dollars." So all four are members of the same phylum. Is there an answer that says that? Yes — Choice (C) looks like your answer. The rest of the information in this paragraph regards only sea urchins and doesn't apply to the other species. Choice (A) is wrong because although the passage indicates that echinoderms are invertebrates, it doesn't say that all echinoderms eat algae; you only know that sea urchins eat algae. As far as you know, only sea urchins were devastated by the bacterium in 1983, so Choice (B) is wrong. Choice (D) is a bit tricky because the second paragraph does say that all echinoderms have spiny shells, but it doesn't say that all the spines are long and sharp. Choice (E) happens to be true of echinoderms, but the passage doesn't tell you that. So Choice (C) is the best answer.

    Note: This passage doesn't really require you to know much about invertebrate taxonomy, but the LSAT-makers do assume that you remember some rudiments from your science classes, such as the meaning of the word *phylum.* (You don't have to know a very specific meaning, but you should remember that it's a kind of category into which scientists sort animals and plants based on their physical characteristics.)

11. **E. A bacterium carried by a ship entering the Atlantic from the Pacific spread throughout the population and killed nearly all sea urchins.**

    Refer to this quotation: "In 1983 a barge traveled from the Pacific to the Atlantic through the Panama Canal carrying a bacterium that proved devastating to the sea urchin population. Nearly all long-spined urchins in the tropical western Atlantic died as a result of this exposure." Choice (E) is the only answer that sums up this tragedy. The other answers are simply wrong. The author does mention people killing sea urchins but doesn't connect this with their near eradication, so Choice (A) is wrong. Choice (B) is wrong because the passage says that coral is dying because it's covered with algae, not that it was killed by a plague. Nowhere does the author mention triggerfish, so Choice (C) is wrong. Choice (D) isn't right either, because a bacterium killed the urchins, not a virus (they're very different), and it didn't come from other echinoderms. That makes Choice (E) the answer.

12. **C. Coral reefs in regions that still have healthy sea urchin populations have almost no algae growing on them.**

What would support the claim that sea urchins are key to solving the algae on reefs problem? Well, if someone had examined reefs with and without sea urchins, and the reefs without urchins had algae overgrowth problems and those with urchins didn't, all other conditions being equal, that would tend to support this hypothesis. Choice (C) looks like the best answer. Choice (A) doesn't work because knowing that damselfish could also take care of the algae problem would actually weaken the author's claim that sea urchins are key to algae removal from coral reefs. Choice (B) is irrelevant because the issue is algae elimination, not coral elimination. Choice (D) has no effect on the author's claim because the article never differentiates among different types of algae. Choice (E) is interesting, but the passage doesn't distinguish types of coral, so it's not clear how this point about coral would affect the claim that sea urchins will take care of the algae problem. Choice (C) is by far the best answer.

13. **C. provide an example of how the scientific community has altered its view of sea urchins**

To answer a question about the purpose of a part of the passage, you need to view it in a larger context, which often means reading at least a sentence or two before and after the part the question references. The Environmental Protection Agency (EPA) is one of two examples showing scientists' changing views on the importance of sea urchins. Choice (A) is wrong because, though it describes the EPA's actions, it doesn't explain that the reason the author mentions those actions is to provide an example of scientists' changing views. Choice (B) is wrong; nowhere does the author mention any relationship between government and shipping. Choice (C) addresses the inclusion of the EPA as an example and therefore looks like a potential right answer. Choice (D) is wrong and, in fact, backward, because EPA scientists *have* recognized the significance of sea urchins. Choice (E) is also wrong because nowhere does the author mention voters. Choice (C) is the correct answer.

14. **A. Humans can take an active role in assisting the recovery of ecosystems that have been harmed by human actions.**

The correct answer is probably a statement that recaps the author's main point or one of her items of evidence. Choice (A) looks like something the author would say. In the last paragraph, she writes approvingly of the scientists who are currently relocating sea urchins to algae-covered reefs. Choice (B) contradicts Choice (A); if the author likes the statement in Choice (A), she won't agree with the one in Choice (B). Choice (C) is just plain wrong; in the first paragraph, the author writes of the ignorant folks who used to kill sea urchins for sports, not realizing the importance of their victims. Choice (D) may well be true in the real world, but you can't really tell from this passage because the author never mentions punishment for the shipping company that introduced the deadly bacterium; Choice (A) still looks better. Choice (E) is almost certainly not something the author would say. Based on her evidence, no creature has yet adapted itself to the sea urchins' niche, and that's why corals are now covered with algae. Choice (A) is the best answer.

15. **D. nonprofits may face difficulties staying true to their overall mission**

The two passages discuss potential problems in running a nonprofit. Passage A concentrates on the difficulties some nonprofits have with leadership and finances. Passage B's focus is on the potential for fraud and corruption in nonprofits.

Choices (A) and (C) involve concerns cited by the author of Passage A but not B, and only Passage B mentions Choice (B). Only Passage B suggests that board members may put their own financial interests above the mission of the nonprofit, so Choice (E) isn't correct. Both authors discuss Choice (D).

The author of Passage A notes that one of the most important challenges is ". . . to keep the mission in mind in all decision making," and Passage B's author notes that one of the primary responsibilities of a nonprofit's governing board is to "make sure the organization remains true to its mission."

16. **A. Managing the Nonprofit Sector: An Overview**

Questions that ask for a title are main idea questions, and the best answer to a main idea question is the one that's neither too general nor too specific. Eliminate answers that concern only one of the passages and select the one that is general enough to pertain to both.

Passage A briefly discusses Choice (B) when the author discusses the decline in government support and the growing number of for-profit businesses occupying areas once traditionally occupied by nonprofit organizations, but it's not the main idea and isn't even mentioned by Passage B. Both passages briefly touch on the conflict between nonprofits' missions and funders' missions, but that conflict isn't the main idea of either passage, so Choice (C) is too specific. If you picked Choice (D), the last line of Passage B is probably still fresh in your mind, but while both passages discuss the role of the board in managing nonprofits, they also consider other factors. You may wish to keep Choice (D) in mind as you look for a better option. Choice (E) implies that the passages focus on the nonprofit sector and how it has changed and advanced over time, and with the exception of a reference here or there as to how things have done in the past, neither passage focuses on the history of nonprofits. Choice (A) is a bit vague but at least summarizes the overall purpose of both passages to discuss the management challenges experienced by nonprofits. It's more on point than Choice (E) and less issue-specific than the other choices, making Choice (A) the best choice of those available. Remember, sometimes the correct answer will be the best one out of five lousy choices.

17. **E. Both passages suggest that the challenges nonprofits face are often exacerbated by the fact that they are organizations intended to serve the public good.**

First, examine the answer choice options for each passage separately. Passage A presents challenges but doesn't offer ways to overcome them, so Choice (A) is wrong. Choice (B) may work for Passage A; it discusses fiscal challenges in the last paragraph. Choice (C) can't be correct because Passage A doesn't offer an opinion on nonprofit management. Passage A definitely presents an overview of nonprofits' challenges, so Choice (D) may work for the first passage. Choice (E) also works for Passage A; it states in the last paragraph that nonprofits are pressured by funders to show proof that they make a positive impact, which means they must prove that they provide a public good. Examine the three remaining choices, (B), (D), and (E), for Passage B. Choice (B) isn't exactly right. Passage B discusses fraud and corruption but never states that these issues present the biggest challenge for nonprofits. Choice (D) is wrong. Passage B presents potential ways to confront fraud and corruption, but these issues aren't the challenges presented by Passage A. Choice (E) is the best answer. The second paragraph of Passage B indicates that nonprofits' problems are particularly disturbing because nonprofits are supposed to provide public benefit.

18. **D. The public should hold managers, leaders, and boards of nonprofit organizations liable for their decisions.**

Choice (C) is an assertion made by *only* Passage A, so there's no way to know whether the author of Passage B would agree. The same goes for Choices (A), (B), and (E). So you've already narrowed down your answer to Choice (D). Because Choice (D) also sounds like something relevant to only Passage A, spotting the wrong answers to this question may be easier than finding the right answer. Note that the author of Passage B states that a nonprofit board is "responsible for making sure the organization remains true to its mission, safeguards it assets and *operates in the public interest*." Similarly, the author of Passage A notes that "the real owner of a nonprofit is the public. It is the public to whom they are ultimately accountable." So you can safely pick Choice (D).

19. **B. The nonprofit sector does not benefit from oversight by a "watchdog" organization whose purpose is to promote integrity, as businesses and the government do.**

Choice (B) is essentially a paraphrase of the entire second paragraph of Passage B, so it's clearly something indicated by the passage. If you picked Choice (A), you misread the first line of Passage B, which actually says that nonprofits are *not* immune from any damage that could be inflicted by unscrupulous or fraudulent solicitors. Choices (C) and (D) are statements included in Passage A rather than Passage B, so nix those options as well. As for Choice (E), while Passage B does indeed mention the media, it does so in reference to the fact that they monitor business and government, not nonprofits. Stick with Choice (B).

20. **C. Most people do not understand how nonprofit organizations are regulated and monitored.**

If you didn't pick Choice (C), you may have forgotten the general rule that you must rely *solely* on the information contained in the passage, regardless of what your own personal knowledge (or common sense) tells you. While both authors may theoretically agree with Choice (C), it's only brought up in Passage B, so you can't make the assumption that both authors would agree.

Choice (A) is stated in one way or another by both passages; Passage A states that "The real owner of a nonprofit is the public," and Passage B says that "All nonprofits are governed by a board of directors or trustees." Both imply that more than one individual is leading the show. Choice (B), while vague, conveys a central point from both passages and is, to some degree, a paraphrase of the information contained in each. So it can't be right. Choice (D) is also an underlying theme present in both passages, so you can knock that one out of contention as well. Regarding Choice (E), Passage A refers to pressure from funders in its final line when it says that funders demand to see positive, measurable results stem from the money they contribute. Passage B references pressure from stakeholders when it says that nonprofits are threatened by board members who are more concerned with their personal financial well-being than the overall mission. Stick with Choice (C).

21. **E. indicate the role that government plays in the operation of nonprofits**

Focus on the context in which each passage mentions the government. Passage A brings up the government to show how the decrease in government funding has negatively affected the well-being of nonprofits. Passage B talks about the government to emphasize that the government doesn't do much to regulate nonprofits. Both show that the government has some role in relation to nonprofits, so Choice (A) is out. Choice (B) can't be right because the second paragraph of Passage A lists "all levels of government" as one of the stakeholders in nonprofits. Choice (C) relates to only Passage A, so it doesn't work. Neither passage suggests that nonprofits and government agencies are alike, so Choice (D) is wrong. Whenever the passages mention the government, they provide one of the ways the government does or doesn't influence the running of nonprofits. So Choice (E) is the best answer.

22. **D. Cloning: Just Another Way of Making a Baby**

A title question is similar to a main idea question. To come up with an accurate title, you have to understand what the whole passage is about. In this case, what is the author's point? She's arguing that the ethical debates about cloning don't make sense because cloning is more similar than dissimilar to regular reproduction and faces many of the same issues.

Choice (A) doesn't make a very good title. The author is explicitly arguing that cloning would *not* harm families. Choice (B) is wrong because this article isn't about the dangers of cloning. Although it does mention several dangers that people have suggested, both ethical and physical, they're not the point. Choice (C) isn't right; the author briefly discusses the mechanics of cloning in the first paragraph but by way of introducing the subject, not as a thesis. Choice (D) makes a perfect title; that cloning is just another way of conceiving a child is exactly the author's point. Choice (E) doesn't work because the passage isn't about the government's role in the debate or about emphasizing the unethical aspects of cloning. In fact, aside from a quick reference to the Clinton administration in the first paragraph and a brief mention of the government's lack of interference in reproduction issues, the government doesn't play a role in this passage. Choice (D) looks like the right answer.

23. **D. Most critics of cloning are worried about aspects of cloning that are not substantially different from the potential problems associated with methods of reproduction already in common use.**

The author's point is that the criticisms of cloning are aimed at fanciful concerns and fantasies about "natural" relationships between parents and children. She would probably think that the people who have criticized cloning based on these concerns are arguing from emotion, not fact, and that their arguments are flawed because they could potentially apply to normal reproduction as well. Choice (A) doesn't work; the author doesn't ever suggest that cloning critics are religious fanatics. Choice (B) is definitely wrong; the author raises the point about creating a master race as an illustration of an outrageous fear so unlikely as to be laughable. Choice (C) is wrong; though the author doesn't state this explicitly, she implies that foes of cloning don't object to other techniques of assisted reproduction. Choice (D) does match up with the author's point; she would argue that children already enter the world in difficult and unpredictable circumstances and that parents already treat children differently depending on their expectations even when they conceive their kids the usual way. Choice (E) is clearly wrong; the author says that cloning critics tend to ignore these practical considerations in favor of fanciful ones. Choice (D) is correct.

24. **A. argue that most critics of cloning are focusing on drawbacks that are either outlandish or no different from the drawbacks of normal reproduction and that ethically cloning is not very different from normal reproduction**

Based on the main idea of the passage, Choice (A) looks like a very good answer. The author is arguing that cloning critics have seized on concerns that aren't really valid and that cloning shouldn't be all that different from other techniques of conception. Choice (B) isn't right because most of the passage isn't concerned with the mechanics of cloning or other genetic engineering processes. Choice (C) doesn't work; the author doesn't address scientists particularly and makes no explicit recommendations. Choice (D) looks like it might work because the author does list some potential benefits of cloning, but it's really not her main purpose. So Choice (A) still looks like the best answer. Choice (E) is definitely wrong; if anything, the author is doing the opposite, suggesting that many so-called dangers of cloning are nothing of the kind. Choice (A) is the best choice.

25. E. show that the worries of cloning critics are exaggerated and based more in fantasy than fact

"Nefarious" and "abominable" are very strong words, commonly used to describe only the most evil of people and deeds. They're definitely too strong to describe the personalities and intentions of most scientists. The author uses them here in a tongue-in-cheek fashion to emphasize the fantastic nature of many criticisms of cloning and to suggest that these fears are probably derived from science fiction rather than real information. Note, too, that these two words are an aberration from the writer's usual vocabulary, which is generally down-to-earth. The best answer is Choice (E).

26. D. In vitro fertilization is a sensible and positive use of technology to help people accomplish a natural human goal.

Based on her comments, the author seems to believe assisted reproduction is a perfectly acceptable way to have children. She wouldn't agree with Choice (A); her statements in the last paragraphs show that she doesn't find much difference in the results of various reproductive techniques. Choice (B) is definitely wrong. Though the author doesn't explicitly state that the government should regulate according to ethics, she implies that the benefits of cloning outweigh the risks and that the government ban on cloning research is misplaced. She would almost certainly extend this opinion to regulation of other types of reproductive technology. Choice (C) is wrong because the author's point is that, although an imbalance in the way parents treat children conceived through assisted reproduction is a hypothetical risk, in fact, regardless of how they're conceived, all kids face parental expectations. And in any case, placing higher expectations on a child doesn't mean a parent values that child more highly. Choice (D) looks good; the author obviously thinks reproductive techniques should be allowed and that they're not all that different from normal conception. The author wouldn't agree with Choice (E); among the benefits of cloning, she includes helping same-sex or infertile couples reproduce, and if she would allow it for cloning, she would allow it for other forms of assisted reproduction. Choice (D) is the best answer.

27. E. discussing the premises of two positions and then dismissing the validity of one position because its argument relies on nonscientific considerations

The passage begins with historical context for the debate over cloning, but the author ultimately suggests that the benefits of cloning may outweigh its risks. Choice (A) is wrong. Choice (B) is also incorrect. That cloning research was banned is only mentioned in the first paragraph; the rest of the passage addresses the pros and cons of cloning rather than specific reasoning behind the administration's ban. Choice (C) is close, but the author doesn't mention specific scientific documentation during the discussion of the critics' position in the third paragraph. The author initially argues in favor of cloning, citing its benefits. At the end of the passage, the author remains largely in favor of cloning. Choice(D) is wrong. Choice (E) remains. In the first two paragraphs, the author introduces cloning and states its benefits. The third paragraph presents the premises of the critics of cloning and rejects the position based on its reliance on biased thinking and science fiction. At the end, the author suggests that a critique of cloning could be made based on physical risks, but the critics' position doesn't go there. Choice (E) is the best answer.

Section III: Analytical Reasoning

To create a game board for this grouping set of questions, consider the fact that you have two types of game pieces: instructors and types of yoga. First, abbreviate the instructors by initials: C, J, M, S, and V. Abbreviate the kinds of yoga as a, b, and i. You're grouping yoga types by the instructors who teach them, and each instructor teaches anywhere from one to three types of yoga. Keep track of this knowledge on your game board.

Write the rules in shorthand under the game board. Two and only two instructors must teach the same class or classes. M and S both teach iyengar, so add "i" under them on the game board. For the next rule, write C < J and M < J to designate that C and M teach fewer kinds of yoga than J. For the last two rules, write V = no C and its contrapositive, that C = no V, and write J = no V and its contrapositive, V = no J.

Now consider the ramifications of the rules. If C and M both teach fewer classes than J, then they must teach either one or two classes, and J must teach either two or three. But you know that J doesn't teach any classes that V teaches, which means J can't teach three classes and must teach two: create two boxes beneath J on your gameboard. Therefore, C and M must each teach one class. Record these rules on your game board by creating only one box beneath C and M. You already know that M teaches iyengar, so M never teaches ashtanga or bikram. You also know that V can teach only one class, because she doesn't overlap with J's two classes, so create one box beneath V. What about S? Well, at this point it looks like she could teach one, two, or three classes; you can't decide. Put three boxes beneath S for now. Here's what your game board may look like:

a b ī

C	J		M	S		V
			ī	ī		

2 = same
M < J; C < J
If V, then no C and no J
If C, then no V
If J, then no V

---

1. **D. Virginia teaches fewer kinds of yoga than Janice does.**

   You can answer this question by eliminating answers that must be false or could be true. Your game board reveals that Caroline and Virginia each teach one kind of yoga, so Choice (A) is wrong. You don't know how many kinds of yoga Suzanne teaches, so Choice (B) doesn't have to be true, though it could be. Suzanne might teach fewer kinds of yoga than Janice, but she doesn't have to, so Choice (C) is wrong. You know that Virginia can teach only one kind of yoga, and Janice teaches two, so Choice (D) looks right. Double-checking Choice (E), Virginia may or may not teach fewer kinds of yoga than Suzanne, so Choice (E) is wrong. Choice (D) it is.

2. **B. Janice teaches iyengar.**

   This question adds a temporary rule. If Virginia doesn't teach iyengar, she must teach either ashtanga or bikram. You know that Janice teaches the classes Virginia doesn't teach, which means Janice must teach iyengar. When you record these new conditions on your game board, it looks like this:

a b ī

C	J		M	S		V
	ī	a or b	ī	ī	a or b	÷ a or b

It looks like Choice (B) should be the answer. But you can check the other answers just in case. Janice will teach either bikram or ashtanga, whichever one Virginia doesn't teach, but you can't know which one from the given information; that knocks out both Choices (A) and (E). Marty can teach only iyengar, which eliminates Choice (C). Suzanne may be able to teach ashtanga, but she doesn't have to, which knocks out Choice (D). Choice (B) is correct.

3. **A. Caroline**

Can you eliminate any choices? You know Janice teaches two classes, so any choice including her can't be right; cross off Choice (B). You know Caroline and Virginia can't teach the same class, so cross off Choices (C) and (E). You know Marty teaches only iyengar, so cross off Choice (D). Could Caroline teach only bikram? Yes, she could teach only one kind of yoga, and it could be bikram. So the answer must be Choice (A).

4. **E. Janice, Marty, Suzanne**

You know Marty and Suzanne must teach iyengar, so you can eliminate any choice that doesn't include both of them; cross off Choices (B) and (C). Consider Choice (A) a possible right answer, but test the other choices to see if the list could be expanded; remember, you want a complete list. Could Caroline teach iyengar? No, if Caroline teaches iyengar, Virginia can't teach iyengar, but if Virginia can't teach iyengar, then Janice must teach iyengar. Choice (D) doesn't include Janice, so it's not a complete list. How about Choice (E)? Sure; if Janice teaches iyengar, she can also teach ashtanga, Caroline could teach ashtanga, too, which would leave bikram for Virginia. If Suzanne also teaches ashtanga, Suzanne and Janice satisfy the condition that two instructors teach the same yoga types. The grouping looks like this:

a b ī

C	J		M	S		V
a	ī	a	ī	ī	a	b

The answer is Choice (E).

5. **C. three**

Caroline, Marty, and Virginia must teach only one kind of yoga. Janice must teach two kinds, and you don't know about Suzanne. She could teach only one but could also teach two or three, so you can't say she must teach only one kind. The answer is three, Choice (C).

Pay attention to "must," "can" and "could," and "all/except" questions. Underline these words and think about what the right and wrong answers will mean *before* you begin working out the question. In this case, if only one "must" be true, all the other choices are merely possible or false. By thinking this through beforehand, you're less likely to jump at the first possible choice.

6. **D. Suzanne teaches bikram.**

Consider the temporary new rule offered by this question. Three instructors must teach ashtanga, so who could those three be? They can't include Marty because she teaches only iyengar. That eliminates Choice (C). The three also can't include Virginia because then neither Caroline nor Janice would be able to teach ashtanga, making it impossible to have three ashtanga teachers. So the three ashtanga teachers must be Caroline, Suzanne, and Janice. That's enough to eliminate Choices (A), (B), and (E).

There are several ways to satisfy the rule that two instructors teach the same kinds of yoga. One is to let both Janice and Suzanne teach ashtanga and iyengar. The other is to let Janice teach ashtanga and bikram, meaning that Marty and Virginia are identical in teaching only iyengar. In this scenario, Suzanne must teach ashtanga and iyengar, but it's optional whether she teaches bikram. The answer must be Choice (D), and the possible groupings look like this:

a b ī

C	J		M	S			V
a	a	ī	ī	a	ī		b
a	a	b	ī	a	ī		ī
a	a	b	ī	a	ī	b	ī

When you realize that the three ashtanga instructors have to be Suzanne, Janice, and Caroline to keep Virginia separate from both Caroline and Janice, Choices (B) and (E) can't be right and the answer must be Choice (D).

Questions 7–12

The first step in solving this grouping question set is to abbreviate all the names as initials. So you have A, B, C, D, O, S, and V. Use lowercase letters to mark Patriots and Liberators (p and l). You're going to be sorting these people into two categories, so write two headings — p and l — on your game board and record members under them.

The most important step is to explore the rules. Write them down in shorthand on your game board. Knowing that O and C don't join the same group is the same as saying that O and C occupy different groups, so when O = p, C = l and vice versa. The same is true for A and D. They can't both be p or l together. That also means that there must be a minimum of two and a maximum of five noblemen in each group. The third condition is that if D = p, S = p. The contrapositive is also true: if S = l, D = l. The fourth rule is if B = p, C and V = l, and its contrapositive is if C or V ≠ l, B = l, because whenever at least one of either C or V is p, they can't both be l. When you record the final rule that if O = p, S = l, you see an intersection with the first rule. You can conclude that when O = p, both C and S = l. The second and third rules intersect as well. If A = l, D = p and S = p. The game board looks something like this:

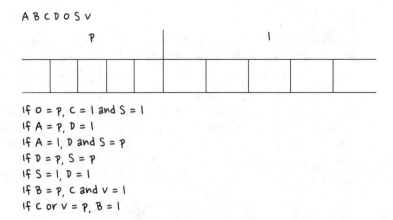

A B C D O S V

P   l

If O = p, C = l and S = l
If A = p, D = l
If A = l, D and S = p
If D = p, S = p
If S = l, D = l
If B = p, C and V = l
If C or V = p, B = l

7. **B. Brutus joins the Liberators.**

Add the temporary new rule provided by this question to the game board. Jot O down under the Liberators. That automatically puts C under the Patriots. Look at your list of rules; if C ≠ l, then B = l, so put B under the Liberators. Choice (B) must be the answer.

You can check the other answers to be sure. If Antonius joins the Liberators, Decimus and Servilius must be Patriots, and Vipsanius can be either a Patriot or Liberator. Choice (E) is wrong. If Antonius joins the Patriots, Decimus is a Liberator, so Choice (C) is wrong. Servilius or Vipsanius can be either Patriots or Liberators, so Choices (A) and (D) are wrong. Possible groupings look like this:

P				l			
C	D	S	V/__	O	B	A	V/__
C	A	S/N		O	B	D	S/N

The answer is Choice (B).

8. **E. Servilius joins the Patriots.**

According to the temporary rule posed by the questions, plug the game pieces into the appropriate groups. Eliminate answers that could or must be true. If Cassius is a Liberator, then Octavius is a Patriot. If Octavius is a Patriot, then Servilius is a Liberator. If Servilius is a Liberator, Decimus is a Liberator and Antonius is a Patriot. That leaves Brutus undecided; he could go either way. The groups look like this:

P					l				
O	A	B/__			C	V	S	D	B/__

Skimming the choices, the only one that doesn't match up is Choice (E); Servilius must be a Liberator, so that's the only false statement.

9. **A. Brutus and Cassius both join the Liberators.**

Jot down A and V under Patriots. Place the other men you know — D goes under Liberators, and so does B because V is under Patriots. Now consider your options, eliminating rule violators first. Choice (B) can go because Brutus isn't a Patriot. Choices (C) and (E) can go because Decimus can't be a Patriot. Choice (D) is definitely wrong because Cassius and Octavius can't be on the same side, which leaves Choice (A). Try Cassius as a liberator; that makes Octavius a Patriot, which makes Servilius a Liberator, like this:

P					l				
A	V	O			D	B	C	S	

Choice (A) looks good.

10. B. Antonius and Servilius

Approach this question by applying the rules to each answer one at a time, until you've placed everyone. Put A and O in the Liberator group. If Antonius is a Liberator, then Decimus is a Patriot. If Decimus is a Patriot, then Servilius is a Patriot. If Octavius is a Liberator, then Cassius is a Patriot. If Cassius is a Patriot, then Brutus is a Liberator, and Vipsanius could go either way. That works, so Choice (A) is possible. Your groups look like this:

	P					I				
(A)	D	S	C	V/__		A	O	B	V/__	

Try Choice (B), A and S as Liberators. If Antonius is a Liberator, then Decimus must be a Patriot, which means Servilius must be a Patriot, so Antonius and Servilius can't both be Liberators. Choice (B) is the answer. If you're confident, go ahead and leave it at that; if you have time, work through the rest of the possibilities to be sure you haven't missed something.

Choice (C) gives you this roster of Liberators: Antonius, Vipsanius, Octavius, and Brutus. It gives you these Patriots: Decimus, Servilius, and Cassius. How? If Antonius is a Liberator, Decimus must be a Patriot, which makes Servilius a Patriot, which makes Octavius a Liberator, which makes Cassius a Patriot, which makes Brutus a Liberator. Choice (D) gives you these Liberators: Cassius, Vipsanius, Servilius, and Decimus. It gives you these Patriots: Octavius, Antonius, and Brutus. How? If Cassius is a Liberator, then Octavius is a Patriot, which makes Servilius a Liberator, Decimus a Liberator, and Antonius a Patriot. Cassius and Vipsanius are both Liberators, which makes Brutus a Patriot, too. Choice (E) gives you this roster of Liberators: Octavius, Servilius, Decimus, and Brutus. It gives you these Patriots: Cassius and Antonius. Vipsanius could be either. If Octavius is a Liberator, Cassius is a Patriot, which makes Brutus a Liberator. If Servilius is a Liberator, Decimus must be a Liberator. Vipsanius could go on either side.

The possible groupings for the last three answer choices are these:

	P					I				
(C)	D	S	C			A	V	O	B	
(D)	O	A	B			C	V	S	D	
(E)	C	A	V/__			O	S	D	B	V/__

11. D. four

Based on work in previous questions, you can immediately eliminate Choices (A) and (B); you already know you can have at least three Patriots. See if you can concoct a roster with five Patriots (because you're looking for a maximum, and five is the largest number the answer choices offer). Try making Decimus and Servilius Patriots, which forces Antonius to be a Liberator. Brutus isn't a good choice for a Patriot, because he forces Cassius and Vipsanius over to the Liberators, so instead make Cassius and Vipsanius Patriots and let Brutus be a Liberator. That makes Octavius a Liberator, too, because he doesn't play on the same team as Cassius. There doesn't seem to be any way to get five guys onto the Patriots, but you know you can do four. That makes the answer Choice (D).

12. A. Antonius, Cassius, Vipsanius

Look for obvious rule violations first. Antonius and Decimus can't be on the same side, which nixes Choice (B). Making Servilius a Patriot forces Octavius to be a Liberator, which nixes Choice (C). Now try the others. For Choice (A), if Antonius is a Patriot, then Decimus is a Liberator. If Cassius is a Patriot, then Octavius and Brutus are both Liberators. You can make Servilius a Liberator without violating any rules, so Choice (A) is a good choice. Now try Choice (D). If Decimus is a Patriot, then Servilius must also be a Patriot. Servilius isn't in that list, so Choice (D) is wrong. Now for Choice (E): If Decimus is a Patriot, then Antonius must be a Liberator. If Servilius is a Patriot, then Octavius must be a Liberator. If Vipsanius is a Patriot, then Brutus must be a Liberator. Cassius can't be in Octavius's group, so Cassius must be a Patriot, so the list in Choice (E) isn't complete. The answer is Choice (A).

Questions 13–18

This ordering problem is pretty straightforward, but it can be tricky if you don't sketch it out correctly. As always, start your game board by abbreviating your game pieces: A, C, E, F, H, and O. You have to put the plays in order by days of the week, so make the days the foundation of the game board: Write T, W, R, F, Sa, Su across the page, leaving space underneath to fill in information. You know H must be performed on Thursday, so record that in the Thursday column.

Now consider the other rules. If A comes after O, A doesn't play on Tuesday and O doesn't play on Sunday. Record this information on your game board, and write the rule underneath as O → A. The third rule states that at least one play comes between A and F. It doesn't say that A must come before F. F could come before A, but there will still be at least a one-day break between them. You can record this rule as "no AF or FA" on the game board. The last rule is similar. You know that C and F don't play consecutively, but you also know that exactly one play separates their performances. You can record this rule as C_F or F_C.

Take a look at your game board. Because H is scheduled for Thursday, you know neither C nor F can be performed on Tuesday or Saturday. So Tuesday's only options are E and O and Saturday's performance can be only A, E, or O. Record this information on your game board, like so:

A C E F H O

T	W	R	F	Sa	Su
~~A~~				~~C~~	~~O~~
~~C~~				~~F~~	
~~F~~					
E O		H		A E O	

O → A
No AF or FA
C_F or F_C

13. D. *Orestes, Frogs, Helen, Clouds, Antigone, Electra*

Answering the first question in the set is usually as simple as working through the rules to find which option doesn't create a violation. Check answers for violations of the first rule. Which choice has *Helen* on a day other than Thursday? Choice (E) does, so you can cross it off. Consider the second rule. Choice (A) has *Orestes* perform before *Antigone,* so it's wrong. Does any choice put *Antigone* and *Frogs* next to each other? Choice (B) does, so eliminate it.

Choice (C) violates the final rule by failing to separate *Clouds* and *Frogs* by exactly one day. That leaves Choice (D), which observes all the rules and is therefore correct.

14. **D. Either *Clouds* or *Frogs* is performed on Friday.**

The question asks for what must be true, so eliminate answers that could be true or must be false. The play with the most restrictions is *Frogs*, so first consider the two choices that include *Frogs*. *Clouds* and *Frogs* can be performed only on Wednesday, Friday, or Sunday. There must be one and only one day between them. The only way to accomplish that is to perform either *Clouds* or *Frogs* on Wednesday and Friday or on Friday and Sunday. Either way, you have to perform either *Clouds* or *Frogs* on Friday. You can add this information to your game board for future questions. That makes the answer Choice (D).

15. **E. *Orestes***

This question is pretty simple. What play must be performed before another play? *Orestes* must come before *Antigone*, which means that *Orestes* can never be performed on Sunday. The answer is Choice (E).

16. **C. *Electra* and *Orestes* are performed on consecutive days, with no other play between them.**

Sketch out the possibilities presented by the answer choices on your game board. Eliminate those that could or must be true. Try Choice (A). If you put *Orestes* on Tuesday and *Antigone* the next day, Wednesday, there's room for *Helen* on Thursday, *Clouds* on Friday, *Electra* on Saturday, and *Frogs* on Sunday. Choice (A) is possible and therefore incorrect. Try Choice (B). The ordering possibility that worked for Choice (A) also works for Choice (B), so it can't be right either. Consider Choice (C). Friday is reserved for *Clouds* or *Frogs*, so it's off limits, as is Thursday. You could put *Electra* and *Orestes* on Tuesday and Wednesday, *Frogs* on Friday, and *Clouds* on Sunday, but that would force *Antigone* next to *Frogs*, which is forbidden. If you put *Electra* and *Orestes* on Saturday and Sunday, that would place *Orestes* after *Antigone*, which is also a rule violation. Choice (C) must be false. Just to make sure you haven't missed something, you may wish to consider the other possibilities. You know Choice (E) is possible from the ordering you used for Choices (A) and (B). If you put *Orestes* on Tuesday and *Frogs* next to it on Wednesday, there's space for *Helen* on Thursday, *Clouds* on Friday, and *Antigone* and *Electra* on Saturday and Sunday. Choices (D) and (E) are possible, so they can't be right. The possible orders for Choices (A), (B), (D), and (E) could look like this:

ACEFHO

	T	W	R	F	Sa	Su
	~~A~~ ~~C~~ ~~F~~ E O		H	~~A~~ ~~E~~ ~~O~~ C or F	~~C~~ ~~F~~ A E O	~~O~~
(A), (B) & (E)	O	A	H	C	E	F
(D)	O	F	H	C	A	E

O → A
No AF or FA
C _ F or F _ C

The answer is Choice (C).

17. **D. Wednesday, Friday, Sunday**

You know from your game board that the possible performance dates for *Frogs* are Wednesday, Friday, and Sunday, so you can eliminate any choice that has a day other than those three: Choices (A), (B), and (E). Double-check Sunday to make sure it really can work for *Frogs*. If you put *Frogs* on Sunday, *Clouds* plays on Friday. To avoid scheduling *Antigone* next to *Frogs*, put *Orestes* on Tuesday and *Antigone* on Wednesday, which leaves Thursday open for *Helen* and Saturday available for *Electra*. *Frogs* can definitely play on Sunday. The answer is Choice (D).

18. **B. *Electra* is performed on Wednesday.**

Based on your answers to other questions, you know that *Frogs* and *Clouds* can be performed on Wednesday, so cross off Choices (A) and (C). Try Choice (B). If *Electra* is performed on Wednesday, then *Clouds* and *Frogs* must be performed on Friday and Sunday. But you run into a problem. With *Helen* on Thursday, only Tuesday and Saturday remain for the performances of *Orestes* and *Antigone*. If you put *Orestes* on Tuesday, *Antigone* gets stuck next to *Frogs* on Saturday. If you put *Antigone* in the Tuesday spot, *Orestes* improperly performs after *Antigone*. Either way you violate a rule, as shown in this potential ordering:

A C E F H O

T	W	R	F	Sa	Su
~~A~~ ~~C~~ ~~F~~ E O		H	~~A~~ ~~E~~ ~~O~~ C or F	~~C~~ ~~F~~ A E O	~~O~~
O/A	E	H	C/F	O/A	C/F

O → A
No AF or FA
C_F or F_C

Choice (B) is your answer. The last two choices work and therefore can't be right. Put O on Tuesday and several acceptable schedules result, such as O, F, H, C, A, E or O, A, H, C, E, F. With O performed on Saturday, you could have the schedule look like this: E, C, H, F, O, A. The answer is Choice (B).

Questions 19–25

This question set involves grouping attorneys with specialties. Because there will always be only four specialties, and attorneys have multiple specialties, this grouping problem is the more complex, open type.

Begin arranging your game board by listing the game pieces. There are four attorneys: B, C, D, and H. The four possible areas of law are e, i, r, and t.

At most each attorney specializes in three of the four areas. As you read the rules, notice that they specify exactly how many attorneys practice each specialization. This tells you that it may be easier to set up your game board with the spots for attorneys listed under each specialty. Put one spot under tax, two under employment and real estate, and three under immigration.

Now consider the other two conditions. The first rule is the same as saying "if C then D." The contrapositive is also true: If no D, then no C. It does *not* mean that if D specializes in the area of law, then C does. The other rule is that "if C, no B and no H." The contrapositive is "if B and H, then no C." Write these rule shortcuts on your game board so that it looks something like this:

t	e	r	i		

B C D H

1 ≤ areas of law ≤ 3

If C, then D

If no D, then no C

If C, no B

If C, no H

If B, no C

If H, no C

You may come up with a few other deductions that will make your thinking process easier as you answer questions about this problem. First, if D must share C's specialties, then C is never the sole specialist in an area. That means C can't specialize in tax. Second, if C can't share a specialty with B or H, that means the only three attorneys who can specialize in the same area must be B, H, and D. They must be the three who specialize in immigration. Third, C must be paired with D in any specialty, and only the two of them can specialize in that particular area, which means that they must practice either employment or real estate law, because those areas need exactly two attorneys. This information is valuable; note it on your game board:

B C D H

t	e	r	i		
~~C~~				B	H	D

1 ≤ areas of law ≤ 3

If C, then D

If no D, then no C

If C, no B

If C, no H

If B, no C

If H, no C

19. C. Duway does not specialize in tax law.

Eliminate answers that could be true or must be false. You know from your game board that Duway has to specialize in immigration. You also know that Duway must specialize in either employment or real estate, but it doesn't matter which one. That puts Burton or Howard in tax, and Burton and Howard in either employment or real estate. Working out the possible combinations on your game board looks like this:

B C D H

t	e		r		i		
~~C~~					B	H	D
B/H	C	D	B	H	B	H	D
B/H	B	H	C	D	B	H	D

1 ≤ areas of law ≤ 3

If C, then D

If no D, then no C

If C, no B

If C, no H

If B, no C

If H, no C

C/D = e or r

Looking at the choices, Choice (A) is wrong because B can specialize in tax if H doesn't. Choice (B) is wrong because it could be true that C specializes in employment law with D. Choice (C) must be right because D can't specialize in tax. To double-check your answer, check the last two choices. Choice (D) is wrong because H can specialize in employment, and Choice (E) is wrong because H, like B, can specialize in tax. So Choice (C) is correct.

20. D. Duway specializes in more areas of law than Cheatham.

You already know one attorney who must specialize in more areas than another: Duway must specialize in more areas than Cheatham because Duway must specialize in immigration. It looks like the answer must be Choice (D). Check the other possibilities if you have time. Burton can specialize in more areas of law than Cheatham but doesn't have to, so Choice (A) is wrong. Howard can specialize in more areas of law than Duway but doesn't have to, so Choice (B) is wrong. Duway can specialize in more areas than Howard but doesn't have to, so Choice (C) is wrong. Burton can specialize in more areas than Howard, but then Howard can also specialize in more areas than Burton, so Choice (E) is wrong. Choice (D) it is.

21. B. Burton

The way to approach this exception question is to eliminate answers that present a complete and accurate list of attorneys who can specialize in both employment and immigration. You know Duway specializes in immigration and could also specialize in employment law with Cheatham, so the correct answer isn't Choice (A). Consider Burton alone in Choice (B). You already know Burton practices immigration law. When you add Burton to employment law, you have to pair him with someone. If you pair him with either Howard or Duway, the complete list of immigration and employment specialists would also have to include either Howard or Duway because both of them also practice immigration law. You can't pair Burton with Cheatham as an employment law specialist because that violates the "if C, then D" rule. You can't eliminate Choice (B).

You *can* eliminate Choice (C) because Burton and Howard have to practice immigration law and easily could be the only attorneys to practice employment law. Likewise, Burton and Duway must practice immigration law and could be the two attorneys who practice employment law. Cheatham and Duway would then be the real estate attorneys, and Howard or Burton would practice tax law. Cross out Choice (D). The same is true for the combination of Howard and Duway, so Choice (E) is out. The possible combinations for each of the answer choices look like this on your game board:

B C D H

	t	e		r		i		
	~~€~~					B	H	D
(A)	B/H	C	D	B	H	B	H	D
(B)		B				B	H	D
(C)	D	B	H	C	D	B	H	D
(D)	H/B	B	D	C	D	B	H	D
(E)	H/B	H	D	C	D	B	H	D

1 ≤ areas of law ≤ 3
If C, then D
If no D, then no C
If C, no B
If C, no H
If B, no C
If H, no C
C/D = e or r

Choice (B) is the only answer you can't eliminate.

22. D. Howard specializes in tax law.

The only two areas of law that Cheatham can specialize in are employment and real estate. If Cheatham occupies those areas, so does Duway. Those two specialties with immigration give Duway the maximum three specialties, so Burton or Howard must specialize in tax. Your diagram looks like this:

t	e		v		i		
~~t~~					B	H	D
B/H	C	D	C	D	B	H	D

Now read the choices and see which answer could be true. Eliminate answers that must be false. Choice (A) is false because Duway can't specialize in tax. Choice (B) is false because Duway must specialize in three areas. Choice (C) is false because Howard can't specialize in employment. Choice (D) may be true because Howard can specialize in tax. Choice (E) is false because Howard can't specialize in three areas of law. Choice (D) is the only one that can be true, and it's your answer.

23. **C. Burton specializes in tax law.**

Consider the temporary rule this question adds. If Burton is to specialize in three fields, one of them must be immigration. You know Cheatham and Duway specialize in either employment or real estate law, so Burton can specialize in one of those but not both, which excludes Choices (A) and (B). Burton must specialize in tax law to get a third specialty. It looks like Choice (C) is the answer. Choice (E) is wrong because Howard can't specialize in tax law when Burton does. Choice (D) is wrong, too, because you don't know anything about Howard aside from the fact that he must specialize in immigration. Howard could specialize in employment law along with Burton but doesn't have to; Burton could share the employment law specialty with Duway just as easily. Choice (C) is correct.

24. **C. The attorney also specializes in real estate but not in immigration.**

From your original game board, you know that the only attorneys who can specialize in tax are Burton, Duway, and Howard; these three also happen to be the attorneys who must specialize in immigration. Any answer choice that doesn't have the attorney specifically specializing in immigration must be false, and because you're looking for something that *can't* be true, that would be the right answer. Do any choices say that the attorney doesn't specialize in immigration? Yes, Choice (C). That's the answer, but if you want to test the other propositions, you can use Burton as a hypothetical. Can Burton specialize in immigration but not in real estate? Yes, if Cheatham and Duway take real estate, so Choice (A) is wrong. Can Burton specialize in both immigration and real estate? Yes, if Cheatham and Duway take employment, so Choice (B) is wrong. Can Burton specialize in employment but not real estate? Yes, if Cheatham and Duway take real estate, so Choice (D) is wrong. Can Burton specialize in neither employment nor real estate? Yes, Cheatham and Duway can possibly take both of these specialties. Choice (C) is the only answer that can't be true.

25. **C. Duway specializes in three areas: employment, immigration, and real estate.**

Look for rule violations. You know Burton can't share specialties with Cheatham, and you know that Cheatham must specialize in either employment or real estate. Choices (A) and (B) have Burton specializing in both of those specialties, which is impossible. Can Duway specialize in employment, immigration, and real estate? Yes, consider Choice (C) a good prospect. Choices (D) and (E) are easy to eliminate because both Duway and Howard must specialize in immigration law, and neither answer includes immigration law in the list of their three specialties. Choice (C) is correct.

Section IV: Logical Reasoning

1. **C. These soccer shoes must be the best because all the best soccer players use them, and the best players wear only the best shoes.**

   The question asks you to identify the argument's pattern of reasoning. You know that the reasoning is flawed because the question tells you so. So what's the flaw? This argument's reasoning is circular: The car seat is safest because the most conscientious parents bought it; they're the most conscientious because they bought the car seat that claims to be safest. No external evidence is available; each half of the argument depends on the other half to support it. So look for an answer that has two conclusions, each of which depends on the other conclusion for support.

   Choice (A) is wrong. A taste test is a perfectly good indicator of a soft drink's good taste, so this reasoning isn't flawed. Choice (B) is wrong, though it may look a bit like the argument. The difference is that attending a good preschool could help kids do better in elementary school, so the conclusion in the second statement isn't circular; it's just a repetition of the reasonable conclusion in the first sentence (the two don't depend on each other). Choice (C) does duplicate the reasoning in the argument. The writer bases the claim that the soccer shoes are the best on the fact that the best soccer players use them and justifies the claim that those players are the best with the evidence that the best players wear only the best shoes. That's completely circular, so Choice (C) looks like a good answer. Choice (D) is wrong because it makes sense; the fact that technologically savvy people use a particular browser is valid evidence that a browser is good, and the argument doesn't use the fact that these people buy this browser to prove that they're technologically savvy. Choice (E) is also wrong; if the curl-enhancing lotion really works for curly haired people, then maybe it is the best. Choice (C) is the right answer.

2. **A. Homeowners with interest-only mortgages won't accumulate equity based on the increasing value of their homes.**

   This logical reasoning question requires you to identify the assumption or, in other words, determine which statement connects the premises to the conclusion. As a general rule, assumptions are not directly stated in the premises, and you have to accept that the stated premises are true, regardless of whether there is evidence to back them up in the text.

   Locate the answer choice that best links the premises to the conclusion that interest-only mortgages should be eliminated because buyers will never accumulate equity. You can eliminate Choice (B) because it mentions a concept that's too general and that appears in only the conclusion and not the premises. Choices (C) and (D) are, in essence, restatements of the premises, so they can't be assumptions that provide a link to the conclusion. Choice (E) may at first seem plausible, but notice that this assumption is about homeowners in general, not only homeowners who take out interest-only loans. The author doesn't assume that all homeowners can't afford to pay the principal on their home loans. This answer doesn't directly link the possibility of defaulting due to lack of equity to the conclusion that interest-only mortgages should be eliminated entirely. The only assumption listed on which the conclusion depends is Choice (A). If the author wants to discontinue interest-only loans because they lead to loan default due to lack of equity, he must assume that the only way to build equity is by paying loan principal and not by benefiting from increases in the home's market value.

3. **A. Healthy human beings always anticipate the sounds of their own voices and differentiate them from other voices.**

   You may have noticed at some point in your life that it's virtually impossible to tickle yourself. If not, go ahead and try it — you'll see. Note that the question asks you to make an inference that extends the reasoning in the statements.

You're seeking an answer that logically flows from one of the premises but isn't stated directly. Choice (B), while appealing, goes too far. The passage states that anticipating the sensation of tickling is true for "normal, healthy human beings," but others may exist who can tickle themselves. Eliminate Choice (C) because the argument doesn't allude to future research at all. Choice (D) inappropriately extends the information regarding schizophrenics (that they can't recognize their own voices) to a healthy human. Choice (E) contradicts the assertion in the passage that humans feel a heightened sense of another's touch when they simultaneously tickle themselves with another, so it can't be correct, either. Choice (A) is supported by the premise that healthy humans can't mistake their voices and provides a reason that the passage suggests (with the information in the last sentence that schizophrenics don't recognize their voices because they don't anticipate the sound of their voices) but doesn't state directly.

4. **C. confuses the defense's failure to prove that someone else committed the crime with proof that the accused is guilty**

The question asks you to spot the flaw in the argument's reasoning. What is that flaw? The prosecutor says that the defense hasn't proven that someone else committed the crime, thus proving that the accused did commit it. That's wrong. Even if you don't know about the principle of "innocent until proven guilty," failing to show who did commit a crime isn't the same as proving that the accused did commit it. Look for an answer that shows the prosecutor's confusion of the defense's inability to furnish the proper criminal with evidence of the accused's guilt.

Choice (A) is wrong because the argument doesn't mention any evidence of the accused's innocence. Some evidence may exist, and the prosecutor may be ignoring it, but if it's not in the argument, you can't put it in an answer. Choice (B) is wrong because the prosecutor does name a flaw in the defense's arguments: The defense has failed to prove that someone else committed the crime. Whether or not that is a valid criticism is beside the point. Choice (C) is exactly what you're looking for; it looks like the right answer. Choice (D) is a bit tricky because the defense has agreed that the crime did occur, but the prosecutor isn't trying to use this admission as proof that the defendant committed the crime. Rather it's the defense's inability to pin the crime on someone else that the prosecutor provides as proof of the accused's guilt. Choice (E) is wrong. Whether the prosecutor has considered that someone else may have committed the crime isn't really the point. The prosecutor is trying to prove that the accused is guilty and has some evidence to back that up. The possibility that someone else committed the crime is irrelevant. The flaw isn't in the prosecutor's case; it's in the prosecutor's critique of the defense's case. Choice (C) is the correct answer.

5. **E. As the Basin and Range area continues to sink, Phoenix, Arizona, will become drier, while areas to the north will receive more moisture.**

You're tasked with drawing a conclusion from the premises. An appropriate conclusion covers all the information in the premises and doesn't include any outside information. There isn't enough information in the paragraph to draw the conclusion in Choice (A). It says Phoenix is low but still states that its elevation is 1,100 feet, which is more than 1,000 feet above sea level. The argument isn't about the expansion of the region but rather its sinking, so Choice (B) isn't right. Choice (D) addresses the compression of the Earth's crust, while the passage says that expansion causes the region to sink, so Choice (D) can't be a conclusion. Choices (C) and (E) come up with opposite conclusions, but the one that's supported by the passage is Choice (E), so eliminate Choice (C). Choice (E) correctly implies, based on the pattern described in the last sentence of the premises, that the sinking will continue in the southern area, making the climate drier and passing even more moisture to the north. Therefore, you can conclude from the premises that the southern area will continue to get drier.

6. **B. Even after hundreds of years of use, names like Patrick, Seamus, and Sean are still not truly Irish.**

This argument provides reasons for the choosing of Irish boys' names. The author explains that many names thought to be traditionally Irish were actually imposed on the Irish by Anglo-Norman invaders. The question asks you to make an inference based on the statements.

Choice (A) is wrong; the argument indicates that the Anglo-Norman invasion introduced non-traditional names to Ireland, but that doesn't mean the invasion marked the end of traditional Irish names. The passage says that parents are free to name their children Cathal, Aodh, and Brian, but that doesn't necessarily mean parents actually choose these names, so Choice (C) is wrong. Choices (D) and (E) contain information that isn't stated in the premises, so you also don't have enough information to infer them from the premises. Concluding that Irish parents prefer the most traditional names available is beyond the scope of the argument as is making value judgments regarding criminal laws in Ireland. The only answer choice that works is Choice (B). If the author of the argument speaks of traditional names as those that were Irish before the 12th century, the author must think that Seamus, Sean, and Patrick are not traditional names.

7. **D. Americans have universally adapted to the QWERTY keyboard and aren't interested in learning an entirely new system.**

The question asks you to weaken the conclusion that everyone would buy keyboards with efficient key arrangements if they were available. To weaken this conclusion, you need to choose an answer that gives a reason why people wouldn't want the new keyboard. Choice (A) moderately weakens the conclusion by implying that the human brain is capable of adapting to the QWERTY keyboard, but it doesn't weaken the idea that consumers will flock to a more efficient arrangement. Choice (B) actually strengthens the conclusion somewhat by arguing that the justification for the QWERTY keyboard no longer exists. Choice (C) is out because the presence of more keys on the computer keyboard doesn't necessarily mean that the keys can't be arranged efficiently and that people wouldn't want to use the resulting efficient arrangement. Choice (E) neither strengthens nor weakens the argument, so you can eliminate that one, too. It may take a lot of testing to develop the new keyboard, but that doesn't prove that people wouldn't want it.

Choice (D) provides the strongest rebuttal to the notion that everyone will want the new keyboard. If people have used the QWERTY system for their entire lives, they aren't likely to want to learn a whole new keyboard arrangement and therefore won't buy the new keyboards.

8. **A. The price of a gallon of gasoline that is quoted at the pump and on gas station signs includes all fuel taxes and fees.**

This question requires you to weaken the conclusion that the quoted price for travel expenses isn't the final price. To weaken this conclusion, you should find an area of travel that doesn't include hidden fees. Choices (C), (D), and (E) point out scenarios in which hidden fees exist (inside and outside of travel), so they don't at all weaken the argument. Choice (B) points out the fact that some final prices are actually lower than the quoted price, but the final price is still different from the quoted price, so Choice (B) also strengthens the argument. Choice (A) points out one instance involving travel where the final price is the same as the advertised price. This finding weakens the conclusion that there isn't "one aspect of traveling where the quoted price is the final price." Choice (A) is the best answer of the five.

9. **D. It confuses a correlation with causation.**

The author asserts that the drop in the number of cigarette smokers has been caused by the increase in advertisements warning against smoking. Without proof that other factors didn't contribute to the decrease in smoking, the increase in advertising and the decrease in smoking is, at most, a correlation. Choice (D) is the best answer. Choice (A) is wrong because the argument doesn't contain personal stories. Choice (B) is wrong because the author doesn't directly compare circumstances from three years ago to present-day realities. No experiment is mentioned, so Choice (C) is wrong. Choice (E) is wrong because the author never argues that all people stopped smoking. Choice (D) is correct.

10. **A. The mandatory fitness classes will improve the physical health of Claar & Carlisle's employees.**

This question requires you to identify the assumption. The assumption is often the statement that links the last premise to the conclusion, so home in on the argument's premises and conclusion.

To make this argument, the author states the premise that better physical health equals greater productivity. The author's conclusion is that Claar & Carlisle should have mandatory fitness classes, so look for the assumption that links better physical health to mandatory fitness programs. That would be Choice (A). You can eliminate Choices (B) and (D) because they require you to read too much into the argument, which doesn't necessarily rely on the assumption that these morning classes are the absolute best way to improve health and productivity. That is, you can't know that the author assumes that morning workouts are better than evening workouts. The reason the author advocates mandatory morning workouts may be that mornings are more convenient than evenings. And the argument doesn't mention nutrition classes, so you can't know how the author feels about them. Choice (E) is wrong because the argument says nothing about the value of sleep or its link to good physical health and productivity. There may be a link, but it's not made in this argument. Finally, whether employees resent mandatory programs is irrelevant to the conclusion that fitness programs would actually increase employee productivity, so you can forget about Choice (C). Stick with Choice (A).

11. **C. Some former members of Rising Stars contribute to the dance school because they enjoy attending the annual showcase.**

This question asks for an underlying assumption. Generally, the best answer for an assumption question is the choice that links an element of the last premise to the author's conclusion.

The last premise of this argument is that the annual dance showcase was canceled. The conclusion is that donations will go down. So find the answer choice that links the canceled concert to a decrease in donations. Eliminate Choice (A) right away because it simply restates one of the premises. An assumption, by definition, isn't a direct assertion. You can cross out Choices (B) and (D); both reference what will likely happen next year. Nothing in the argument points to events that will happen next year. It's concerned only with this year's possibilities. Choice (E) is backward. It links donations to the annual showcase rather than the other way around. The only answer that connects the occurrence of the holiday concert to donation amounts is Choice (C). If donations will decrease as a result of the lack of an annual showcase, there must be at least some segment of the donor population who give to the organization based on the occurrence of the showcase.

12. C. **The majority of the customers who have spent in excess of $500 on a single rental since the fuel discounts began are regular customers who now make lengthier but less frequent rental arrangements.**

Approach this problem methodically. First, isolate the claim you're supposed to weaken. The executives claim that the fuel discount program has been massively successful, so you're supposed to weaken the claim that the program has been successful. The basis for the claim is the increase in single rentals of $500 or more.

Eliminate answers that suggest the program has indeed been successful. Choices (A), (B), and (E) present positive outcomes of the program and therefore strengthen rather than weaken the executives' claim.

The remaining choices are Choices (C) and (D). Choice (D) concerns only those customers who spend less than $500 per rental. It says nothing about customers who spend more. Perhaps the program has been successful because of new customers or because it has provided incentives to customers who normally spend more than $500 per rental at other companies to switch their business to Exploration. So the best answer is Choice (C). If the increase in $500 single rentals is primarily due to a switch in the rental practices of regular customers, Exploration will experience no increase in overall earnings. When the Joe Citizen changes from spending $250 on two separate rentals at Exploration to spending $500 on one single rental, the company's overall sales numbers don't change.

13. E. **Parents who care for their child full time immediately after birth when the child is most vulnerable are likely to develop a stronger emotional connection with the child than parents who do not.**

This question isn't particularly difficult if you keep in mind exactly what it asks for. It's often easier to answer questions that require you to find an exception by rephrasing them. In this case, you're looking for the answer that doesn't rebut the argument. It's likely the choice that reinforces the argument that paid family leave should be mandatory for new parents.

Choice (A) calls into question whether the leave would achieve the goal of creating meaningful relationships between parents and their children, while Choice (B) shows that the leave isn't necessary for establishing meaningful relationships. Choice (C) questions whether the government has the right to mandate family leave. Choice (D) casts doubt on whether the mandated leave is sufficient to realize its purpose as a decision-making tool. That leaves Choice (E), which actually strengthens the argument by reinforcing that family leave may indeed result in meaningful relationships between parents and their children.

14. A. **Taxes on a scarf imported from Taiwan to the United States are less than 35 percent of the cost of manufacturing the scarf in the United States.**

The point of the argument concerns saving on the cost of scarf production. Eliminate Choice (D) immediately because it concerns production time rather than production cost. Likewise, get rid of Choice (C) because it relates to job reduction, not production costs. Eliminate any choices that contradict the statement that it's more cost effective to produce scarves in Taiwan. If transportation costs wipe out the amount the manufacturer saves in production costs, manufacturing in Taiwan isn't cost effective. So Choice (B) is out. That leaves Choices (A) and (E). Both substantiate the claim that manufacturing in Taiwan is more cost effective, but Choice (E) regards labor costs, and the argument doesn't identify what component of production in Taiwan lowers the overall costs. Therefore, the best answer is Choice (A). If producing a scarf in Taiwan is more profitable for the company than producing it in the United States, the taxes on the scarf coming from Taiwan have to be less than the 35 percent saved by producing it there.

15. **E. Music is meaningful when it is creative and inventive.**

   Assumption questions ask you to find the missing premise. If distinguishing among the answer choices for an assumption question overwhelms you, concentrate on the argument's premises and conclusion. The answer that links the last premise to the conclusion is usually the correct answer.

   The conclusion is that music has lost much of its creativity and artistry. It bases this assertion on three premises:

   - Musicians focus more on making a profit than they did before digital downloads and MP3 music sharing.

   - Musicians focus more on attracting technologically savvy fans than they did before digital downloads and MP3 music sharing.

   - Musicians focus less on producing quality, meaningful music than they did before digital downloads and MP3 music sharing.

   The answer that connects the idea that musicians are focusing less on making meaningful music to the conclusion that music is less creative and artistic is Choice (E). For the author to draw the conclusion that music is less creative based on the premise that music is less meaningful, the author must assume that creativity and artistry are what make music meaningful. Choices (A) and (B) don't relate to the conclusion about the innate creativity and artistry of digital music, so they can't be assumptions. Choice (C) is merely a restatement of one of the premises. The argument doesn't go into what makes music popular; its concern is the changing focus of musicians. Therefore, the author's conclusion isn't dependent on what makes music popular, and Choice (D) can't be correct. Stick with Choice (E).

16. **E. The ratio of male to female employees at Goodman-Horning is about the same as the ratio of male to female job applicants.**

   To counter the claim that it discriminates against women, Goodman-Horning would have to show that there is a reason other than gender-biased hiring practices for the discrepancy between the number of men and the number of women who work there. Choices (A) and (C) address only the current employees and therefore shed no light on the company's practices concerning prospective employees. They don't answer the question about why there aren't more women. Choice (D) could account for the discrepancy among executives, but it doesn't say anything about the difference in the number of male and female staff members. Choice (B) essentially states that similar companies have the same male to female employee ratio, but that doesn't prove that Goodman-Horning doesn't discriminate. Maybe all companies similar to Goodman-Horning discriminate against females. Choice (E) is the choice that offers another explanation for the discrepancy at Goodman-Horning. If the company has significantly fewer female applicants for its jobs, it may not have a choice to hire more women.

17. **B. Motorcycle insurance rates for all motorcycle owners have risen by 5 percent over the last decade to offset the medical costs associated with head injuries incurred by motorcycle riders who fail to wear helmets.**

   Focus on the exact nature of the conclusion you're supposed to weaken. Notice that you're supposed to weaken the argument *against* helmet mandates, and the opponents to helmet requirements say that they should be able to go without wearing a helmet because their behavior doesn't potentially hurt anyone but themselves. The answer that deals a blow to that assertion is Choice (B). It reveals that others are, in fact, negatively affected because they have to pay more in insurance rates. Choices (A) and (E) provide reasons why wearing a helmet is a good idea, but they don't specifically address the reasoning of the opponents to helmet requirements, which is focused on the right to take the safety risks, not on denying risks exist. Whether governments do or don't require helmets for motorcycle riders has nothing to do with whether they *should* have those requirements, so Choices (C) and (D) aren't relevant in weakening the opponents' argument. Choice (B) is best.

18. **A. The level of discretion and common sense people exhibit when they use social media directly mirrors their use of the same in day-to-day personal and business interactions.**

You approach questions that ask you to strengthen the argument in the same way you approach questions that ask you to weaken the argument. Isolate the argument you're supposed to strengthen and examine the method it uses to reach a conclusion.

The question asks you to strengthen the executives' position that they have the right to request access to potential employees' social media pages. You don't know why executives feel this way, but you *do* know that their opponents claim that social media pages don't reveal information that's pertinent to job performance. If you can weaken this claim, you'll strengthen the executives' position. Look for answers that show that a correlation does indeed exist between an employee's social media pages and the way that employee performs on the job.

Choice (B) regards social media use and how that reveals something about the user, but it doesn't address access to the content of an individual's private pages, nor does it directly refer to attributes that would affect employment. Choice (C) weakens the executives' position, so it's clearly wrong. Choices (D) and (E) don't specifically address the propriety of allowing employer access to social media pages, so they're not as good as other answers that do regard that issue. The correct answer is Choice (A) because it directly challenges the proponents' assertion that what people post and how they behave through social media is no indication of how they'd perform on the job.

19. **B. Women are not choosing elective Cesarean section deliveries for cosmetic and other personal reasons.**

This question draws the conclusion that the cause of the increased percentage of expensive Cesarean section procedures is that hospitals want to make money and don't care about patients. To reach this conclusion, the author would have to assume that it's the hospitals that are dictating whether a mother delivers by Cesarean section and not the mother herself. You can eliminate Choice (A). The argument depends on a percentage of births, so total numbers are irrelevant. Choice (C) restates the conclusion and therefore isn't an assumption. Choice (D) doesn't affect the conclusion, so it can't be a relevant assumption. That leaves Choices (B) and (E). Of the two, Choice (B) presents the underlying assumption that hospitals and not mothers are choosing the birth method. Choice (E), comparison of the number of surgeons, is irrelevant. Choice (B) is correct.

20. **A. At the same time that businesses began imposing stiffer sanctions for employee theft, the average number of employees per business increased.**

The conclusion of this weaken-the-argument question is that penalties don't work, and the proof is that the number of thefts hasn't gone down. You weaken the argument by showing that the reason for the static number of employee thefts is something other than the failure of the stiffer penalties.

Choice (B) actually strengthens the conclusion. If businesses have fewer employees overall, you'd expect the number of employee thefts to also decrease.

You can eliminate Choice (C) because it isn't specific enough to allow you to determine that a different definition of theft would affect the number of employee theft incidents (you don't know whether the more recent definition is stricter or more lenient). Choice (E) is out because it's irrelevant. Choice (D) addresses theft in general and, therefore, doesn't relate specifically to employee theft.

That leaves you with Choice (A). If employee numbers have increased, you'd expect to see a simultaneous increase in the number of employee thefts. The fact that the number of thefts hasn't increased as employee numbers increase suggests that the penalties may indeed be working because the number of thefts per employee is actually decreasing.

21. **A. The women in the study who smoked marijuana were from the same village, one whose residents were of a substantially higher socioeconomic status than the rest of the country, with better access to prenatal care.**

The researchers conclude that smoking marijuana during pregnancy has little effect on the health of the unborn child. They reached this conclusion because few health differences occurred between the babies of the mothers who smoked and those who didn't. Choice (A) is the answer that most seriously weakens the conclusion because it shows that the two groups had something else distinguishing them other than marijuana smoking. If the marijuana smokers were receiving better prenatal care while the others weren't, it's difficult to say whether the babies were unaffected by marijuana or whether the effects were minimized by better medical care.

Choice (B) is irrelevant. The conclusion regards the health of babies, not mothers. Choice (C) would more likely strengthen the argument because these mothers weren't just smokers but heavy smokers, and their babies still ended up fine. Choice (D) is irrelevant because the study concerned pregnant women who smoked marijuana, not tobacco. The argument doesn't discuss how damaging tobacco is. Knowing that smoking marijuana is less damaging to a fetus than tobacco doesn't tell you much about how much marijuana affects a fetus. Saying that a toothache is less painful than a kidney stone doesn't mean that a toothache isn't painful. Likewise, Choice (E) doesn't weaken the argument because the conclusion regards the health of the babies after they were born, so the differences in the stage of pregnancy at the time of the study are irrelevant given the information provided by the argument.

22. **C. Students in poorer neighborhoods cannot afford the transportation costs required to attend schools that are not located nearby.**

This question doesn't give you much to work with. The conclusion is that the government should implement a school voucher system because students would benefit greatly. Then it defines a school voucher system as a tuition waiver. To weaken the argument, find an answer that calls into question the premise that students would benefit. Choices (A), (B), and (D) actually strengthen the argument by showing ways that school vouchers may provide benefits. Choice (E) is irrelevant. If vouchers allow students to choose to attend any school, and public schools are better, the students can simply attend a public school where these vouchers may also apply. The only possible answer is Choice (C). If students can't afford to travel to the school they prefer, they won't be able to benefit from attending that school because the voucher doesn't cover transportation costs.

23. **C. Anthropologists are incorrect in their estimation of the cumulative death rate due to diseases brought to the Western Hemisphere.**

Read through the answer choices to determine whether Serena would agree or disagree with them. Then do the same for Maeve. When you discover a statement that one agrees with and the other disagrees with, you've found your answer. Eliminate answers they both disagree or agree with or answers that one or both have no opinion about.

Choice (A) is wrong. Maeve agrees that the Black Death was the most virulent disease in recorded history, but Serena has no opinion on the virulence of the Black Death. Choice (B) is out. Serena claims that the Europeans brought a number of diseases to the Western Hemisphere, including those listed in the answer choice, but Maeve doesn't comment on whether the Europeans were the source of those diseases. Regarding Choice (C), Serena bases her argument on the premise that anthropologists estimate that European diseases killed 95 percent of the Native American population, so she agrees. Maeve argues that 95 percent is too high based on death rates associated with other diseases, so she disagrees with the anthropologists' estimation. Check the last two options. Serena likely agrees with the statement in Choice (D) based on her assertion that only 4.75 percent of the Native American population would have died if it had been 20 times greater. Maeve doesn't express an opinion on whether Europeans would have conquered the Native Americans under different circumstances. Choice (D) is incorrect. At first, Choice (E) may seem correct, but Serena and Maeve aren't at odds over the percentage of infected people. They disagree about the percentage of those who *died* from the diseases. Choice (C) is the best answer.

24. **D. The NCAA tournament is appropriately named because of the "madness" it creates among employees in March of every year.**

This question is — despite the slightly different wording — essentially asking you to determine the most appropriate conclusion you can draw from the prompt. Remember that a conclusion encompasses all the premises and brings in no outside information. You can eliminate Choice (A) because it talks about the NCAA basketball tournament being the world's most popular sporting event, which isn't in the premises. Choice (B) also relies on outside information — in this case, details about the way people pick winners. You may agree with Choice (E), that employees shouldn't check sports scores, or with Choice (C), that employers should just indulge their employees, but either way, these statements are opinions and not appropriate conclusions to a set of primarily descriptive premises that are neither judgmental nor supportive of employees. Choice (D) is the best answer. It covers all the premises without adding outside information and therefore is the most logical answer choice to follow the original statement.

25. **E. There has been an exponential increase in the number of people around the world with cellphones that could be disrupted by solar activity.**

For this question, you're asked to provide a reason that would explain the paradox that weaker solar activity causes disruption in communications and power transmission for a greater number of people than did stronger such activity a decade ago. Look for an answer choice that indicates that population has increased over the decade and explains why so many more of them will be affected.

You can begin by eliminating Choice (D). The argument mentions northern lights but not in the context of disruption. You can then eliminate Choices (A) and (C) because they both tend to explain a lessening of the impact of solar activity and fail to mention the increased numbers of disrupted people. Choice (B) seems like a possible choice because it mentions the increased use of satellite signals for radio reception. However, the answer also mentions that regular radio signals are stronger than they used to be, so the effect on communications may be balanced — neither stronger nor weaker than a decade ago. The answer doesn't give you enough information to explain the "many more people" who will be inconvenienced next time. Choice (E) is the best answer because a substantial increase in cellphone use would mean that solar flares cause more disruption to more people than they did when cellphones were less popular.

Answer Key for Practice Exam 3

Section I: Logical Reasoning

1.	D	8.	B	15.	D	22.	B
2.	D	9.	E	16.	D	23.	A
3.	E	10.	A	17.	A	24.	B
4.	C	11.	D	18.	D	25.	D
5.	C	12.	B	19.	C		
6.	A	13.	C	20.	D		
7.	A	14.	D	21.	E		

Section II: Reading Comprehension

1.	E	8.	A	15.	D	22.	D
2.	A	9.	B	16.	A	23.	D
3.	B	10.	C	17.	E	24.	A
4.	C	11.	E	18.	D	25.	E
5.	C	12.	C	19.	B	26.	D
6.	E	13.	C	20.	C	27.	E
7.	A	14.	A	21.	E		

Section III: Analytical Reasoning

1.	D	8.	E	15.	E	22.	D
2.	B	9.	A	16.	C	23.	C
3.	A	10.	B	17.	D	24.	C
4.	E	11.	D	18.	B	25.	C
5.	C	12.	A	19.	C		
6.	D	13.	D	20.	D		
7.	B	14.	D	21.	B		

Section IV: Logical Reasoning

1.	C	8.	A	15.	E	22.	C
2.	A	9.	D	16.	E	23.	C
3.	A	10.	A	17.	B	24.	D
4.	C	11.	C	18.	A	25.	E
5.	E	12.	C	19.	B		
6.	B	13.	E	20.	A		
7.	D	14.	A	21.	A		

TIP

Refer to Chapter 16 for tips on computing your score.

7

The Part of Tens

Realize you *can* study for the LSAT and significantly improve your score.

Distinguish what's true about how law school admissions committees evaluate your LSAT score.

Discover intriguing areas of law to pursue after you receive your law degree.

Notice that you can practice law in a variety of venues, including law offices, corporations, and government agencies.

Chapter **21**

Ten (Plus One) Myths about the LSAT

P eople who go to law school tend to be particular and precise about how they do things. They study law school rankings, fret about their grades and LSAT scores, and generally grasp at any apparent "truth" that helps them tackle the daunting process of launching a legal career. That's why myths about the LSAT abound. Nervous would-be law students looking for certainty in an uncertain endeavor try to come up with principles that can guarantee them the results they want. Unfortunately, life isn't certain, and the LSAT is no exception. This chapter contains some of the most common beliefs and explanations of why they aren't true.

The LSAT Doesn't Have Anything to Do with Law School

People may tell you that the LSAT and law school are unrelated, and on its face it does seem that analytical reasoning and the other sections don't pertain to law school. But think about it; the LSAT-writers have to concoct a test that in about four hours can spot the people who are likely to succeed in legal education. So they've boiled down law school to its essence, which is the ability to read carefully and apply rules. They realize that what you read in law school and later as a lawyer is often boring, arcane, likely to put you to sleep, and extremely complicated, so they've made a test that spots people with the ability to overcome these obstacles. They realize that law students and lawyers have to apply themselves steadily to particular tasks for hours on end, so they've made the LSAT a test of endurance. The LSAT is quite impressive when you think of it that way. And the test works — high LSAT scores do in fact match up with good performance in law school. (Also, to the Law School Admission Council's [LSAC's] credit, it constantly works to improve the test and make it more accurate.)

You Can't Study for the LSAT

This book is all about studying for the LSAT. At the very least, getting familiar with the test's format *before* you sit down to take it for real is bound to make your experience easier; you don't have to waste time reading instructions. At best, studying can make a substantial difference in your score. Improving your performance on analytical reasoning problems is especially achievable because you don't likely deal with logical games much as a daily activity. Likewise, logical reasoning and reading comprehension questions get easier the more you expose yourself to them. Anyone can improve an LSAT score with strategic practice.

You Must Take a Prep Course to Do Well on the LSAT

Plenty of people ace the LSAT after studying on their own at home. You must be self-disciplined, but you can do it. If you think you need a class to make you accountable to regular practice or just enjoy company for your misery, you may find a test prep course helpful. Many people do see dramatic improvements in their scores after taking a prep course. When choosing a test prep course, do some due diligence. You don't have to spend a fortune. Affordable quality options are available, often through continuing education programs at colleges and community colleges.

TIP

If you do decide to study on your own, you can't get better practice materials than actual LSATs, sold by the LSAC. Try to work through at least two or three of those before you take the LSAT.

Some People Just Can't Do Analytical Reasoning Problems

Analytical reasoning problems may be scary and a little weird. They may freak you out the first time you see them, but you can figure out how to do them. They're actually the most teachable part of the LSAT. Studying for a few weeks before the test isn't likely to improve your reading speed, and it probably won't improve your vocabulary much, but it can definitely help your ability to work analytical reasoning problems.

Read Chapters 4, 5, and 6 of this book carefully. Work through the analytical reasoning sections and answer explanations in the practice tests in Chapters 15 through 20 and online, and then practice some more by working on official LSAT exams. The more analytical reasoning problems you work, the more manageable they become.

You Can Spot Difficult Questions Before You Work Them

Digesting the material in any LSAT question takes a certain amount of time; that's especially true in the case of the longer questions in the reading comprehension and analytical reasoning sections. A problem that may look incredibly difficult at first glance may turn out to be incredibly easy after you start on it. You'll likely need to skip around while you work the test, but don't waste too much precious time on the ultimately fruitless task of rating the questions by difficulty.

After you delve into a question, though, if you discover that it's too difficult, don't fret; give it your best guess and move on. Mark it to revisit later and go back to it if you have time at the end of the section. See Chapter 2 for a discussion of guessing and test-taking strategies.

B Is the Best Letter to Guess

The sad fact is that you can't predict what letter is the most prevalent on any given test section. You can test this proposition by reading the answers to several LSATs. The most common letter changes with dismaying regularity. What is true about completely random guessing is that you maximize your chances of getting some answers right if you stick to the same letter; statistically you should get about 20 percent right that way. Twenty percent is nothing to strive for, but it's better than nothing. A better strategy is to guess based on at least some knowledge; you stand a better chance of correctly getting one out of three than one out of five.

No One Reads the Writing Sample

Would you stake your future law school career on that belief? We didn't think so. Assume that everyone on every admissions committee is reading every single LSAT essay. They're not, but what if your essay happens to be the one they *do* pull out of the pile for scrutiny? You'd better be prepared. What'll it hurt, anyway? You have to spend 35 minutes of your LSAT experience writing the thing, so you may as well do a good job. You'll have to write essays for the next several years as a law student, and then perhaps as a lawyer. You may as well put a little effort into discovering a quick method of cranking out a decent document in limited time.

Finishing a Section Is Better Than Concentrating on Two-Thirds of It

This notion isn't necessarily true. Take the analytical reasoning section. You have four problems per section, each with five, six, or seven questions. If you take your time and work the three problems with the most questions and get most of them right, you're looking at about 75 percent correct — a good score even if you completely ignore one problem. If instead you force yourself to tackle every problem and you rush and miss about half (a typical result), then even though you've finished the section, you answer only about 50 percent correct.

A good general rule to follow while practicing is to first try to answer all the questions within the given time. If you score less than 60 percent (or so) correct on a section, you may want to slow down and increase the percentage you get right. You'll likely find, however, that with practice, you'll have time to give all questions in a section your full attention.

A Great LSAT Score Guarantees Admission to a Great Law School

Alas, a near perfect LSAT score is pretty much a requirement for admission to a top law school, but it doesn't guarantee admission. Harvard, Yale, Stanford, and their compatriots at the top of the law school pyramid see so many applicants with scores of 180 that they can afford to toss some in the trash. A 170 won't impress them; they see hundreds of those. What is true, though, is that you need that high score for them even to begin to consider you. This is true of all tiers of law schools; you must achieve a certain score level or they just plain won't let you in. Some schools even use computers to weed out unacceptable applicants, doing some computations that combine LSAT score with GPA to see whom the admissions committee will consider. The moral of this story? Aim high; it never hurts to score higher than you need.

The LSAT Is Used Only for Admissions Purposes

Actually, if your LSAT score is attractive enough to a law school, the admissions folks may reward you with all sorts of financial perks. For instance, if your LSAT score is off the charts, don't be surprised if you get a notice from a law school allowing you to waive the application fee. In addition, schools may consider your LSAT score when granting merit-based scholarships, which could pay more than 70 percent of your tuition!

The lesson here is that even if you're happy with your score, improving it a little may pay off big time in the end.

Your Score Won't Improve if You Retake the LSAT

You may have a bad day the first time you take the LSAT. Maybe you stayed out too late the night before or came down with a case of the sniffles the morning of the test. Or maybe you didn't bother to study the first time around, so you didn't produce a score that represents your true abilities. Plenty of factors can change that can result in a higher score. If you think you can do better given a second chance, look on your first attempt as a practice run and go back and give it another shot.

REMEMBER

But be sure that you prepare well for the second test. The LSAT has a high retest predictability, which means that without a significant change in your circumstances (you didn't properly prepare or you were feeling ill the first time you took it), chances are your score will be very similar to your first try. However, adequate preparation *can* significantly increase your score. Make sure that you get serious about studying and that you chart your progress on real, timed, practice LSATs provided by LSAC. That's the best indicator of your score on test day.

Some schools average your LSAT score, so for it to make a difference, your score needs to improve quite a lot. For instance, if you get a 145 the first time and a 155 the second time, your score would be averaged to a 150. But do your homework on this one. Many schools look at your latest or best score.

Chapter 22

Ten Kinds of Law You Can Practice

So you're seriously considering law school. Have you thought about what you'd do with a law degree? A degree of Juris Doctor (JD — that's the degree you get when you graduate from law school) can lead down all sorts of roads. A lawyer isn't a multipurpose legal expert; different lawyers specialize in different fields. Don't assume that just because someone is a lawyer she can handle any legal task. Just as you'd never go to a plastic surgeon to get a liver transplant, you wouldn't want to hire a criminal lawyer to write your will.

This chapter contains some common areas of legal practice. *Note:* We have room to list only the most common ones. Many specialties aren't listed. Within most of these listed specialties, some lawyers are primarily *litigators* — they go to court and talk to judges — and other lawyers specialize in *transactional work* — they sit in offices, writing documents and negotiating deals. The law offers something for nearly everyone!

Business/Corporate

Some lawyers spend all their time working on behalf of corporations. They negotiate deals, write and review contracts, and handle venture capital, securities, mergers, acquisitions, commercial paper, and plenty of other big-money topics. Some lawyers work directly for individual corporations as corporate counsel. Others work in firms that do the work for big and small businesses. If you're into deal making and especially like to wear fancy clothes, this field could be for you.

Criminal

Do you want to put bad guys behind bars or fight to keep wrongfully accused people out of jail? Perhaps what interests you most is the theoretical study of criminal justice, the rationale behind such concepts as the insanity defense, the death penalty, and lengthy incarcerations. These topics all fall under the heading of criminal law. Criminal lawyers include prosecutors, who work for the state prosecuting people accused of crimes, and public defenders, who defend these same people accused of crimes. This field is a great area to pursue if you want to spend a lot of time in court.

Domestic Relations/Family Law

Domestic relations and family law encompass all the legal aspects of family life — prenuptial and postnuptial agreements, divorce, custody, child support, division of marital property, visitation, child abuse, adoption, and so on. Some family lawyers specialize in even more particular matters, such as divorces involving wealthy people, though the relatively small number of super-wealthy people in the world limits the number of lawyers who can find work in this area. More typically, family lawyers handle the unfortunate situations confronting everyday people. Many family lawyers work closely with social services, particularly to monitor the welfare of children who may get lost in unfortunate family situations.

Employment/Labor

Employment law concerns itself with all aspects of the workplace — compensation, discrimination, sexual harassment, hiring and firing, benefits, and workplace safety. When employees sue employers for wrongful termination or national origin discrimination, employment lawyers get to participate in the fracas.

REMEMBER

Labor law isn't the same thing as employment law. Labor law involves labor unions and collective bargaining agreements. Labor law has tons of federal regulation, such as the National Labor Relations Act, and various other state and federal statutes that cover specific industries, such as railroads.

Intellectual Property

Intellectual property includes copyrights, trademarks, and trade names. It also includes patents, though patent lawyers tend to specialize primarily in that area. (Patent law often involves inventions, so many patent lawyers are former engineers or engineering majors.) Intellectual property lawyers help their clients register trademarks, file lawsuits for trademark or trade name violations, watch out for unfair competition, and regularly consider matters such as the value of celebrity endorsements. The Internet has opened up a vast new arena of intellectual property matters, so if you're into software and electronically distributed texts, you may want to pay more attention while you're in intellectual property class.

International

You've heard of the United Nations, but there are hundreds of other less well-known international organizations in the world, such as the Association of Southeast Asian Nations (ASEAN), the Organization of the Petroleum Exporting Countries (OPEC), and Mercosur (or Southern Cone

Common Market — that's in South America). International law comes from all sorts of different sources. Countries enter into treaties and conventions with one another. International organizations such as the International Court of Justice decide some international disputes, and the vague but important principle known as *customary international law* provides guidance for nations interacting with one another. International lawyers figure out all this stuff. International law is complicated but interesting, and involvement in international affairs carries significant prestige, so many people study this field.

TIP

If you think international law is for you, brush up on your foreign languages; speaking several definitely helps you find jobs.

Personal Injury/Insurance Defense

Have you been injured in an accident? We hope not, but if you become a plaintiff's attorney and specialize in personal injury cases, you may want to find people who have. Plaintiffs' attorneys file lawsuits on behalf of people who've been injured in some way and hope to recover damages. These lawsuits are usually based on *torts*, which are injuries such as battery, trespass, fraud, products liability, intentional infliction of emotional distress — anything that injures someone but isn't a crime under state or federal law. (This kind of lawsuit is called *civil*, not because the parties are especially polite to each other but because the lawsuits are brought by private citizens, unlike criminal lawsuits, which are always brought by the state.)

Of course, someone has to defend the people and companies who get sued in personal injury lawsuits. Defense lawyers rise to the occasion here. In any given year, many personal injury lawsuits are filed against companies with malpractice insurance, and the insurance companies often end up paying for the legal defense. Lawyers who defend defendants in certain kinds of personal injury cases are called *insurance defense attorneys.*

REMEMBER

One big difference between plaintiffs' and defense lawyers is in the way they get paid for their work. Plaintiffs' attorneys often collect a *contingency fee*, which is a percentage of whatever amount the plaintiff recovers if he wins the lawsuit. If the lawsuit fails, the attorney doesn't get paid. Defense attorneys typically bill by the hour, so the more hours they work on a case, the more they get paid.

Real Estate

If you've ever bought property, like a house, you've probably met a real estate attorney. Real estate lawyers are the folks who oversee *closings*, those quaint ceremonial occasions in which the parties to a transaction sit around a table and pass around myriad forms that everyone has to sign, at the end of which the buyer is poorer and owns the property and the seller is richer and doesn't. Real estate lawyers also do title searches, investigate zoning laws, and come to a deeper understanding of arcane concepts such as the rule against perpetuities (go to law school to figure out that one). Real estate tends to be a fairly stable field that attracts people who want relatively regular hours, though things can get crazy in real estate offices at the end of every month or whenever interest rates do something exciting.

Tax

Ever read the Internal Revenue Code? Become a tax lawyer and you'll experience that sublime pleasure on a daily basis. Tax lawyers almost have to specialize in this one area; the state and federal tax codes are so complex and change so often that being a generalist with a sideline in tax is difficult. Good tax lawyers have mastered a delicate balancing act, making sure that their clients pay exactly as much tax as they need to in order to avoid prosecution but also ensuring that they don't pay a penny more than they absolutely must.

REMEMBER

Attorneys who specialize in tax are unusual in that they very often have an advanced legal degree, called a Master of Laws (LLM).

Trusts and Estates/Probate

When people die, they usually leave stuff behind. Trusts and estates is the field of study concerned with how all that stuff gets disposed of, a process known as *probate*. Sometimes people die without wills, and it's the lawyer's job to figure out who gets what according to state laws of descent and distribution. Rich people don't like to let the state decide who gets their money and property, so they usually write wills or create trusts to ensure that particular people get particular things. Lawyers who do estate planning are usually in demand, especially if they combine this specialty with some specialized knowledge of tax laws.

Index

civil lawsuits, 393

claims, 81, 113–114

classification grouping games

  defined, 64

  practice problems, 72–75

clothing, 22

combining rules, 53–54

completely determined order questions, 58

complex questions, 93

conditions (rules), in analytical reasoning section, 36–39, 65–68

  arranging rules, 51–52

  combining rules, 53–54

  consequential truths, 38

  contingencies, 54–55

  expanding rules, 52–53

  if/then rules, 67–68

  joining rules, 66–67

  possible listing/assignment questions, 40–41

  rule shortcuts, 37–38

  spacing rules, 50–51

  target rules, 37, 49–50, 65–66

  temporary conditions, 42–43

contingencies, 54–55

contingency fees, 393

contrapositive statements, 67–68

corporate law, 391

Credential Assembly Service (CAS), 11, 15, 31

criminal law, 391–392

customary international law, 393

D

deductive reasoning, defined, 85, 108

dictionaries, 22

Digital LSAT, 1, 8–9

  prep materials and practice tests, 13–14

  reading comprehension section, 127–128, 130

direct information questions, 122

discrepancies, 81, 103–105

  examples of questions involving, 104–105

  identifying discrepancy questions, 103–104

domestic relations law, 392

drinks, 21

E

eating, 21–22

eliminating answers, 20

  analytical reasoning section, 44

  logical reasoning section, 83–84

  reading comprehension section, 124, 128, 132

employment law, 392

erasers, 20, 22

exception questions

  reading comprehension, 125

  strengthen- or weaken-the-argument questions, 100–102

expanding rules, 52–53

extremes, 124

F

fallacies

  of ambiguity, 93

  of analogy, 93–94

  of presumption, 93

  of relevance, 93

  of weak induction, 93

false dichotomies, 93

family law, 392

fees

  contingency fees, 393

  law schools, 30

  LSAT, 12

flawed argumentative strategy (flawed reasoning strategy)

  pattern-of-reasoning questions, 108–109

  questions involving, 81, 92–94

G

game board (box chart)

  creating, 37

    grouping games, 68–69

    ordering games, 49

  taking time to develop, 44

Get Acquainted With LSAT Writing tool, 145

grading practices, 27

GRE, 7

grouping games, 63–75

  classification grouping games

    defined, 64

    practice problems, 72–75

complex grouping games, 64, 72–75

creating game board/box chart, 68–69

defined, 36

identifying, 63

ordering games vs., 36

in/out grouping games

  defined, 64

  practice problems, 69–72

possible assignment questions, 40–41

rules/conditions, 65–68

  if/then rules, 67–68

  joining rules, 66–67

  target rules, 65–66

guidance offices, 25

H

hasty generalizations, 93

humanities reading passages, 119–120

I

identification, 20, 22

if/then rules, 67–68

inductive reasoning, 85–86

  analogy arguments, 86, 97–98, 108

  cause-and-effect arguments, 86, 96–97, 108

  defined, 85–86, 108

  statistical arguments, 86, 98–99, 108

inference questions, 122–124

inferences, 81, 89–90

in/out grouping games, 64, 69–72

insurance defense law, 393

intellectual property law, 392

international law, 392–393

J

joining rules, 66–67

Juris Doctor (JD), 391

L

labor law, 392

law practice, types of, 391–394

  business/corporate law, 391

  criminal law, 391–392